SCHOLARS' GUIDE
TO WASHINGTON, D.C.
FOR LATIN AMERICAN
AND CARIBBEAN STUDIES

THE WILSON CENTER

W

LATIN AMERICAN
PROGRAM

SCHOLARS' GUIDE

TO WASHINGTON, D.C. FOR

LATIN AMERICAN
AND
CARIBBEAN STUDIES

MICHAEL GROW

Consultants
WILLIAM GLADE
MARTIN C. NEEDLER
JOSEPH S. TULCHIN

Editor
ZDENEK V. DAVID

LATIN AMERICAN PROGRAM

OF THE

WOODROW WILSON INTERNATIONAL CENTER FOR SCHOLARS

SMITHSONIAN INSTITUTION PRESS
WASHINGTON, D.C.
1979

The Organization of American States provided financial support for the *Guide*'s preparation, and the Morris and Gwendolyn Cafritz Foundation partially defrayed the cost of its printing.

Library of Congress Cataloging in Publication Data

Grow, Michael.
  Scholars' guide to Washington, D.C. for
Latin American and Caribbean studies.

  At head of title: Woodrow Wilson International
Center for Scholars, Smithsonian Institution,
Washington, D.C.
  Bibliography: p.
  Includes indexes.
  1. Latin America—Library resources—
Washington, D.C. 2. Caribbean area—Library
resources—Washington, D.C. I. Woodrow Wilson
International Center for Scholars. II. Title.

Z1601.G867   [F1408]   026.98   78-21316
ISBN 0-87474-486-5
ISBN 0-87474-487-3 pbk

Printed in the United States of America

Designed by Elizabeth Dixon and Natalie Babson

CONTENTS

FOREWORD

This is the second in a series of *Guides* to the scholarly riches of the Washington area published by the Woodrow Wilson International Center for. Scholars. The series exemplifies the center's "switchboard function" of facilitating connections between the vast resources of the nation's capital and individuals with scholarly or practical needs, or simply curiosity. These *Guides*, like the Wilson Center's annual fellowship program, are designed largely to serve the national and international scholarly communities. Approximately 20,000 visiting scholars annually come to Washington from this country and abroad, and we hope that the *Guides* will be useful to this ever-growing constituency. We also hope that those scholars, many of them outside the major university research centers in the United States, will be aided in knowing what possibilities exist of engaging in research on particular topics in Washington.

The series of *Guides* is under the general editorship of Zdenek V. David, the Wilson Center librarian, who has devised the basic format. Elizabeth Dixon is largely responsible for the design and the publication arrangements. The preparation of this particular volume has been sponsored by the center's Latin American Program under the leadership of Abraham F. Lowenthal. Its author, Dr. Michael Grow, is lecturer in Latin American history at George Washington University.

The center wishes to thank the Organization of American States for its indispensible financial support of the *Guide*'s preparation, as well as the Morris and Gwendolyn Cafritz Foundation for partially defraying the cost of its printing.

The first center *Guide* was developed for scholars in the Russian/Soviet field and appeared in 1977. Forthcoming volumes will include surveys of resources in the Washington area for scholars interested in the study of East Asia, Africa, Central and Eastern Europe, the Middle East, and of film and video materials.

James H. Billington, *Director*
Woodrow Wilson International Center for Scholars

INTRODUCTION

Purpose. This volume is intended to serve as a basic reference aid for scholars interested in utilizing the extraordinarily rich intellectual resources of the nation's capital for research on Latin America and the Caribbean. Although aimed primarily at serious researchers, the volume should also prove useful and informative to a broader reading audience with related Latin American/Caribbean interests.

Scope and Content. The *Guide* is designed to be neither a rudimentary directory of names and addresses nor an exhaustive, itemized inventory of source materials, but rather a descriptive and evaluative survey of research resources. The body of the work is divided into two parts.

Part I examines Washington-area resource *collections*: libraries; archives and manuscript depositories; art, film, music, and map collections; and data banks. Individual entries succinctly describe the size, content, and organizational format of each collection's Latin American holdings, and evaluate the subject/country-strengths and most distinctive materials within those holdings.

Part II focuses on Washington-based *organizations*, public and private, which deal with Latin America and are potential sources of information or assistance to researchers. Included are sections on United States government agencies; Latin American embassies; international/inter-American organizations; private professional and cultural associations; cultural-exchange and technical-assistance organizations; research centers; and academic departments and programs at local universities. Each entry describes the organization's Latin American-related functions, delineates its pertinent research activities, materials, and products (published and unpublished, classified and unclassified), and discusses restrictions on scholarly access to unpublished and classified materials. The section on U.S. government agencies contains information on Freedom-of-Information Act processes (see particularly that section's Introductory Note). The volume concludes with a series of appendixes (Latin American-oriented publications, media, and bookstores in Washington, etc.) and indexes (name, subject, personal-papers collections, and library subject-strengths).

The *Guide*'s topical coverage concentrates on the disciplines of the social sciences and humanities traditionally considered to fall under the rubric of "Latin American studies," although the fields of science and technology have been included where relevant. The volume's geographic scope includes not only Iberic Latin America but also all former and current Caribbean possessions of Great Britain, France, and the Netherlands. Resources relating to Puerto Rico and other United States territories in the Caribbean are included only up to the date at which those territories came under U.S. administrative jurisdiction. Coverage does not include research resources for the study of Chicano or other Hispanic-American communities in the United States. Nor was an attempt made to include coverage of ephemeral organizations representing Washington's ever-shifting population of Latin American emigrants and exiles.

Methodology. Preparation of the volume began with the compilation of a list of all Washington-area collections and organizations thought to be potential sources of information or assistance for scholarly research on Latin America and the Caribbean. (The reference sources consulted in the compilation of that list are indicated in the bibliography at the end of the volume.) Each pertinent collection and organization was then investigated by the author in person and/or by telephone. Information was gleaned from on-site examinations, from discussions with staff members, and from printed materials. Data should be considered current through early- to mid-1978.

Acknowledgments. The author owes much to the support of Abraham F. Lowenthal, Secretary of the Latin American Program at the Woodrow Wilson International Center for Scholars; to the conceptual guidance of Zdenek David, editor of the Wilson Center's *Scholars' Guide* series; to advice and consultation by William Glade of the University of Texas at Austin, Martin C. Needler of the University of New Mexico, Joseph S. Tulchin of the University of North Carolina at Chapel Hill, and Carl Deal of the University of Illinois; to the financial support of the Organization of American States; and to the pathbreaking labors of Steven A. Grant, author of the first *Guide* in the series. Allan Kessler provided research assistance for the sections devoted to nongovernmental organizations. Manuscript deadlines could not have been met without the superb typing assistance of Patricia R. Sheridan. Finally, the author extends his appreciation collectively to the hundreds of men and women on the staffs of the institutions discussed below who contributed their time and knowledge to this project. Many, but by no means all, of these individuals are mentioned in the pages which follow.

INSTRUCTIONS FOR USE OF *GUIDE*

Format. The main body of the volume is divided into 14 sections, each of which corresponds to a sub-category of collection or organization. Within each section, entries are arranged alphabetically by the name of the individual collection or organization.

Standard Entry Forms. At the beginning of each section of the *Guide* (and in Appendix III, as well), a standard entry form indicates, in outline format, the categories and sequence of information contained within each entry. These standard entry forms must be consulted closely in using the *Guide*. The numerical sequence of data presented within each entry corresponds to the numerical content-arrangement of that section's standard entry form. Where a number does not appear in an entry, that category of information was not relevant to that particular collection or organization.

Indexes. Four indexes provide access to information in the text from several perspectives.

The Name Index contains the names of organizations and institutions, but not of individuals.

The Personal-Papers Index includes the names of individuals whose papers and manuscripts are located in libraries or other depositories in the Washington, D.C. area.

The Library Subject-Strength Index ranks the major library collections in the Washington, D.C. area by subject, based upon a scale of evaluation explained in the Introductory Note to the "Libraries" section. Categorization is based on standard Library of Congress subject-headings, or, in the case of geographic headings, on regional- and country-holdings in selected sub-categories of history, economics, political science, and literature. Some ratings are based on sub-categories of major subject-headings (for example, collections with particular strength in finance or trade are ranked within the broader Economics category).

The Subject Index is limited to non-geographic subject-headings, because the overwhelming majority of collections and organizations discussed in this volume focus on all of the nations of Latin America and the Caribbean rather than concentrating exclusively on any single country or group of countries. Thus, to have included geographic subject-index terms would have resulted in the repetitious indexing of virtually every entry in the *Guide* under the name of each separate country in the region.

Names, Addresses, and Telephone Numbers. These data are highly subject to change, and should be considered up-to-date only through early- to mid-1978. For long-distance dialing of telephone numbers, use the following area codes: District of Columbia, area code 202; suburban Maryland, area code 301; suburban Virginia, area code 703.

COLLECTIONS

A. Libraries

Library Entry Format (A)

1. General Information
   a. *address; telephone numbers*
   b. hours of service
   c. conditions of access (including availability of inter-library loan and reproduction facilities)
   d. name/title of director and heads of relevant divisions

2. Size of Collection
   a. general
   b. Latin American

3. Description and Evaluation of Collection
   a. narrative assessment of Latin American holdings—subject and area strengths/weaknesses
   b. tabular evaluation of subject strength:

Subject Category	Number of Titles (t.)	Rating (A-D)*
1. Philosophy and Religion		
2. History		
3. Geography and Anthropology		
4. Economics		
5. Sociology		
6. Politics and Government		
7. International Relations		
8. Law		
9. Education		
10. Art and Music		
11. Language and Literature		
12. Military Affairs		
13. Bibliography and Reference		

   14. Argentina
   15. Bolivia
   16. Brazil
   17. Caribbean (excluding Cuba)
   18. Central America

19. Chile
20. Colombia
21. Cuba
22. Ecuador
23. Guianas (Guyana, Surinam, French Guiana)
24. Mexico
25. Paraguay
26. Peru
27. Uruguay
28. Venezuela

*A—comprehensive collection of primary and secondary sources (Library of Congress collection to serve as standard of evaluation)

B—substantial collection of primary and secondary sources; sufficient for some original research (holdings of roughly one-tenth those of the Library of Congress)

C—substantial collection of secondary sources, some primary; sufficient to support graduate instruction (holdings of roughly one-half those of B collection)

D—collection of secondary sources, mostly in English; sufficient to support undergraduate instruction (holdings of roughly one-half those of C collection)

4. Special Collections
   a. periodicals
   b. newspapers
   c. government documents
   d. miscellaneous vertical files
   e. archives and manuscripts
   f. maps
   g. films
   h. tapes

5. Bibliographic aids (catalogs, guides, etc.) facilitating use of collection

---

Introductory Note

In the following section, the Latin American-related book holdings in most large, general collections, and in several smaller, specialized collections, are evaluated on a scale of A through D. These rankings are based on the quantity and quality of 13 major subject categories and 15 geographic categories. The Library of Congress' holdings were taken as the standard of evaluation for an A collection—which is here defined as a comprehensive collection of primary and secondary source materials. The B collection is defined as a substantial collection (approximately one-tenth the size of the Library of Congress collection) of primary and secondary sources, sufficient for some original research. The C collection is considered to be a substantial collection (roughly one-half the size of a B collection) of secondary sources, with some primary, sufficient to support graduate instruction. Finally, a D collection is defined as a collection (approximately one-half the size of a C collection) of predominantly secondary sources, sufficient to support undergraduate instruction.

Numbers of titles in the various subject and geographic categories were derived primarily through the measurement of library shelflists, on the basis of a Library of Congress formula of 33.8 titles per centimeter of shelflist catalog-cards. Only those call-numbers with a geographic sub-section devoted to the region and nations of Latin America were measured. Numerical totals in geographic categories were arrived at by combining the shelflist measurements of selected call-numbers in history, economics, political science, and literature for each country or subregion, and must accordingly be considered merely reflective of geographic strengths in a relative and impressionistic sense. The current lack of a comprehensive Library of Congress classification schedule for the field of law made it impracticable to measure the legal materials in many area collections (necessitating frequent use of the word "unmeasured" in the law subject-category). Consequently, as a result of these various factors, the quantitative figures given for Latin American holdings in the collections discussed below tend inevitably to underestimate their true numbers.

The reader's attention is called to Appendix III—Library Collections: A Listing by Size of Latin American Holdings, and to the Library Subject-Strengths Index.

Academy for Educational Development—Clearinghouse on Development Communication See entry I1

A1 Academy of American Franciscan History Library

1. a. *9901 Carmelita Drive*
        Potomac, Maryland 20854
        365-1763

    b. 9 A.M.-5 P.M. Monday-Saturday

    c. Open to serious researchers, by appointment. There is no interlibrary loan service. Photoreproduction facilities are available.

2. The total collection numbers more than 15,000 volumes, almost all of which are on Latin America. The library also receives more than 60 journals, the majority of which are historical and ecclesiastical publications from Latin American archives and Franciscan academies.

3-4. Primarily a research collection for the staff of the Academy, the library's holdings are a major resource for the study of colonial Latin American religious history. The core of the book collection is Franciscan history and bibliography, and the range of titles is probably as extensive as can be found in any library in the United States. Holdings include Franciscan laws (from the 14th century), annals, and missionary manuals, original editions of Franciscan works on history, theology, and exploration, published collections of documents, and a strong range of secondary literature on Franciscan activities in Latin America, by region and country. A particular focus of the collection is Franciscan bibliography, including catalogs and indexes of Franciscan-related documents in Latin American and European archives.

    Among the most unique resources of the library are its extensive collections of copies of original Franciscan documents in Latin American and European archives. One collection consists of more than 100 bound volumes of photocopies of colonial documents from Franciscan missions in California, Mexico (especially Jalisco), the Caribbean, Venezuela, Brazil, and Peru, and related documents from the Vatican Archives, the College of San Isidro in Rome, and the Archivo de Indias in Seville. A second collection contains microfilm copies of Franciscan documents in repositories in Peru (for example, the Convento de San Francisco and the Archivo de la Provincia de los Doce Apóstoles), Venezuela (e.g., the Archivo Arzobispal de Caracas), Bolivia (the Convento Franciscano de Tarija, etc.), Ecuador, Argentina, Paraguay, and Mexico. Made by, or for, the Academy staff, these photo- and microfilm copies are frequently the only extant copies of the original documents.

The library also has a card index to Franciscan materials in the Archivo de Indias in Seville (six drawers) and the National Archives of Mexico (nine drawers). Copies of many indexed documents are available.

5. A badly dated catalog, Rev. Leo Adasiewicz and Rev. Donald Bilinski (comp.), *Catalog of Books in the Academy of American Franciscan History Library* (Pulaski, Wisconsin: Provincial Library, 1951), is available.

Note: Also see entry M1.

A2 ACTION Library (formerly Peace Corps Library)

1. a. *Room 407*
806 Connecticut Avenue, NW
Washington, D.C. 20525
254-3307

 b. 8:30 A.M.-5:15 P.M. Monday-Friday

 c. Open to the public for on-site use. Reference services (particularly by telephone or mail) limited by staff's work schedule. Interlibrary loan services available. No coin-operated photocopying machines.

 d. Rita Warpeha, Chief Librarian

2. The ACTION Library collection, the bulk of which consists of the holdings of the former Peace Corps Library, contains some 35,000 books and documents, approximately 5,000 of which pertain specifically to Latin America.

3. Latin American book holdings consist largely of English-language secondary literature in the areas of history, economics, and general culture. Holdings are insufficient to warrant a subject evaluation.

4. c. The ACTION Library's major research resource is its collection of Peace Corps program documents, dating from the organization's inception to the present. Included are country training manuals, project reports, country-program evaluations, Latin American regional plans and analyses, and volunteers' newsletters. Most pre-1970 program evaluations are restricted, but are obtainable through Freedom-of-Information Act requests. (Researchers should consult with reference staff members to determine whether any pertinent pre-1970 program evaluations have already been cleared for release.)

 d. A large vertical file contains miscellaneous Peace Corps news releases and planning documents, as well as State Department post reports. There are folders for Latin America, by country. Additional folders with "Peace Corps" subject-headings may also contain Peace Corps operational records relating to Latin America.

5.   The library's alphabetically arranged dictionary card catalog has Latin American country headings, as well as "U.S. Peace Corps" headings by country. All books and documents pertaining to Latin America are shelved together, by region and country.

Note: Also see entries F22 and J26.

A3   Agency for International Development (AID) Reference Center

1.   a.   *State Department Building, Room 1656*
              320 21st Street, NW
              Washington, D.C. 20523
              632-9345

       b.   8:45 A.M.-5:30 P.M. Monday-Friday

       c.   The reference center is primarily for the use of AID personnel. Private scholars engaged in substantive research may gain access to the facility by obtaining prior approval from the AID Office of Public Affairs, an AID technical-bureau staff-member (see entry J1), or the reference center chief. (Located within the State Department Building, the Reference Center can also be visited freely by scholars working in the State Department Library [see entry A49].) Materials must be used on the premises (only AID personnel have borrowing privileges). There is no interlibrary loan service. Photoreproduction services are available.

       d.   Edna A. Falbo, Chief

2.   The collection totals approximately 56,000 cataloged reports and documents, and an indeterminate quantity of uncataloged materials. Cataloged Latin American holdings number more than 6,100 titles.

3.   The AID Reference Center is the agency's development-research information center and its primary collection-point for in-house research. As such, it is a major resource for Latin American development studies (particularly in the fields of development economics, agriculture, education, health/nutrition, housing, population, and technical-assistance methodology) and research on U.S. development-assistance programs. The reference center's collection contains research reports and related technical documents (both classified and unclassified) produced by AID and predecessor U.S. development-assistance agencies dating back to the World War II-era Institute of Inter-American Affairs. Included are development-assistance program and project reports (feasibility studies, field surveys, program evaluations); AID discussion papers, sector profiles, and country analyses (for example, "Land Reform in Mexico, 1970"); AID contract-research studies; end-of-tour reports by AID field officials; annual AID budget-presentations to Congress; historical surveys of U.S. aid programs (e.g., *"Servicio Técnico Interamericano de Cooperación Agrícola* in Paraguay, 1943-1968"); and scattered country-studies by other U.S. government agencies, the Organization of American States, Inter-American Development Bank, and World Bank. A

survey revealed the following numbers of titles, virtually all of which focus on development-related topics: Latin America (regional), 1,014 t.; Argentina, 199 t.; Bolivia, 220 t.; Brazil, 973 t.; Caribbean (excluding Cuba), 335 t.; Central America, 1,251 t.; Chile, 237 t.; Colombia 554 t.; Cuba, 17 t.; Ecuador, 227 t.; Guianas, 127 t.; Mexico, 142 t.; Paraguay, 142 t.; Peru, 439 t.; Uruguay, 91 t.; Venezuela, 179 t.

Reference materials include AID research bibliographies, a complete set of the 33-volume *AID Organization Handbook* containing internal agency regulations and management policies, and a set of the State Department Foreign Affairs Document and Reference Center's *Country Fact Sheets*.

The reference center's small staff can provide outside researchers with invaluable reference and referral assistance in working with AID's voluminous research reports and the agency's rather labyrinthine functional structures. It can also assist researchers in obtaining declassification of classified materials.

4. d. A separate vertical file contains some 30 drawers of AID project-files (working papers, budgetary submissions, appraisals, and other key documents), arranged alphabetically by country.

5. There are three card catalogs: a dictionary catalog (alphabetically arranged by author, title, and subject—with development-related subjects subdivided by country), a geographic catalog, and an AID research-contract catalog (arranged by contract number). Containing references to both classified and unclassified materials, these catalogs are an outstanding source of bibliographic data on classified AID research reports, and accordingly they can be of great value to scholars in filing Freedom-of-Information Act requests.

Note: A recently created AID Bureau for Development Support—Technical Information Center (Room 105, Rosslyn Plaza "C" Building, 1601 Kent Street, Arlington, Virginia) is attempting to combine the collections of several AID technical-assistance office libraries. This facility has, on microfiche, copies of all research studies listed in the agency's *A.I.D. Research and Development Abstracts*. It is open to the public. For information, call 235-8936.

The AID Office of Population's Population Reference Library (235-9675), which has not as yet been integrated into the Bureau for Development Support—Technical Information Center, maintains a separate collection of some 6,000 monographs, periodical articles, and research reports (governmental and private) dealing with population, fertility, and family planning. Located in Room 215, Rosslyn Plaza "E" Building, 1621 N. Kent Street, Arlington, Virginia, it too is open to outside researchers.

Note: Also see entries F1, G1, G2, and J1.

Agriculture Department Library See National Agricultural Library, entry A35

A4 **American Federation of Labor and Congress of Industrial Organizations (AFL-CIO) Library**

1. a. *Room 102*
815 16th Street, NW
Washington, D.C. 20006
637-5297

b. 9 A.M.-4:30 P.M. Monday-Friday

c. Open to the public for on-site use. Photoreproduction facilities available.

d. Jean Webber, Librarian

2-4. The AFL-CIO Library possesses a small number of English-language books on labor relations and trade unionism in Latin American nations. The library's vertical file contains miscellaneous clippings, pamphlets, and correspondence (again, primarily English-language) relating to inter-American labor relations. Contents date back to approximately World War I.

Within the AFL-CIO General Files, housed one floor above the library, are archival records relating to U.S. labor leaders Samuel Gompers and William Green, as well as general AFL-CIO "international" records, 1950s-1970s. Contact Logan Kimmel (637-5138) for further information.

Note: Also see entry 19.

A5 American Institute of Architects Library

1. a. *1735 New York Avenue, NW*
Washington, D.C. 20006
785-7293

b. 8:30 A.M.-5 P.M. Monday-Friday

c. Open to the public for on-site use. Limited inter-library loan and photocopying facilities available.

d. Susan Cosgrove, Librarian

4. a. The library receives the major architectural journals published in Latin America. Retrospective holdings range sporadically back into the 1950s.

American Red Cross—National Headquarters Library See entry I10

American Society of International Law Library See entry H13

A6 American University Library

1. a. *Massachusetts and Nebraska Avenues, NW*
Washington, D.C. 20016
686-2325 (Reference)

b. Academic year:
8 A.M.-midnight Monday-Friday
9 A.M.-6 P.M. Saturday
1 P.M.-midnight Sunday
Summer:
9 A.M.-11 P.M. Monday-Thursday
9 A.M.-5 P.M. Friday-Saturday
Closed Sunday

    c. Open to the public for use of materials within the library, with borrowing of books limited to the university community. Interlibrary loan and photore-production services available.

    d. Donald D. Dennis, University Librarian

2. The library contains approximately 390,000 volumes, with Latin American holdings totaling some 6,500 volumes. The library also currently receives 3,100 periodicals (20 from Latin America) and 50 newspapers (one Latin American: Buenos Aires' *La Nación*).

3. b. Subject categories and evaluations:

1. Philosophy and Religion	96 t.	C
2. History	3,543 t.	C
3. Geography and Anthropology	13 t.	Below D
4. Economics	810 t.	C/D
5. Sociology	250 t.	C
6. Politics and Government	302 t.	C/D
7. International Relations	376 t.	B
8. Law	3 t.	Below D
9. Education	69 t.	Below D
10. Art and Music	48 t.	Below D
11. Language and Literature	927 t.	Below D
12. Military Affairs	6 t.	Below D
13. Bibliography and Reference	22 t.	Below D

14. Argentina	308 t.	Below D
15. Bolivia	49 t.	D
16. Brazil	368 t.	Below D
17. Caribbean (excluding Cuba)	388 t.	C
18. Central America	483 t.	C
19. Chile	220 t.	C/D
20. Colombia	189 t.	C/D
21. Cuba	209 t.	C/D
22. Ecuador	46 t.	Below D
23. Guianas	19 t.	D
24. Mexico	923 t.	C
25. Paraguay	42 t.	D
26. Peru	179 t.	D
27. Uruguay	85 t.	Below D
28. Venezuela	179 t.	C/D

4. a. The library's microfilm collection contains scattered issues of Brazilian leftist periodicals, mostly from the 1940s and 1950s.

Arms Control and Disarmament Agency Library See entry J3

A7 Army Library (Army Department)

1. a. *The Pentagon, Room 1A518*
Washington, D.C. 20310
697-4301 (Reference)

b. 9:30 A.M.-4 P.M. Monday-Friday

c. Entrance to the Pentagon is restricted. Private researchers may use the Army Library collection at the discretion of its staff. Interlibrary loan and photo-copying facilities are available.

d. Mary L. Shaffer, Director

2-3. The Army Library has within its total collection of some 275,000 volumes only a few hundred volumes on Latin American history, international relations, and military affairs. Except for a handful of Latin American army publications (largely from the 1940s and 1950s), the collection consists of English-language secondary literature.

4. a. The library currently receives armed-forces periodicals from Argentina, Brazil, Chile, Peru, and Venezuela. Retrospective holdings do not appear to be extensive.

5. Card catalogs and a list of currently received periodicals are available.

A8 Association of American Railroads—Economics and Finance Department Library

1. a. *Room 523*
   1920 L Street, NW
   Washington, D.C. 20036
   293-4068/4069

   b. 8:30 A.M.-5:15 P.M. Monday-Friday

   c. Open to the public (stacks restricted). Interlibrary loan and photocopying facilities available.

   d. John McLeod, Librarian

2-3. The collection includes an estimated 2,000-3,000 volumes pertaining to Latin American railroads. The majority of the holdings are annual reports of private and state-run railroad companies in Latin America, dating from the late 19th century to ca. 1950. Mexican and Argentine materials appear to be in greatest abundance, although most countries are represented.

5. An extensive dictionary card catalog contains references to a considerable quantity of pre-1950 Latin American railroad literature (books, periodicals, government reports, legislation) beyond that which is in the library's collection. Substantial quantities of Latin American titles appear under country headings and under the subject heading "Railroads" (which is subdivided by country).

   All Latin American holdings are shelved together in the stacks, by country. Researchers, if persistent, may be permitted to examine the stacks.

A9 Augustinian College Library

1. a. *3900 Harewood Road, NE*
   Washington, D.C. 20017
   529-5606

   b. 8:30 A.M.-4:30 P.M. Monday-Friday

   c. Open to the public.

   d. Father John E. Bresnahan, Librarian

2. Within the library's 18,000-volume collection are an estimated two dozen Latin American titles.

3. Holdings consist of published works—mostly in Spanish—on Augustinian missionary activities in colonial Latin America.

A10   Brazilian-American Cultural Institute (BACI) Library

1.   a. *Suite 211*
        4201 Connecticut Avenue, NW
        Washington, D.C. 20008
        362-8334

   b. 10 A.M.-7 P.M. Monday-Friday

   c. Open to the public. Lending privileges available to persons who, for a moderate fee, become members of the institute. Photocopying facilities available.

   d. Paulo Costa, Librarian

2. Approximately 3,500 volumes, almost all in Portuguese.

3. The BACI Library collection ranks within the "B" range for research on Brazilian culture, history, literature, art, and education. Among its holdings are many major titles in Brazilian history and social science (including sets of the complete works of Gilberto Freyre, Rui Barbosa, and several other major Brazilian authors), as well as many of the classics of Brazilian literature. There are no government serials in the collection.

4.   a. The library receives the *Revista de História*, various periodicals on cinema and the arts, and several popular Brazilian magazines (*Veja, Manchete,* etc.).

   b. *Folha de Sao Paulo* and *Jornal do Brasil* are currently received. Issues are retained for two or three months.

   g. BACI maintains a collection of some 300-400 photographs of contemporary general scenes of Brazil.

Note: Also see entries D1 and I12.

Brookings Institution Library See entry M6

A11   Catholic University of America—Mullen Library

1.   a. *620 Michigan Avenue*
        Washington, D.C. 20017
        635-5155 (Reference)

   b. Academic year:
        9 A.M.-10 P.M. Monday-Thursday

9 A.M.-5 P.M. Friday-Saturday
1 P.M.-10 P.M. Sunday
(Summer hours may vary considerably. Call Reference Division for further information.)

c. Open to the public for use of materials within the library. Visiting scholars may be eligible for temporary courtesy borrowing of books, and should inquire at the Office of the Director (635-5055). Interlibrary loan and photoreproduction services are available.

d. Fred M. Peterson, Director

2. The total collection numbers nearly one million volumes, with Latin American holdings of more than 4,700 volumes. In addition, the library receives some 5,100 periodicals, at least 105 of which emanate from Latin America. No Latin American newspapers are received.

3. a. The library's Latin American collection is strongest in early Catholic Church history and theology. The staff estimates, for example, that nearly every source cited by Las Casas is available, "from Gratian and Aquinas to Vitoria—probably in editions contemporaneous with Las Casas."

b. Subject categories and evaluations:

1. Philosophy and Religion	337 t.	B/A
2. History	2,451 t.	C/D
3. Geography and Anthropology	33 t.	D
4. Economics	320 t.	Below D
5. Sociology	233 t.	C
6. Politics and Government	99 t.	Below D
7. International Relations	179 t.	C/D
8. Law	unmeasured	
9. Education	75 t.	Below D
10. Art and Music	91 t.	D
11. Language and Literature	869 t.	Below D
12. Military Affairs	5 t.	Below D
13. Bibliography and Reference	42 t.	Below D
14. Argentina	299 t.	Below D
15. Bolivia	35 t.	Below D
16. Brazil	281 t.	Below D
17. Caribbean (excluding Cuba)	231 t.	D
18. Central America	266 t.	D
19. Chile	147 t.	D
20. Colombia	118 t.	D
21. Cuba	98 t.	Below D
22. Ecuador	51 t.	Below D
23. Guianas	20 t.	D
24. Mexico	638 t.	C/D
25. Paraguay	35 t.	D
26. Peru	194 t.	D
27. Uruguay	50 t.	Below D
28. Venezuela	87 t.	Below D

4. Several special collections contain materials on Latin America. The 9,800-volume Clementine collection, comprising part of the library of the Italian Clementine family (which included among its members Pope Clement XI), features a wide range of rare books on church law and history, 1473-1870. Included are several early European travel accounts of the New World, descriptions of Catholic missionary enterprises, and original editions of the writings of the Spanish theologian and legal theoretician Francisco Suárez.

The 10,000-volume Canon Law library collection features original editions of works by Aquinas, Erasmus, and other major church writers, European travel accounts of Spanish America dating from 1590, a substantial number of early facsimiles of Aztec codices, and an original 15-volume set of *Obras* of Juan de Palafox y Mendoza, 17th-century viceroy of New Spain. The collection also contains a wealth of primary source material on the Catholic missionary orders—constitutions, annals, journals, bio-bibliographies, histories, bishops' synods, provincial council reports—as well as a full run of CIDOC publications.

In addition, a closed vault area holds a large number of medieval European manuscripts, incunabula, and rare books—with the emphasis again on ecclesiastical matters.

Unfortunately, none of these collections has been cataloged, and the staff admits that it cannot fully define or describe their contents. The most knowledgeable source of information is Theology-Philosophy division librarian Carolyn Lee (635-5088).

e. The Department of Archives and Manuscripts holds the following items of interest to Latin Americanists:

An 1823 manuscript copy of Agustín de Iturbide's *Plan de Iguala*, with attachments.

Twenty documents, dating from 1607 to 1796, on the Mexican Inquisition (contained in the Rev. Arthur T. Connolly collection).

The Rev. Charles W. Perrier papers (Perrier was bishop of Matanzas, Cuba during World War I; his papers also contain scattered materials on the Mexican Revolution).

The Rev. Francesco Lardone papers (Lardone was Papal Nuncio to the Dominican Republic in the early 20th century).

The 1919-1970 records of the National Catholic Welfare Council (predecessor to the United States Catholic Conference), and the personal papers of William Montavon, NCWC legal counsel active in Mexican affairs.

Finding aids for these materials are exceedingly rudimentary. For information, contact archivist Anthony Zito (635-5065).

Note: Catholic University's Biology Library, 207 McCort Ward (635-5272), has a good collection dealing with Latin American flora and fauna.

A12 Census Bureau Library (Commerce Department)

1. a. *Federal Office Building 3, Wing 4, Room 2451*
Suitland Road and Silver Hill Road
Suitland, Maryland
763-5042 (Reference)

Mail: Department of Commerce
Washington, D.C. 20233

(Note: A daily Commerce Department shuttle-service operates between the Census Bureau Library and the Main Commerce Building [see entry J5] in downtown Washington.)

b. 8 A.M.-5 P.M. Monday-Friday

c. Open to the public. Interlibrary loan and rather expensive photoreproduction services are available.

d. Betty Baxtresser, Chief of the Library Branch

2. Total holdings number some 375,000 volumes. Approximately 3,400 periodicals are currently received. The bulk of the collection consists of U.S. and foreign statistical materials (censuses, yearbooks, bulletins), and monographs on statistics and demography.

3. The Census Bureau Library has one of the fullest collections of recent Latin American national censuses (along with scattered provincial and state censuses), statistical yearbooks, and statistical bulletins in the Washington area. Its holdings of post-1930 materials are, according to some researchers, superior to those of the Library of Congress and Organization of American States. Among its holdings are the *Aussenhandel des Auslandes* Latin American country-series of the German Federal Republic's *Statistisches Bundesamt,* and, on microform, the on-going "International Population Census" microfilm series containing every Latin American and Caribbean national census taken between ca. 1950 and ca. 1960. The collection is also strong in official Latin American foreign-trade bulletins and central-bank reports, CELADE publications, and U.S. Census Bureau population estimates and projections.

   Many current items in the collection are on loan to the Census Bureau's International Demographic Statistics staff (see entry J5), but will be recalled for private researchers.

5. There are two separate dictionary card catalogs, each of which must be consulted: a retired catalog for holdings cataloged prior to March 1976, and an active catalog for post-March 1976 acquisitions. The contents of the retired catalog have been published in *Catalogs of the Bureau of the Census Library*, 20 vols. (Boston: G.K. Hall and Co., 1976).

   A *List of Periodicals Currently Received by the Census Library* is also available.

Center for Defense Information Library See entry M8

Center for National Security Studies Library See entry M10

Central Intelligence Agency Library See entry J4

A13   Commerce Department Library

1. a. *Room 7046*
14th Street and Constitution Avenue, NW
Washington, D.C. 20230
377-5511

   b. 8:30 A.M.-5 P.M. Monday-Friday

   c. Open to the public for on-site use. Interlibrary loan and photoduplication facilities are available.

d. Stanley J. Bougas, Librarian

2. The collection totals 250,000 volumes, with Latin American holdings of some 3,000 volumes. Approximately 1,800 periodicals are currently received.

3. a. The Latin American holdings of the Commerce Department Library consist predominantly of Latin American government serials relating to international trade and commerce. Included are the reports and statistical bulletins of government ministries, trade bureaus, tariff commissions, commercial agencies, and central banks, along with scattered research reports and country studies by U.S. government agencies, the World Bank, Organization of American States, and other international organizations. Materials range intermittently back into the 19th century for many countries, although the library staff periodically weeds out older materials. Holdings of Commerce Department publications—current and retrospective—are strong.

b. Within the Economics category, the collection ranks in the "A" range for research on Latin American international trade and U.S.-Latin American commercial relations. For recent statistical data, the Inter-American Development Bank Library (see entry A26) and Joint Bank-Fund Library (entry A31) may be stronger, while for historical data the Library of Congress (entry A33) or OAS Columbus Memorial Library (entry A43) probably have more comprehensive holdings. Nevertheless, the Commerce Department Library may well contain individual items not available elsewhere. Country strengths (primarily serials titles) are as follows:

Argentina	209 t.
Bolivia	77 t.
Brazil	345 t.
Caribbean (excluding Cuba)	144 t.
Central America	412 t.
Chile	193 t.
Colombia	355 t.
Cuba	148 t.
Ecuador	78 t.
Guianas	46 t.
Mexico	222 t.
Paraguay	48 t.
Peru	144 t.
Uruguay	55 t.
Venezuela	90 t.

5. There are two dictionary card catalogs, each of which must be consulted: an inactive catalog of holdings cataloged between 1914 and 1974, and a current catalog of post-1974 acquisitions. The staff cautions researchers that the 1914-1974 catalog may overstate the library's actual holdings because some older materials have been culled from the stacks without a corresponding removal of cards from the catalog.

The library publishes a descriptive brochure, as well as a monthly *Commerce Library Bulletin* listing selected recent acquisitions.

Note: Several bureaus and sub-agencies of the Commerce Department maintain separate libraries and/or reference collections. These are discussed in entry J5. Also see Census Bureau Library, entry A12.

Defense Mapping Agency Topographic Center Libraries
See entry E1

A14 Dominican College Library

1. a. *487 Michigan Avenue, NE*
   Washington, D.C. 20017
   529-5300

   b. 8:30 A.M.-4:30 P.M. and 7 P.M.-10 P.M. Monday-Friday (mornings only during summer months).

   c. Open to the public. Interlibrary loan and photoreproduction facilities available.

   d. Rev. J. Raymond Vandegrift, O.P., Librarian

2-3. The collection contains some 40,000 volumes (including a sizable rare-book collection), concentrating on Thomas Aquinas, Thomist philosophy, and the history of the Dominican order. The librarian estimates that Latin American holdings are extremely small, but researchers interested in medieval theology or the Dominican missionary enterprise in colonial Latin America might wish to examine the card catalog.

A15 Dumbarton Oaks (Harvard University)—Center for Pre-Columbian Studies Library

1. a. *1703 32nd Street, NW*
   Washington, D.C. 20007
   232-3101

   b. 9 A.M.-5 P.M. Monday-Friday

   c. Open to qualified researchers, contingent upon severe space limitations. Appointment required. No interlibrary loan. Photocopying facilities are available.

   d. Elizabeth Benson, Director

2-3. The collection, some 7,500 volumes and 21 periodicals on Pre-Columbian art and archeology, is primarily designed to support the research activities of the Center for Pre-Columbian Studies' staff and fellows. Book holdings are strongest on Meso-American subjects, and include reprints of early works dating to the 16th century, a large collection of codex facsimiles, Mayan-language dictionaries, and an original edition of A.P. Maudslay's *Biologia Centrali-Americana*. The library also has a large selection of catalogs of museum holdings and art exhibits, and a growing collection on ethnography and natural history.

Note: Also see entries C2, F6, and M15.

Embassy of Brazil Library See entry K5

Embassy of Chile Library See entry K6

Embassy of Venezuela Library See entry K27

A16 Export-Import Bank Library

1. a. *811 Vermont Avenue, NW*
      Washington, D.C. 20571
      566-8320

   b. 7:30 A.M.-5:30 P.M. Monday-Friday

   c. Open to the public. Interlibrary loan and photocopying facilities available.

   d. Theodora McGill, Librarian

4. a. The Export-Import Bank Library receives some 85 Latin American and Caribbean periodicals, including selected statistical, economic, and banking bulletins, and a number of bank newsletters. The greatest numbers of titles are from Brazil (17), Mexico (10), Argentina (9), Colombia (7), and Venezuela (6). Items are retained for approximately two years (after which they are sent to the Library of Congress). The Library of Congress, Joint Bank-Fund Library, Inter-American Development Bank Library, and Federal Reserve Board Library all receive a greater number of Latin American economic periodicals, but there may be individual titles in the Export-Import Bank Library which are not currently received elsewhere.

5. A *Periodicals* list is available upon request.

Note: Also see entry J11.

A17 Federal Reserve System—Research Library of the Board of Governors

1. a. *20th Street and Constitution Avenue, NW*
      Washington, D.C. 20551
      452-3332 (Reference)

   b. 8:45 A.M.-5:15 P.M. Monday-Friday (Closed 2-4 P.M. Tuesdays and Thursdays)

   c. Open to the public for on-site use. Interlibrary loan service and extremely limited photoreproduction facilities available.

   d. Ann Clary, Chief Librarian

2-3. The Federal Reserve Board's Research Library has an excellent collection of materials on Latin American banking, finance, and monetary policy. The library's major strength lies in its serial holdings. Included are: Latin American central-bank annual reports and bank superintendents' reports dating back at least to the 1920s or 1930s for most countries; the official statistical yearbooks of most countries back to the mid- or late-1950s; and sporadic holdings of Latin American government financial reports, foreign-trade reports, treasury bulletins, national development corporation reports, and national development plans. Other strengths are holdings in 20th-century Latin American monetary and banking law; individual reports and special publications of Latin American central banks; and a large number of studies from the *Centro de Estudios Monetarios Latinoamericanos* (CEM-LA) in Mexico City. There are also scattered reports, dating as far back as the 1920s, from international financial and monetary commissions in Latin America. Overall, the collection ranks within the "A" range for financial aspects of the Economics category.

4.   a.   The library currently receives some 145 Latin American financial periodicals (more, in fact, than any other U.S. government-agency library). Included are bank bulletins and newsletters, and general statistical bulletins, from every Latin American and Caribbean nation, as well as a good selection of non-governmental economic, financial, and commercial reviews. The largest numbers of titles are from Argentina (21), Mexico (15), Brazil (14), Venezuela (10), Chile, Colombia, Peru, and Jamaica (6 each). Many of the periodical holdings are retained by the library for only one or two years. Holdings of major bank bulletins from some countries, however, extend back to the 1930s.

5.   A dictionary card catalog is the primary finding-aid. The library's computer-printout list of currently-received periodicals is available upon request.

Note: Also see entry J12.

A18   Folger Shakespeare Library

1.   a.   *201 East Capitol Street, SE*
      Washington, D.C. 20003
      546-4800

  b.   8:45 A.M.-4:45 P.M. Monday-Friday
      8:45 A.M.-4:30 P.M. Saturday

  c.   The Folger Shakespeare Library is an advanced research library, open to serious researchers (usually persons at the graduate- or postdoctoral levels). There is no interlibrary loan, but photoduplication and microfilming services are available.

  d.   O.B. Hardison, Jr., Director

2.   Within the total collection of 220,000 volumes and 40,000 manuscripts are approximately 800 Latin American-related volumes and a handful of Caribbean-related manuscripts.

3.   The collection focuses not only on Shakespeare, Shakespearean England, and English literature, but also on all aspects of 16th- and 17th-century Western civilization. Works on the European voyages of discovery and exploration are well represented, as are early descriptive, historical, and travel accounts relating to Latin America. There are a number of 16th-, 17th-, and 18th-century imprints on Latin America and British America, including

several 17th- and 18th-century items pertaining to the British Caribbean. The manuscript collection contains a handful of late-16th- and 17th-century Spanish and English documents pertaining to the Caribbean basin.

5.   A dictionary card catalog is available. For manuscript holdings, see the three-volume *Catalog of Manuscripts of the Folger Shakespeare Library* (Boston: G.K. Hall & Co., 1971), specifically entries under "Spanish America" and "West Indies."

A19 Food and Agriculture Organization (FAO) (United Nations)— Liaison Office for North America Library

1. a. *1776 F Street, NW*
Washington, D.C. 20437
634-6215

   b. 8 A.M-5:30 P.M. Monday-Friday

   c. Open to the public. No interlibrary loan. Limited photocopying services available (for small numbers of pages).

2-3. The Food and Agriculture Organization's Washington Office library contains a small but useful collection of FAO documents and publications, including budgets and conference reports, FAO statistical yearbooks on world agricultural production and trade, fisheries, forest products, and animal health, world agricultural commodity reviews and projections, FAO nutritional and agricultural studies, and the organization's international *Food and Agriculture Legislation* series, as well as three FAO periodicals—the *Monthly Bulletin of Agricultural and Economic Statistics*, the bimonthly magazine *Ceres: FAO Review on Agriculture and Development*, and the Washington Office's *Notes for North America.*

In addition, FAO Washington Office staff member Teresa Clark (634-6214) has handled FAO liaison matters with the OAS and Inter-American Development Bank, and maintains a valuable reference collection of documents and reports, including OAS country-reviews, on agricultural development, land reform, and land tenure, which she will make available to researchers. She has also prepared a useful *Directory of International, Inter-American, U.S., and Canadian Organizations Concerned with Latin American Development* (1974), which may be consulted in the office.

5.   FAO documents-indexes are available in the library. Also see the sales pamphlet *FAO Books in Print*, which contains information on how to order FAO publications from United Nations headquarters in New York City.

Note: Also see entry F7.

A20 Geological Survey Library (Interior Department)

1. a. *12201 Sunrise Valley Drive, Fourth Floor*
Reston, Virginia 22092
860-6671 (Reference)

   b. 7:45 A.M.-4:15 P.M. Monday-Friday

c. Open to the public. Interlibrary loan and photocopying facilities available.

d. George H. Goodwin, Jr., Librarian

2. The library has approximately 600,000 monographic and serials titles, at least 2,000 of which focus on Latin America.

3. The bulk of the library's Latin American holdings are in the earth sciences and other physical sciences, particularly the fields of geology (general, structural, dynamic, historical, and economic), physical geography, mineralogy, and petrology. The official publications (serials, periodicals, individual reports) of Latin American government geological services, mining bureaus, and minerals institutes are well represented, with coverage extending back into the mid- or late-19th century in many instances. Other holdings include sporadic nongeological government serials on agriculture, natural resources, irrigation, etc., private nongovernmental geological periodicals, and periodicals in sciences other than geology (geography, natural history, etc.). Also scattered throughout the collection are copies of mining and natural-resource legislation, 19th- and early-20th-century reports from U.S. petroleum and mining companies in Latin America, and field reports by 19th-century scientific expeditions.

4. f. The library's map collection is discussed in entry E2

5. A subject catalog and an author-title catalog are maintained. Within the subject catalog, Latin American titles may appear under country headings or under geographic subdivisions of scientific subject headings. For a thorough search of the collection by country, researchers might wish to peruse the library's shelflist, aided by a copy (available on request) of the *Geological Survey Library Classification Scheme and Index.*

Within the library's open stacks, Latin American government geological publications, private geological periodicals, periodicals in nongeological sciences, and nongeological government serials are shelved together in separate sections, each of which is subdivided by country.

The library's card catalog has been reproduced as *Catalog of the United States Geological Survey Library,* 25 vols. (Boston: G.K. Hall, 1964), with on-going supplements.

A brochure, *U.S. Geological Survey Library,* is available without charge.

Note: Also see entries A27 and J16

A21 George Washington University Library

1. a. *2130 H Street, NW*
Washington, D.C. 20052
676-6047 (Reference)

b. Academic year:
8:30 A.M.-midnight Monday-Friday
10 A.M.-6 P.M. Saturday
Noon-midnight Sunday
(Hours may vary during examination periods, holidays, intersessions, and summer sessions. For information on library hours, call 676-6845.)

c. Open to the public for on-site use. Interlibrary loan and photoreproduction facilities are available.

d. Rupert C. Woodward, University Librarian

2. The library contains approximately 500,000 volumes. Latin American holdings total more than 7,600 volumes. The library also currently receives 7,700 periodicals (42 emanating from Latin America) and 67 newspapers (one Latin American: Havana's *Granma* weekly review).

3. a. The library's principal Latin American strength is in literature, particularly Mexican and Colombian.

b. Subject categories and evaluations:

1. Philosophy and Religion	95 t.	C/D
2. History	2,658 t.	C/D
3. Geography and Anthropology	38 t.	D
4. Economics	602 t.	D
5. Sociology	215 t.	C/D
6. Politics and Government	181 t.	D
7. International Relations	379 t.	B
8. Law	unmeasured*	
9. Education	72 t.	Below D
10. Art and Music	67 t.	Below D
11. Language and Literature	3,128 t.	B/C
12. Military Affairs	4 t.	Below D
13. Bibliography and Reference	157 t.	C

14. Argentina	689 t.	C/D
15. Bolivia	54 t.	D
16. Brazil	573 t.	D
17. Caribbean (excluding Cuba)	353 t.	C
18. Central America	453 t.	C
19. Chile	365 t.	C
20. Colombia	415 t.	B/C
21. Cuba	249 t.	C
22. Ecuador	74 t.	D
23. Guianas	28 t.	C/D
24. Mexico	1,475 t.	B
25. Paraguay	42 t.	D
26. Peru	225 t.	C/D
27. Uruguay	173 t.	C
28. Venezuela	173 t.	C/D

*George Washington University's Jacob Burns Law Library, located on campus at 716 20th Street, NW (676-6646), has a small collection of some 150 titles on Latin American law.

4. f. The George Washington University Library is the Washington, D.C. Consortium of Universities' depository library for Defense Mapping Agency Topographic Center maps.

g. The library's Audiovisual Department (676-6378) is a regional center for Vanderbilt University's Television News Archive, and as such can supply videotapes of news stories on Latin America aired by the three major U.S. commercial television networks. An annual index, Vanderbilt Television News Archive, *Television News Index and Abstracts: A Guide to the Videotape Collection of the Network Evening News Programs,* has been published since 1968.

A22   Georgetown University—Lauinger Library

1. a. *37th and O Streets, NW*
        Washington, D.C. 20057
        625-4173 (Reference)

    b. Academic year:
        8:30 A.M.-midnight Monday-Thursday
        8:30 A.M.-10 P.M. Friday
        10 A.M.-10 P.M. Saturday
        11 A.M.-midnight Sunday
        (For summer hours, call 625-3300)

    c. Open to scholars for on-site use. Interlibrary loan and photocopying facilities are available.

    d. Joseph E. Jeffs, University Librarian

2.   The library collection numbers some 750,000 volumes, with Latin American holdings of at least 13,500 volumes. The library also currently receives 3,450 serials (an estimated 50 from Latin America) and 26 newspapers (four from Latin America: Buenos Aires' *La Prensa,* Mexico City's *Excelsior,* Havana's *Granma,* and *Estado de Sao Paulo*).

3. a. One of the strongest university collections in the area. Principal strengths are in religion, history (particularly Argentine and Brazilian), and international relations.

    b. Subject categories and evaluations:

1. Philosophy and Religion	195 t.	B
2. History	5,810 t.	B
3. Geography and Anthropology	28 t.	D
4. Economics	1,703 t.	B/C
5. Sociology	587 t.	B
6. Politics and Government	562 t.	C/B
7. International Relations	463 t.	B
8. Law	41 t.*	Below D
9. Education	106 t.	D
10. Art and Music	118 t.	D
11. Language and Literature	3,723 t.	B/C
12. Military Affairs	10 t.	Below D
13. Bibliography and Reference	212 t.	B/C

14. Argentina	1,518 t.	B
15. Bolivia	192 t.	B
16. Brazil	1,886 t.	B
17. Caribbean (excluding Cuba)	707 t.	B
18. Central America	673 t.	B/C
19. Chile	549 t.	B/C
20. Colombia	392 t.	B/C
21. Cuba	347 t.	C
22. Ecuador	157 t.	C
23. Guianas	33 t.	C
24. Mexico	1,332 t.	B/C
25. Paraguay	235 t.	B
26. Peru	466 t.	B/C
27. Uruguay	305 t.	B/C
28. Venezuela	294 t.	C

*Georgetown University's Fred O. Dennis Law Center Library, located off-campus near Capitol Hill at 600 New Jersey Avenue, NW, has a Foreign Law Section (624-8375) containing approximately 130 Latin American titles.

4. c. Georgetown's Lauinger Library is the only selective depository library for United States government documents in the Washington, D.C. Consortium of Universities. Its holdings total some 71,000 government publications. The library also has complete sets of OAS (1961-present) and UN (1946-present) publications on microfilm.

  e. The Archives, Manuscripts, and Rare Books Division (625-4567/4160) possesses a variety of unique materials dealing with the Panama Canal, Mexico, and Peru. Contact George M. Barringer, Special Collections librarian, or John Reynolds, University Archivist and Manuscripts Curator.

  Panama Canal materials feature the papers of Tomás Herrán, Colombian envoy to the United States in 1903. The Herrán Collection, measuring 2.5 linear feet, contains cable communications between Herrán and Bogotá as well as correspondence with Philippe Bunau-Varilla, John Hay, William Nelson Cromwell, and others. The Earl Harding papers (6 linear feet) contain correspondence, photographs, and documents dealing with the 1903 Panamanian revolution by a reporter for Joseph Pulitzer. Other collections of interest are the papers of three U.S. Congressional leaders active in Canal-oversight committee matters in the post-World War II era—Sen. Thomas E. Martin (2.25 linear feet), Rep. Clark W. Thompson (4.5 linear feet), and Rep. Leonor K. Sullivan (3 linear feet). The papers of two American lobbyists interested in the Canal's enlargement during the 1950s, William McCann and Miles DuVal, are also here.

  Mexican materials include one uncataloged box of Agustín de Iturbide's papers, a box of papers pertaining to José Antonio López, a Mexican priest who served as tutor and guardian to Iturbide's children from 1816 to the mid-1920s, and a box of Antonio López de Santa Anna's papers (including letters and field reports from his generals during the Mexican War). Other collections of interest are the papers of Fathers Antonio Rey and John McElroy, Catholic chaplains serving in the U.S. army during the Mexican War, and the papers of three Jesuit officials involved with Mexican affairs during the late 1920s—the Revs. Richard Tierney, Wilfrid Parsons, and Edmund Walsh.

  Peruvian materials include one bound volume of Jesuit mission reports, primarily from Brazil and Paraguay, ca. 1675-1682 (located in the George

Schwarz collection), a box of 18 annual letters (some unpublished) from Jesuit missions in Peru on Jesuit activities there and in Chile, 1591-1704 (contained in the John B. Molloy collection), and a folder of miscellaneous Peruvian documents dating from 1650 to 1820.

The Rare Books collection has approximately 10 shelves devoted to Latin America. Holdings include travel accounts, early titles on the Spanish borderlands, and a 1571 edition of Alonso de Molina's Spanish-Nahuatl dictionary with manuscript annotations in a second Indian language.

g-h. Among the Audiovisual Department's various materials are approximately 40 slide collections focusing on Latin American art, architecture, archeology, and culture, by country; some 25 audiotaped interviews of, and readings by, Iberian and Latin American authors; and two short films—"Peron and Evita," and "Cuba: Art and Revolution."

Housing and Urban Development Department (HUD) Library See entry J15

A23 Howard University—Founders Library

1. a. *500 Howard Place, NW*
   Washington, D.C. 20059
   636-7253 (Reference)

   b. Open continuously from noon, Sunday until 5 P.M. Saturday.
   Limited services, midnight-8 A.M.

   c. Open to serious researchers for on-site use. Interlibrary loan and photoreproduction facilities available.

   d. Binford Conley, Director of University Libraries

2. The entire library system—comprising Founders and 10 smaller collections—contains some 880,000 volumes. Latin American holdings total at least 3,000 volumes. Use of these holdings is complicated by the fact that the Founders Library collection is classified partly under the Library of Congress system and partly under the older Dewey Decimal system.

3. b. Subject categories and evaluations:

1. Philosophy and Religion	54 t.	D
2. History	1,577 t.	D
3. Geography and Anthropology	6 t.	Below D
4. Economics	235 t.	Below D
5. Sociology	144 t.	D
6. Politics and Government	82 t.	Below D
7. International Relations	103 t.	D
8. Law	unmeasured	
9. Education	28 t.	Below D
10. Art and Music	54 t.	Below D
11. Language and Literature	658 t.	Below D

12. Military Affairs	6 t.	Below D
13. Bibliography and Reference	57 t.	Below D

14. Argentina	165 t.	Below D
15. Bolivia	40 t.	D
16. Brazil	262 t.	Below D
17. Caribbean (excluding Cuba)	361 t.	C
18. Central America	166 t.	Below D
19. Chile	100 t.	Below D
20. Colombia	42 t.	Below D
21. Cuba	128 t.	D
22. Ecuador	23 t.	Below D
23. Guianas	19 t.	D
24. Mexico	384 t.	D
25. Paraguay	22 t.	Below D
26. Peru	102 t.	Below D
27. Uruguay	43 t.	Below D
28. Venezuela	56 t.	Below D

A24 Howard University—Moorland-Spingarn Research Center Library

1. a. *500 Howard Place, NW*
      Washington, D.C. 20059
      636-7239

   b. 9 A.M.-9 P.M. Monday-Thursday
      9 A.M.-5 P.M. Friday-Saturday

   c. Open to the public for on-site use. There is no interlibrary loan service. Photocopy and microfilming facilities are available.

   d. Michael R. Winston, Director

2-3. The 90,000-volume Moorland-Spingarn collection, located in Howard University's Founders Library, specializes in works written by or about persons of African descent, worldwide. Its Latin American holdings are extensive, and are a significant resource for research on black history, literature, and culture in the English-, French-, and Spanish-speaking Caribbean, the circum-Caribbean basin, and Brazil. (A staff member estimates, for example, that the collection contains at least 100 titles on the British Caribbean not found in the Library of Congress.) A selective survey of the two subject catalogs (one for the Moorland collection, one for the Spingarn collection) revealed the following number of titles: Brazil, 1,105 t.; Cuba, 425 t.; Haiti, 1,934 t.; Jamaica, 553 t.; West Indies, 744 t.

   Particular strengths of the collection are works on slavery (including a number of rare, first-edition, slave memoirs and autobiographies) and black literature (especially Haitian, Afro-Cuban, and Afro-Brazilian). In addition, patient exploration of the stacks can result in the discovery of uncataloged primary materials such as original 18th-century manuscripts and documents dealing with the French colonial administration of Saint Domingue.

4. a-b. The library holds a large collection of Caribbean literary, historical, and scientific journals, dating from the 1920s to the present. Twenty Caribbean newspapers and magazines are available on microfilm.

   d. A Vertical File contains a substantial amount of miscellaneous materials (pamphlets, newspaper clippings, magazine articles, newsletters, etc., in varying stages of deterioration) on blacks in the Americas, by country and subject.

   e. The Manuscript Division (636-7239) contains several items of interest to Caribbeanists, including an indeterminate number of Toussaint L'Ouverture letters (part of an as-yet-unprocessed collection), the papers of Archibald Grimke (U.S. Consul in Santo Domingo, ca. 1894-98), and writings by Frederick Douglass on Haiti. There are indications that the unprocessed papers of several other American blacks contain manuscript materials on the Caribbean. For further information, contact Archivist Thomas C. Battle.

5. For the library's holdings, see *Dictionary Catalog of the Arthur B. Spingarn Collection of Negro Authors, Howard University Library, Washington, D.C.* (Boston: G.K. Hall and Co., 1970), and *Dictionary Catalog of the Jesse E. Moorland Collection of Negro Life and History, Howard University Library, Washington, D.C.* (Boston: G.K. Hall and Co., 1970) plus three-volume 1976 supplement.

   In addition, guides and descriptive brochures are available upon request.

Inter-American Defense Board Library See entry L4

A25 Inter-American Defense College Library

1. a. *Fort Lesley J. McNair*
      Washington, D.C. 20319
      693-8133

   b. 7:30 A.M.-4 P.M. Monday-Friday

   c. Primarily for the use of the students and faculty of the college. Permission to use the library may be granted upon request. Interlibrary loan service and photoreproduction facilities are available.

   d. Mercedes Mendez Bailey, Librarian

2. The total collection numbers approximately 20,000 volumes, with Latin American holdings of at least 5,000 volumes (50 percent in Spanish or Portuguese). The library receives 300 current periodicals, a substantial number of which are military-related journals (including Latin American armed-forces *revistas* from Argentina, Brazil, Colombia, the Dominican Republic, Mexico, and Venezuela). Back issues are retained for five years. Thirteen Latin American newspapers are currently received; copies are not retained.

3. The library's holdings do not concentrate on Latin American military affairs. Rather, they are eclectic, with a worldwide focus designed to support the wide-ranging curriculum of abstract and global, as well as hemispheric, topics taught at the Inter-American Defense College (see entry L5). The

Latin American collection is strongest in history and economics. Holdings on Latin American military affairs, internal security, and military civic-action, while not extensive, may include titles not available elsewhere in the area. Materials on inter-American military relations are well represented, and include pamphlets and studies produced by the United States Army's School of the Americas in the Canal Zone.

5. A list of "Periodicals Currently Received in the IADC Library" is available.

A26 Inter-American Development Bank Library

1. a. *801 17th Street, NW*
      Washington, D.C. 20577
      634-8382/83/84

   b. 9 A.M.-5:30 P.M. Monday-Friday

   c. Open to qualified researchers with permission of the director.

   d. R. Alberto Calvo, Chief of the Library

2. The library contains 34,000 volumes on Latin American socioeconomic matters and a separate 8,000-volume collection on Latin American "cultural" topics. It also has a periodicals collection of some 1,200 titles and receives 40 Latin American newspapers.

3. The Inter-American Development Bank Library has one of the Washington area's three strongest Latin American collections. Its holdings of post-1950 Latin American economic source materials (books and serials) equal or surpass those of the Library of Congress and the OAS Columbus Memorial Library. The book collection, 40 percent of which is in Spanish or Portuguese, contains a full range of works by Latin American economists and social scientists, and rates as an "A" collection in economics. The library is also a repository for IDB publications and program descriptions of bank-funded development projects.

   Perhaps the library's most significant resource is its serial collection. The library has extensive holdings of serial publications from every Latin American government—statistical bulletins, censuses, the annual reports of central banks, development corporations, and a wide range of governmental ministries, etc. The official publications of international economic organizations, regional-integration bodies (LAFTA, CACM, SELA, etc.) and regional development banks are also well represented, as are periodicals from the major Latin American research centers. In addition, the library maintains a large card-index (arranged by author, title, subject, and country) to periodical articles on any aspect of social or economic development in Latin America.

   The texts of a large number of Latin American national development plans are available on microfiche.

   The separately-cataloged Cultural Library has a good selection of titles, almost entirely in Spanish and Portuguese, on Latin American history, politics, philosophy, and literature, by country. There are many works here, particularly relating to the smaller republics, which are not found in area university libraries.

A survey of the combined holdings of the library's economics collection and the cultural collection produced the following country-totals and ratings:

Argentina	1.764.t.	B
Bolivia	453 t.	B/A
Brazil	1.193 t.	C
Caribbean (excluding Cuba)	460 t.	C
Central America	1.176 t.	B/A
Chile	963 t.	B
Colombia	879 t.	B
Cuba	179 t.	C/D
Ecuador	267 t.	B
Guianas	7 t.	Below D
Mexico	1.305 t.	B
Paraguay	220 t.	B
Peru	690 t.	B
Uruguay	446 t.	B
Venezuela	717 t.	B/A

In addition, the bank's Law Library (Room 1216a) has a 3,000-volume collection of current Latin American legal codes, commercial and financial legislation, international treaties, and related materials. A 13-drawer vertical file (card-indexed) contains recent official *gacetas* from every Latin American nation.

4 h. The library is currently in the process of building a record and tape collection of Latin American music.

5. The library publishes a quarterly *Boletín,* listing new acquisitions by country and subject. A 121-page *Lista de Publicaciones Periodicas* (1973), which itemizes the serials received by the library, is also available. In addition, the library prepares occasional bibliographies on topics of interest to the Bank staff (e.g., finance, land reform, financing of higher education).

A27 Interior Department—Natural Resources Library

1. a. *C Street, between 18th and 19th Streets, NW*
Washington, D.C. 20240
343-5815 (Reference)

   b. 7:45 A.M.-5 P.M. Monday-Friday

   c. Open to the public, for on-site use only. Interlibrary loan and photocopying facilities available.

   d. Mary A. Huffer, Director

2. The collection numbers some 800,000 volumes, with Latin American holdings of approximately 2,300 titles.

3. Latin American holdings consist largely of Latin American government serials and reports on natural resources, particularly minerals, mines, and fisheries. Latin American geological, hydrological, and mining bulletins are well represented. The collection also includes national law codes and regulations concerning the exploitation of natural resources, as well as substantial material on national parks. Geographic coverage is strongest for

Brazil (390 t.), Mexico (350 t.), Argentina (340 t.), Venezuela (175 t.), and Peru (170 t.). The majority of titles appear to be 1930s-1950s imprints. The staff warns that some of the pre-1950s titles which appear in the library's card catalog may have been discarded or lost.

5. A dictionary card catalog is available. Also see U.S. Department of the Interior, *Dictionary Catalog of the Departmental Library,* 37 vols. (Boston: G.K. Hall, 1967) and four supplements (1969-1975).

Note: Also see entries A20 and J16.

International Center for Research on Women Library Collection
See entry M23

A28 International Communication Agency (ICA) Library

1. a. *Room 1011*
      1750 Pennsylvania Avenue, NW
      Washington, D.C. 20547
      724-9214 (Librarian)
      724-9126 (Reference)

   b. 8:45 A.M.-5:30 P.M. Monday-Friday

   c. Closed to the public, but qualified researchers may obtain permission to use unique materials. Interlibrary loan service and photocopying facilities are available.

   d. Jeanne R. Zeydel, Librarian

2. The ICA (formerly United States Information Agency) Library collection comprises some 63,300 volumes, approximately 1,100 of which deal with Latin America. Sizable special collections focus on government documents and Communist propaganda (see point four, below).

3. The book collection of the ICA Library is not a significant resource for Latin Americanists. Primarily a reference collection for ICA staff members, its topical and geographic focus is on "Americana." Latin American holdings are insufficient to warrant a subject-strength evaluation.

4. a-b. The library receives 21,900 newspapers and periodicals. Those emanating from Latin America are not retained in the library, but are sent to the various Latin American area divisions within ICA.

   c. Documents Branch
      Room 1011
      Mary Woods, Chief
      724-9364

   The Documents Branch of the library contains more than 3.5 million items, dating from 1944 to the present. Included are unclassified U.S. government reports and press releases, reports issued by international organizations and research centers, and clippings from eight U.S. newspapers. The collection is organized by geographic areas and by subjects. There are six large drawers of materials on Latin America as a general region, five in Cuba, three each on

Mexico and Brazil, etc. Within each country and area file, materials are arranged by subject ("agriculture," "foreign relations," etc.). In addition, the Documents Branch maintains biographic files of similar materials on some 100,000 persons, including major Latin American governmental and cultural figures. The staff is in the process of weeding out materials over two years old, and microfilms the least expendable items. A file index to microfilmed items is available.

d. Propaganda Collection
Room 1014
Carol Ryczek, Librarian
724-9292

This specialized collection contains some 25,000 pieces of Communist propaganda—books, magazines, newspapers, pamphlets, leaflets, posters, etc.—in Western languages. Approximately 25 percent of the collection consists of Soviet propaganda disseminated in Latin America and materials produced by indigenous Latin American Communist movements. Holdings are organized by country, and are most extensive for the years 1965-1973. The librarian is available only on a part-time basis, Monday through Wednesday, 9 a.m. to 4 p.m.

5. An information pamphlet and an index of periodical holdings are available.
The Library regularly publishes accessions lists of books (biweekly), documents (weekly), and classified documents (weekly)—each organized by geographic area.

Note: Also see entry J17.

International Food Policy Research Institute Library Collection
See entry M26

International Institute for Environment and Development—Washington Office Library Collection See entry M27

A29 International Labour Organization (ILO) (United Nations)—Washington Branch Office Library

1. a. *Room 330*
1750 New York Avenue, NW
Washington, D.C. 20006
634-6335

b. 8:30 A.M.-5 P.M. Monday-Friday

c. Open to the public. No interlibrary loan. Photocopying facilities available.

d. Patricia S. Hord, Librarian

2-3. The International Labour Organization (ILO) Washington Branch Office library collection consists of between 6,000 and 8,000 ILO documents and publications dating from 1919 to the present. It is an excellent resource for research on Latin American labor conditions, employment, trade-unionism, workers' standards of living, and social security. Among the holdings are ILO conference documents; the minutes of the ILO Governing Body; reports, resolutions, and proceedings of ILO regional (including Latin American) and industrial (mining, petroleum, plantations, etc.) conferences; the ILO *Yearbook of Labour Statistics;* the ILO's *Legislative Series* of national laws and regulations on labor and social security (in English); ILO studies and reports on international labor conditions, trade-unionism, labor-management relations, social security, occupational health and safety, etc.; International Social Security Association publications; and documents from International Conferences of Labour Statisticians. The collection also includes selected research studies from ILO affiliates in Latin America—the Inter-American Center for Labor Administration, the Center for Inter-American Vocational Training—Research and Documentation Center, and the Regional Employment Program for Latin America.

Of particular interest to Latin Americanists will be the library's collection of "technical assistance program" ("TAP") reports presented to Latin American national governments by ILO field-investigation missions. Among the subjects covered by various of these reports are employment and labor conditions, national labor codes, wages, consumer prices, cost-of-living, social security, trade unionism, occupational safety, vocational training, and worker rehabilitation. Some of the reports are classified "confidential" by the Latin American governmental recipient, but many of these restricted reports will be made available to researchers under the condition that the researcher will agree not to quote directly from the report. A card-index to the reports, by country, is available.

Note: The Washington Branch Office also sells ILO publications. An *ILO Catalogue of Publications in Print* and a subscription order-form will be supplied on request.

4.   a.   Also available are complete collections of most ILO periodicals, including the *Official Bulletin, International Labour Review, Bulletin of Labour Statistics, Social and Labour Bulletin, Labour Education, Cooperative Information,* and *Women at Work.*

      d.   The Office also maintains a separate country-file of national laws and regulations on labor and social security, 1920-present, drawn from the ILO Legislative Series.

5.   There is no card catalog. The key finding-aids for identifying documents and publications on Latin America are the ILO's *Subject Guide to Publications of the International Labour Office, 1919-1964* (Geneva, 1967); *International Labour Documentation* (Boston: G.K. Hall, 1968-1972), a 12-volume index to the holdings of the ILO Central Library in Geneva, Switzerland, with on-going monthly supplements; and the *ILO Catalogue of Publications in Print.*

Note: Also see entry F10.

A30 International Trade Commission Library

1.   a.   *701 E Street, NW*
           Washington, D.C. 20436
           523-0013

      b.   8:45 A.M.-5:15 P.M. Monday-Friday

    c. Open to the public. Interlibrary loan and photoreproduction facilities available.

    d. Dorothy J. Berkowitz, Chief, Library Division

2-3.   The International Trade Commission (formerly Tariff Commission) Library receives official foreign-trade serials and statistical yearbooks from almost every Latin American and Caribbean country. Holdings extend back to 1950 for most countries. The library also features a full set of International Customs Journal translations of the customs laws, past and present, of every Latin American nation.

  4. c. Of particular interest to researchers will be the library's separate "Foreign Service collection" of recent economic reports from U.S. embassies throughout the world. This collection consists of official airgrams—the vast majority of which are unclassified—reporting general economic conditions, trade developments, agricultural and industrial production, investment climate, etc., in each foreign country in which the United States has diplomatic representatives. The reports are kept on file for two years and are then destroyed. Private researchers will be given access to unclassified reports.

Note: Also see entry J18.

A31 Joint Bank-Fund Library (Library of the International Bank for Reconstruction and Development [World Bank] and the International Monetary Fund)

1. a. *1800 G Street, NW*
        Washington, D.C. 20431
        477-3125 (Librarian)
        477-3167 (Reference)

    b. 8:30 A.M.-6 P.M. Monday-Friday
       8 A.M.-1 P.M. Saturday

    c. Open to serious researchers with permission of the librarian. Interlibrary loan and photocopying facilities are available.

    d. Charles O. Olsen, Librarian

2.   The library contains some 85,000 monograph and serial titles, with Latin American holdings exceeding 11,500. The library receives 3,000 current periodicals and newspapers, approximately one-eighth of which emanate in Latin America.

3.   The library has a good collection of Latin American materials on topics of interest to the World Bank and IMF: banking, commerce, finance, agriculture, industry, labor, economic policy, planning, production, and development. For the "Economics" subject-category, the collection falls between an "A" and "B" rating. Country totals in economics are:

Argentina	662 t.
Bolivia	288 t.
Brazil	947 t.
Caribbean (excluding Cuba)	1,402 t.
Central America	1,614 t.

Chile	632 t.
Colombia	820 t.
Cuba	207 t.
Ecuador	337 t.
Guianas	334 t.
Mexico	820 t.
Paraguay	187 t.
Peru	518 t.
Uruguay	298 t.
Venezuela	534 t.

The collection is particularly strong in serials holdings: annual reports, statistical digests, bulletins, etc., from central banks, government ministries, regional and international organizations, and private research centers. Although its Latin American serials holdings are less extensive than those of the Inter-American Development Bank Library, the Joint Bank-Fund Library is considerably older than the IDB Library, and its *retrospective* serials holdings are probably fuller (dating from the 1930s, in some cases).

5.   For a complete catalog of the library's Latin American collection, see *The Developing Areas, A Classed Bibliography of the Joint Bank-Fund Library: Volume I, Latin America and the Caribbean* (Boston: G.K. Hall and Co., 1976).

     The library has also produced *Economics and Finance: Index to Periodical Articles, 1947-1971*, 4 vols., (Boston: G.K. Hall and Co., 1972) and a *First Supplement, 1972-1974*. A card index to periodical articles since 1974 is maintained.

     A *Guide to the Joint Bank-Fund Library* and a *Current List of Periodicals Received by the Joint Bank-Fund Library* (with periodicals listed by country of origin) are available upon request.

Note: The World Bank's Latin America and the Caribbean Regional Information and Documents Center (477-5446) maintains a reference collection of internally and externally produced documents, restricted and non-restricted, to support the bank's Latin American research activities. The facility is not open to the public.

A32   Labor Department Library

1.   a.   *New Department of Labor Building, Room 2439*
     200 Constitution Avenue, NW
     Washington, D.C. 20210
     523-6992 (Reference)

     b.   8:15 A.M.-4:45 P.M. Monday-Friday

     c.   Open to the public for on-site use. Interlibrary loan and photoreproduction facilities available.

     d.   Andre C. Whisenton, Librarian

2.   The Labor Department Library contains some 500,000 volumes, more than 8,000 of which focus specifically on Latin America. Of approximately 2,500 periodicals currently received, about 100 (primarily labor and social security reviews, trade union publications, national statistical bulletins, and some industrial and general economic periodicals) emanate from Latin America.

3. The library's collection rates in the "A" range for research on Latin American labor topics. Subject strengths include rural and urban labor forces, labor legislation, trade unionism, wages, cost-of-living, industrial and agricultural production, labor disputes and arbitration, social insurance, and workers' health, safety, and welfare. The majority of the Latin American holdings are government documents and reports—including labor codes and decree-laws, the reports of government ministries, banks, commissions, institutes, and conferences, national censuses and other statistical surveys, presidential addresses, and government proclamations. Holdings of government labor bulletins range sporadically back to World War I or earlier in some instances. Overall, the collection appears to be strongest in materials printed between ca. World War I and 1950, although earlier and later imprints are also fairly well represented. From a geographic perspective, Central America (1,500 t.), Mexico (800 t.), Brazil (760 t.), Argentina (580 t.), and Chile (530 t.) are represented in greatest abundance.

    Other strengths are International Labour Organization publications, and literature on Mexican-Americans and Mexican laborers in the United States.

4. a. A special "Foreign Trade Union Periodicals" collection, arranged alphabetically by country, contains Latin American materials dating from the late 1950s to the present.

    d. A separate vertical file called the "I.M.I. collection" consists in part of miscellaneous uncataloged Latin American government publications (on labor, education, business, human resources, etc.) assembled by the Labor Department's former International Management Institute. The materials are arranged by country, and date roughly from the 1950s and 1960s.

5. Two dictionary card catalogs must be consulted: an "Old Catalog" of publications cataloged prior to February, 1975, and a "New Catalog" of subsequent acquisitions. The Old Catalog has been printed, in 38 volumes, as *U.S. Department of Labor Library Catalog* (Boston: G.K. Hall, 1975).

    A 1973 list of *Journals Treating Foreign Countries Currently Received by the U.S. Department of Labor Library* is being updated.

Note: Also see entry J20.

A33   Library of Congress (LC)

1. a. *10 1st Street, SE*
        Washington, D.C. 20540
        426-5000

    b. General Reading Rooms:
        8:30 A.M.-9:30 P.M. (stack service to 9 P.M.) Monday-Friday
        8:30 A.M.-5 P.M. (stack service to 4 P.M.) Saturday
        1 P.M.-5 P.M. (stack service to 4:30 P.M.) Sunday
        Closed on all holidays except Washington's Birthday, Columbus Day, and Veterans Day.
        Divison hours noted below.

    c. Open to postsecondary-school researchers for on-site use. Interlibrary loan service (exclusive of periodicals and newspapers) is available to other libraries. Self-service, coin-operated, photocopying machines are available in the general reading rooms. In addition, the Photoduplication Service, Room G-1009, Annex Building (426-5640) will, for a fee, provide photostats, microfilms, and other photocopies of any materials in the Library of Congress collections.

    d.   Daniel J. Boorstin, The Librarian of Congress
        Division chiefs listed below.

2-3.   It is difficult to discuss the Library of Congress (LC) without a certain ambivalence. On one hand, LC undoubtedly possesses the largest and most comprehensive collection of Latin American research materials in the United States, and probably in the world. On the other hand, frustrations and obstacles abound in identifying and retrieving those materials. Holdings are so massive, and so diffused among various divisions of the library, that it is often difficult to identify everything that is available for research on a given topic. Large quantities of materials (for example, a 6,000-volume Costa Rican book collection, a Spanish theater collection, and vast holdings of Latin American film and music materials) remain totally uncataloged. Cataloged materials are divided, frequently at random, among several divisions (for Latin American periodicals one must look in the main book collections, the Serial Division, the Hispanic Law Division, and the Microform Reading Room; colonial manuscripts and government documents can be found in the main book collection, the Manuscript Division, the Microform Reading Room, etc.). To be thorough, researchers must visit the various divisions described below, explore the catalogs and other "finding aids" available in each division, and discuss their research projects with as many library staff members as possible.

    Poor stack service in the Main Reading Room has been a traditional source of irritation to researchers. ("Horror-stories" are legion about three-hour waits for a "Not-on-Shelf" response to book requests.) The library is, nevertheless, diligently attempting to improve its services. The Collections Management Division (426-5455), located in the Main Reading Room, responds to readers' complaints regarding stack service. The Study Facilities Office of the General Reading Rooms Division (426-5530), also located in the Main Reading Room, will provide scholars with special research/study facilities—including private desks (for which there is currently a six-month waiting list), reserved book shelves, advance book-reserve service, and limited stack passes. In addition, the Hispanic Division (discussed below) provides separate study facilities to Latin Americanists and can be of assistance in obtaining stack materials.

    Negativism aside, however, the Library of Congress is an extraordinary resource for substantive primary research in virtually any field of Latin American studies. Within its total collection of more than 75 million items are an estimated one million Latin American-related items. For books, and for retrospective runs of government serials (national and provincial), newspapers, and other periodicals, there is no more extensive a collection in the United States. So voluminous and diverse are LC's Latin American holdings that it would be an injustice (if not an impossibility) to attempt to itemize or categorize "significant" topical or geographic strengths. Suffice it to say that visiting Latin American scholars consistently report the discovery of materials in LC that are not available in their home countries.

3. b. Subject categories and evaluations:

1. Philosophy and Religion	2,167 t.	A
2. History	64,886 t.	A
3. Geography and Anthropology	1,308 t.	A
4. Economics	25,370 t.	A
5. Sociology	5,520 t.	A
6. Politics and Government	8,736 t.	A
7. International Relations	4,287 t.	A
8. Law	41,780 t.	A
9. Education	4,554 t.	A
10. Art and Music	3,931 t.	A
11. Language and Literature	50,140 t.	A
12. Military Affairs	663 t.	A
13. Bibliography and Reference	3,339 t.	A

---

14. Argentina	17,873 t.	A
15. Bolivia	2,238 t.	A
16. Brazil	22,707 t.	A
17. Caribbean (excluding Cuba)	8,167 t.	A
18. Central America	8,126 t.	A
19. Chile	6,645 t.	A
20. Colombia	5,516 t.	A
21. Cuba	5,874 t.	A
22. Ecuador	2,809 t.	A
23. Guianas	724 t.	A
24. Mexico	16,535 t.	A
25. Paraguay	1,636 t	A
26. Peru	6,253 t.	A
27. Uruguay	4,086 t.	A
28. Venezuela	4,664 t.	A

4. HISPANIC DIVISION

Main Building, Second Floor
426-5400 (Administration)
426-5397 (Reference)

8:30 A.M.-5 P.M. Monday-Friday

William E. Carter, Chief
John Hebert, Assistant Chief
Georgette Dorn, Head—Reference Section
Everette Larson, Area Librarian

The Hispanic Division (until recently called the Latin American, Spanish, and Portuguese Division, and previously the Hispanic Foundation) is the Library of Congress' reference and bibliographic center for all fields of Latin American studies except law. It should serve as the Latin Americanist's initial and primary contact point at the library. The staff will orient researchers regarding LC's diverse Latin American collections, answer bibliographic and reference questions, and assist in securing materials from the stacks. Research materials obtained in the Main Reading Room may be brought to the division's public reading area, where they will be held for up to 90 days.

The division maintains a 4,000-volume reference collection, a 16-drawer vertical file of current directories, bibliographic reports, and other reference aids, and a clipping collection of Latin American-related items appearing in major U.S. newspapers. In addition, it houses a 200-box pamphlet collection of miscellaneous political, economic, literary, and general-information materials, arranged geographically and topically. The collection, dating primarily from the 1940s and 1950s, but with items ranging back into the 19th century, contains a diversity of intriguing materials in addition to pamphlets, including scattered literary manuscripts and photocopies of rare books and documents not found elsewhere in the library. Another 200 boxes of uncataloged pamphlet materials, dating from 1900-1930, are presently in storage.

The division also administers the Archive of Hispanic Literature on Tape. Begun in 1943, this facility features tape-recordings of nearly 350 Latin American and Iberian poets and prose writers reading selections from their original works, as well as interviews and commentaries. Virtually every major Latin American literary figure of the past three decades is represented. In addition to its literary significance, the tape collection documents distinctive regional dialects and speech patterns. Listening equipment is available, as are notebooks containing lists and texts of recorded selections. Surveys of the collection include Francisco Aguilera (comp.), *The Archive of Hispanic Literature on Tape: A Descriptive Guide* (Washington, D.C.: Library of Congress, 1974); Georgette Dorn, "The Archive of Hispanic Literature on Tape," *Federal Linguist 7* (nos. 1-4, 1976); and an author/country list, available without charge from the division.

The major publication of the Hispanic Division is the well-known *Handbook of Latin American Studies,* an annual bibliography containing descriptive and evaluative comments on recent books and articles in the social sciences and humanities. It is estimated that 95 percent of all titles listed in the *Handbook* can be found in the Library of Congress collection. Among the division's other publications are the *National Directory of Latin Americanists,* 2nd ed. (1972), and *Latin America, Spain, and Portugal: An Annotated Bibliography of Paperback Books,* 2nd rev. ed. (1976).

SERIAL DIVISION

Newspaper and Current Periodical Room
Annex (Thomas Jefferson Building), Room 1026
426-5690

Hours: same as Main Reading Room

Donald Wisdom, Chief

LC's Newspaper and Current Periodical Room has what is generally regarded as the world's largest collection of Latin American newspapers and recent periodicals. Unless the researcher arrives with specific titles in mind, however, adequate catalogs or indexes to these materials do not always exist.

The 98 Latin American newspapers currently received are listed in an LC publication, *Newspapers Received Currently in the Library of Congress,* 5th ed. (1976). Retrospective newspaper holdings are indeterminate but extensive. No comprehensive newspaper card catalog is maintained—researchers are instead referred to Steven M. Charno's 1968 work *Latin American*

Newspapers in United States Libraries: A Union List for information on LC's holdings. The staff also relies heavily on *A Check List of Foreign Newspapers in the Library of Congress* (1929) and loose-leaf supplementary updates through the 1960s. All newspaper acquisitions since 1962 have been microfilmed, and a card catalog for these holdings is available, as is an LC publication, *Newspapers in Microform: Foreign Countries, 1948-1972* (1973), and an annual supplement, *Newspapers in Microform.* The staff indicates that the entire pre-1962 retrospective collection is scheduled to be microfilmed within the next decade. Active efforts are currently being made to develop microfilm-exchange programs with Latin American libraries, and will soon result in the acquisition of complete holdings of two major Brazilian newspapers on microfilm, *O Estado de São Paulo* and Rio de Janeiro's *O Jornal do Commercio.* Potential future microfilm acquisitions are *El Comercio* (Lima), *El Universal* (Caracas), and *El Tiempo* (Bogotá).

The Newspaper and Current Periodical Room also receives an impressive range of Latin American government serial publications and other periodicals (official *gacetas* and law journals, however, go to the Hispanic Law Division). It should be noted that, unlike newspapers, periodical items are eventually transferred to LC's main book collection as they become dated. The primary finding aid for current periodicals is a somewhat unreliable dictionary card catalog which is currently in the process of being updated. A selective survey of this catalog produced the following numbers of currently received periodicals by country: Argentina, 304 t.; Brazil, 450 t.; Chile, 118 t.; Mexico, 254 t.; Peru, 85 t.; Venezuela, 47 t. The survey also turned up a total of 466 *"revistas"* and 108 *"boletines."* Holdings of recent Brazilian and Cuban government serials appear to be particularly strong. Further information on LC's Latin American serial holdings can be obtained from the five-volume *Union List of Serials* (1965) and an ongoing supplement (*New Serials Titles*), as well as from Rosa Quintero Mesa's multivolume series, *Latin American Serials Documents: A Holdings List* (R.R. Bowker and University Microfilms, 1968-1973).

Division staff member Robert Schaaf specializes in the publications and documents of international organizations—including the UN, OAS, LAFTA, CACM, and other Latin American regional organizations. He can aid researchers in locating these materials in LC and elsewhere.

RARE BOOK DIVISION

Main Building, Room 256
426-5435

8:30 A.M.-5 P.M. Monday-Friday

William Matheson, Chief

Within the division's general collection of incunabula and rare books can be found a large number of Latin American travel accounts, government decrees, military documents, miscellaneous literary works, and early periodicals, dating primarily from the 17th through 19th centuries. A selective survey of the division's alphabetically arranged card catalog revealed the following number of titles by country: Argentina, 51 t.; Brazil, 189 t.; Chile, 78 t.; Colombia, 50 t.; Mexico, 568 t.; Paraguay, 21 t.; Peru, 210 t.; Venezuela, 20 t. Several special collections will be of particular interest to Latin Americanists:

Spanish American Imprints Collection. Approximately 400 of the earliest monographs and pamphlets produced in the Spanish colonies, 1540-1820. Holdings are most extensive for Mexico, Peru, and Guatemala, although other areas are also represented. Included are religious works (catechisms, sermons, missionary manuals, statutes of the Inquisition), juridical/political writings, general histories, and indian-language grammars and vocabularies. Among the collection's treasures are a 1544 copy of Zumarraga's *Doctrina Breve* and original editions of Arriaga, Bautista, Grijalva, Molina, Palafox y Mendoza, Peralta Barnuevo, and Siguenza y Góngora.

Thacher Collection. An extensive collection of early works, some in manuscript, relating to the voyages of discovery. Included are several editions of Ptolemy; the ca. 1503 Trevisan manuscript on Spanish exploration in America, 1492-1500, and Portuguese voyages to India, 1497-1502; numerous facsimiles of Columbus letters; copies of several Papal bulls related to the discovery; and many 16th- and 17th-century titles relating to exploration of the New World. A three-volume catalog, *The Collection of John Boyd Thacher in the Library of Congress* (Washington, D.C.: Library of Congress, 1915-1931) is available.

Rosenwald Collection. Writings, illustrations, and maps (predominantly European imprints) relating to the conquest and early post-conquest period. Among the holdings are a rare 1543 legal treatise, *Leyes...de las Indias,* on treatment of indians, and works by De Bry, Gomara, Cieza de León, Molina, and others. See *The Rosenwald Collection: A Catalogue of Illustrated Books and Manuscripts, of Books from Celebrated Presses, and of Bindings and Maps, 1150-1950, The Gift of Lessing J. Rosenwald to the Library of Congress* (Washington, D.C.: Library of Congress, 1954).

Broadsides Collection. Nearly 1,200 Latin American items, ranging in date from the 16th to the mid-20th century. The collection is strongest in 19th- and 20th-century political broadsides, with particular strength in the early post-independence period. A four-volume reference work, *Catalog of Broadsides in the Rare Book Division* (Boston: G.K. Hall, 1972) is available.

Two general-information brochures, *The Rare Book Division: A Guide to its Collections and Services* (1965) and *Some Guides to Special Collections in the Rare Books Division* (1974), can be obtained from the division.

HISPANIC LAW DIVISION

Main Building, Second Floor
426-5070

8:15 A.M.-4:15 P.M. Monday-Friday

Rubens Medina, Chief
Armando Gonzalez, Assistant Chief

The Hispanic Law Division maintains the most complete collection of Iberian and Latin American (excluding English- and French-speaking Caribbean) legal materials in the world. Holdings total more than 155,000 volumes, with new acquisitions averaging some 5,000 volumes annually. Included in the collection are a full range of constitutions, official *gacetas,* legal codes covering every field of law (civil, criminal, commercial, real estate, etc.), international treaties, and legal periodicals for every Latin American nation. Materials relating to Latin American regional-integration organizations are also well represented. Retrospective holdings are strong for every period and region (with particularly noteworthy strength in 19th-century Mexico), and extend back through colonial legislation to the legal heritage of medieval Iberia. A 1,500-volume rare-book collection includes a 13th-century Spanish manuscript (the *Fuero Juzgo*) on Visigothic law, several early editions of *Siete Partidas,* and an original copy of the 1563 Mexican *Cedulario de Puga,* believed to be the first law book printed in the New World.

The division has produced a long list of guides to the law and legal literature of many Latin American nations. Indispensable for modern Latin American legal research is its *Index to Latin American Legislation, 1950-1960,* 2 vols. (Boston: G.K. Hall, 1961) and supplements for 1961-1965 (1970), 1966-1970 (1973), and 1971-1975 (in press). A program is currently under way in the division to computerize all post-1975 Latin American legal legislation.

Assistant Chief Armando Gonzalez maintains a useful card index to periodical articles on Latin American law, by subject and country. The staff, comprised of three attorneys and three paralegal specialists, is well equipped to answer questions on virtually any aspect of Latin American law.

MUSIC DIVISION

Main Building, Basement Level
426-5507

8:30 A.M.-5 P.M. Monday-Saturday

Donald L. Leavitt, Acting Chief

The Music Division contains an extraordinary collection of books, periodicals, manuscripts, original scores, sheet music, opera librettos, and sound recordings from throughout the world. Total holdings exceed 4.5 million items. Although no systematic effort has ever been made to build a comprehensive Latin American collection, it is certain that the division contains voluminous material for research on any major Latin American composer or Latin American musical form—from classical to folk to popular.

The division staff estimates that some 60 percent of its scores, sheet music (including large quantities of Cuban and other Latin American dance music), and holograph manuscripts remain completely uncataloged, and are identifiable and retrievable only with the assistance of staff members. Furthermore, few of the division's cataloged materials appear in LC's Main Card Catalog. The Music Division reading room, however, has a variety of reference tools to assist researchers in locating cataloged items. Several card catalogs based on LC's classification schedule for the field of music are available. Through the "M Class" catalog, the researcher can identify printed holdings of Latin American music by medium and type, title of work, and name of composer. A brief survey of this catalog produced the following totals: Villa Lobos, 321 t; Ginastera, 61 t. The "ML Class" catalog contains holdings on the literature and history of music. The "MT Class" catalog contains works on music theory, teaching, appreciation, and analysis. Still another catalog is available for the Music Division's massive collection of opera librettos. There is also a card index to articles appearing in U.S. and foreign music periodicals, 1902-ca. 1940.

The division's cataloged holdings appear in a comprehensive published catalog, *Music, Books on Music, and Sound Recordings,* which is part of the

National Union Catalog. Issued semiannually, with annual and quinquennial cumulations, this publication has replaced the *Library of Congress Catalog: Music and Phonorecords; a cumulative list of works represented by Library of Congress printed cards,* an earlier quinquennial publication also issued as part of the *National Union Catalog.* A general-information brochure, *The Music Division: A Guide to its Collections and Services* (1972), is available from the division office.

The division's collections of sound recordings are described in the "Collections of Music and Other Sound Recordings" section, entry D2.

MICROFORM READING ROOM

Main Building, Room 140-B
426-5471

8:30 A.M.-9:30 P.M. Monday-Friday
8:30 A.M.-5 P.M. Saturday
1 P.M.-5 P.M. Sunday

Robert Gross, Head
Pablo Calván, Reference Librarian

The Microform Reading Room contains, among its nearly 1.5 million titles, a heterogeneous but significant collection of Latin American materials on microform. Included are large holdings of copies of colonial documents from archives in Mexico (the Archivo Nacional de la Nación and provincial archives in Jalisco, Oaxaca, Puebla, Parral, and elsewhere) and Peru; Bolívar manuscripts; rare books; miscellaneous runs of 19th- and 20th-century Latin American government documents and legislative records; and scattered early periodicals. Other highlights are microform copies of materials in the Archivo Nacional de Panama; the Mangones collection of books and manuscripts on independence and the early national period in Haiti; 19th-century Chilean bibliophile José Toribio Medina's collection of rare 17th-19th-century Latin American imprints; and University of Chicago research material on Middle American cultural anthropology. Also available are full microform runs of OAS, United Nations, and League of Nations official publications; FBIS and JPRS transcripts; substantial quantities of British state papers from the Public Record Office in London; and an estimated 98 percent of all U.S. doctoral dissertations which appear in *Dissertation Abstracts.* Researchers should not fail to explore the Microform Reading Room's card catalog, since most of these microform holdings are available nowhere else in the Library of Congress in any format and many are not cataloged in the Main Reading Room card catalog. Reading machines are available.

GENERAL READING ROOMS DIVISION

Main Building, Room 144
426-5530

Reference staff members from the General Reading Rooms Division are on duty in Alcoves 4 and 5 of the Main Reading Room during its hours of service, and can provide reference assistance to researchers during hours (evenings and weekends) when the specialized divisions discussed above are closed. For reference assistance by telephone, call 426-5522

The division's Union Catalog Reference Section (426-6300) in Deck 33 off the Main Reading Room can provide bibliographic reference assistance regarding both the published and as-yet-unpublished portions of LC's *National Union Catalog*. The section's hours are 8 A.M.-4:30 P.M. Monday-Friday.

In addition, for researchers whose stay in Washington will be of limited duration, the General Reading Rooms Division maintains a list of private, local, free-lance researchers who can be hired for library searches and research assistance in any field or language. For further information, call 426-5515.

5. The primary reference tool for LC's collections is the 20-million-card Main Catalog (a combined author-title-subject dictionary card-catalog) located in the Main Reading Room. The Main Catalog is the most comprehensive finding-aid available for LC's monographic and serial items, but it does not include all specialized materials held by the Rare Book, Serial, Prints and Photographs, Geography and Map, and Music Divisions and Microform Reading Room, and it thus must be used in conjunction with the many other specialized catalogs and finding-aids available in those divisions. Again, it should also be stressed that research consultation with LC staff members and reference librarians is indispensable in identifying and locating relevant materials.

[Researchers should note that, beginning in 1980, LC plans to "freeze" the Main Catalog, and will thereafter catalog new acquisitions only in its new Computerized Catalog. From that point forward, as a result, researchers desiring to undertake thorough searches of LC's holdings, will need to explore *both* the retired Main Catalog and the new Computerized Catalog.]

Currently, LC's two automated, machine-readable, bibliographic data bases can supplement the library's traditional finding-aids in significant ways:

MARC (Machine-Readable Cataloging) system. MARC provides access to the Library of Congress Computerized Catalog (LCCC), which consists of bibliographic records on more than 700,000 books (English-language monographs cataloged by LC since 1968, and Spanish- and Portuguese-language monographs cataloged since 1975). Primarily a catalogers' data system, MARC can be used to conduct bibliographic searches by author and title.

SCORPIO (Subject-Content-Oriented-Retriever for Processing Information On-Line) system. A more generalized data-retrieval system of considerably greater utility to researchers, SCORPIO can be used for general bibliographic searches by subject (based on LC subject-headings) and by LC classification category (call number) as well as by author and title. Four data files can be tapped through SCORPIO:

    a. Library of Congress Computerized Catalog (LCCC). Bibliographic data on recent monographs, described above under MARC.

    b. Bibliographic Citation file. Periodical articles on public-policy issues, subject-indexed by the Congressional Research Service from nearly 1,500 major journals (primarily U.S.). Foreign-affairs articles are indexed by country.

    c. National Referral Center Master File. Data on some 10,000 organizations, institutions, research centers, groups, and individuals (governmental, business, academic, and professional) which can serve as specialized information resources on specific topics in the fields of science (including the social sciences) and technology. The data-file produces neither hard-data nor bibliographic reference information. Rather, it acts as an intermediary referral agent, directing researchers with questions on a specific topic to information sources possessing expertise on the subject of inquiry. It is subject-indexed.

    d. Legislative Information files. Basic data on legislative bills considered by the 93rd, 94th, and 95th U.S. Congresses.

Public computer terminals to MARC and SCORPIO data bases are available in LC's Computer Catalog Center (426-6213), located off the Main Reading Room. The terminals may be used free of charge by researchers. Staff members are on hand to instruct researchers in the use of the terminals. The staff will also perform bibliographic searches for a fee. Data output is available in a variety of formats.

The published finding-aid of greatest value in identifying individual titles in the LC collection is the ongoing *National Union Catalog* project, which includes among its component parts *The National Union Catalog: A Cumulative Author List Representing Library of Congress Printed Cards and Titles Reported by Other American Libraries* (for post-1952 imprints), 274 vols. (1953-1972) with subsequent annual and quinquennial cumulations; and *The National Union Catalog, Pre-1956 Imprints*, 610 vols. projected. Also useful is the *Library of Congress Catalog—Books: Subjects, a Cumulative List of Works Represented by Library of Congress Printed Cards*, 209 vols. (1950-1974), and *Subject Catalog* (1974-), a continuation of the preceding work. Information on LC acquisitions appears in the *Quarterly Journal of the Library of Congress* and the *Annual Report of the Librarian of Congress*.

In addition, by 1979-1980, microform copies of LC's massive shelflist (in its entirety or any individual segment thereof) will be available for purchase—on fiche from University Microfilms International (300 North Zeeb Road, Ann Arbor, Michigan 48106), or on film from United States Historical Documents Institute, Inc. (1911 Fort Myer Drive, Arlington, Virginia 22209).

Other LC publications of particular assistance to Latin Americanists are: *Cuban Acquisitions and Bibliography* (1970), and an accessions list, *The Library of Congress Special Foreign Acquisition Programs: Brazil* (monthly).

A large variety of general-information pamphlets are also available, including *Information for Readers in the Library of Congress, Special Facilities for Research in the Library of Congress*, and *Catalogs: The Major Access Tools to the Collections of the Library of Congress*.

Note: Also see entries B4, D2, E3, and F11.

Marine Corps Historical Center Reference Library See entry B5

A34 Maryland University—McKeldin Library

1. a. *College Park, Maryland 20742*
        454-5704 (Reference)

    b. Academic year:
       8 A.M.-11 P.M. Monday-Thursday

8 A.M.-6 P.M. Friday
10 A.M.-6 P.M. Saturday
Noon-11 P.M. Sunday
(For information on summer hours, call 454-2853.)

c. Open to the public for on-site use. Interlibrary loan and photocopying facilities are available.

d. Joanne Harrar, Director of Libraries

2.   Campus libraries contain some 1,232,000 volumes, with Latin American holdings in excess of 13,000 volumes. Of the 15,847 serials currently received, nearly 100 emanate from Latin America. The 210 newspapers received include five from Latin America: *Excelsior* (Mexico City), *La Prensa* (Buenos Aires), *El Tiempo* (Bogotá), *Granma* (Havana), and *Estado de Sao Paulo*.

3.   One of the strongest university collections in the area. History (particularly Mexican) is very well represented.

b. Subject categories and evaluations:

1. Philosophy and Religion	166 t.	B/C
2. History	6,028 t.	B
3. Geography and Anthropology	133 t.	B
4. Economics	1,238 t.	C
5. Sociology	554 t.	B
6. Politics and Government	400 t.	C
7. International Relations	449 t.	B
8. Law	unmeasured	
9. Education	157 t.	C/D
10. Art and Music	453 t.	B
11. Language and Literature	3,153 t.	C
12. Military Affairs	13 t.	D
13. Bibliography and Reference	298 t.	B

14. Argentina	1,193 t.	C
15. Bolivia	116 t.	C
16. Brazil	987 t.	C
17. Caribbean (excluding Cuba)	900 t.	B
18. Central America	633 t.	B/C
19. Chile	460 t.	C/B
20. Colombia	292 t.	C
21. Cuba	443 t.	B/C
22. Ecuador	111 t.	C
23. Guianas	82 t.	B
24. Mexico	1,832 t.	B
25. Paraguay	86 t.	C
26. Peru	520 t.	B/C
27. Uruguay	200 t.	C
28. Venezuela	259 t.	C

4. c. McKeldin Library is a regional depository library for United States government documents. Its documents collection—in excess of 500,000 items—is virtually complete for the period 1925-present, with a substantial holding of earlier series. The library also has complete collections of OAS, IMF, UN, and League of Nations publications.

e. The Special Collections division (454-2318) has the papers of Brantz Mayer, secretary of the U.S. legation in Mexico City during the 1840s, and miscellaneous Mexican materials collected by American author Katherine Anne Porter.

f. The library has been a Defense Mapping Agency Topographic Center depository since 1950.

g-h. The Undergraduate Library's Nonprint Media Services Department (454-4723) has a small collection of audio- and video-cassettes focusing on Latin American history and literature.

A35 National Agricultural Library (U.S.D.A. Technical Information Systems)

1. a. *Main Library:*
10301 Baltimore Blvd. (at U.S. Route 1 and Interstate 495 [Beltway Exit 27 North])
Beltsville, Maryland 20705
344-3778 (Director)
344-3756 (Reference)
344-3715 (Interlibrary Loan)
344-3750 (After-hours Loan Requests)

D.C. Branch Library and Law Library:
U.S. Department of Agriculture, South Building
Independence Avenue and 14th Street, SW
Washington, D.C. 20250
447-3434 (D.C. Branch Library)
447-7751 (Law Library)

(Note: A shuttle service operates daily between the USDA South Building and the Main Library in Beltsville, Md. Contact the library for departure times.)

b. Main Library: 8 A.M.-4:30 P.M. Monday-Friday
D.C. Branch Library: 8 A.M.-5 P.M. Monday-Friday
Law Library: 8:30 A.M.-5 P.M. Monday-Friday

c. Open to the public. Interlibrary loan and photoduplication facilities (both coin-operated machines and a photocopying service) are available.

d. Richard A. Farley, Director
Kevin Keaney, Chief, D.C. Branch Library
Spurgeon Terry, Law Librarian

2. The library contains more than 1.5 million volumes (monographs and serials), of which at least 20,000 relate specifically to Latin America. Some 23,000 periodicals are currently received. The collection's principal strengths

are technical agricultural subjects, soil and food sciences, botany, entomology, chemistry, forestry, agricultural economics, and agricultural law. The library also contains a fairly complete collection of U.S. Department of Agriculture publications, including the published research reports of the Foreign Agricultural Service and the Economic Research Service, as well as a Translations File of some 22,000 foreign-language research publications (monographs, excerpts, journal articles) translated by USDA during the last three decades.

3.   a.   The National Agricultural Library is a significant resource for research on the rural economy of 19th- and 20th-century Latin America. Although it focuses primarily on the agricultural sciences, the collection contains substantial material on Latin American agricultural economics, rural production (farm, ranch, and forest), rural economic development, land usage, land colonization, rural education, agricultural law, commerce, and trade. Serial holdings are particularly strong. The reports and statistical publications (including agricultural censuses) of government ministries (agriculture, commerce, finance, interior), government agricultural agencies, banks, institutes, and councils are well represented, with sporadic coverage ranging back into the 19th century. Also included are the publications of a number of private stockbreeders' and producers' associations (*Sociedad rural argentina,* etc.), as well as the reports of national and international commissions and regional conferences. Spanish- and Portuguese-language materials constitute a majority of the Latin American holdings.

(Note: Most post-1940 imprints of interest to Latin Americanists are housed in the D.C. Branch Library rather than the Main Library in Beltsville, Md.)

b.   For the study of agricultural aspects of the Latin American economy, the library's holdings rank as an "A" collection. Geographic coverage is as follows:

Argentina	2,775 t.
Bolivia	379 t.
Brazil	3,566 t.
Caribbean (excluding Cuba)	1,129 t.
Central America	2,075 t.
Chile	933 t.
Colombia	1,180 t.
Cuba	1,031 t.
Ecuador	477 t.
Guianas	430 t.
Mexico	2,258 t.
Paraguay	264 t.
Peru	943 t.
Uruguay	642 t.
Venezuela	1,112 t.

4.   A small map collection contains several early-20th-century Latin American agricultural production and acreage maps. The library also has a poster collection, which includes a small number of Argentine, Brazilian, Ecuadorean, Guatemalan, and Venezuelan government agricultural posters.

5.   Researchers must consult two separate card catalogs: an inactive Dictionary Catalog of all library acquisitions from 1862 through 1965, and a Current Catalog for post-1965 acquisitions. The Current Catalog is subdivided into a

Subject Catalog and a Name Catalog for authors and titles. There is also a Translations File catalog (arranged by author only) for foreign-language materials translated by USDA.

The Dictionary Catalog's contents are reproduced in the 73-volume *Dictionary Catalog of the National Agricultural Library, 1862-1965,* published by Rowman and Littlefield (Totowa, N.J.), 1967-1970, with subsequent volumes for 1966-1971 library acquisitions. Recent acquisitions appear in two monthly publications: *The National Agricultural Library Catalog,* containing bibliographic information on all monographic and serials titles acquired by the library since 1966; and the *Bibliography of Agriculture,* which indexes periodical articles on agricultural topics back to 1942 and all monographs acquired since 1971. Both publications have annual cumulations, with author and subject indexes.

An especially valuable aid to researchers is the library's AGRICOLA (Agricultural On-Line Access) computerized bibliographic data system. AGRICOLA contains bibliographic information on nearly 900,000 books, journal articles, government reports, and conference papers acquired by the National Agricultural Library since 1970. Articles from approximately 5,000 journals worldwide are currently indexed in the system. AGRICOLA can be searched by author, title, subject-heading (including geographic codes), language, date of publication, document type, and a variety of other approaches. A geographic search produced some 20,000 Latin American-related citations. Terminals are available in the D.C. Branch Library as well as the Main Library. Library staff members will conduct searches for researchers without charge.

Three useful pamphlets are available: *The National Agricultural Library: A Guide to Services; The Card Catalogs of the National Agricultural Library: How to Use Them;* and *AGRICOLA.*

A36 National Collection of Fine Arts/National Portrait Gallery Library (Smithsonian Institution)

1. a. *8th and F Streets, NW*
      Washington, D.C. 20560
      381-5118

   b. 10 A.M.-5 P.M. Monday-Friday

   c. Open to the public for on-site use. Visitors are required to register at building entrance. Interlibrary loan and photoreproduction facilities available.

   d. William B. Walker, Librarian

2. The library contains some 15,000 volumes, with Latin American holdings of approximately 400 volumes.

3. The collection ranks within the "B" range for research on the fine arts in Latin America. Monographic holdings include imprints dating back to the late 19th century. The library also receives a number of catalogs and publications from Latin American museums, art centers, and institutes.

4. A large vertical file contains miscellaneous exhibit catalogs, illustrations, clippings, and pamphlets pertaining to U.S. and foreign (including Latin American) artists, museums, and art institutes.

A37 National Geographic Society Library

1. a. *1146 16th Street, NW*
      Washington, D.C. 20036
      857-7787

   b. 8:30 A.M.-5 P.M. Monday-Friday

   c. Open to the public for on-site use. No interlibrary loan or photocopying facilities.

   d. Virginia Carter Hills, Librarian

2. The collection totals 63,000 volumes, at least 2,000 of which pertain to Latin America.

3. The majority of the library's Latin American holdings consist of general descriptive literature, 20th-century travel accounts, and guidebooks. There are also scattered titles in geography, ethnography, art, and folklore. Most of the collection is English-language.

   Cataloged and shelved separately from Latin American materials is the library's 700-volume collection on exploration ("voyages and travels"), much of which relates to early explorations in the New World. Included is a complete collection of Hakluyt Society publications. Materials are, again, primarily English-language (or translations).

   The library maintains a card index to photographs and geographic names which have appeared in the *National Geographic* magazine since its inception. Contact the Public Reference Service (857-7059) for inquiries.

4. a. The library receives approximately 360 Latin American periodicals, including geographic, ethnological, archeological, and folklore bulletins, and miscellaneous periodicals from Latin American scientific, cultural, agricultural, and travel organizations. A list of titles, by country, is available. Some of these publications are retained, while others are clipped (see below) and discarded.

   d. The library maintains an extensive vertical file of miscellaneous clippings from U.S. newspapers and foreign periodicals. The folders are arranged by country (subdivided topically—with categories for political and economic activities, travel, transportation, geographic regions, etc.) and by subject ("indians of South America," "national parks," "petroleum," "tin," "railroads," etc.—each of which is subdivided geographically). Contents date from the late 1940s to the present. For further information, contact the library's Clipping Service (857-7053).

A38 National Institute of Education (Health, Education, and Welfare [HEW] Department)—Educational Research Library

1. a. *1832 M Street, NW, 6th Floor*
      Washington, D.C. 20208
      254-5060

   b. 8 A.M.-4:30 P.M. Monday-Friday

   c. Open to the public. Interlibrary loan and photoreproduction facilities available.

    d. Patricia Coulter, Director

2. The library contains some 130,000 volumes, approximately 700 of which pertain to Latin America. No Latin American periodicals are currently received.

3. The collection ranks within the "B" range for research on Latin American education. Holdings include foreign-language monographs on education, Latin American ministry of education serials and reports (ranging sporadically back to the mid-19th century), and national legislation pertaining to public education. The collection is strongest in pre-1950 imprints, and includes a considerable quantity of 19th- and early 20th-century materials.

5. Researchers must consult two separate finding aids—for recent acquisitions: a card catalog (divided by author-title and subject); and for older materials: a 20-volume publication, National Institute of Education, *Subject Catalog of the Department Library* (Boston: G.K. Hall, 1965) with 4-volume supplement (1973.).

A39 National Library of Medicine

1. a. *8600 Rockville Pike*
       Bethesda, Maryland 20014
       496-6095 (Reference)
       496-5511 (Interlibrary Loan)
       496-5405 (History of Medicine Division)

   b. Labor Day to Memorial Day:
       8:30 A.M.-9 P.M. Monday-Friday
       8:30 A.M.-5 P.M. Saturday
       Memorial Day to Labor Day:
       8:30 A.M.-5 P.M. Monday-Saturday
       History of Medicine Division:
       8:30 A.M.-4:45 P.M. Monday-Saturday

   c. Open to researchers for on-site use. Interlibrary loan and photocopying facilities available.

   d. Martin M. Cummings, Director

2. The collection numbers about 750,000 volumes, including at least 9,000 Latin American titles (books, serials, and periodicals). The library currently receives some 20,000 serial and periodical titles each year, approximately 1,500 of which come from Latin America.

3. The National Library of Medicine has the world's largest collection of literature in the biomedical sciences. Latin American holdings are substantial both in technical medical fields and in several nontechnical categories as well. Government serials are well represented, particularly the annual reports and bulletins of national, state, and municipal public-health agencies (for example: Mexico City Board of Health bulletins, 1900-1920; Cuban rural health service reports, 1963-present); along with the reports of national departments of hygiene and sanitation; reports of national disease-control agencies (malaria, yellow fever, leprosy, tuberculosis); and the publications of military medical services. National statistical materials (vital and health

statistics, general statistical yearbooks and bulletins) are well represented, with holdings extending back into the 19th century in some instances (e.g., 1879 for Trinidad). Other strengths of the collection are national legislation and international treaties pertaining to health and sanitation; government nutrition and mortality studies; private Latin American medical journals; and publications from health-related conferences and symposia. In addition, there are numerous Spanish- and Portuguese-language monographs on public health and public-health administration, the history of medicine in Latin America, nutrition, hospitals, medical education, and nursing, with holdings ranging in date from 1870 to the present. (A separate historical collection of pre-1870 materials is described in point 4, below.) From a geographic perspective, Mexican materials appear to be particularly abundant.

The collection ranks within the "A" range for research on health-related aspects of sociology, the history of medicine in Latin America, and related topics in Latin American social history.

[For comparative purposes, it can be tentatively suggested that, in the areas of Latin American public health and health statistics, the Pan American Health Organization (PAHO) Library (see entry A47) may have the greater range of current and recent materials, while the National Library of Medicine's collection may be more extensive in retrospective and historical titles.]

4. The library's separate 400,000-item History of Medicine collection contains an indeterminable but significant number of pre-1870 Latin American materials. Included are many obscure, late-18th- and early/mid-19th-century books and periodical articles on health conditions, epidemics, the state of medical science and health care, military medicine, and the history of medicine in Latin America; early medical texts, treatises, and pamphlets; several early 19th-century Latin American (particularly Mexican) government *reglamentos* and surveys relating to health and medicine; and some 19th-century dissertations from Brazil, Argentina, and elsewhere. Scattered among the collection's approximately 50,000 rare books are 16th-, 17th-, and 18th-century European imprints focusing on New World and Latin American topics. Finally, the collection also contains numerous manuscripts, including personal papers of a few North Americans involved in Latin American disease eradication and/or inter-American public-health administration—notably the papers of Fred L. Soper (South America/Caribbean, 20th century), and the 1924 Central American diary of Philip Connors.

The History of Medicine collection is not totally cataloged. For books and periodical articles, the most comprehensive finding-aid is the multivolume *Index-Catalogue of the Library of the Surgeon General* (1880-1961). Organized by medical subject-headings (and therein subdivided geographically—e.g., "Medicine—Peru") as well as by country and city of the world, the extensively cross-referenced *Index-Catalogue* is a valuable bibliography of obscure literature (foreign-language and English-language) on health conditions, diseases, and the history and state of medicine in 19th-century Latin America.

The History of Medicine collection's 1801-1870 monographic imprints are cataloged in the main National Library of Medicine card catalogs. The collection also has its own card catalogs for pre-1801 holdings (by century of publication) and for pre-1820 Western Hemisphere imprints (the "Americana" catalog).

5.   Card catalogs include a "Name Catalog" (with entries for corporate authors and individual authors), and two "Subject Catalogs" (one each for pre- and post-1959 cataloged titles) arranged by medical subject-headings and therein subdivided by country. Latin American government serial titles in the collection are cataloged together by country (call numbers W2/DA5-W2/DV4) in a separate "Documents" shelflist catalog located in the main card-catalog room.

For published bibliographic guides to the collection, see the *Index-Catalogue of the Library of the Surgeon General* (five multivolume series, 1880-1961) for pre-1950 acquisitions, and the on-going *National Library of Medicine Current Catalog* (varying titles) for post-1950 acquisitions. An *Index of NLM Serial Titles* is also available. In addition, the library produces the monthly *Index Medicus,* a bibliography of periodical literature in the biomedical field.

Among the several computerized bibliographic data bases which are available to researchers at the library are: CATLINE (Catalog On-Line), which contains references to some 175,000 books and serials cataloged by the library since 1965, and MEDLINE (MEDLARS [Medical Literature Analysis and Retrieval System] On-Line), containing references to approximately 600,000 periodical articles indexed from some 3,000 journals published in the United States and 70 foreign countries, 1966-present. Each system can be searched geographically. A small search fee is charged.

A40   National Museum of Natural History (Smithsonian Institution)—Department of Anthropology Library

1.   a.   *Natural History Building, Room 330*
Constitution Avenue at 10th Street, NW
Washington, D.C. 20560
381-5048/5095

b.   9 A.M.-5 P.M. Monday-Friday

c.   Open to researchers for on-site use only. Visitors are requested to call for an appointment in advance of their arrival. Interlibrary loan and photoreproduction services are available.

d.   Janette Saquet, Librarian

2.   The total collection numbers some 50,000 volumes, with Latin American holdings of approximately 6,000 volumes.

3.   The collection ranks within the "A" range (indeed, rivaling the Library of Congress) for research in Latin American archeology, anthropology, and ethnology. Monographic holdings are strong in Latin American indian cultures, archeology (codex-facsimiles are very well represented), indigenous arts, crafts, and music, as well as in colonial and 19th-century histories and travel accounts. There is also an excellent collection of Latin American indian-language dictionaries. A substantial proportion of the library's Latin American holdings consist of non-English-language materials and/or pre-20th-century imprints.

In addition, a majority of the library's separately shelved, 600-volume "rare-book" collection consists of archeological works or early histories pertaining to Latin America.

4. a. The library also possesses a fine collection of periodicals from Latin America, including archival and museum journals, and academic bulletins in the fields of anthropology, archeology, history, and philosophy. Complete holdings of several titles extend back well into the 19th century. All Latin American periodicals are shelved together in the stacks, by country.

    d. Within the library's extensive vertical file are some 40 boxes of Latin American materials (arranged by region, country, or subject). Contents include Latin American museum catalogs, archeological and anthropological journal reprints, and miscellaneous papers, pamphlets, and bibliographies. Most of the holdings are in Spanish. Late 19th- and early 20th-century materials are particularly abundant.

6. There are separate card catalogs for each of the library's two main component parts: the Bureau of American Ethnology collection and the Smithsonian Office of Anthropology collection.

Note: Also see entries B8, C8, and F16

National War College (National Defense University) Library
See entry J8

A41   Navy Department Library

1. a. *Washington Navy Yard, Building 220*
        9th and M Streets, SE
        Washington, D.C. 20374
        433-4131/32/33

    b. 8 A.M.-4:30 P.M. Monday-Friday

    c. Open to the public for on-site use. Interlibrary loan and photoduplication services available.

    d. Stanley Kalkus, Director

2. The collection totals some 130,000 volumes, with Latin American holdings of more than 1,500 volumes. No Latin American naval periodicals are currently received.

3. The strengths of the collection are naval history, general history, and naval affairs. Researchers will find an abundance of 19th-century travel literature, predominantly English-language. In addition, miscellaneous Latin American naval studies, reports, and regulations, along with naval and hydrographic journals dating into the 19th century, are scattered throughout the collection. There may be specialized titles here which are not available at the Library of Congress. Much of the early material is in storage, but will be retrieved for researchers.

4. The library has a special collection of unpublished unit histories produced by naval historians on active duty during World War II. Included are studies of wartime U.S. naval operations in the south Atlantic, the Caribbean, and the Canal Zone. The histories are described in William C. Heimdahl and Edward J. Marolda (comps.), *Guide to United States Naval Administrative Histories*

of World War II (1976), published by the Naval History Division of the Naval Historical Center (see entry B9)

5.   Two dictionary card catalogs must be consulted: an inactive catalog of pre-1968 acquisitions and an active catalog of subsequent acquisitions. A descriptive pamphlet, *Navy Department Library,* is available.

A42   Oliveira Lima Library (Catholic University)

1. a. *620 Michigan Avenue, NE*
     Washington, D.C. 20017
     635-5059

   b. 1 P.M.-8 P.M. Tuesday
     Noon-7 P.M. Wednesday-Friday
     9 A.M.-5 P.M. Saturday
     Closed Sunday-Monday

   c. Open to the public for on-site use. Researchers are advised to contact the curator in advance. Holdings cannot be removed from the library, but the staff will supply photocopies within reasonable limits.

   d. Manoel Cardozo, Curator

2-3.   The Oliveira Lima Library, housed in the basement of Catholic University's Mullen Library, is generally considered the finest collection of Luzo-Brazilian materials in the United States. The original collection, the personal library of Brazilian diplomat, historian, journalist, and book collector Manoel de Oliveira Lima (1867-1928), has been expanded significantly in size through the active acquisitions program of curator Cardozo, and today numbers more than 50,000 printed items and several thousand manuscripts. It is extremely strong in late 19th- and early 20th-century Brazilian cultural, intellectual, and diplomatic history, and contains major research materials on Brazilian and Portuguese history, literature, and culture, 17th through 19th centuries, with earlier and later periods also well represented. Many of the materials are available nowhere else in the United States.

    Within the library's collection of printed materials on Brazil, the following categories are particularly well represented: colonial history and literature; travel accounts dating from 1507; literature of the imperial period and the Old Republic; 19th-century political pamphlets and broadsides; the proceedings of the first constituent assembly and the annals of the national legislature, virtually complete, since 1823; 17th-century books and pamphlets on the Dutch incursion; the annual reports of the Foreign Office since 1831; the publications of the Brazilian Historical and Geographical Institute since 1839; and the publications of the National Library, the National Archives, and the Public Archives of Sao Paulo.

    Focal points for Latin Americanists among the Portuguese holdings include chronicles of the realm, *nobiliarios* (genealogies of the Portuguese nobility) dating back to the 17th century, and an abundance of material on the Age of Discovery, the worldwide overseas empire, the missionary enterprise (particularly the Jesuits), Pombal, Portuguese theater prior to 1800, and 19th-century liberalism.

    Among the many noteworthy individual items in the collection may be mentioned Bento Teixeira's *Prosopopeia* (1601), a 1647 Barlaeus with colored illustrations from the Huth collection, and the only existing copy of the *Preciso* of the 1817 Pernambuco Revolt.

There are also substantial holdings, largely pre-20th-century, on Spanish America, especially Argentina, Paraguay, Venezuela, Chile, and Mexico.

4. a-b. The library also maintains a major collection of Brazilian periodicals (an estimated 800 titles) dating to the first half of the 19th century. Early newspaper holdings are sporadic. In addition, more than 30 periodicals (academic publications, government serials, etc.) and newspapers are currently received.

   e. Manuscript holdings include a wealth of Portuguese historical documents (particularly for the War of the Spanish Succession), 19th-century Brazilian documents, and a large quantity of materials on 19th- and early 20th-century Brazilian diplomacy—notably, the papers of Brazilian diplomat Artur de Sousa Correia (1852-1900), the Oliveira Lima family papers, and the 1908-1914 records of the Brazilian legation in Brussels.

   g. The library's photograph collection is described in entry F19

5. The *Catalog of the Oliveira Lima Library: The Catholic University of America, Washington, D.C.* 2 vols. (Boston: G.K. Hall and Co., 1970) reproduces the library's card catalog, and contains special sections on manuscripts, periodicals, and iconography.

A descriptive brochure on the collection is available on request.

Note: Also see entries C9 and F19.

A43 Organization of American States—Columbus Memorial Library

1. a. *Constitution Avenue and 17th Street, NW*
Washington, D.C. 20006
381-8209 (Librarian)
381-8259/8408 (Reference)

   b. 9:30 A.M.-5:30 P.M. Monday-Friday
(Stack service until 4:30 P.M.)

   c. Open to the public (stack access restricted). Interlibrary loan service is available, as is a relatively expensive photoduplication service. There are no individual photocopying machines.

   d. Ana Maria Clark, Chief Librarian
Myriam Figueras, Head, Reference Section

2. The collection totals more than 100,000 Latin American-related volumes, some 4,560 serials titles (both currently received and retrospective), and approximately 150,000 government (largely OAS) documents. Twelve Latin American newspapers are currently received on an intermittent basis (utilized by OAS staff-members, they are seldom available to library users).

3. a. The OAS Columbus Memorial Library has the second largest Latin American collection in the Washington area, after the Library of Congress. Holdings are strongest in works produced between 1890 and 1950, although the collection also includes many pre-1890 imprints as well as major post-1950 titles in international relations, the social sciences, history, and

literature. All subject areas are well represented, with ca. 1890-1950 imprints in inter-American relations (monographs, conference proceedings, treaties, and Pan American Union/OAS publications), economics, philosophy, education, geography, and bibliography approximating or surpassing those at the Library of Congress. While every Spanish- and Portuguese-speaking country of Latin America is extremely well represented, Chilean titles are particularly extensive. A 540-volume rare-book collection consists primarily of 18th- and 19th-century travel literature.

b. Subject categories and evaluations:

1. Philosophy and Religion	2,074 t.	A
2. History	20,141 t.	B/A
3. Geography and Anthropology	1,440 t.	A
4. Economics	21,610 t.	A
5. Sociology	3,420 t.	A
6. Politics and Government	4,376 t.	A/B
7. International Relations	3,629 t.	A
8. Law	1,957 t.	C
9. Education	4,509 t.	A
10. Art and Music	2,264 t.	A/B
11. Language and Literature	13.858 t.	B/A
12. Military Affairs	481 t.	A/B
13. Bibliography and Reference	1,192 t.	B/A

14. Argentina	8,893 t.	A/B
15. Bolivia	1,646 t.	A
16. Brazil	8,768 t.	B/A
17. Caribbean (excluding Cuba)	2,072 t.	B
18. Central America	7,057 t.	A
19. Chile	8,960 t.	A
20. Colombia	4,107 t.	A
21. Cuba	3,583 t.	A/B
22. Ecuador	2,258 t.	A
23. Guianas	164 t.	B/A
24. Mexico	8,298 t.	A/B
25. Paraguay	1,007 t.	A
26. Peru	6,253 t.	A
27. Uruguay	2,741 t.	A/B
28. Venezuela	3,566 t.	A

4. a. Serial holdings include official gazettes (fairly complete runs dating from the 1890s for most countries, and from the late 1870s for Chile, Colombia, and Mexico), government statistical publications and ministerial reports, and major academic and scholarly journals from every Latin American nation. Retrospective holdings, encompassing a broad range of subject areas, are most comprehensive for the early decades of the 20th century, although there is sporadic coverage of some government serials extending back to the mid- or early-19th century in several instances. The approximately 700 Latin American serials currently received focus largely on government statistics,

social and economic development, and international relations. A survey of the library's periodicals card catalog revealed the following numbers of titles (including both retrospective and currently received holdings) by country: Argentina, 680 t.; Bolivia, 125 t.; Brazil, 525 t.; British West Indies, 8 t.; Chile, 240 t.; Colombia, 340 t.; Costa Rica, 120 t.; Cuba, 230 t.; Dominican Republic, 110 t.; Ecuador, 160 t.; El Salvador, 100 t.; Guatemala, 130 t.; Haiti, 65 t.; Honduras, 90 t.; Jamaica, 10 t.; Mexico, 700 t.; Panama, 85 t.; Paraguay, 60 t.; Peru, 270 t.; Trinidad and Tobago, 8 t.; Uruguay, 200 t.; Venezuela, 300 t.

The library also has an extensive card catalog of Latin American periodical articles published between 1929 and 1970.

b. A collection of newspapers on microfilm includes the following: *La Prensa* (Buenos Aires), 1938-1950; *Jornal do Brasil* (Rio de Janeiro), 1938-1943; *Journal do Commercio* (Rio de Janeiro), 1944-1955; *El Mercurio* (Santiago, Chile), 1938-1955; *El Tiempo* (Bogotá), 1938-1955; *La Prensa Libre* (Costa Rica), 1946-1955; *El Mundo* (Havana), 1938-1947; *Diario de la Marina* (Havana), 1953-1959; *Revolución* (Havana), 1959-1963; *Granma* (Havana), 1966-1972; *El Telégrafo* (Guayaquil), 1938-1939; *El Comercio* (Quito), 1940-1946; *El Universal* (Mexico City), 1938-1955; *El Comercio* (Lima), 1938-1955; and *El Universal* (Caracas), 1944-1955.

c. The library maintains a separate collection of some 150,000 documents and publications of the OAS and specialized inter-American agencies. The primary finding aid for this collection is an on-going annual OAS cumulation, *Documentos Oficiales de la Organización de los Estados Americanos.*

   The library is also a depository for United Nations documents, and has strong collections of ECLA, UNCTAD, and GATT materials.

d. The reference staff maintains a 40-drawer vertical file of reference material (pamphlets, U.S. newspaper clippings, miscellaneous OAS and other publications, dating back to the 1950s) on Latin American-related individuals, associations, organizations, and an enormous range of subjects (organized topically and by country). Many folders contain bibliographies prepared by the library staff. Some 16 drawers are devoted to OAS agencies, conferences, and related topics.

e. The library administers a small archive containing copies of Pan American Union and OAS documents, from 1890 to the present. Included are the minutes, proceedings, and reports of inter-American conferences and congresses (and many collections of related newspaper clippings), the minutes of the Governing Board of the Pan American Union, and the records of OAS council sessions. Miscellaneous materials include World War II records of the Inter-American Defense Board and the Inter-American Emergency Advisory Committee for Political Defense, and copies of the records of the first meeting (1960) of the Board of Governors of the Inter-American Development Bank. Many of these archival copies are not duplicated in the library's general collection or documents collection.

   In addition, some 27 linear feet of personal papers pertaining to Dr. Leo Rowe, director-general of the Pan American Union from 1920 to 1947, are housed in the library's rare-book collection.

f. A poorly maintained and completely uncataloged 40-drawer map file contains miscellaneous topographic, hydrographic, agricultural, military, transportation, and city maps, etc., dating predominantly from 1910-1940, with a few late-19th-century items. Using a rough estimate of 40 maps per file-drawer, the collection consists of the following numbers of maps per area: Central America (region), 40; South America (region), 80; Argentina, 120; Bolivia, 40; Brazil, 160; Chile, 120; Colombia, 40; Cuba, 80; Dominican Republic, 40; Ecuador, 40; El Salvador, 40; Guatemala, 40; Haiti, 40; Honduras, 40; Mexico, 160; Nicaragua, 40; Panama, 80; Paraguay, 40; Peru, 120; Uruguay, 40; Venezuela, 40.

5.   The principal finding aids are the main card catalog (a dictionary catalog) and the periodicals card catalog. Separate shelflists are available for OAS and UN documents and for the rare-book collection. A quarterly *List of Recent Accessions* is published. The quarterly *Inter-American Review of Bibliography,* prepared by the OAS Department of Cultural Affairs, also contains bibliographic information on the library's accessions.

The library's formerly extensive publications program, which included several bibliographic series and periodicals indexes, has been curtailed almost completely due to budgetary considerations. Still useful are the eight-volume *Index to Latin American Periodical Literature, 1929-1960* (Boston: G.K. Hall and Co., 1962) with two-volume 1961-1965 supplement, and the ten-volume annual *Index to Latin American Periodicals (1961-1970).* A recently inaugurated "Documentation and Information series" includes a *Guide to Latin American Business Information Sources* (1977) and a forthcoming bibliography of monographic and periodicals titles on the OAS.

Researchers should note that two offices of the OAS General Secretariat maintain their own separate library collections: the Department of Educational Affairs—Documentation and Information Service Library (see entry A44) and the Statistical Office—Statistical Reference Collection (see entry A45). The Columbus Memorial Library's card catalogs do not reflect the holdings of either of these collections.

Note: Also see OAS entries B11, C10, D4, F20, L2, L3, L7, and L10

A44   Organization of American States—Department of Educational Affairs—Documentation and Information Service Library

1.   a.   *Paramount Building, Room 923*
1735 Eye Street, NW
Washington, D.C. 20006
381-8345/8128

b.   9 A.M.-5:15 P.M. Monday-Friday

c.   Open to researchers. Limited interlibrary loan and photocopying services available.

d.   Alice Brooks, Documentation Assistant
Tereza Davis, Documentation Assistant

2-3.   The office library of the OAS Department of Educational Affairs contains some 12,000-15,000 publications on all aspects of Latin American education (primary, secondary, higher, nonformal, technical, adult, professional), curriculum, educational administration and finance, educational psychology, educational development planning, and educational statistics. The overwhelming majority of holdings are reports and publications of Latin

American government ministries of education and technical reports of the OAS and other international organizations (including the World Bank and Inter-American Development Bank), dating from World War II to the present. The collection also includes the proceedings of inter-American educational conferences and a substantial number of Latin American educational journals.

The collection ranks within the "A" range for research on contemporary Latin American education.

4. c. The facility also features an eight-drawer vertical file, arranged by country, containing Latin American national legislation pertaining to educational matters, 1940s-present.

5. A card catalog (arranged by author, subject, title, and country) is available. Researchers should note that this collection is maintained and cataloged separately from that of the OAS' Columbus Memorial Library (entry A43).

A45 Organization of American States—Statistical Office—Statistical Reference Collection

1. a. *Premier Building, Room 815-A*
1725 Eye Street, NW
Washington, D.C. 20006
381-8409/8333

   b. 9 A.M.-5:30 P.M. Monday-Friday

   c. Open to researchers for on-site use only, subject to space limitations. Appointment recommended. Photocopying facilities extremely limited.

   d. Silvia Sacks, Librarian

2-3. The Statistical Reference Collection of the OAS' statistical office contains several thousand volumes of Latin American government statistical publications, including censuses, statistical yearbooks and bulletins, and central-bank reports, as well as specialized statistical reports and periodicals pertaining to demography, economics, education, geography, government and politics, health, labor, and living conditions. Holdings date back to approximately the 1930s-1940s. There are few post-1959 Cuban materials. The collection is strong in OAS and United Nations publications and in reference works on Latin American statistical compilation and statistical methodology.

5. An extensive card catalog (arranged by country, and therein by subject) contains bibliographic references to a large number of Latin American national statistical publications beyond those contained in the Statistical Reference Collection.

Researchers should note that the Statistical Reference Collection is maintained and cataloged separately from the holdings of the OAS' Columbus Memorial Library (entry A43).

Overseas Private Investment Corporation Library See entry J24

A46   Panama Canal Company Library

1. a.   *Pennsylvania Building, Room 312*
         425 13th Street, NW
         Washington, D.C. 20004
         724-0104

    b.   8 A.M.-4:30 P.M. Monday-Friday

    c.   Open to private researchers for on-site use only. No interlibrary loan. The staff requests that visitors call in advance for an appointment. Extremely limited photocopying facilities are available.

    d.   Hazel Murdock

2-3.   The Panama Canal Company's small reference collection includes a comprehensive set of annual reports from the Canal Zone Government, the Panama Canal Company, and the original Isthmian Canal Commission; the minutes of the Panama Canal Company board of directors' quarterly meetings (including budgetary, commercial, and policy materials); bound copies of the *Panama Canal Record,* a weekly newspaper and official record of Canal and Canal Zone operations, 1907-1941; a full set of U.S. General Accounting Office audits of the Panama Canal Company, 1950-present; private research studies (commercial and financial analyses, transportation studies and estimates, environmental impact statements, technical engineering reports, etc.) on the Canal; pertinent U.S. legislative materials; and a small number of published monographs on the history of the Canal's construction.

4. g.   Slide sets and black-and-white prints of the Canal are available for distribution. The staff also possesses an index to the extensive collection of Panama Canal photographs held by the National Archives.

Note: Also see entry J25.

A47   Pan American Health Organization (PAHO) Library

1. a.   *Room 607*
         525 23rd Street, NW
         Washington, D.C. 20037
         331-5386

    b.   8:30 A.M.-5:30 P.M. Monday-Friday

    c.   Open to the public. Interlibrary loan and limited photoreproduction services available. There are no coin-operated photocopying machines.

2.   The PAHO Library collection numbers approximately 50,000 bound volumes. Some 350 periodicals are currently received.

3.   The majority of the collection consists of technical literature in the fields of medicine and public health. In addition, however, there are ample materials

for Latin American health-related, demographic, and statistical research which social scientists and historians may find nowhere else in Washington. Included are the annual reports of Latin American public-health agencies extending back to the early 20th century (to 1895 in the case of Brazil), national public-health and nutrition surveys, national health plans, government documents on population and family planning, reports on vital statistics, legislation pertaining to public health and welfare, and reports from inter-American technical conferences. There are also incomplete runs of national censuses (back to the 1940s for some countries) and of national statistical yearbooks and bulletins back into the 1920s/1930s, as well as scattered holdings of national development plans and planning documents, and World Bank economic studies.

The library also holds a complete collection of Pan American Health Organization official documents, country agreements, country-representatives' reports, and PAHO publications and technical studies.

The collection ranks within the "A" range for research on health-related aspects of sociology and selected topics in 20th-century social history.

4.   a.   Shelved separately is an excellent collection of Latin American public-health bulletins and medical journals, with runs dating back to the early 20th century in some cases.

     d.   There are vertical files of miscellaneous pamphlet materials and family-planning documents, by country.

5.   The principal finding-aid is an author/subject card catalog. A list of currently received periodicals is also available.

Note: Also see entries F21 and L11. For research on aspects of Latin American public health and health statistics, attention is also called to the National Library of Medicine, entry A39.

Patent Office (Commerce Department) Scientific Library
See entry J5

Peace Corps Library See ACTION Library, entry A2

Population Crisis Committee Library See entry H35

Population Reference Bureau Library See entry M31

A48   School of Advanced International Studies (SAIS) (Johns Hopkins University)—Mason Library

1.   a.   *1740 Massachusetts Avenue, NW*
          Washington, D.C. 20036
          785-6296

     b.   Academic Year:
          8:30 A.M.-10 P.M. Monday-Thursday

8:30 A.M.-6 P.M. Friday
10 A.M.-5 P.M. Saturday
Noon-9 P.M. Sunday
When classes are not in session:
8:30 A.M.-5 P.M. Monday-Friday

c. Open to serious researchers for on-site use, for limited periods of up to one month. For borrowing privileges, and for on-site reading privileges of more than one month's duration, a fee is charged. Interlibrary loan and photocopying facilities available.

d. Peter J. Promen, Director

2. The total collection numbers 83,000 volumes, with Latin American holdings of approximately 3,900 volumes. Of the approximately 800 periodicals currently received, 45 emanate from Latin America (predominantly economic and commercial journals, and central-bank reports). The library also receives three Latin American newspapers—*Jornal do Brasil, Granma,* and *La Prensa* (Buenos Aires).

3. a. The collection consists largely of English-language secondary literature published since 1950. Subject strengths are economics and international relations.

   b. Subject strengths and evaluations:

1. Philosophy and Religion	39 t.	Below D
2. History	1,623 t.	D
3. Geography and Anthropology	10 t.	Below D
4. Economics	1,200 t.	C
5. Sociology	177 t.	C/D
6. Politics and Government	243 t.	C/D
7. International Relations	439 t.	B
8. Law	Unmeasured	
9. Education	43 t.	Below D
10. Art and Music	0 t.	Below D
11. Language and Literature	66 t.	Below D
12. Military Affairs	10 t.	Below D
13. Bibliography and Reference	35 t.	Below D

14. Argentina	172 t.	Below D
15. Bolivia	47 t.	D
16. Brazil	220 t.	Below D
17. Caribbean (excluding Cuba)	213 t.	D
18. Central America	189 t.	D
19. Chile	128 t.	D
20. Colombia	59 t.	Below D
21. Cuba	120 t.	D
22. Ecuador	33 t.	Below D
23. Guianas	19 t.	D
24. Mexico	196 t.	Below D
25. Paraguay	28 t.	D

26. Peru	92 t.	Below D
27. Uruguay	105 t.	D
28. Venezuela	98 t.	Below D

4. b. The library has the following Latin American newspapers on microfilm: *Jornal do Brasil,* 1973-present; *O Estado de Sao Paulo,* 1960-1970; *La Prensa* (Buenos Aires), 1960-1970; *Excelsior* (Mexico City), 1960-1971; and *El Siglo* (Santiago, Chile), 1962-1970.

A49 State Department Library

1. a. *State Department Building, Room 3239*
   2201 C Street, NW
   Washington, D.C. 20520
   632-0372 (Librarian)
   632-0535/1099/0486 (Reference)

   b. 8:45 A.M.-5:30 P.M. Monday-Friday

   c. The library is primarily for the use of State Department, Agency for International Development, and Arms Control and Disarmament Agency personnel. Outside researchers are permitted to use materials which are not available elsewhere in the metropolitan area. Call in advance for clearance. Interlibrary loan and photocopying services are available.

   d. Conrad Eaton, Librarian

2. The library contains nearly 800,000 volumes, including approximately 30,000 Latin American titles. Of the roughly 1,000 periodicals currently received, some 80 (primarily statistical and economic bulletins) emanate in Latin America. No Latin American newspapers are received.

3. a. Latin American holdings are strongest in the fields of politics/government, diplomatic history, international relations/inter-American affairs, and economic and social conditions. U.S. and Latin American government publications (including official gazettes) are well represented. The library's collections of international-treaty materials and State Department publications (notably foreign-service and consular lists and State Department press releases) are probably the most comprehensive of any in the area. From a geographic perspective, Central American holdings are particularly strong.

   b. Subject categories and evaluations:

1. Philosophy and Religion	67 t.	D
2. History	6,459 t.	B
3. Geography and Anthropology	35 t.	D
4. Economics	6,140 t.	B/A
5. Sociology	482 t.	B
6. Politics and Government	1,899 t.	B
7. International Relations	2,194 t.	B/A
8. Law	1,310 t.	D
9. Education	307 t.	C/B
10. Art and Music	24 t.	Below D
11. Language and Literature	141 t.	Below D

12. Military Affairs	58 t.	B
13. Bibliography and Reference	361 t.	B

14. Argentina	1,818 t.	B
15. Bolivia	970 t.	B/A
16. Brazil	2,741 t.	B
17. Caribbean (excluding Cuba)	1,237 t.	B
18. Central America	4,239 t.	A/B
19. Chile	1,535 t.	B
20. Colombia	1,376 t.	B
21. Cuba	1,437 t.	B
22. Ecuador	811 t.	B
23. Guianas	429 t.	A/B
24. Mexico	2,694 t.	B
25. Paraguay	608 t.	B
26. Peru	1,382 t.	B
27. Uruguay	619 t.	B
28. Venezuela	1,149 t.	B

5.　　There are two card catalogs: a dictionary catalog (alphabetically arranged by author, title, and subject) and a geographic catalog. A geographically-arranged index of currently-received periodicals is available at the library information desk.

The library publishes a monthly acquisitions list, as well as an irregular series of bibliographies on topical foreign-affairs issues. (Recent bibliographies have dealt with "The North-South Dialogue," "Human Rights," and "The Trilateral Commission.") In addition, the library prepares short subject- and country-oriented bibliographies for publication each month in the Department of State *Newsletter.*

A brief guide, *Department of State Library* (1976), is available without charge.

Note:　The State Department's Foreign Service Institute Library (Room 300, 1400 Key Boulevard, Arlington, Virginia) maintains a general collection of some 1,250 monographs in Latin American area studies, including language-training materials. Librarian Mary Schloeder (235-8717) answers inquiries.

In addition, the State Department's Foreign Affairs Research Documentation Center, administered by the Bureau of Intelligence and Research's Office of External Research, maintains a collection of some 15,000 recently completed governmental and scholarly research studies on foreign areas and international affairs. For further information, see entry J28.

Note:　Also see entry F23.

Textile Museum Library See entry C11

A50　Transportation Department Library

1.　a.　*Department of Transportation Headquarters Building, Room 2200*
400 7th Street, SW
Washington, D.C. 20590
426-1792

b. 7:30 A.M.-5:30 P.M. Monday-Friday

c. Open to the public for on-site use. Interlibrary loan and photoreproduction facilities available.

d. Lucile E. Beaver, Library Director

2-3. The Department of Transportation Library has, within its 500,000-volume collection, a modest number of works—largely post-1960, English-language—relating to Latin American roads and highways, railroads, urban mass transit, and transportation history.

Of potentially greater interest to researchers is the library's sizable uncataloged collection of miscellaneous foreign materials—including Latin American national ministry of transportation publications and reports, road plans, travel guides, and other items, dating primarily from the early 1920s to the 1950s. This collection, which is shelved separately in the stacks (alphabetically, by country), contains a wealth of statistical data on Latin American transportation systems.

The library also maintains a large card index to periodical literature on transportation, ca. 1920-present, which includes some references to Latin American transportation.

5. The library's dictionary card catalog is broken down primarily by transportation mode (highways, railroads, etc.), each of which is subdivided geographically.

Note: Also see entry J29.

A51 Treasury Department Library

1. a. *Room 5030*
   15th Street and Pennsylvania Avenue, NW
   Washington, D.C. 20220
   566-2777/8 (Reference)

b. 9 A.M.-5:30 P.M. Monday-Friday

c. Open to the public for on-site use. Interlibrary loan and photoreproduction facilities available.

d. Anne Stewart, Chief—Library Division

2-3. The Treasury Department Library receives the official statistical bulletin and central-bank annual report from almost every Latin American nation. Its collection also includes scattered holdings of national budgets, official financial and foreign-trade serials, and reports from specialized state banks (development, agriculture, etc.). Holdings are largely post-1960, with sporadic coverage extending back into the late 1940s for some serials.

All of the library's Latin American serials are shelved by country in a special "Foreign Documents" section.

Note: Also see entry J30.

United Nations Food and Agriculture Organization (FAO)—Liaison Office for North American Library See entry A19

A52   United Nations Information Centre

1.   a.   *Suite 209*
2101 L Street, NW
Washington, D.C. 20037
296-5370

b.   9 A.M.-1 P.M. Monday-Friday

c.   Open to the public. Interlibrary loan service and photocopying facilities are available.

d.   Vera Gathright, Reference Librarian

2.   The collection totals between 8,000 and 10,000 items.

3.   The Information Centre maintains an up-to-date reference library of United Nations documents and publications. Included among its holdings are official UN records, council and committee proceedings, statistical publications, and reports of special conferences such as UNCTAD and Law-of-the-Sea. Documents from UN regional commissions such as ECLA are incomplete, but the centre can provide liaison with the UN's New York City documents library and with ECLA headquarters in Santiago, Chile.

4.   g.   The centre maintains a small collection of still photographs and motion pictures dealing with UN activities and programs. Some of the materials have a Latin American focus. The centre can also obtain items from the UN's extensive photograph and film files in New York City.

United Nations—International Labour Organization—Washington Branch Office Library See entry A29

United States Catholic Conference—Office of International Justice and Peace Library See entry H38

Woodrow Wilson International Center for Scholars Library See entry M40

A53   Woodstock Theological Center Library (Georgetown University)

1.   a.   *37th and O Streets, NW*
Washington, D.C. 20057
625-3120

b.   9 A.M.-5 P.M. Monday-Friday

c.   Open to serious researchers for on-site use. Interlibrary loan and photocopying facilities available.

d. Henry Bertels, S.J., Director
   William Sheehan, C.S.B., Assistant Librarian

2-3. The 150,000-volume Woodstock Library, located in the lower level of Georgetown University's Lauinger Library, has a specialized collection focusing on theology, ecclesiastical history and law, and spirituality studies. Its collection of "Jesuitica" is believed to be as strong as any in the United States. The library's Latin American holdings are substantial, and the collection ranks with those of the Library of Congress, Catholic University, and the Academy of American Franciscan History as a resource for the study of Latin American church history and theology.

4. a. The library currently receives 1,548 periodicals, with Latin American ecclesiastical journals extremely well represented.

   d. An uncataloged pamphlet file contains a variety of primarily 19th-century materials—historical pamphlets, letters, orders, etc.—on the Jesuits and other Catholic missionary orders, by country.

B. ARCHIVES

Archive Entry Format (B)

1. General Information
    a. *address; telephone numbers*
    b. hours of service
    c. conditions of access
    d. reproduction services
    e. name/title of director and heads of relevant divisions
2. Size of holdings pertaining to Latin America
3. Description of holdings pertaining to Latin America
4. Bibliographic aids (inventories, calendars, etc.) facilitating use of collection

---

Academy of American Franciscan History Library—Documents Collection See entry A1

Agriculture Department—Agricultural History Branch See entry J2

B1 American Red Cross Archives

1. a. *17th and D Streets, NW*
        Washington, D.C. 20006
        857-3706/3712

    b. 8:30 A.M.-4:45 P.M. Monday-Friday

    c. Open to researchers.

    d. Photoreproduction services available. No charge for small numbers of copies.

    e. Irma Lucas, Archivist

2-3. Holdings include post-1947 records relating to Latin American natural disasters, American Red Cross disaster-relief activities in the aftermath of several Central and South American earthquakes, Red Cross involvement in the 1962-1963 U.S.-Cuban "prisoner exchange," and general correspondence between officials of the American Red Cross and Latin American National

Red Cross organizations. All pre-1947 American Red Cross records have been transferred to the National Archives (see entry B6).

4. Indexes are available to both the American Red Cross Archives' post-1947 records and to pre-1947 records at the National Archives.

Note: Also see entries F4 and I10.

B2 Archives of American Art (Smithsonian Institution)

1. a. *Fine Arts and Portrait Gallery Building*
      8th and F Streets, NW
      Washington, D.C. 20560
      381-6174

   b. 10 A.M.-5 P.M. Monday-Friday

   c. Open to researchers. Access to some archival materials is restricted.

   d. Photoreproduction services are available.

   e. Arthur Breton, Curator of Manuscripts

2-3. Among the archives' approximately five million manuscripts, letters, notebooks, sketchbooks, clippings, exhibit catalogs, and rare publications pertaining to United States artists, craftsmen, critics, dealers, collectors, art historians, museums, societies, and institutions, there may be scattered papers from artists who emigrated to the United States from Latin America as well as some correspondence and catalogs pertaining to Latin American artists.

4. See Garnett McCoy, *Archives of American Art: A Directory of Resources* (New York: R.R. Bowker, 1972) and the archives' periodically updated *Checklist of the Collection.* A card index is also available.

Catholic University of America, Mullen Library—Manuscript Collections See entry A11

B3 Church of Jesus Christ of the Latter Day Saints (Mormon Church) —Genealogical Libraries

1. a. *Annandale Branch Genealogical Library*
      3900 Howard Street
      Annandale, Virginia 22003
      256-5518

   Oakton Genealogical Library
   2719 Hunter Mill Road
   Oakton, Virginia, 22124
   281-1836

   Silver Spring Branch Genealogical Library
   500 Randolph Road
   Silver Spring, Maryland 20904
   622-0088

b. Annandale Branch Genealogical Library:
9:30 A.M.-2 P.M. Monday-Tuesday and Thursday-Saturday
7 P.M.-10 P.M. Tuesday-Wednesday

Oakton Genealogical Library:
9 A.M.-2 P.M. Monday-Friday
7 P.M.-10 P.M. Tuesday-Friday
9:30 A.M.-2 P.M. Saturday

Silver Spring Branch Genealogical Library:
9 A.M.-5 P.M. Monday and Wednesday
7 P.M.-10 P.M. Tuesday-Friday
1 P.M.-5 P.M. Saturday

c. Open to the public.

d. Microfilm copies can be ordered, for a fee, from the genealogical library in Salt Lake City.

e. David T. Pryor, Librarian (Annandale)
Mickey Beard, Librarian (Oakton)
Barton Howell, Librarian (Silver Spring)

2-3. The Genealogical Society of the Church of Jesus Christ of the Latter Day Saints in Salt Lake City, Utah, has undertaken a massive program of microfilming religious and civil records in archives throughout the world. The resulting microfilm collection currently totals some one million reels and is growing rapidly. These microfilmed records can be obtained on loan from Salt Lake City by researchers through any of the church's three genealogical libraries in the Washington, D.C. area for the price of mailing. (Allow four to six weeks for delivery of reels.)

Microfilming of records in Latin America has been in progress since 1953, and is expected to continue for another quarter-century. Among the records filmed thus far are Catholic Church parish registers, civil registers, the records of *audiencias* and ecclesiastical councils, Inquisition records, notarial, financial, and census records from provinces, states, and municipalities, diocesan minutes, parish histories, and personal wills. Contents range in date from the 16th into the 20th centuries. Filming of parish records in Argentina, Chile, Guatemala, Mexico, and Panama, and of civil records in Costa Rica, Guatemala, and Mexico, is well advanced or already completed. Other microfilming projects are in varying stages of progress in Argentina, Brazil, Chile, Costa Rica, Ecuador, El Salvador, Nicaragua, Paraguay, Uruguay, Venezuela, and various Caribbean islands. Mexican and Guatemalan records are the most extensive. The collection currently contains a vast wealth of primary historical data on births, deaths, baptisms, marriages, titles, land-ownership, property taxes, mortgages, etc., and, although still far from completion, already constitutes a virtually inexhaustible resource for research on Latin American social, economic, or demographic history, for either the colonial or the national period.

4. Each branch library has a microfilm index to the Salt Lake City microfilm collection, arranged by country and therein by parish, municipality, etc. A guide to the microfilm index is also available.

For Latin American materials in the collection, a useful introduction is Roger M. Haigh and Frank J. Sanders, "A Report on Some Latin American Materials in the Genealogical Library of the Church of Jesus Christ of the Latter Day Saints at Salt Lake City, Utah," *Latin American Research Review* Vol. X, No. 2 (Summer, 1975), 193-196.

Defense Department—Office of the Secretary of Defense, Historian's Office See entry J8

Georgetown University, Lauinger Library—Manuscript Collections See entry A22

Howard University, Moorland-Spingarn Research Center—Manuscript Collections See entry A23

International Communication Agency (ICA) Archive See entry J17

Joint Chiefs of Staff (Defense Department)—Historical Divison See entry J8

B4 Library of Congress—Manuscript Division

1. a. *Room 3004*
        Library of Congress Annex (Thomas Jefferson Building)
        10 1st Street, SE
        Washington, D.C. 20540
        426-5383 (Administration)
        426-5387 (Reading Room)

    b. 8:30 A.M.-5 P.M. Monday-Saturday (stack service until 4:15 P.M.)

    c. Open to serious researchers.

    d. Photocopying machines and microfilm copiers are available. Special permission required for use of cameras.

    e. John C. Broderick, Chief
        Carolyn Sung, Head—Reference and Reader-Service Section

2. The Manuscript Division of the Library of Congress has, scattered among its massive holdings of documents and personal papers, a large and exceedingly heterogeneous collection of Latin American materials.

3. The division's holdings are not organized on a geographic basis. Nevertheless, for expository purposes, Latin American materials may be said to fall within two categories: a) collections containing Latin American source materials, and b) papers of U.S. citizens involved in inter-American diplomatic, economic, military, or cultural affairs.

A. Collections containing Latin American source materials:

Archiv Kaiser Maximilians von Mexico collection. Photocopies of Austrian archival documents pertaining to the French occupation of Mexico, 1861-1865.

Archive of West Florida collection. Seven volumes of transcripts of 1763-1781 documents, from Seville's Biblioteca Colombiana.

Juan and Nicolás Arnao papers. One box of materials relating to the activities of two Cuban revolutionaries, 1869-1898, including revolutionary publications and letters from José Martí, Máximo Gomez, Antonio Maceo, and others.

Luis Berlandier papers. Five boxes of manuscript items relating to exploration of northern Mexico and the Mexican War, 1826-1846.

Ramón Blanco papers. Correspondence of the governor-general of Cuba, 1881.

Philippe Jean Buneau-Varilla papers. Sixty boxes of materials on the Panama Canal, 1884-1923.

George Chalmers collection. Correspondence and administrative/commercial documents pertaining to the British West Indies, 1670-1825, with some materials on other areas of the Caribbean, Honduras, Brazil, and West Florida.

Sir George Cockburn papers. Logbooks of the British admiral involved in Spanish American revolutionary activities, 1788-1812.

Jeannette Thurber Connor collection. Transcripts of 16th-19th-century documents from Spanish archives relating to Florida.

George R. G. Conway collection. Large quantity of transcripts of documents pertaining to the Mexican Inquisition and British subjects in Spanish colonial possessions, 1559-1786.

Domingo del Monte collection. Fourteen boxes and two bound volumes of manuscripts pertaining to Cuban history, 1500-1869, with substantial holdings on early exploration, colonial administrative and military affairs, and 19th-century abolitionist and revolutionary activities.

Dutch West India Company materials, 1568-1695.

Peter Force collection. Miscellaneous documents (originals and copies) relating to Spain's American empire, 1527-1811, including transcripts of Las Casas and Hidalgo materials.

Harry Friedmann collection. Mexican manuscripts, 18th-19th centuries, with materials on economics, missionary affairs, and *hacienda* records.

Alice Gould Puerto Rican Memorial collection. Seventeen boxes of 18th-19th-century materials on Puerto Rican politics, religion, and education.

Guatemalan documents collection. Some 35,000 items pertaining to government agencies, political parties, and labor unions, 1944-1954, with some 1809-1849 ecclesiastical papers and 1826-1915 broadsides.

Edward S. Harkness collection. Twenty-three boxes and 31 volumes of Mexican and Peruvian documents, 1493-1829. Mexican materials focus on the early post-Conquest period; included are the 1531 Huejotzingo Codex and numerous documents relating to the Cortés family (with emphasis on legal proceedings connected with the Avila-Cortés conspiracy). Peruvian materials include heterogeneous colonial records—notarial registers, viceregal decrees, *cédulas, cabildo* records, and documents on mining and agriculture—dating from the 1530s onward. Published catalogs are available: Stella R. Clemence, *The Harkness Collection in the Library of Congress: Calendar of Spanish Manuscripts Concerning Peru, 1531-1651* (Washington, D.C.: Government Printing Office, 1932); Stella R. Clemence, *The Harkness Collection in the Library of Congress: Documents from Early Peru, the Pizarros and the Almagros, 1531-1578* (Washington, D.C.: Government Printing Office, 1936); and J. Benedict Warren, *The Harkness Collection in the Library of Congress: Manuscripts Concerning Mexico, A Guide* (Washington, D.C.: Library of Congress, 1974).

Agustín de Iturbide papers. Twenty-six boxes of manuscripts (military diaries, correspondence with associates, estate documents), 1799-1876.

Hans P. Kraus collection. Some 162 major Spanish-American manuscript items, 1497-1819. Included is a copy of a 1504 Vespucci letter discussing his voyages, 49 Verrazzano manuscripts, and decrees and letters (relating to Cabeza de Vaca, Luis de Velasco, Fernando Alvarado Tezozomoc, Antonio de Mendoza, Zumárraga, Las Casas, Juan Ruiz de Apodaca, and others) which document exploration, Spanish-indian relations, political and ecclesiastical administration of New Spain (including the Inquisition), economic conditions, taxation, and loss of parts of the Spanish empire to Anglo-Saxon encroachments. A descriptive catalog, J. Benedict Warren, *Hans P. Kraus Collection of Hispanic American Manuscripts: A Guide* (Washington, D.C.: Library of Congress, 1974), is available.

Toussaint L'Ouverture papers. Six letters and a collection of original addresses and proclamations, 1798-1800.

Woodbury Lowery collection: Some 40 volumes of documents (including transcripts) relating to the Spanish borderlands, 1551-1803.

Medieval Manuscripts Miscellany. Several Vespucci manuscripts.

Mexican Archives of New Mexico collection. Miscellaneous documents, 1821-1846.

Mexican Miscellany collection. Miscellaneous documents, 1720-1771.

Luis de Onís papers. Correspondence of Ferdinand VII's envoy to the United States, 1810-1816.

Charles Pinfold collection. Manuscripts of the governor of Barbados, 1756-1766.

Vicente Pintado papers. Materials relating to the surveyor-general of Spanish West Florida, 1803-1817.

Portugal Miscellany collection. Miscellaneous Brazilian items, including papers of Alexandre de Gusmao, Joao V's secretary of state, and a 1774-1779 letter-book of Manoel de Cunha Menezes, captain-general of Pernambuco and Bahia.

Recife and San Francisco Pernambuco Railway Company papers. Minutes of directors' meetings, 1854-1861.

José Ignacio Rodríguez papers. Papers of a Cuban international lawyer active in inter-American claims commissions, 1860-1907. Included is a substantial quantity of material on 19th-century Cuban politics and revolutionary movements.

D'Ossier Roume papers. One box of papers of an administrative agent in Santo Domingo, 1791-1802, including correspondence with Toussaint L'Ouverture.

Antonio López de Santa Anna papers. Ninety-six items of correspondence.

Rudolph R. Schuller collection. Thirty-five boxes of transcripts of documents on Latin American archeology, ethnography, and indian languages.

Spanish American Affairs collection. Miscellaneous documents, 1810-1816.

Spanish Archives of New Mexico collection. Miscellaneous documents, 1621-1821.

Spanish Government of East Florida collection. Some 65,000 administrative and military documents, 1777-1821.

Ephraim George Squier papers. Materials relating to Central American archeology and the Honduras Interoceanic Railroad, 1853-1870.

Vernon-Wager papers. Correspondence of two British admirals pertaining to pirates and naval operations in the Caribbean, 1666-1743.

Irene Wright collection. Transcripts of documents in Seville's Archivo General de Indias.

In addition, several sizable "miscellany" collections mentioned in earlier guides have been broken up and their contents (documents, manuscripts, books) dispersed among other collections, including those listed above. Among these former miscellanies were:

Bermudiana collection. Nine boxes of legal, legislative, and journalistic materials, 1690-1893.

Central American collection. Fifteen boxes and six volumes of miscellaneous documents (some relating to indian dialects), 1670-1931.

Cuban Transcripts collection. Copies of documents from the Archivo Nacional de Cuba, including 18th-century material on Florida and Louisiana.

Indian Languages of Mexico and Central America collection. Over 200 boxes and 25 volumes of dictionaries, vocabularies, translations of Aztec dramas, and other early materials.

Mexican collection. Fifty-three boxes and 19 bound volumes of miscellaneous materials, 1590-1910.

New Mexico papers. One hundred eighty portfolios of documents on administrative, military, and ecclesiastical affairs, 1621-1843.

South American miscellany. Twenty boxes, 20 volumes, and 10 portfolios of material, including documents relating to Argentina (1772-1938), Brazil (1568-1861), Chile (1808-1943), Colombia (1862-1904), Ecuador (1854), Peru (1579-1942), and Venezuela (1806-1926).

Spanish Transcripts and Facsimiles collection. Large quantity of copies of colonial documents (*cédulas,* memorials, viceregal decrees, *audiencia* records, trade reports, journals of exploration, missionary reports, etc.).

Texas collection. Ecclesiastical and *cabildo* records, etc., 1689-1836.

West Indies miscellany, 1494-1821. Ten boxes and 28 volumes of materials pertaining to the British West Indies.

West Indies miscellany, 1591-1938. Thirty boxes and 15 volumes of manuscripts relating to Cuba (1762-1938), Haiti (1776-1912), and Puerto Rico (1591-1899).

Portions of these collections may have been transferred to a "Miscellaneous Manuscripts Collection" and to smaller Argentine, Brazilian, Chilean, Colombian, Peruvian, Puerto Rican, Venezuelan, and "Indian Language" miscellanies. For assistance in locating materials from these dispersed collections, Carolyn Sung, head of the Reference and Reader-Service Section, can be helpful.

The Manuscript Division also possesses a significant microfilm collection of documents from foreign archives, including materials from the Real Academia de la Historia, Archivo Histórica Nacional, and Biblioteca Nacional (Madrid); the Archivo General de Indias and Biblioteca Colombiana (Seville); Archivo General de Simancas; Biblioteca Pública (Toledo); the national archives of Argentina (diplomatic correspondence, 1810-1854), Chile, Cuba, Puerto Rico, Venezuela, the Vatican (Peruvian dispatches, 1603-1875), and Great Britain (British Foreign Office papers on Panama, 1827-1919); and several Mexican archives, including the Archivo General de la Nación, Archivo de la Secretaría de Relaciones Exteriores, Biblioteca Nacional, Biblioteca Benjamín Franklin, Archivo General de Mérida, the Archive of the Bishop of Mérida, and the Biblioteca Nacional de Arqueología, Historia y Etnografía. A card catalog of the Manuscript Division's microfilm collections is maintained. Also see Richard B. Bickel (comp.), *Manuscripts on Microfilm: A Checklist of the Holdings in the Manuscript Division* (Washington, D.C.: Library of Congress, 1974).

B. Papers of U.S. citizens involved in inter-American affairs:

Presidents: John Adams, James Madison, James Monroe, John Quincy Adams, James K. Polk, Zachary Taylor, Millard Fillmore, Franklin Pierce, James Buchanan, Abraham Lincoln, Ulysses S. Grant, Grover Cleveland, William McKinley, Theodore Roosevelt, William Howard Taft, Woodrow Wilson, and Warren G. Harding.

Secretaries of State: Henry Clay, William Marcy, William Seward, Hamilton Fish, James G. Blaine, Frederick Frelinghuysen, Thomas Bayard, Richard Olney, John Hay, Elihu Root, Philander C. Knox, Robert Lansing, Bainbridge Colby, Charles Evans Hughes, Cordell Hull, and Henry Kissinger (restricted access).

Diplomats: Jeremy Robinson (U.S. agent, Peru, southern South America during Spanish American wars of independence), Joel R. Poinsett (Mexico, South America, early 19th century), John Mitchell (early 19th-century U.S. consul, Cuba, Martinique), Nicholas B. Trist (consul, Havana, and agent, Mexico, Mexican War era), Edward Lee Plumb (Cuba, Mexico, 19th century), John T. Pickett (Confederate agent, Mexico, 1860-1862), Thomas Henry Nelson (Mexico, Chile, 1860s), William Henry Trescot (Caribbean, 1851-1889), John Wheeler (Nicaragua, 19th century), Whitelaw Reid (U.S. delegate, Spanish-American War peace commission), John Barrett (Pan American Union, 1898-1920), William Culbertson (Chile, 1928-1933), Leland Harrison (assistant secretary of state, post-World War I period), Henry Fletcher (Mexico, undersecretary of state, post-WWI), Wilbur J. Carr (assistant secretary of state, post-WWI), Harry F. Guggenheim (Cuba, 1920-1933), Josephus Daniels (Mexico, 1933-1942).

Military figures: Christopher Raymond Perry (naval officer, Caribbean, 1812-1814); Winfield Scott, George B. McClellan, P.G.T. Beauregard, David Connor, John Hatch, George W. Morgan, and John Loyall Saunders (Mexican War); Andrew Talcott (military engineer, Imperial Mexican Railway, 1865-1866); George Dewey, Henry Clark Corbin, George Collier Remy, Edgar Alexander Mearns, and Pascual Cervera (Spanish-American War); Leonard Wood and John E. McMahon (U.S. army of occupation, Cuba); George Washington Goethals (chief engineer, Panama Canal project, and early governor of Canal Zone); William Gorgas (army surgeon-general, Panama and elsewhere, 1885-1919); John Pershing (Mexican Punitive Expedition); and a large number of U.S. secretaries of war and navy.

Private citizens and organizations: John Kennion (Caribbean slave-dealer, 1760s), Lewis Brantz (journal of an 1829-1831 trip through Cuba and Mexico), William Jones (Cuba, 1830s), Mary (Mrs. Horace) Mann (correspondence with Sarmiento, Mitre, and other 19th-century Argentine notables), B. Jay Antrim (diaries and sketchbooks of California and Mexico, 1848-1849), William Walker and David Deaderick (Central American filibusterers), Lewis Haupt (engineer, Nicaraguan canal project, 1861-1923), R. Cleary (Brazil, 1865-1885), Clara Barton (Spanish-American War), Chandler Parsons Anderson (international arbitrator, Caribbean/Central America, 1911-1932), and Women's Auxiliary Conferences of Pan American Congresses (minutes and correspondence, 1915-1927). Inter-American commercial materials can be found in the papers of the following: Nicolas Low

(Honduras Bay trade, 1785-1808), Providence Merchant (Peru, 1805-1849), Riggs and Company (Central and South America, 1816-1854), Jonathon Meredith (South America, first half of 19th century), Nicaragua Canal Construction Company (1886-1891), Alexander Shepherd (Mexican mining, 1879-1902), General Society of Merchants and Business Men of the Island of Cuba (correspondence with Theodore Roosevelt and Leonard Wood, 1901), National Citizens Committee on Relations with Latin America (financial and banking matters, 1905-1921), and Henry Clay Pierce (owner of Mexican Central Railway, 1914). Papers of academicians include those of James A. Robertson, Samuel Guy Inman, and Howard Cline.

4.   No comprehensive finding-aid to the Manuscript Division's Latin American-related materials presently exists. The above lists of collections (lists which are by no means exhaustive) were gleaned from a variety of guides and catalogs, which the researcher should rely upon collectively. These include an unpublished three-volume *Reference Guide to Hispanic Manuscripts in the Library of Congress* (1964), copies of which are available in the Manuscript Reading Room and in the Library of Congress' Hispanic Division; an unpublished, alphabetically-arranged, 1976 computer print-out of the Manuscript Division's holdings; the Manuscript Reading Room's dictionary card catalog (presently in two parts, both of which must be consulted); and the excellent volume by Russell H. Bartley and Stuart L. Wagner, *Latin America in Basic Historical Collections: A Working Guide* (Stanford, Calif.: Hoover Institution Press, 1972). Unpublished registers or other finding aids exist for some individual collections. A card file of collections for which such aids are available is maintained in the division.

    The ongoing annual publication *National Union Catalog of Manuscript Collections,* 15 vols. (1959-1976) describes many of the division's holdings. Manuscript accessions are also described in the *Annual Report of the Librarian of Congress* (1897-   ) and, since 1943, in the *Quarterly Journal of the Library of Congress* (formerly the *Library of Congress Quarterly Journal of Acquisitions*). Dated, but still useful, inventories include the *Handbook of Manuscripts in the Library of Congress* (1918); Curtis W. Garrison, *List of Manuscript Collections in the Library of Congress to July 1931* (1932); C. Percy Powell, *List of Manuscript Collections Received in the Library of Congress, July 1931 to July 1938* (1939); and Philip Hamer, *A Guide to Archives and Manuscripts in the United States* (New Haven: Yale University Press, 1961).

    Two brief guides, *Manuscript Division: Library of Congress* and *Catalogs, Indexes, Finding Aids,* are available without charge from the division.

B5   Marine Corps Historical Center (Navy Department)

1.   a.   *Washington Navy Yard, Building 58*
    9th and M Streets, SE
    Washington, D.C. 20374
    433-3439 (Archives Section)
    433-3396 (Personal Papers Collections)
    433-3840 (Oral History Section)
    433-3447 (Library)
    433-3634 (Still-Photo Archive)

  b.   8 A.M.-4:30 P.M. Monday-Friday

c. Open to researchers. Some holdings are classified or otherwise restricted.

d. Photoreproduction facilities are available.

e. Joyce E. Bonnett, Head—Archives Section
Charles A. Wood, Personal Papers Curator
Benis M. Frank, Head—Oral History Section

2-4. The Archives Section contains Marine Corps operational records (including command diaries, field reports, operations plans, and intelligence estimates), ca. World War I-present. Included are materials on Marine Corps activities in Nicaragua, 1912-1936; Haiti, 1914-1934; the Dominican Republic, 1920-1921 and 1965; Cuba, 1962; and Panama, 1964. Many of the earlier records are stored in the Washington National Records Center (Suitland, Maryland), but will be retrieved for researchers. Much, but not all, of the 1960s material on Cuba, Panama, and the Dominican Republic is classified. There is a card index to individual documents (both classified and unclassified), arranged by geographic area.

A separate personal-papers collection contains manuscript materials from 30 Marine Corps officers or enlisted personnel who participated in the Mexican War, the 1885 Panamanian intervention, Spanish-American War, or early 20th-century interventions in Mexico, Cuba, the Dominican Republic, Haiti, and Nicaragua. For a detailed description of the collection's contents, see the Marine Corps Historical Reference Pamphlet *Marine Corps Personal Papers Collection Catalog* (1974).

In addition, the center has an expanding oral-history collection, which contains taped interviews with more than 50 Marine Corps officers and enlisted personnel involved in 20th-century Mexican, Central American, and Caribbean operations. Indexed transcripts of most of the tapes are available. This collection is described in detail in a 1975 Marine Corps Historical Reference Pamphlet, *Marine Corps Oral History Collection Catalog.*

The Still Photo Archive contains primarily post-1940 materials, including some 1960s coverage of Cuba and the Dominican Republic, as well as a limited quantity of early 20th-century Caribbean basin photos. Most pre-World War II materials have been transferred to the National Archives, although the Still Photo Archive hopes to eventually develop a duplicate collection of transferred photographs for its own use.

The Marine Corps Historical Center's 25,000-volume reference library has, within its collection, a small number of Marine Corps field reports and historical studies pertaining to interventions in the Caribbean.

Note: Also see entry J8.

Maryland University, McKeldin Library—Manuscript Collection
See entry A34

B6 National Archives and Records Service (General Services Administration)

1. a. *8th Street and Pennsylvania Avenue, NW*
Washington, D.C. 20408
523-3218 (General Information)
523-3232 (Central Research Room)

    b. Central Research Room and Microfilm Reading Room:
8:45 A.M.-10 P.M. Monday-Friday
8:45 A.M.-5 P.M. Saturday
Branch Research Rooms:
8:45 A.M.-5 P.M. Monday-Friday

    c. Open to all serious researchers with a National Archives research pass, obtainable from the Central Reference Division, Room 200-B.

    d. Extensive photocopying and microfilming services are available. Rates are expensive.

    e. James B. Rhoads, Archivist of the United States.

2-3. The National Archives and Records Service is the official repository for the records of the United States Government. Current holdings total more than three billion records, amounting to some one million cubic feet of material. These holdings are organized into some 400 "record groups," each of which consists of the records of an individual department, agency, bureau, or other U.S. governmental unit. Some form of "finding aid"—card index, inventory, preliminary inventory, special list, etc.—exists for most record groups.

Nearly half of the National Archives record groups contain material relating to foreign nations and their dealings with the United States. The indispensable starting-point for research on Latin America is a 489-page publication prepared by Archives staff members George S. Ulibarri and John P. Harrison, *Guide to Materials on Latin America in the National Archives of the United States* (Washington, D.C.: National Archives and Records Service, 1974), which provides a detailed description of the Archives' extraordinarily vast range of Latin American holdings, by record group. Additional materials and record groups have been opened since that volume appeared, however, and researchers may wish to consult with Mr. Ulibarri (523-3126) regarding recent developments.

It should be noted that some Latin American-related documents in the fields of post-1940 diplomatic and military affairs are occasionally withheld from researchers due to security-classification or other restrictions. Persistent researchers, however, have become increasingly successful in gaining access to such materials by maintaining careful lists of identifying information on withheld documents (date, file number, author), and then pursuing Freedom-of-Information Act processes to request a mandatory review of the restriction by the document's originating agency.

There follows a brief summary of some of the Latin American holdings within each record group (RG), grouped according to the archival division or branch which maintains administrative control over that record group:

CIVIL ARCHIVES DIVISION (NNF)
Jane Smith, Director
523-3239

Diplomatic Branch
Milton Gustafson, Chief
523-3174

RG 11: General Records of the United States Government. Treaties and other international acts (executive agreements, postal conventions) between the U.S. and Latin American nations, 1778-1968. See Preliminary Inventory (PI) 159.

RG 43: Records of International Conferences, Commissions, and Exposi-tions. Materials dealing with U.S. participation in the Panama Congress of 1826-1827, the Spanish-American War peace settlement, and a wide range of inter-American conferences and organizations (multilateral and bilateral), 1889-1951. See PI 76.

RG 59: General Records of the Department of State. This massive record group contains the basic source materials for research in U.S.-Latin American diplomatic history, from 1789 through the latest year for which the State Department has authorized the release of its records (currently 1949; the cut-off date always corresponds to the latest year for which the State Department's *Foreign Relations of the United States* documents-series has been published). Included in RG 59 are the State Department's instructions to U.S. diplomats in Latin America, the reports, dispatches, and letters of U.S. diplomatic and consular officials, departmental memoranda and communications with Latin American governmental representatives, the records of special agents and special missions, and an enormous variety of additional material. Reports from U.S. embassies, legations, and consulates in Latin America contain a wealth of descriptive and statistical information on local politics and socioeconomic conditions. Newspaper clippings, political pamphlets, and copies of official Latin American governmental decrees are frequently attached as enclosures. Recent accessions include a series of State Department "lot files" (office files and working papers not integrated into the central files), which contain materials from the Office of American Republic Affairs and its predecessors, 1905-1947; the 1921-1933 records of Assistant Secretary of State for Latin American Affairs Francis White; and "Research and Analysis" reports from the Office of Intelligence Research (successor to the OSS), 1944-1948. See PI 157, Special Lists (SL) 7 and 37, and lot-file indexes. The complete State Department central files through 1910 (and substantial materials through 1929) are available on microfilm.

RG 76: Records of Boundary and Claims Commissions and Arbitrations. Materials dealing with U.S. commercial and territorial claims against Latin American governments, and U.S. participation in Latin American boundary disputes, 1795-1930.

RG 84: Records of the Foreign Service Posts of the Department of State. The field records of all U.S. diplomatic and consular posts in Latin America, dating from 1797. Much of the material consists of copies of documents found in RG 59 (duplicates of documents missing from RG 59 can frequently be found here). In addition, there is valuable additional material on local conditions and the commercial activities of U.S. businessmen and corpora-tions in Latin America. See PI 60 and SL 9.

RG 256: Records of the American Commission to Negotiate Peace. Reports on Latin American attitudes toward World War I and the Versailles Peace Conference. See PI 89.

RG 353: Records of the Interdepartmental and Intradepartmental Com-mittees (State Department). Includes "lot files" of materials from the State-War-Navy Coordinating Committee and other hemispheric-defense commit-tees, 1938-1949; the Interdepartmental Advisory Council on Technical Cooperation and its predecessors, 1938-1953; and the Latin American Working Group of the Foreign Military Assistance Correlation Committee, 1950. An unnumbered Preliminary Inventory is available from the Diplo-matic Branch staff.

RG 360: Records of the Continental and Confederation Congresses and the Constitutional Convention. Reports and letters on commercial and other matters in Spanish Florida and the Caribbean, 1776-1788. See SL 26.

Judicial and Fiscal Branch (NNFL)
Clarence Lyons, Chief
523-3059

RG 26: Records of the United States Coast Guard. Materials on maritime commerce, customs collections, and efforts to prevent smuggling and filibustering in the Caribbean, dating from the 1790s.

RG 36: Records of the Bureau of Customs. Correspondence between the Treasury Department and its special agents in Mexico and the Caribbean dealing with smuggling, filibustering, and local conditions, 1854-1915. See PI 122 and SL 22.

RG 39: General Records of the Department of the Treasury, Bureau of Accounts. Country files containing material on U.S. loans to Latin America in the post-World War I period.

RG 56: General Records of the Department of the Treasury. Includes correspondence between the Secretary of the Treasury and customs collectors at Atlantic and Gulf of Mexico ports, 1789-1833; letters from foreign bankers, 1833-1855; miscellaneous letters on tariffs, 1844-1849; and 20th-century office files of the Secretary of the Treasury.

RG 60: General Records of the Department of Justice. Material relating to Spanish land grants in Florida, ca. 1818-1845; California land claims, 1851-1856; and claims against Spain arising out of the Spanish-American War.

RG 63: Records of the Committee on Public Information. World War I propaganda activities in Argentina, Chile, and Mexico.

RG 65: Records of the Federal Bureau of Investigation. Reports of Axis activities in Latin America during World War II. Largely restricted.

RG 85: Records of the Immigration and Naturalization Service. Material on the entry of Latin Americans (including Cuban, Mexican, and Central American revolutionaries) into the United States, dating from the 1820s.

RG 123: Records of the United States Court of Claims. Claims arising out of seizures of U.S. merchant vessels in the Caribbean and South America by French warships and privateers, 1793-1801. See PI 58.

RG 154: Records of the War Finance Corporation. Material on post-World War I government loans to U.S. exporters, with folders on trade and economic conditions in Latin America.

RG 217: Records of the United States General Accounting Office. Accounts of living expenses of U.S diplomatic, consular, and naval officials in 19th-century Latin America.

RG 220: Records of Presidential Committees, Commissions, and Boards. Material from the 1930 President's Commission for Study and Review of Conditions in Haiti.

RG 267: Records of the Supreme Court of the United States. Materials dealing with land claims and ship seizures in the Caribbean and Central America, 1792-1915. See PI 139.

Industrial and Social Branch (NNFS)
Jerome Finster, Chief
523-3119

RG 12: Records of the Office of Information. Scattered material on Latin American education and inter-American educational and student congresses. See PI 178.

RG 20: Records of the Office of the Special Adviser to the President on Foreign Trade. Materials on Latin American reciprocal trade agreements, 1934-1935.

RG 23: Records of the Coast and Geodetic Survey. Geographic and cartographic data on Latin America, 1844-1910. See PI 105.

RG 25: Records of the National Labor Relations Board. Case files involving U.S. firms engaged in business in Latin America.

RG 28: Records of the Post Office Department. Inter-American postal conventions and congresses, 1856-1929. See PI 168.

RG 29: Records of the Bureau of the Census. Reports and records on the Virgin Islands, Canal Zone, and Puerto Rico, 1910-1950. See PI 161.

RG 32: Records of the United States Shipping Board. Extensive Latin American commercial shipping reports, 1917-1933. See PI 97.

RG 40: General Records of the Department of Commerce. Limited materials on Latin America from the offices of the Secretary and Assistant Secretaries of Commerce, 1903-1950.

RG 41: Records of the Bureau of Marine Inspection and Navigation. Scattered material from the 1890s on suspected violations of neutrality laws, filibustering, and efforts of insurgents to smuggle arms into Cuba.

RG 86: Records of the Women's Bureau. Bulletins on women workers in Latin America, by country, dating from 1920 through the 1940s.

RG 90: Records of the Public Health Service. Reports and correspondence on Latin American health and sanitation problems, 1879-1944. See PI 141.

RG 122: Records of the Federal Trade Commission. Early 20th-century Latin American commercial data in the files of the FTC's predecessor, the Bureau of Corporations. See PI 7.

RG 151: Records of the Bureau of Foreign and Domestic Commerce. Reports of Commerce Department commercial attaches, 1931-1940; and extensive bureau files on Latin American trade, resources, and transportation, ca. 1914-1945.

RG 174: General Records of the Department of Labor. Materials on Mexican labor, 1907-1961; and records of U.S. participation in the 1949 Conference of American States' Members of the International Labor Organization.

RG 188: Records of the Office of Price Administration. Reports on Latin American price trends and price controls during World War II. See PI 95.

RG 211: Records of the War Manpower Commission. Materials on Mexican labor during World War II. See Inventory 6.

RG 234: Records of the Reconstruction Finance Corporation. World War II and early postwar records of the Rubber Development Corporation, the U.S. Commercial Company, and the American Republics Aviation Divison of the Defense Supplies Corporation. See PI 173.

RG 250: Records of the Office of War Mobilization and Reconversion. Material on the production and acquisition of strategic Latin American raw materials during World War II. See PI 25.

RG 259: Records of the Board of War Communications. Substantial information on Latin American radio and telecommunications systems during World War II.

RG 262: Records of the Foreign Broadcast Intelligence Service. Transcripts and analyses of propaganda and news broadcasts beamed to Latin America from the Axis nations or originating in Latin America, 1941-1946. See PI 115.

RG 275: Records of the Export-Import Bank of the United States. Case files of Eximbank loan transactions involving Latin America, 1934-1951.

Legislative and Natural Resources Branch (NNFN)
Harold Pinkett, Chief
523-3238

RG 7: Records of the Bureau of Entomology and Plant Quarantine. Reports and correspondence on the control of insects and prevention of the spread of Latin American plant diseases, 1878-1951. See PI 94.

RG 16: Records of the Office of the Secretary of Agriculture. Diverse Latin American materials in the correspondence of the Secretary, 1893-1959. See PI 37.

RG 22: Records of the Fish and Wildlife Service. Information on the introduction of fish and game into Latin America, 1899-1920; records of the U.S.-Mexican International Fisheries Commission, 1925-1937.

RG 27: Records of the Weather Bureau. Nineteenth-century meteorological records on Latin America. Consult PI 38 and SL 1.

RG 46: Records of the United States Senate. Senate documents and committee hearings on Latin American policy matters, treaties, etc. See PI 23.

RG 48: Records of the Office of the Secretary of the Interior. Miscellaneous 19th- and 20th-century materials on Latin America, predominantly Central America and the Caribbean. See PI 81.

RG 49: Records of the Bureau of Land Management. Private land claims involving land grants made by the Spanish and Mexican governments in territories eventually ceded to the United States, 1773-1917. See PI 22.

RG 54: Records of the Bureau of Plant Industry, Soils, and Agricultural Engineering. Material on Latin American agricultural production, ca. 1849-1950. See PI 66.

RG 55: Records of the Government of the Virgin Islands. Documents and other materials relating to the Danish colonial administration of the Virgin Islands, 1672-1917. See PI 126.

RG 57: Records of the Geological Survey. Topographic and resource surveys of the Caribbean, 1912-1925; and a U.S. Commercial Company report series on Brazilian strategic minerals, 1941-1946.

RG 66: Records of the Commission of Fine Arts. Project files on Latin American art, architecture, and decorations, 1910-1952. See PI 79.

RG 70: Records of the Bureau of Mines. Reference material on Mexican petroleum production and mining operations, 1910-1949, and additional Latin American materials, 1917-1922.

RG 83: Records of the Bureau of Agricultural Economics. Correspondence and statistical reports dealing with Latin American agricultural production, labor, marketing, etc., 1912-1952. See PI 104.

RG 95: Records of the Forest Service. Research files and survey projects on Latin American forest resources, 1897-1947; and records of the World War II Emergency Rubber Project. See PI 18.

RG 97: Records of the Bureau of Agricultural and Industrial Chemistry. Agricultural and scientific correspondence and reports, primarily relating to Cuba and the Caribbean, late 19th/early 20th century. See PI 149.

RG 103: Records of the Farm Credit Administration. Data from the 1930s on Brazilian coffee.

RG 115: Records of the Bureau of Reclamation. Material on Latin American irrigation and water-control projects, 1919-1945; and records of the U.S.-Mexican dispute over the Colorado River, 1902-1949. See PI 109.

RG 136: Records of the Agricultural Marketing Service. Market-research materials on Latin American agricultural production, 1923-1942.

RG 139: Records of the Dominican Customs Receivership, 1905-1941. See PI 148.

RG 140: Records of the Military Government of Cuba, 1899-1902. See PI 145.

RG 166: Records of the Foreign Agricultural Service. Extensive documentation on Latin American agricultural and forestry production, markets, competition, and policy, 1904-1954.

RG 186: Records of the Spanish Governors of Puerto Rico, 1754-1898, including royal decrees, fiscal, military, and ecclesiastical matters, slave records, and material on the *Virginius* affair.

RG 199: Records of the Provisional Government of Cuba, 1899-1902. See PI 146.

RG 224: Records of the Office of Labor (War Food Administration). U.S. utilization of Mexican and Caribbean farm laborers during World War II. See PI 51.

RG 233: Records of the United States House of Representatives. House files and committee records on Latin American issues. See PI 113.

RG 253: Records of the Petroleum Administration for War. World War II materials on Latin American oil production. See PI 31.

RG 350: Records of the Bureau of Insular Affairs. Material relating to Caribbean and Central American areas where the United States exercised administrative authority, 1898-1939. See Inventory 3 and Special Lists 3-5.

MILITARY ARCHIVES DIVISION (NNM)
Meyer Fishbein, Director
523-3089

Navy and Old Army Branch (NNMO)
Robert Krauskopf, Chief
523-3229

RG 24: Records of the Bureau of Naval Personnel. Logs of U.S. naval vessels active in Latin American waters, 1801-1942. See PI 123.

RG 37: Records of the Hydrographic Office. Field notes of exploring and surveying expeditions, 1837-1946; correspondence and reports relating to hydrographic surveys, 1854-1907. See PI 39.

RG 38: Records of the Office of the Chief of Naval Operations. Major series of Office of Naval Intelligence/naval-attache intelligence reports, 19th century-1945. Also substantial material on the U.S. military government of Santo Domingo, 1916-1924.

RG 45: Naval Records Collection of the Office of Naval Records and Library. Extensive range of Latin American materials, largely 19th and early 20th century, in the correspondence between the Secretary of the Navy and U.S. squadron commanders in Latin American waters; naval intelligence reports, 1888-1914; and private naval logbooks and journals.

RG 78: Records of the Naval Observatory. Scientific correspondence on Latin America, 1842-1861, and the records of U.S. Naval Astronomical Expedition to the Southern Hemisphere, 1848-1861.

RG 80: General Records of the Department of the Navy. Intelligence reports and documents on U.S. naval intervention in the Caribbean, Central America, and Mexico, 1885-1926.

RG 92: Records of the Office of the Quartermaster General. Materials on U.S. Army activities in the Mexican and Spanish-American Wars and other Caribbean operations.

RG 94: Records of the Adjutant General's Office, 1780s-1917. Military records dealing with a variety of subjects, including southwestern frontier operations, the Mexican War, the Spanish-American War, the Mexican Revolution, and U.S. interventions in Mexico. See PI 17. Much of RG 94 has been microfilmed.

RG 108: Records of the Headquarters of the Army. Limited material dealing with the Spanish-American War and Texas-Mexico border problems in the 1860s-1870s.

RG 127: Records of the United States Marine Corps. Miscellaneous reports and field records on Marine Corps activities in Central America and the Caribbean, 1915-1932. See PI 73.

RG 393: Records of the United States Army Continental Commands, 1821-1920. Records of U.S. military posts along the Mexican border.

RG 395: Records of United States Army Overseas Operations and Commands, 1898-1942. Army records dealing with the Spanish-American War, the Veracruz expedition and Punitive Expedition in Mexico, and Army commands in Panama.

Modern Military Branch (NNMM)
Robert Wolfe, Chief
523-3340

RG 160: Records of Headquarters Army Service Forces. Materials relating to Latin American airbases, lend-lease, and other hemisphere-defense matters during World War II.

RG 218: Records of the Joint Chiefs of Staff. Strategic assessments of Latin America in the early Cold War period.

RG 226: Records of the Office of Strategic Services. Numerous intelligence analyses of Latin American political, social, and economic conditions during World War II.

RG 242: Foreign Records Seized. Documents on Latin America from the German Foreign Ministry, 1855-1945, and the Italian Foreign Office and Ministry of Culture, 1922-1940, captured by the Allies at the end of World War II.

RG 263: Records of the Central Intelligence Agency. One-half box containing nothing more than FBIS transcripts of foreign broadcasting, 1947-1949.

RG 319: Records of the Army Staff. Post-1940 G-2 military intelligence reports on Latin America.

RG 330: Records of the Office of the Secretary of Defense. Not currently open to researchers. Nevertheless, an inventory of documents can be obtained from the Modern Military Branch staff. Contact Edward Reese.

RG 333: Records of International Military Agencies. World War II and postwar records of the Joint Brazil-U.S. Military Commission. See PI 127.

[The Modern Military Branch also maintains artificial files containing recently declassified Central Intelligence Agency and National Security Council documents (including a comprehensive index of NSC papers, 1947-1953), duplicates of which have been found in the Branch's military records.]

Note: Certain 20th-century U.S. military record groups are administered jointly by the two branches of the Military Archives Division listed above, with pre-1940 records assigned to the Navy and Old Army Branch and post-1940 records held by the Modern Military Branch. These include:

RG 18: Records of the Army Air Forces. Contains material on U.S.-Latin American cooperation in military aviation, 1920s through World War II.

RG 77: Records of the Office of the Chief of Engineers. Includes material on Mexican War military-construction activities, Nicaraguan and Panama Canal surveys, etc.

RG 107: Records of the Office of the Secretary of War, 1791-1948.

RG 165: Records of the War Department General and Special Staffs. Military Intelligence Division reports from U.S. military attaches stationed in Latin America, 1917-1941.

RG 407: Records of the Adjutant General's Office, 1917-. An extension of RG 94, with substantial pre-World War II intelligence reporting on Mexico.

GENERAL ARCHIVES DIVISION (NNG)
Washington National Records Center
4205 Suitland Road
Suitland, Maryland
763-7410

Mail: Washington, D.C. 20409

Daniel T. Goggin, Director

(Daily shuttle service available from main Archives building.)

RG 4: Records of the United States Food Administration. Material on the procurement of Latin American agricultural commodities (notably Yucatán *henequen*) during World War I. See PI 3.

RG 6: Records of the United State Sugar Equalization Board, Inc. Material dealing with the importation of Latin American (primarily Cuban) sugar and coffee, 1918-1920.

RG 17: Records of the Bureau of Animal Industry. Correspondence on Latin American livestock matters, 1895-1939. Consult PI 106.

RG 21: Records of District Courts of the United States. Court files of piracy and privateering cases involving vessels seized in the Caribbean and South America, 1757-ca. 1900. See PI 116.

RG 30: Records of the Bureau of Public Roads. Reports and correspondence dealing with Latin American highways and U.S. roadbuilding activities in Mexico and Central America (including the Pan-American Highway), 1920-1950. See PI 134.

RG 111: Records of the Office of the Chief Signal Officer. Textual materials on Mexican, Caribbean, and Panamanian communications, 1889-1940. See PI 155.

RG 141: Records of the Military Government of Veracruz, 1914. See PI 138.

RG 152: Records of the Bureau of Dairy Industry. Limited materials on the Latin American dairy industries and international dairy congresses, largely 1920s-1930s.

RG 169: Records of the Foreign Economic Administration. Copious descriptive and statistical material relating to Latin American economic conditions and inter-American economic affairs during World War II. See PI 29.

RG 182: Records of the War Trade Board. Research and statistics on Latin American commerce and inter-American trade, 1911-1919. See PI 100.

RG 185: Records of the Panama Canal. Materials dealing with the Panama Railroad Company, 1849-1938; French canal companies, 1879-1904; Nicaragua canal commissions, 1895-1899; and the Isthmian Canal Commission, 1899-1901. See PI 153.

RG 208: Records of the Office of War Information. Limited quantity of intelligence reports and propaganda material from World War II. Consult PI 56.

RG 229: Records of the Office of Inter-American Affairs. Material related to Coordinator of Inter-American Affairs Nelson Rockefeller's propaganda, cultural, and economic-assistance programs during World War II. See Inventory 7 and PI 41.

RG 265: Records of the Office of Foreign Assets Control. World War II census of American-owned assets in Latin America.

RG 313: Records of Naval Operating Forces. Material on U.S. naval operations in the Caribbean, 1896-1907.

MACHINE-READABLE ARCHIVES DIVISION
711 14th Street, NW
Washington, D.C. 20408
724-1080

In response to the federal government's increasing reliance on computer technology for data-processing, the National Archives recently created this division to store machine-readable magnetic tapes. Data of interest to Latin Americanists can presently be found in:

RG 77: Records of the Office of the Chief of Engineers. Transportation data related to U.S. foreign trade during 1970, including air- and water-borne commodity shipments, by world area.

RG 90: Records of the Public Health Service. World Health Organization survey (based on household interviews) of international attitudes toward health care, 1968-1969. Includes Argentine data.

RG 166: Records of the Foreign Agricultural Service. Statistics on U.S. agricultural imports and exports, 1967-1974, derived from the Bureau of the Census' foreign trade statistics program. Coverage is worldwide, by commodity.

RG 354: Records of the Economic Research Service. International trade statistics prepared by the Organization for Economic Cooperation and Development (OECD), 1961-1971.

A *Catalog of Machine-Readable Records in the National Archives of the United States* (1977), which also contains information on the division's extensive data-reproduction facilities and fees, is available without charge.

4.   In addition to the *Guide to Materials on Latin America in the National Archives* and the published "finding aids" referred to above, researchers may find the following National Archives publications to be of assistance:

Guide to the National Archives of the United States (1974) and an annually-updated loose-leaf version used by the Archives staff.

Catalog of National Archives Microfilm Publications (1974) and 1977 supplement.

Milton O. Gustafson (ed.), *The National Archives and Foreign Relations Research* (1974).

A series of "reference information papers" describes materials in the National Archives relating to:

The Mexican States of Sonora, Sinaloa, and Baja California (Reference Information Paper No. 42, 1952).

The Independence of Latin American Nations (Reference Information Paper No. 45, 1968).

Commerce Data Among State Department Records (Reference Information Paper No. 53, 1973).

Nineteenth-Century Puerto Rican Immigration and Slave Data (Reference Information Paper No. 64, 1973)

Useful general-information leaflets include:

Regulations for the Public Use of Records in the National Archives and Records Service (1972).

Select List of Publications of the National Archives and Records Service (1976).

Location of Records and Fees for Reproduction Services in the National Archives and Records Service (1975).

General Restrictions on Access to Records in the United States (1976).

Information on recent National Archives accessions appears in *Prologue: The Journal of the National Archives* (quarterly), as well as in the American Historical Association's *AHA Newsletter* (nine issues per year) and Phi Alpha Theta's *The Historian* (quarterly). Much useful information on foreign-affairs research in the National Archives is also contained in the Society for Historians of American Foreign Relations' quarterly *Newsletter*.

Note: Also see entries D3, E4, and F13.

B7   National Geographic Society Archives

1.   a.   *17th and M Streets, NW*
             Washington, D.C. 20036
             857-7072

      b.   8:30 A.M.-5 P.M. Monday-Friday

      c.   Not open to the public. Permission to use National Geographic Society archival records must be obtained from a Society officer, usually an associate secretary. Requests for permission should be submitted in writing.

      d.   Photocopying facilities are available.

      e.   Marguerite Northwood, Archivist

2-3.   The archives' Latin American holdings include records pertaining to Hiram Bingham's Peruvian expeditions and to various 20th-century National Geographic Society expeditions to Meso-America.

B8   National Museum of Natural History (Smithsonian Institution) —National Anthropological Archives

1.   a.   *Natural History Building, Room 60-A*
             Constitution Avenue at 10th Street, NW
             Washington, D.C. 20560
             381-5225

      b.   9 A.M.-5 P.M. Monday-Friday

      c.   Open to the public. Visitors are requested to notify the staff prior to their arrival.

    d.   Photoduplication facilities are available.

    e.   Herman Viola, Archivist

2-3.   Within the National Anthropological Archives' approximately 3,500 cubic feet of records are a few thousand Latin American manuscript items, which were acquired by staff-members of the Smithsonian Natural History Museum's Department of Anthropology (see entry C8) or its predecessors (the Bureau of American Ethnology and others), or which have come to the archives through private donations. Included are a large number of Latin American indian vocabularies and other linguistic materials (classifications, maps, charts), transcripts of indian songs, archeological and anthropological field notes and journals, scattered 17th- and 18th-century historical documents and manuscripts (including some governmental and private correspondence from Mexico and Central America), along with translated excerpts from colonial-era publications.

    The archives also houses several personal-papers collections (containing correspondence, field notes, maps, and some sound recordings) from individuals active in the fields of Latin American anthropology, archeology, or ethnology: William H. Crocker, John P. Harrington, Sister Inez Hilger, Ales Hrdlicka, Herbert Krieger, Weston LaBarre, Robert M. Laughlin, and William Duncan Strong.

    Institutional collections of potential interest to Latin Americanists are the records of the Bureau of American Ethnology, 1878-1965; the records of the Bureau of American Ethnology's Institute for Social Anthropology (which conducted anthropological training programs throughout Latin America), 1942-1952; and the records of the Department of Anthropology, 1897-present.

    Also available, in the public research room, is a complete collection of Bureau of American Ethnology reports and publications.

4.   See the four-volume *Catalog to Manuscripts at the National Anthropological Archives* (Boston: G.K. Hall, 1975). An alphabetically arranged card catalog of individual manuscript holdings is maintained. Registers or other finding-aids are available for most of the personal-papers collections.

Note: Also see entries F12 and F16.

───

B9 Naval Historical Center (Navy Department)—Operational Archives

1.   **a.** *Washington Navy Yard, Building 210 (Fourth Floor)*
          9th and M Streets, SE
          Washington, D.C. 20374
          433-3170

    b. 7:30 A.M.-4:30 P.M. Monday-Friday

    c. Open to the public. Some materials are classified or otherwise restricted. Researchers are requested to notify the staff prior to their arrival.

    d. Photoduplication services available.

    e. Dean C. Allard, Head—Operational Archives Branch.

2-3.   The Naval Historical Center's Operational Archives contain a large quantity of 20th-century U.S. Navy operational records pertaining to Latin America.

They include naval intelligence reports dating back to World War II; action and operational reports of naval commands, 1939-1950; war diaries of naval commands, 1941-1953; strategic and operational planning documents (including U.S. war plans relating to Mexico and Cuba), 1939-1950; documents from the files of naval operating commands (1941-1963); central security-classified records of the offices of the Secretary of the Navy and Chief of Naval Operations, 1940-1950; records of the War Plans (later Strategic Plans) Division, Office of the Chief of Naval Operations, 1917-1950; records of the Base Maintenance Division, Office of the Chief of Naval Operations (including histories of overseas bases), 1939-1957; records of the Organization, Research, and Policy Division, Office of the Chief of Naval Operations, 1947-1949; records of the Top Secret Control Office, Office of the Chief of Naval Operations, 1944-1950; records of the Politico-Military Affairs Division, Office of the Chief of Naval Operations, 1944-1950; records of the U.S. Atlantic Fleet, 1939-1944; records of the U.S. Naval Air Station, Bermuda, 1942-1945; and records of the General Board of the Navy (including material on Caribbean bases), 1901-1951. Foreign records held by the Operational Archives include translated records of the German Navy, essays by German officers, and related studies, 1922-1945; World War II German U-boat records; and previously classified publications of the British Navy, 1914-1945. Among the other holdings of potential interest to Latin Americanists are unpublished World War II unit histories prepared by wartime U.S. naval historians.

In addition, the archive has office files and personal papers of several 20th-century U.S. naval officers and officials, including Secretary of the Navy James Forrestal, 1934-1951; Secretary of the Navy Frank Knox, 1940-1944; Captain Miles P. Duval (Panama Canal), 1943-1949; Captain Glenn F. Howell (naval attaché in Brazil), 1923-1924; and others.

There is also an oral-history collection.

4.   A list of "Declassified and Unclassified Groups and Collections in the Operational Archives" will be provided on request.

There are detailed finding-aids available for most of the individual collections. For the unpublished World War II unit histories, see the Naval Historical Center's *Partial Checklist: World War II Histories and Historical Reports in the U.S. Naval History Divison* (1973).

Note: Also see entry J8.

B10   Office of Air Force History (Air Force Department)

1.   a.   *Forrestal Building, Room 8E082*
1000 Independence Avenue, SW
Washington, D.C. 20314
693-7399 (Reference)

b.   7:45 A.M.-4 P.M. Monday-Friday

c.   Open to qualified researchers, who should call ahead to arrange a visit. Many of the holdings are classified or otherwise restricted.

d.   Photoreproduction and microfilm-copying facilities are available.

e.   Stanley L. Falk, Chief Historian

2-3.　　　The Office of Air Force History possesses an extensive collection of microfilm copies of official Air Force archival records housed in the Albert F. Simpson Historical Research Center at Maxwell Air Force Base, Alabama. Included are Air Force unit histories, strategic assessments, policy and planning documents, intelligence reports, end-of-tour reports, attache debriefings, records of Air Force commands and units responsible for hemispheric air defense (e.g., the U.S. Southern Command, Caribbean Air Defense Command, and Antilles Air Command, as well as the Inter-American Air Force Academy, and, presumably, the records of the U.S. units associated with Latin American air force units which participated in World War II and the Korean War), and Latin American intelligence studies prepared by CIA, DIA, the State Department, and the Defense Department. Also available are microfilm copies of materials from personal-papers and oral-history collections located at the Simpson Historical Research Center, including materials relating to various U.S. Air Force officers involved in inter-American military affairs. The bulk of the collection dates from World War II to the present, with some earlier coverage. Much of the post-World War II material is restricted. Staff members, however, can assist researchers in obtaining declassification of classified documents.

　　　The facility also has a small reference library, which contains a collection of Air Force historical studies (largely classified) and a multivolume collection of "Selected Statements" by principal Air Force and/or Defense Department officials, 1958-present.

4.　　　There is an index (on microfilm) to the microfilmed records collection, arranged alphabetically, by subject, with entries for "Latin America" and individual countries. This index contains detailed references to both classified and unclassified documents, and should prove useful to researchers in compiling data for Freedom-of-Information Act requests. Also useful in working with the collection is the *Air Force Historical Archives Document Classification Guide* (1971). For materials in the personal-papers and oral-history holdings, consult *Personal Files in the U.S. Air Force Historical Collection* (1975) and *U.S. Air Force Oral History Catalog of Selected Interviews* (1975), respectively.

　　　Two Office of Air Force History publications will also be of interest to researchers: *United States Air Force History: A Guide to Documentary Sources* (1973) and *United States Air Force History: An Annotated Bibliography* (irregularly updated).

Oliveira Lima Library (Catholic University)—Documents Collection
See entry A42

B11　Organization of American States—Records Management Center

1.　a.　*B-10, Administrative Building*
　　　19th Street and Constitution Avenue, NW
　　　Washington, D.C. 20006
　　　381-8255/8281

　　b.　9:30 A.M.-5 P.M. Monday-Friday

　　c.　Open to researchers. An appointment is recommended.

　　d.　OAS photoreproduction services are available.

e. Mercedes Fritzsching, Chief

2. The records-collection numbers some 11 million documents.

3. This valuable and largely untapped collection consists of the internal staff papers, conference material, and correspondence of the OAS and its predecessor, the Pan American Union. The records, which date back to 1889, are almost entirely open to researchers. Among the few exceptions are 15 boxes of restricted U.S. military records pertaining to 1965 inter-American "peace-keeping" operations in the Dominican Republic.

In addition, the Records Management Center administers a locked vault containing the original copies of inter-American treaties, agreements, conventions, and final acts. Also in the vault are many items of physical evidence presented to, or collected by, the OAS relating to inter-American boundary violations (including the 1960s Cuban-Venezuelan dispute).

4. Mercedes Fritzsching, Chief of the Records Management Center, maintains lists of all records under her jurisdiction, arranged by originating office and date. She will be happy to assist outside researchers.

Note: Additional OAS archival materials are administered by the OAS Columbus Memorial Library. See entry A43.

B12 Smithsonian Institution Archives

1. a. *Arts and Industries Building, Room 133*
900 Jefferson Drive, SW
Washington, D.C. 20560
381-4075

b. 8:45 A.M.-5:15 P.M. Monday-Friday

c. Open to the public.

d. Photoduplication facilities are available.

e. Richard H. Lytle, Archivist

2-3. Included in the Smithsonian Institution Archives' approximately 5,500 cubic feet of records are personal-papers collections relating to some 50-75 U.S. biologists, zoologists, naturalists, and other scientists who participated in scientific expeditions in Latin America during the 19th and 20th centuries. Contents include field notebooks, diaries, correspondence, photographs, and maps. Also in the archives are the 1918-1965 records of the Smithsonian's Tropical Research Institute in the Panama Canal Zone.

4. Individual collections are described in the *Guide to the Smithsonian Institution Archives* (Washington, D.C.: Smithsonian Institution Press, forthcoming). A periodically updated computer index to the archives' holdings will also prove useful. Detailed finding-aids to individual collections are available.

State Department Historical Office See entry J28

United States Army Center of Military History See entry J8

C. Museums, Galleries, and Art Collections

Museum, Gallery, and Art Collection Entry Format (C)

1. General Information
   a. *address; telephone number(s)*
   b. hours of service
   c. conditions of access
   d. reproduction services
   e. name/title of director and heads of relevant divisions

2. Size of holdings pertaining to Latin America

3. Description of holdings pertaining to Latin America

4. Bibliographic aids facilitating use of collection

C1 "Daniel C. Stapleton" Private Collection

1-4. This privately owned collection—which was assembled by U.S. miner Daniel C. Stapleton during the late 1800s, primarily in Colombia, Ecuador, and Peru—is reputed to be the most magnificent collection of colonial and 19th-century Latin American fine-arts pieces in the Washington, D.C. area. Included are paintings (some 82), sculptures, jewelry, furniture, silver (200 pieces), books, and maps. Cataloging efforts have been in progress for some time. Unfortunately, the present owners regretfully state that they lack the facilities to permit general scholarly access to the collection as of this writing.

C2 Dumbarton Oaks (Harvard University)—Pre-Columbian Collection

1. a. *1703 32nd Street, NW*
      Washington, D.C. 20007
      232-3101

   b. 2 P.M.-5 P.M. Tuesday-Sunday
      Closed Monday

   c. Open to the public.

   e. Elizabeth Benson, Curator

2. The collection totals some 500-600 pieces, of which more than 250 are on exhibit.

3.   Originally the private collection of United States diplomat Robert Woods Bliss, the Dumbarton Oaks Pre-Columbian Collection covers the major Amerind cultures of Meso-America and South America. Holdings are small in number, but of extremely high quality—each piece having been chosen for the aesthetic beauty of its craftsmanship and artistic expression as well as for its archeological significance. The pieces are displayed in an extraordinarily attractive setting.

The exhibit is arranged by geographical and chronological sequence. Olmec artifacts feature a number of finely carved objects of jade and serpentine. The great classic period in Middle America is represented by a wealth of material: carved stone masks, pottery, and a mural from Teotihuacán; Mayan sculpture, relief panels, painted and carved pottery and figurines, jade and shell ornaments; ceremonial ballgame equipment, carved stone yolks and *hachas* from central Veracruz. From the later Mixteca-Puebla culture of Oaxaca, there is cast gold jewelry, while the Aztec period is represented by stone sculptures of dieties and animals. Central American materials feature polished jade "axe-god" pendants and cast gold ornaments from Costa Rica, gold pendants cast in the lost-wax process from Panama, and gold ornaments from the area of the Canal Zone. From Colombia there are intricately detailed gold objects. Peruvian materials include textiles, polychrome pottery and masks, lapidary work, small objects of carved stone, and ornaments and tools of gold, silver, bronze, and copper—ranging in date from very early Chavín to Inca.

4.   Guides include two Dumbarton Oaks publications: *Handbook of the Robert Woods Bliss Collection of Pre-Columbian Art* (1963), with 1969 supplement; and Michael D. Coe, *Classic Maya Pottery at Dumbarton Oaks* (1975).

A free brochure, *The Robert Woods Bliss Collection of Pre-Columbian Art,* is also available.

Note: Also see entries A15, F6, and M15.

Embassy of Panama Art Collection See entry K21

Embassy of Peru Art Collection See entry K23

C3 Fondo del Sol

1. a. *2112 R Street, NW*
        Washington, D.C. 20008
        483-2777

    b. Noon-7 P.M. Tuesdays and Saturdays

    e. Marc Zuver, Curator
        Rebecca Kelley Crumlish, Curator

2-3.   The Fondo del Sol is a commercial art gallery and studio focusing on contemporary Latino, Hispanic, Chicano, and Puerto Rican art—painting, lithographs, murals, sculpture, film, and photographs. Artists-in-residence conduct workshops.

C4 Hirshhorn Museum and Sculpture Garden (Smithsonian Institution)

1. a. *Independence Avenue at 8th Street, NW*
      Washington, D.C. 20560
      381-6753

   b. April 1-Labor Day: 10 A.M.-9 P.M. Daily
      Labor Day-April 1: 10 A.M.-5:30 P.M. Daily

   c. Open to the public. For permission to see items in the permanent collection which are not on public display, contact the curatorial staff of the Department of Painting and Sculpture (381-6708/6718).

   d. Photographic copies of many works in the collection are available for purchase. Cameras are permitted.

   e. Abram Lerner, Director

3. Within the Hirshhorn's collection are several pieces of 20th-century Latin American art, including:
   Paintings by Horacio Garcia-Rossi, Romulo Maccio, and Antonio Segui (Argentina); Roberto Matta (Chile); Fernando Botero (Colombia); Francisco Zuñiga (Costa Rica); José Cuevas, Ricardo Martinez, José Clemente Orozco, David Alfaro Siqueiros, and Rufino Tamayo (Mexico); Joaquin Torres-Garcia (Uruguay); and Jesus Rafael Soto (Venezuela).
   Sculpture by Martha Boto, Hugo de Marco, Lucio Fontana, Julio Le Parc, and Alicia Penalba (Argentina); Marina Nuñez del Prado (Bolivia); Amilcar de Castro (Brazil); Marta Colvin and Roberto Matta (Chile); Francisco Zuñiga (Costa Rica); Joaquin Torres-Garcia (Uruguay); and Jesus Rafael Soto (Venezuela).
   The Hirshhorn has also periodically hosted temporary exhibits of Latin American art.

4. See the museum's inaugural catalog *Selected Paintings and Sculpture from the Hirshhorn Museum and Sculpture Garden* (1974), and a periodically updated checklist of holdings. A card index to holdings, arranged by name of artist, is also maintained.

C5 National Collection of Fine Arts (Smithsonian Institution)

1. a. *8th and G Streets, NW*
      Washington, D.C. 20540
      381-6543

   b. 10 A.M.-5:30 P.M. Daily

   c. Open to the public. Contact the Office of the Registrar (381-4034) to see works in the permanent collection which are not on public display.

   d. Photographic copies of most works in the collection are available for purchase. Cameras are permitted.

   e. Joshua Taylor, Director

2-3. Within the permanent collection are two prints by the Mexican Rufino Tamayo and a single lithograph by Mexico's José Clemente Orozco.

The National Collection of Fine Arts occasionally hosts temporary exhibitions of Latin American art and furnishings.

4.   The Office of the Registrar (381-4034) maintains an index of works in the collection, by artist's name.

C6   National Gallery of Art

1.   a.   *Constitution Avenue at 6th Street, NW*
          Washington, D.C. 20565
          737-4215

     b.   April 1-Labor Day:
          10 A.M.-9 P.M. Monday-Saturday
          Noon-9 P.M Sunday

          Labor Day-April 1:
          10 A.M.-5 P.M. Monday-Saturday
          Noon-9 P.M. Sunday

     c.   Open to the public.

     d.   Photographic copies of many works in the collection are available for purchase. Works may also be photographed by visitors.

     e.   J. Carter Brown, Director

2-3.   The collection contains a small number of single works by Latin American artists, including paintings by David Alfaro Siqueiros and Rufino Tamayo (Mexico), Enrique Castro-Cid and Roberto Matta (Chile), and Carlos Scliar (Brazil); and prints by Diego Rivera and José Clemente Orozco (Mexico).
          The National Gallery of Art also periodically hosts temporary, traveling art exhibits from Latin America.

C7   National Museum of History and Technology (Smithsonian Institution)

1.   a.   *History and Technology Building*
          12th Street and Constitution Avenue, NW
          Washington, D.C. 20560
          628-4422 (Information)

     b.   Public Exhibits:
          April 1-Labor Day: 10 A.M.-9 P.M. Daily
          Labor Day-April 1: 10 A.M.-5:30 P.M. Daily

          Departmental offices and research collections:
          8:45 A.M.-5:15 P.M. Monday-Friday

     c.   Exhibit areas and departmental research offices are open to the public. Visitors to the latter are requested to call or write for an appointment in advance of their arrival.

     d.   Cameras permitted. Photoreproduction services available.

     e.   Otto Mayr, Acting Director

2-3.   *Department of Cultural History*

The department's Division of Community Life (381-5652) possesses some 2,000-3,000 culturally significant artifacts representing the European cultural heritage in Spanish North America. Ninety percent of the artifacts are from New Mexico, most of the remainder from Mexico. The majority of the items date from the 19th century, although earlier and later materials are also represented. Included in the collection are costumes and textiles (for example, 19th-century soldiers' leather jackets and a complete Mexican *rurales* uniform), horse gear (rare saddles, spurs, etc.), domestic household furnishings (furniture, tools, utensils, looms, secular folk art), religious art and paraphernalia (rosaries, medals, reliquaries, *santos, retablos, ex votos,* etc.), and miscellaneous items (a Cuban *garrote,* an 1840s ox-cart, a property map and public proclamations from Spanish California). Curator Richard Ahlborn is a specialist in the cultural and artistic history of Spanish America and the Spanish borderlands.

Department of National and Military History

The Division of Military History (381-5115) has a few (probably less than a dozen) locally manufactured weapons from Brazil and other South American nations. Also in the division's research collections are substantial numbers of U.S. weapons, uniforms, insignia, and other military equipment from the Mexican War, Spanish-American War, and early 20th-century Mexican incursions.

The Division of Naval History (381-5505) possesses several artifacts from underwater sites along Spanish colonial shipping routes in the Caribbean.

Department of Applied Arts

The Division of Postal History (381-5024) possesses some 30 specialized Latin American collections, containing an estimated one million postal stamps, postal stationery items, and other philatelic research material. Museum technician Lowell Newman maintains a card file on the contents of the Latin American collections. The division also has a specialized reference library.

The Division of Numismatics (381-5026) possesses a large collection of Latin American metallic coins (with items dating back to the early colonial period) and paper currency. Included is a substantial special collection of Latin American gold coins. Curator Elvira Clain-Stefanelli can provide detailed information.

C8   National Museum of Natural History (Smithsonian Institution)

1.   a.   *Natural History Building*
          Constitution Avenue at 10th Street, NW
          Washington, D.C. 20560
          628-4422 (Information)
          381-5626 (Department of Anthropology)

     b.   Public Exhibits:
          April 1-Labor Day: 10 A.M.-9 P.M. Daily
          Labor Day-April 1: 10 A.M.-5:30 P.M. Daily

          Department of Anthropology offices and research collections:
          8:45 A.M.-5:15 P.M. Monday-Friday

c. Exhibit areas and departmental research offices are open to the public. Visitors to the latter are requested to call or write for an appointment in advance of their arrival.

d. Cameras permitted. Photoreproduction services available.

e. Porter Kier, Director
William H. Crocker, Associate Curator (South American Ethnology)
Clifford Evans, Curator (Latin American Archeology)
Robert M. Laughlin, Curator (Meso-American and Caribbean Ethnology)
Douglas H. Ubelaker, Associate Curator (New World Physical Anthropology)

2-3.   There are two permanent Latin American exhibits on public display: "Native Peoples of the Americas" (First Floor) and "South America: Continent and Cultures" (Second Floor).

In addition, the archeological, anthropological, and ethnological research collections of the museum's Department of Anthropology contain an extensive range of Latin American artifacts and specimens. Holdings are stored, by country, in drawers. The following estimated numbers of drawers per country within each collection provide a general sense of geographic representation. The quantity of individual items within each drawer, however, varies widely.

Archeology research collection (pre-Columbian ceramics, textiles, metals, stone, wood, leather, shells, etc.): Argentina, 42 drawers; Bolivia, 3; Chile, 30; Colombia, 15; Costa Rica, 80; Dominican Republic, 62; Ecuador, 775; Guatemala, 10; Honduras, 35; Mexico, 790; Nicaragua, 75; Panama, 305; Peru, 245; Puerto Rico, 65; Venezuela, 120; other Caribbean islands, 70. Unaccessioned materials, which are included in the above figures, are stored together separately, by country. In addition, a collection of oversized items is stored in a fourth-floor attic, and a collection of South American precious metals is stored in an attic safe.

Ethnology research collection (Amerindian ceramics, textiles, jewelry, musical instruments, weapons, tools, masks, baskets, gourds, etc.): Argentina, 25 drawers; Bolivia, 10; Brazil, 110; Chile, 20; Colombia, 15; Costa Rica, 20; Ecuador, 45; El Salvador, 3; Guatemala, 55; Guianas, 70; Honduras, 5; Mexico, 190; Nicaragua, 5; Panama, 50; Paraguay, 20; Puerto Rico, 15; Venezuela, 20; other Caribbean islands, 30. There is also a small quantity of oversized material, and a separate "Abbott Room collection" containing a number of South American indian spears.

Physical anthropology research collection (skulls, femurs, and other skeletal remains): Peru, 450 drawers; Mexico, 30-40; Argentina, Bolivia, Brazil, Chile, Colombia, Cuba, and Ecuador, 20 or fewer.

4.   Card catalogs are maintained for individual accessioned items within each of the three research collections. Staff members of the Department of Anthropology's Processing Lab, located in room 311 (381-5758), assist private researchers in working with the collections.

C9 Oliveira Lima Collection (Catholic University)

1. a. *620 Michigan Avenue, NE*
Washington, D.C. 20017
635-5059

    b. 1 P.M.-8 P.M. Tuesday
Noon-7 P.M. Wednesday-Friday
9 A.M.-5 P.M. Saturday
Closed, Sunday-Monday

    c. Open to the public. Cameras are permitted.

    d. Manoel Cardozo, Curator

2.   The Oliveira Lima Library contains a varied collection of several hundred pieces of Luzo-Brazilian materials acquired by Brazilian diplomat Manoel de Oliveira Lima (1867-1928).

3.   Museum pieces include momentos of the Brazilian and Portuguese royal families, memorabilia of the Oliveira Lima family, several pieces of 19th-century furniture, a lady's fan from the court of John VI, a headcomb belonging to Simón Bolívar's mother, busts of Pedro I and several other 19th-century Brazilian statesmen, a photograph of Francisco Solano López taken during the Paraguayan War, and assorted coins, medals, and medallions.

    An iconography collection contains a large number of rare paintings and engravings, including portraits of Brazilian and Portuguese royalty, a landscape of Pernambuco by the 17th-century Dutch master, Frans Post, ten 1782 watercolors of the Amazon region by Spanish commissioner Francisco de Requeña, engravings of Count Maurice of Nassau, the Marquess of Pombal, and Francisco de Miranda, and 18th-century maps of the New World by Cano y Olmedilla.

4.   A brochure, *The Art Collection of the Oliveira Lima Library: A Catalog of Selected Items,* is available free upon request.

C10 Organization of American States—Museum of Modern Art of Latin America

1.   a. *201 18th Street, NW*
Washington, D.C. 20006
381-8381/8261

    b. 10 A.M.-5 P.M. Tuesday-Saturday

    c. Open to the public.

    d. Cameras permitted. Slides and postcards of some items within the collection are available for purchase.

    e. José Gomez-Sicre, Director
Angel Hurtado, Curator

2.   The collection numbers some 360 works, at least half of which are on public display at any one time.

3.   The museum, which opened in 1976, is devoted entirely to contemporary Latin American and Caribbean art. Included within its growing collection are:

    Paintings by Hector Basaldua, Luis F. Benedit, Ary Brizzi, Víctor Chab, Miguel Diomede, Raquel Forner, Domingo Gatto, Sara Grilo, Rogelio

Polesello, Ricardo Supisiche, and Miguel Angel Vidal (Argentina); Rudy Ayoroa and María Luisa Pacheco (Bolivia); Tikashi Fukushima, Manabu Mabe, Cândido Portinari, Danilo di Prete, Yutaka Toyota, and Kazuya Wakabayashi (Brazil); Jaime Bendersky, Roberto Matta, and Mario Toral (Chile); Enrique Grau, Alejandro Obregón, and Eduardo Ramírez Villamizar (Colombia); Lola Fernández (Costa Rica); Cundo Bermúdez and Amelia Peláez (Cuba); Ramón Oviedo and Darío Suro (Dominican Republic); Estuardo Maldonado and Enrique Tábara (Ecuador); Mauricio Aguilar and Benjamín Cañas (El Salvador); Carlos Mérida and Elmar Rojas (Guatemala); Joseph Jean-Gilles (Haiti); José Antonio Velasquez (Honduras); Rafael Coronel, José Luis Cuevas, Leonardo Nierman, and Rufino Tamayo (Mexico); Asilia Guillén, Armando Morales, and Rodrigo Peñalba (Nicaragua); Guillermo Trujillo (Panama); Enrique Careaga (Paraguay); Julio Rosado del Valle (Puerto Rico); Ciro Palacios and Fernando de Szyszlo (Peru); M. P. Alladin (Trinidad and Tobago); Rafael Barradas, Pedro Figari, and Joaquín Torres-García (Uruguay); and Angel Hurtado, Carmen Millan, Alejandro Otero, Héctor Poleo, Humberto Jaimes Sanchez, and Jesús Rafael Soto (Venezuela).

Sculptures by Raúl Valdivieso (Chile); Beatriz Echeverri, Edgar Negret, and Eduardo Ureta (Colombia); Juan José Sicre (Cuba); Georges Liautaud (Haiti); Everald Brown (Jamaica); and Rafael Ferrer (Puerto Rico).

Graphics by Antonio Berni, Aida Carballo, and Juan C. Liberti (Argentina); Ruth Bess and Aldemir Martins (Brazil); Gerardo Caballero and David Manzur (Colombia); Osvaldo Guayasamín (Ecuador); Rodolfo Abularach (Guatemala); David Alfaro Siqueiros and Rufino Tamayo (Mexico); and José Sabogal (Peru).

In the future, the museum hopes to sponsor film and lecture series on Latin American art. An artists' workshop and reference library are also planned.

4.   An illustrated descriptive brochure, *Museum of Modern Art of Latin America*, may be purchased through the museum or the OAS Department of Publications. An illustrated catalog of the museum's holdings is planned. Many of the museum's works are featured in films and slide collections prepared by the Visual Arts unit of the OAS Department of Cultural Affairs (see entry L10).

Note: In addition, rotating exhibits of Latin American art (usually focusing on a single artist or nation) are always on display in a permanent gallery located outside the OAS Council Chamber in the original Pan American Union (now called the Main) Building, 17th Street and Constitution Avenue, NW. These temporary exhibits, which usually are sponsored jointly by local Latin American embassies and the OAS Visual Arts Unit, change on an average of every six weeks. The Visual Arts Unit, which administers the Museum of Modern Art of Latin America, also holds, in storage in a small building next to the museum, a large and valuable collection of paintings, prints, and drawings left on consignment by Latin American artists.

C11   Textile Museum

1.   a.   *2320 S Street, NW*
Washington, D.C. 20008
667-0441

b.   10 A.M.-5 P.M. Tuesday-Saturday

    c. Open to the public. Items in the permanent collection which are not on public display may be viewed by researchers on an appointment basis.

    d. Black-and-white photographs of some items in the collection are available for purchase. The museum also maintains a large file of black-and-white negatives (as well as some color transparencies), including coverage of most of the museum's major pre-Columbian Peruvian textiles.

    e. Andrew Oliver, Jr., Director
Ann P. Rowe, Assistant Curator (Western Hemisphere Textiles)

2.   Approximately 4,000 of the museum's 9,000 textiles are of Latin American origin.

3.   The focus of the collection is on hand-woven articles—primarily tapestries and clothing—ranging in date from ca. 600 B.C. to the present. The vast majority of Latin American items (more than 3,000) are pre-Columbian archeological textiles (tapestries, tunics, etc.) from Peru. Most of the remainder are ethnographic textiles (predominantly 20th-century indian clothing—*rebozos,* skirts, belts, etc.), including approximately 250 items from Peru and southern South America, 400 from Guatemala (primarily village costumes), 300 from Mexico, and 50 from Panama (*molas,* etc.). Also in the collection are a few colonial-era Peruvian indian tapestries, colonial Mexican embroideries, and 19th-century Mexican samplers and *serapes.* Only a very small percentage of the total collection is on public display at any one time. The museum also periodically hosts temporary, travelling exhibits from Latin America.

    The Textile Museum's 7,000-volume library contains an estimated 900 volumes on Latin American art, archeology, textiles, and weaving. Approximately one-quarter of the Latin American titles are Spanish-language imprints. Also included in the collection are U.S. doctoral dissertations on Latin American textiles. The library is open to researchers, 10 A.M.-4 P.M., Wednesday-Friday, and at other times by appointment.

4.   For individual items in the collection, see the curator's card catalog, which is arranged by country and therein by region or village.

    Several of the museum's publications will also provide at least partial inventories of Latin American holdings. See Ann P. Rowe, *Warp-Patterned Weaves of the Andes* (1977); *Ancient Peruvian Textiles from the Collection of the Textile Museum, Washington, D.C. and the Museum of Primitive Art, New York* (1965); and various exhibition catalogs, including: *A Heritage of Color: Textile Traditions of the South Coast of Peru; The Guatemalan Huipil; Molas: Art of the Cuna Indians;* and *Peruvian Costume: A Weaver's Art.* Also see the published proceedings of Textile Museum conferences devoted to pre-Columbian textiles (1973) and ethnographic textiles in the Western Hemisphere (1976). An annual *Journal* and a quarterly *Newsletter* are disseminated to the museum's Associate membership.

C12 Washington World Gallery

1.   **a.** *3065 M Street, NW*
Washington, D.C. 20007
338-7414

      b. 10 A.M.-6 P.M. Tuesday, Wednesday, Saturday
Noon-9 P.M. Thursday, Friday

    c. Open to the public.

    d. Cameras permitted.

    e. José Font, Director

2-3.   This commercial art gallery (which is owned by a Cuban and a Chilean) offers a changing variety of Latin American art works for sale, including colonial and contemporary paintings, contemporary sculpture, tapestries, Indian ceramics, and handicrafts.

Note: In addition, the following institutions periodically host temporary exhibitions of Latin American art and/or artifacts:

Brazilian-American Cultural Institute, Inc. 362-8334
4201 Connecticut Avenue, NW
Washington, D.C. 20008
Hours: 9 A.M.-7 P.M. Monday-Friday

Corcoran Gallery of Art 638-3211
17th Street and New York Avenue, NW
Washington, D.C. 20006
Hours: 11 A.M.-5 P.M. Tuesday-Sunday

Inter-American Development Bank 634-8000
801 17th Street, NW
Washington, D.C. 20577
Hours: 8 A.M.-5:30 P.M. Monday-Friday

International Monetary Fund 393-6362
700 19th Street, NW
Washington, D.C. 20431
Hours: 9 A.M.-5:30 P.M. Monday-Friday

National Geographic Society 857-7588
17th and M Streets, NW
Washington, D.C. 20036
Hours: 9 A.M.-6 P.M. Monday-Friday
       9 A.M.-5 P.M. Saturday
      10 A.M.-5 P.M. Sunday

Phillips Collection 387-2151
1600 21st Street, NW
Washington, D.C. 20009
Hours: 10 A.M.-5 P.M. Tuesday-Saturday
      2 P.M.-7 P.M. Sunday

Renwick Gallery (National Collection of Fine Arts) 381-5811
17th Street and Pennsylvania Avenue, NW
Washington, D.C. 20006
Hours: 10 A.M.-5:30 P.M. Daily

D. Collections of Music and Other Sound Recordings

Music Collection Entry Format (D)

1. General Information
   a. *address; telephone number(s)*
   b. hours of service
   c. conditions of access
   d. name/title of director and key staff members

2. Size of holdings pertaining to Latin America

3. Description of holdings pertaining to Latin America

4. Facilities for study and use
   a. availability of audiovisual equipment
   b. reservation requirements
   c. fees charged
   d. reproduction services

5. Bibliographic aids facilitating use of collection

Archive of Hispanic Literature on Tape See entry A33

D1 Brazilian-American Cultural Institute (BACI) Music Collection

1. a. *Suite 211*
      4201 Connecticut Avenue, NW
      Washington, D.C. 20008
      362-8334

   b. 10 A.M.-7:30 P.M. Monday-Friday

   c. Open to the public.

   d. José Neistein, Director
      Paulo Costa, Record and Tape Librarian

2-3. Approximately 1,000 record albums and 100 tapes of Brazilian music, classical and popular.

4. Taping equipment is available.

5. A 1975 record inventory is available.

Embassy of Argentina Music Collection See entry K1

Embassy of Chile Music Collection See entry K6

Embassy of Jamaica Music Collection See entry K18

Embassy of Venezuela Music Collection See entry K27

Inter-American Development Bank Library Music Collection
See entry A26

D2 **Library of Congress—Music Division—Recorded Sound Section and Archive of Folk Song**

1. a. *Library of Congress Main Building*
10 1st Street, SE
Washington, D.C. 20540
426-5509 (Recorded Sound Section)
426-5510 (Archive of Folk Song)

   b. 8:30 A.M.-5 P.M. Monday-Friday

   c. Open to the public.

   d. Robert Carneal, Head—Recorded Sound Section
Joseph C. Hickerson, Head—Archive of Folk Song

2-3. The Recorded Sound Section of the Library of Congress' Music Division holds a 750,000-item collection of commercial (LP and pre-LP) and noncommercial recordings. No meaningful assessment of Latin American holdings is possible, because 90 percent of the collection remains uncataloged and the available card catalog for processed items is not structured geographically. As a result, researchers must either have specific recordings in mind or rely almost exclusively on staff members for assistance in identifying and locating Latin American materials.

   Commercial recordings include an indeterminate but probably substantial quantity of Latin American classical, popular, and folk recordings. A very brief survey of the dictionary card catalog turned up 206 recorded works by Villa Lobos and 42 by Ginastera. Non-music recordings include 230 shortwave radio monitorings of Fidel Castro's speeches (which the Library of Congress recently acquired from the Central Intelligence Agency); Voice of America broadcasts; speeches delivered by U.S. officials and visiting dignitaries at National Press Club luncheons; CBS and NBC radio broadcasts to Latin America during World War II; and complete recordings of United Nations proceedings (General Assembly sessions, committee meetings, and, within the near future, Security Council sessions), 1945-1965.

   The Archive of Folk Song possesses some 40,000 recordings—tapes, discs, cylinders, and wire spools—containing over 250,000 items of folk song, folk music, folk tale, and other types of folklore. Within the collection are substantial numbers of Latin American field recordings. Although virtually every Latin American nation is represented, coverage is most extensive for the Bahamas, Haiti, Trinidad, Mexico, Brazil, Venezuela, and Panama. Mexican materials include 1910 Charles Lummis recordings of indian languages, and several 1940s field collections of Mexican indian music and folk songs. The extensive field recordings of West Indian and Afro-Bahian folk music are also noteworthy.

Field notes, music transcripts, and printed texts are available for many of the collections. The archive also maintains a sizable reference collection of books, periodicals, and unpublished theses dealing with folk music, folklore, and ethnomusicology. LP recordings of Mexican, Venezuelan, and Puerto Rican folk music and Afro-Bahian religious songs from the archive's collections are available for purchase.

4. a-c. Listening equipment for every form of recorded sound in the various collections may be used without charge, on an appointment basis.

d. Researchers are not permitted to use their own taping equipment to reproduce Music Division materials. Reproduction services are available in the division's recording laboratory, however. Fees are substantial.

5. Dictionary card catalogs are available for cataloged materials in both the Recorded Sound Section and the Archive of Folk Song. Holdings are also listed in *Music, Books on Music, and Sound Recordings,* a semiannual catalog, with annual and quinquennial cumulations, issued as part of the *National Union Catalog.* Free brochures available from the Music Division include *The Music Division: A Guide to its Collections and Services* (1972); *A Guide to the Collections of Recorded Folk Music and Folklore in the Library of Congress* (1976); *The Archive of Folk Song in the Library of Congress* (1977); and lists of recorded LP albums for sale.

D3 National Archives and Records Service—Audiovisual Archives Division

1. a. *8th Street and Pennsylvania Avenue, NW*
Washington, D.C. 20408
523-3208

b. 8:45 A.M.-5 P.M. Monday-Friday

c. Open to researchers with a National Archives research pass, obtainable from the Central Reference Division, Room 200-B.

d. James Moore, Director
William Murphy, Chief—Motion Picture and Sound Recording Branch
Les Waffen, Head of Sound Recording

2-3. The National Archives' Audiovisual Archives contain some 70,000 sound recordings (tapes and phonograph records), dating from the turn of the century. Materials are arranged according to National Archives "record group" (RG). Latin American-related holdings are not extensive, but include:

RG 12: Records of the Office of Education. Radio broadcasts dealing with Domingo Sarmiento, Dom Pedro II, and the 50th anniversary of the Pan American Union.

RG 48: Records of the Office of the Secretary of the Interior. State Department recordings related to the Pan American Union, 1940s.

RG 59: General Records of the Department of State. Public addresses by U.S. secretaries of state, and recordings of the State Department's "Good Neighbor" series on Brazilian economic, cultural, and political history.

RG 200: National Archives Gift Collection. Recordings of speeches and press conferences by U.S. Presidents (beginning with Grover Cleveland), congressmen, and State Department officials (including Sumner Welles). In addition, a recording of Eva Perón's deathbed radio address to the Argentine people, and a recording of a 1942 CBS "Dedication Program of the Network of the Americas" featuring remarks by Sumner Welles, Nelson Rockefeller, and several Latin American chiefs of state and government ministers.

RG 229: Records of the Office of Inter-American Affairs. Twenty-four World War II U.S. propaganda broadcasts to Latin America.

RG 262: Records of the Foreign Broadcast Intelligence Service. Recordings of foreign shortwave radio braodcasts monitored during 1940-1947. Included are Axis broadcasts to Latin America, and Latin American broadcasting (including speeches by Juan Perón).

RG 306: Records of the United States Information Agency. Voice of America recordings, including speeches by U.S. and Latin American political leaders (for example, Juscelino Kubitschek), 1950-1965.

RG 330: Records of the Office of the Secretary of Defense. Recordings of press conferences, briefings, speeches, and statements by Defense Department and other government officials, 1949-1961.

4. a-b. Listening equipment (tape recorders and phonographs) is available on a reservation basis.

   c-d. Materials may be duplicated by researchers with their own recording equipment. The staff will duplicate items for a fee.

5. A free guide, Mayfield S. Bray and Leslie C. Waffen, *Sound Recordings in the Audiovisual Archives Division of the National Archives* (1972), and a card catalog are available.

D4 Organization of American States Voice Archive

1. a. *Administrative Building, Room B-10*
   19th Street and Constitution Avenue, NW
   Washington, D.C. 20006
   381-8255/8281

   b. 9:30 A.M.-5 P.M. Monday-Friday

   c. Open to researchers. An appointment is recommended.

   d. Mercedes Fritzsching, Chief—Records Management Center

2. The collection totals some 50 boxes of records and tapes.

3. The OAS Voice Archive, administered by the OAS Records Management Center, contains records and tape-recordings of speeches and statements on inter-American issues by OAS spokesmen and prominent hemispheric leaders. Included are recordings of the proceedings of the 1938 Lima Conference and addresses by Lyndon Johnson, Eduardo Frei, Alfredo

Stroessner, and other hemispheric presidents at the 1967 Punta del Este Conference. Most holdings date from the 1960s.

In addition, tapes of 1960s-1970s inter-American conferences and OAS General Assembly and council proceedings which have not been entered into the Voice Archive are in storage in the Records Management Center, where they are available to researchers.

4.   Listening equipment can be obtained from the OAS radio and television unit. Researchers may tape Voice Archive materials on their own recording equipment.

5.   A contents-list is available from Miss Fritzsching.

Note: The Music Unit of the OAS Department of Cultural Affairs maintains a small record and tape collection of Latin American music. See entry L10.

D5   Zodiac Record Shop

1. a. *1756 Columbia Road, NW*
        Washington, D.C. 20009
        265-7996

    b. 9 A.M.-9 P.M. Seven days per week

2-3.   The Zodiac Record Shop is a commercial enterprise specializing in popular (some folk) music from Latin America and the Caribbean.

E. Map Collections

Map Collection Entry Format (E)

1. General Information
   a. *address; telephone number(s)*
   b. hours of service
   c. conditions of access
   d. reproduction services
   e. name/title of director and heads of relevant divisions

2. Size of holdings pertaining to Latin America

3. Description of holdings pertaining to Latin America

4. Bibliographic aids facilitating use of collection

Central Intelligence Agency Maps See entry J4

E1 Defense Mapping Agency Topographic Center (Defense Department)

1. a. *6500 Brookes Lane*
      Washington, D.C. 20315
      227-2000
      227-2036 (Information Resources Division)

   b. 7:30 A.M.-4 P.M. Monday-Friday

   c. Defense Mapping Agency facilities are not open to the public. Prior clearance or special permission would be necessary for researchers to use their resources.

2-3. The contents of the Defense Mapping Agency Topographic Center's map collections are, for the most part, classified. Unclassified maps produced by the center are distributed to DMA depository libraries, including the Library of Congress-Geography and Map Division (see entry E3) and the George Washington University Library (entry A21). The Defense Mapping Agency Hydrographic Center, a separate component of the Topographic Center, has a public Sales Office (763-1530) which sells Latin American-related navigational charts and publications.
   The Topographic Center has two main library collections. Its Geodetic Library (227-2227) contains a considerable quantity of Latin American

geodetic-survey material from international organizations, U.S. government agencies, private oil companies, etc. The separate Department of Defense Map Library (227-2036) contains some 1.7 million maps, as well as nearly 700,000 books, periodicals, and documents on cartography, geodesy, and geography. Both libraries have collections of aerial photographs. Both also have inter-library loan service. Researchers should contact the facilities directly for information on contents and accessibility.

E2 Geological Survey Library (Interior Department)—Map Collection

1. a. *12201 Sunrise Valley Drive, Fourth Floor*
        Reston, Virginia 22092
        860-6679

    b. 7:45 A.M.-4:15 P.M. Monday-Friday

    c. Open to the public.

    d. Researchers wishing to obtain copies of maps in the collection are directed to several local commercial-photoduplication firms which provide such services for a fee.

    e. George H. Goodwin, Jr., Librarian

2.   The library has within its total collection of approximately 225,000 sheet maps, an estimated 3,000-4,000 Latin American maps. These are filed together in 86 map drawers, with the following numbers of drawers per geographic area: Latin America (region), 1; Middle America (region), 2; Mexico, 15; Central America (region and individual countries), 8; Caribbean (region and individual islands), 17; South America (region), 5; Brazil, 9; Argentina, 4; Chile, 2; Bolivia, 2; Peru, 4; Colombia, 6; Ecuador, 1; Venezuela, 6; the Guianas, 3; Uruguay and Paraguay, 1.

3.   The collection consists largely of geologic and topographic maps, ranging in date from the 1850s to the present. Coverage includes general topographic, geological, and geophysical features, mineral resources (including a variety of petroleum and mining maps), soils, water, and natural vegetation.

E3 Library of Congress—Geography and Map Division

1. a. *845 South Pickett Street*
        Alexandria, Virginia
        370-1335

        Mail: Washington, D.C. 20540

    b. 8:30 A.M.-5 P.M. Monday-Friday
        8:30 A.M.-12:30 P.M. Saturday

    c. Open to the public.

    d. Complete photoreproduction services are available through the Library of Congress Photoduplication Service.

    e. Richard W. Stephenson, Head—Reference and Bibliography Section.

2-3.   The Geography and Map Division of the Library of Congress contains the world's largest cartographic collection. Included are more than 3.5 million maps and charts, 40,000 atlases, over 250 globes, and a 7,500-volume reference collection. The Latin American collection—little known and seldom used—is magnificent, and includes the following categories of materials:

Single Maps. A massive collection of individual sheet maps (manuscript and printed, originals and facsimiles), dating from the 1480s to the 1960s. Holdings are almost totally uncataloged, but are filed by geographic area—making Latin American materials relatively easy to identify and retrieve. Latin American map-files are organized by region, subregion, and country, and are then further subdivided by chronological period (with coverage extending back at least through the 17th century for every area of Latin America), by subject (agriculture, mining/minerals, transportation and communications systems, military affairs, climate, etc.), by subnational region (e.g., under Brazil, "Amazon"), by political/administrative subdivision (states, provinces), and by city. Included are copies (and some originals) of virtually every major early European map pertaining to the discovery and exploration of the New World (e.g., a facsimile of Christopher Columbus' 1493 map of Hispañola). Indeed, it is not unlikely that the collection contains maps relating to any geographic region, time period, and thematic subject of interest to Latin Americanists. A survey of Latin American map files produced the following total numbers of maps by category (using a rough estimate of 40 maps per file drawer): Latin America (region), 200; Gulf of Mexico (region), 120; Caribbean (region), 200; Mexico, 5,400; Central America (region), 480; Central America (by country), 3,440; Panama Canal Zone, 400; West Indies (region), 520; Cuba, 1,880; other West Indian islands, 3,720; South America (region), 2,280; Argentina, 2,800; Bolivia, 560; Brazil, 6,280; Chile, 1,520; Colombia, 1,760; Ecuador, 560; Guianas, 440; Paraguay, 480; Peru, 2,200; Uruguay, 560; Venezuela, 2,420. Other files of interest are United States: Mexican War, 175; and United States: Spanish-American War, 80.

Single maps acquired by the division since 1968 (but dating from every historical period) are filed separately, following the same geographic organizational format as that referred to above. These maps are to be cataloged in the Library of Congress MARC computerized catalog. Latin American entries (regional and country) number approximately 5,760.

Series Maps. A collection of multiple-sheet map-sets (each series containing from two to several thousand maps). There are some 963 Latin American-related series. Content includes topographic, hydrographic, and thematic maps (geology, soils, city plans, etc.). There are large quantities of nautical/hydrographic maps produced by the Argentine, Brazilian, and Chilean governments. Materials date almost totally from the 20th century. A series-map shelflist is maintained by the division. Post-1968 series-map acquisitions are to be cataloged in the Library of Congress MARC computerized catalog.

Atlases. Among the approximately 830 Latin American atlases in the division, the researcher can find items ranging from general coverage for every country and period to detailed coverage of topics as specific as Cuban sugar warehouses in 1920. A dictionary card catalog is available. The contents of most of the division's atlases are described in detail in the *List of Geographical Atlases in the Library of Congress, with Bibliographical Notes,* 8 vols. (1909-1974).

Rare and Valuable Materials. A large collection of unique maps, atlases, and globes, stored in a special vault. Among the rare-map collections of interest to Latin Americanists are:

Woodbury Lowery Collection. A large quantity of early maps (originals and photostats) of Spanish settlements within the present borders of the United States. Holdings are described in Woodbury Lowery, *The Lowery Collection: A Descriptive List of Maps of the Spanish Possessions Within the Present Limits of the United States, 1502-1820* (Washington, D.C.: Government Printing Office, 1912).

Spanish and Portuguese portolan charts of the Atlantic Ocean and the New World, from the 16th and 17th centuries. A descriptive catalog, Walter W. Ristow and R. A. Skelton (comps.), *Nautical Charts on Vellum in the Library of Congress* (Washington, D.C.: Library of Congress, 1977) is available.

Ephraim Squier Collection. Thirty-eight 19th-century maps of Central America and Peru, by the well-known archeologist. The materials are described in an article by John Hebert in the January, 1972, issue of the *Quarterly Journal of the Library of Congress*.

Lessing J. Rosenwald Collection. Maps of America by Diego Gutierrez (1562) and Andre Thevet (1581).

Henry Harrisse Collection. Manuscript maps of South America drawn in 1639 by Joan Vingboans, cartographer to the Prince of Nassau.

In addition, 18th-century maps relating to the West Indies and Central America are to be found in the William Faden, Richard Howe, Pierre Ozanne, and *Atlantic Neptune* collections. Some 19th-century material is contained in the Johann Georg Kohl, Millard Fillmore, and Montgomery Blair collections.

Also to be found among the vault items are more than 400 rare individual maps of Latin America, filed geographically. Included are a great many 18th-century harbor maps, boundary maps, and town plans. A particular treasure is the Oztoticpac Lands map, a 1540 pictorial plan of an Aztec estate in Texcoco. (The map was analyzed by Howard Cline in the April, 1966, issue of the *Quarterly Journal of the Library of Congress*.) Other representative highlights are a splendid 1674 street plan of Lima; a series of manuscript maps based on boundary surveys made by Spanish commissioners in accordance with the provisions of the 1777 Treaty of San Ildefonso; a 1782 manuscript map of Peruvian royalist forces' troop movements against Tupac Amarú; some 350-400 naval charts of Latin American coastlines by students in the Royal Navigation School of Cadiz, ca. 1750-1800; and an 1816 map of the Buenos Aires-Potosí post road. Rare atlases date from the earliest printed edition of Ptolemy's *Geography* (1482), and include the ca. 1544 Agnese atlas and original 16th-17th-century editions of Ortelius, Blaeu, and Mercator.

A shelflist of the vault's holdings is available.

4. The division maintains a large reference and bibliographic collection related to Latin American cartography. Among the division's many publications are the five-volume *Bibliography of Cartography* (Boston: G. K. Hall, 1973), and John Hebert (comp.), *Population Maps of the Western Hemisphere: A List of National and Regional Population Maps from 1960 in the Geography and Map Division, Library of Congress,* rev. ed. (1971). A brochure, *The Geography and Map Division: A Guide to its Collections and Services* (1975), and a *List of Publications* (1975), are available.

E4 National Archives and Records Service—Cartographic Archives Division

1. a. *8th Street and Pennsylvania Avenue, NW*
      Washington, D.C. 20408
      523-3062

   b. 8:45 A.M.-5 P.M. Monday-Friday

   c. Open to researchers with a National Archives research card, obtainable from the Central Reference Division, Room 200-B.

   d. A variety of photoreproduction services are available.

   e. Ralph Ehrenberg, Director.

2-3. The National Archives' Cartographic Archives Division, containing more than 1.6 million maps and some 2.25 million aerial photographs, is one of the world's largest cartographic collections. Diverse 19th- and 20th-century maps on Latin America produced by U.S. government agencies are scattered throughout the collection. Coverage (both regional and by country) includes Latin American exploration; land settlement (including considerable early 19th-century material on the Spanish borderlands) and land use; boundaries and boundary disputes (including copies of early 17th-century maps in foreign archives); military affairs (particularly U.S. military operations in the Caribbean basin); natural resources; agricultural and mineral production; commerce and trade routes; foreign economic interests; land, water, and air transportation (including canals, railroads, highways, and airfields); communications systems; population distribution; city planning; topography, and meteorology. In addition, there are aerial photographs of nearly every Latin American nation.

Holdings are organized by National Archives "record group" (RG). Pertinent record groups for Latin American materials include:

RG 30: Records of the Bureau of Public Roads.
RG 37: Records of the Hydrographic Office.
RG 43: Records of International Conferences, Commissions, and Expositions.
RG 49: Records of the Bureau of Land Management.
RG 57: Records of the Geological Survey.
RG 70: Records of the Bureau of Mines.
RG 76: Records of Boundary and Claims Commissions and Arbitrations.
RG 77: Records of the Office of the Chief of Engineers.
RG 83: Records of the Bureau of Agricultural Economics.
RG 94: Records of the Adjutant General's Office 1780s-1917.
RG 95: Records of the Forest Service.
RG 127: Records of the United States Marine Corps.
RG 140: Records of the Military Government of Cuba, 1899-1902.
RG 151: Records of the Bureau of Foreign and Domestic Commerce.
RG 165: Records of the War Department General and Special Staffs.
RG 185: Records of the Panama Canal.
RG 199: Records of the Provisional Government of Cuba, 1899-1902.
RG 350: Records of the Bureau of Insular Affairs.
RG 395: Records of the United States Army Overseas Operations and Commands, 1898-1942.

4.   For information on specific items within these record groups, consult two
        National Archives publications: Charlotte M. Ashby, et al., *Guide to
        Cartographic Records in the National Archives* (1971) and George S.
        Ulibarri and John P. Harrison, *Guide to Materials on Latin America in the
        National Archives of the United States* (1974). Card catalogs, inventories,
        and other "finding aids" are also available.

E5 National Geographic Society—Cartographic Division Map Library

1. a. *Membership Center Building*
        11555 Darnestown Road
        Gaithersburg, Maryland 20760
        857-7000 (extension 1401)

    b. 7:30 A.M.-4 P.M. Monday-Friday

    c. Not open to the public, although serious researchers are permitted to use the
        collection on an individual basis. Contact the map librarian for an appoint-
        ment.

    d. Photocopying machines are available.

    e. Margery Barkdull, Map Librarian

2-3.   The collection numbers approximately 100,000 maps, mostly of recent
        origin. Included are U.S. and foreign geological-survey maps, road maps,
        archeological maps, and oil-company maps. There is also a copy of every
        map ever produced by the National Geographic Society.

4.   The collection is arranged by country, etc.

Note: National Geographic Society published maps are available for purchase at
        the Explorers Hall sales desk (857-7589), 17th and M Streets, NW, in
        downtown Washington.

**Organization of American States—Columbus Memorial Library
Map Collection** See entry A43

F. Film Collections (Still Photographs and Motion Pictures)

Film Collection Entry Format (F)

1.   General Information
    a. *address; telephone number(s)*
    b. hours of service
    c. conditions of access
    d. name/title of director and key staff members

2.   Size of holdings pertaining to Latin America

3.   Description of holdings pertaining to Latin America

4.   Facilities for study and use
    a. availability of audiovisual equipment
    b. reservation requirements
    c. fees charged
    d. reproduction services

5.   Bibliographic aids facilitating use of collection

F1 Agency for International Development (AID)—Photo Collection

1. a. *Office of Public Affairs*
      State Department Building, Room 4894
      320 21st Street, NW
      Washington, D.C. 20532
      632-8194

    b. 8:45 A.M.-5:30 P.M. Monday-Friday

    c. Open to researchers, by appointment. Call ahead for clearance.

    d. Carl Purcell, Photographer

2-3.   The collection contains approximately 4,000 recent photographs (primarily black-and-white, some color) of Latin American subjects—including AID-sponsored development projects, activities of AID field personnel, and general scenes of people and living conditions. The photographs are organized by country. In addition, the Office of Public Affairs has available for loan (without charge) four short (15-30 minute) color motion pictures illustrating AID development activities in Guatemala, Nicaragua, Haiti, and the Dominican Republic respectively.

4.   Commercial reproduction services are available for photographs.

Note: The AID Population Reference Library (Room 215, Rosslyn Plaza "E" Building, 1621 N. Kent Street, Arlington, Virginia) possesses an estimated 100 films related to family planning, sterilization, contraception, etc. These are available for loan. Contact Librarian Ann Peters (235-9675) for further information.

F2   Air Force Central Still Photographic Depository (Air Force Department)

1.   a.   *1361st Audiovisual Squadron*
1221 South Fern Street (adjacent to the Pentagon)
Arlington, Virginia 22202
695-1147

b.   7:45 A.M.-4:30 P.M. Monday-Friday

c.   Open to the public.

d.   Margaret Livesay, Chief

2-3.   The depository's "Overseas File" contains an estimated 1,500 unclassified photographs (both color and black-and-white) of Latin American aircraft, airfield sites, air force installations and personnel, and ceremonies involving visiting U.S. officers and dignitaries. The photographs are kept in notebooks and are arranged alphabetically by country. Coverage dates sporadically back to the mid-1950s for some countries, and includes U.S. Air Force aerial-reconnaissance photographs of Cuban military defenses and Russian ships during the 1962 Cuban missile crisis, and photos of U.S. Air Force operations during the 1965 Dominican intervention.

4.   d.   Copies will be made for a fee.

F3   American Film Institute (AFI)

1.   a.   *John F. Kennedy Center for the Performing Arts*
2700 F Street, NW
Washington, D.C. 20566
833-9300

b.   10 A.M.-5 P.M. Monday-Friday

c.   Open to the public.

d.   George Stevens, Jr., Director

2-5.   The American Film Institute, at the Kennedy Center, presents at least one major week-long Latin American film series (with recent and/or retrospective films) each year.

AFI's Information Services library (ext. 52/77) has a "Foreign Information" section containing a small number of monographs on Latin American cinema. The library also maintains a clipping file (which contains some English-language reviews of Latin American motion pictures, by country) and a foreign film-festival file.

For a reference guide to information sources on Latin American film-making, see AFI's *Fact File* series, Volume 10: *Third World Cinema*.

F4 American Red Cross Photograph Collection

1. a. *Office of Public Affairs—Photograph Department*
   18th Street between D and E Streets, NW
   Washington, D.C. 20006
   857-3428

   b. 8:30 A.M.-4:45 P.M. Monday-Friday

   c. Open to the public. Appointment recommended.

   d. Carolyn Smith, Photo Librarian

2. The total collection consists of some 20,000 black-and-white photographs and 1,000 color transparencies. Latin American content numbers approximately 100 black-and-white prints and a small number of color slides.

3. Coverage includes Red Cross nursing and relief activities during the Spanish-American War and Mexican Revolution, Red Cross disaster-relief activities in the aftermath of several 20th-century Central and South American earthquakes, and Red Cross involvement in the 1962-1963 U.S.-Cuban "prisoner exchange."

4. Free photoreproduction service is provided.

5. Latin American prints are found in a "historical file" (arranged chronologically) and an "international services" file (arranged by country).

F5 Army Audiovisual Activity (Army Department)

1. a. *The Pentagon, Room 5A486*
   Washington, D.C. 20310
   697-2806 (Reference Library)

   b. 10 A.M.-4:30 P.M. Monday-Friday

   c. Access to the Pentagon is restricted. Researchers wishing to examine the Army Audiovisual Activity photographic collection may telephone the Reference Library from the Pentagon entrance; escorts will be sent to accompany them. The photographic collection itself is open to the public.

   d. Vickie Destefano, Chief—Reference Library

2. The collection contains more than one million still photographs. Latin American materials consist of approximately 2,000 black-and-white prints and perhaps an equal number of color prints.

3. Coverage includes Latin American army officers (including a number of politically influential officers), troops, equipment, defense installations, U.S. military-assistance activities in Latin America, and U.S.-Latin American military ceremonies. The photographs range in date from the early 1940s to the present. Geographic coverage is particularly strong for Brazil (including the Brazilian Expeditionary Forces in World War II) and the Canal Zone.

4.   Commercial photoreproduction services are available.

5.   There are separate card indexes for black-and-white prints and color prints. Each is arranged geographically, by country.

Brazilian-American Cultural Institute films and photographs See entries A10 and I12

F6 Dumbarton Oaks (Harvard University)—Center for Pre-Columbian Studies Photograph Collection

1.   a.   *1703 32nd Street, NW*
         Washington, D.C. 20007
         232-3101

    b.   9 A.M.-5 P.M. Monday-Friday

    c.   Appointment required.

    d.   Elizabeth Benson, Director
        Ann-Louise Schaffer, Assistant

2-3.   The Center for Pre-Columbian Studies maintains a photographic collection of several thousand slides, prints, and negatives on Mayan art and archeology, the Dumbarton Oaks collection, and other Pre-Columbian subjects.

4.   Print copies will be supplied for a fee.

5.   A partial index is available, and reference service is provided.

Embassy of Argentina Film Collection See entry K1

Embassy of Brazil Film Collection See entry K5

Embassy of Chile Film Collection See entry K6

Embassy of Jamaica Film Collection See entry K18

Embassy of Panama Film Collection See entry K21

Embassy of Venezuela Film Collection See entry K 27

F7 Food and Agriculture Organization (FAO) (United Nations)—Liaison Office for North America Photograph Collection

1.   a.   *1776 F Street, NW*
         Washington, D.C. 20437
         634-6215

b. 8 A.M. 5:30 P.M. Monday-Friday

c. Open to the public.

d. Jay J. Levy, Information Officer

2. The collection consists of approximately 10,000 black-and-white prints, one-quarter to one-third of which relate to Latin America.

3. The collection covers FAO and other UN development activities in the fields of land and water use, animal and plant production, rural welfare, nutrition, fisheries, forestry, wildlife, etc., worldwide. There is a substantial amount of general agricultural, cultural, and environmental coverage. The photos date from the 1950s to the present.

4. A limited number of prints will be supplied to researchers without charge.

5. The photos are rather haphazardly arranged by country and/or major development activity. The collection is drawn from the extensive photo collection (80,000 black-and-white prints, 5,000 color slides) maintained at FAO headquarters in Rome. Photographs not in stock in Washington can be ordered from Rome. See the *FAO Photo Library Catalogue* (Rome, 1972) for further information on content, arrangement, and ordering instructions.

F8 Inter-American Development Bank Photograph Collection

1. a. *808 17th Street, NW, Room 975*
      Washington, D.C. 20577
      634-8154

   b. 9 A.M.-5:30 P.M. Monday-Friday

   c. Open to the public, on an appointment basis.

   d. Mario Traverso, Audiovisual Assistant

2-3. The Office of Information has a collection of 5,000 black-and-white photographs and 6,000 color transparencies dealing with Latin American socioeconomic, agricultural, and technical development projects funded by the Inter-American Development Bank.

4. Prints, slides, and captions supplied without charge.

F9 International Bank for Reconstruction and Development (World Bank) Photo Library

1. a. *701 19th Street, NW*
      Washington, D.C. 20433
      477-2366

   b. 9 A.M.-5:30 P.M. Monday-Friday

   c. By appointment

   d. Susan Watters, Photo Librarian

2-3. The World Bank Photo Library maintains a collection of approximately 30,000 black-and-white prints and 40,000 color slides dealing with bank-funded economic development projects, worldwide. Approximately ten percent of the collection consists of scenes of highway and dam construction, rural development, and family-planning activities in Latin America.

4. Black-and-white print copies and color-slide photocopies are provided without charge.

5. Print and slide catalogs are produced.

F10 International Labour Organization (ILO) (United Nations)—Washington Branch Office Photograph Collection

1. a. *Room 330*
   1750 New York Avenue, NW
   Washington, D.C. 20006
   634-6335

   b. 8:30 A.M.-5 P.M. Monday-Friday

   c. Open to the public.

   d. Patricia S. Hord, Librarian

2. The collection consists of ṣome 2,000 black-and-white prints. A few hundred are on Latin American subjects.

3. The photographs relate to workers and working conditions worldwide. The collection is arranged by topic. Topics include cooperatives, employment, ILO conferences and projects, living conditions, labor conditions, mining, plantations, production, social security, timber industry, trade unions, vocational training, welfare facilities, and women workers. Within each topic-file there may be Latin American coverage. There is also a file on the ILO "Andean Programme." Contents of the total collection date from 1919 to the present, although most Latin American coverage is post-1950.

4. Prints will be supplied to researchers without charge.

5. The prints have been drawn from the much larger photo library at the ILO headquarters in Geneva, Switzerland. The *ILO Photo Library: Catalogue* (Geneva, 1973) describes the content and arrangement of the collection, and provides instructions on how researchers may order prints from Geneva.

F11 Library of Congress—Prints and Photographs Division

1. a. *Room 1051*
   Library of Congress Annex (Thomas Jefferson Building)
   10 1st Street, SE
   Washington, D.C. 20540
   426-5836 (Division Office)
   426-5840 (Motion Picture Section)

   b. 8:30 A.M.-5 P.M. Monday-Friday

   c. Open to the public.

   d. Dale Haworth, Chief
      Jerry Kearns, Head—Reference Section
      Paul Spehr, Head—Motion Picture Section

2. The Library of Congress possesses what is probably the largest film collection in the area, with perhaps 15 million still-picture items and well in excess of 200,000 reels of motion-picture and television-videotape footage. There is no effective way to measure the size of Latin American holdings, because substantial quantities of materials remain completely uncataloged and cataloged materials are not always arranged by geographic area.

3. *Still Photographs.* It is extremely difficult to systematically locate still-picture items on a geographic basis. Those Latin American materials which are cataloged are diffused throughout a massive, general "lot" collection for which a "lot" card catalog (alphabetically arranged by person and place name) is available. "Lots" of interest to Latin Americanists include the following:

    International American Conference collection. Some 40 Mathew Brady photographs of the 1889-1890 Washington, D.C. Pan American conference (lot number 3206).

    William Howard Taft collection. Fifty photographs of Secretary of War Taft's 1907 trip to Panama, Cuba, and Puerto Rico (lot 3307).

    John Pershing collection. Numerous photographs relating to the 1916 Mexican Punitive Expedition and Pershing's subsequent travels in Latin America (various lots).

    Josephus Daniels collection. More than 6,000 photographs, many from Daniels' 1933-1941 ambassadorship in Mexico (numerous lots).

    Hovey collection. One hundred 1868 photographs of Peru and southern South America (lot 4831).

    Depaz and Moreau collection. Sixteen views of village life and sugar-industry operations on Martinique, ca. 1890 (lot 2931).

    Escudero y Arias collection. Nearly 200 photographs of major figures and events in Mexico, 1850-1880, including coverage of Maximilian's execution (lot 3112).

    Detroit Publishing Company collection. Large numbers of photographs dealing with Mexico and the Caribbean, 1884-1914, including 125 prints of the Spanish-American War (lot 3034).

    Shaw collection. Twenty 1884-1885 prints of Panama (lot 2479).

    Molina Barbery collection. Views of Jesuit missions and rural conditions in Bolivia (lot 4721).

    Milhollen collection. Fifty 1895-1905 Peruvian photographs (lot 4720).

    Archambault collection. Views of Nicaraguan Canal Commission dredging operations, 1899-1900, and related street scenes (lot 3863).

    Cuban Department of Public Works collection. Some 225 views of conditions in Cuba, 1907-1908 (lots 3132 and 3166).

    Nadel collection. One hundred Chilean photographs, ca. 1915-1920 (lot 4303).

    Abbott collection. Some 4,200 negatives of local scenes and daily life in Mexico and Guatemala, 1925-1949 (lot 5579).

    Leland Harrison collection. Photographs from a U.S. ambassador's post-World War I tour of duty in Colombia (lots 5954-5958).

    Servicio Cooperativo Inter-Americano de Salud Pública collection. Photographs of public-health activities in the Dominican Republic, 1946-1947 (lot 2377).

    United Fruit Company collection. Some 124 photographs of the company's Central American operations, primarily ca. 1948 but including 1876-1936 materials (lot 4873).

Far from being an exhaustive inventory, the above list merely represents a sampling of the types of materials to be found in the lot collection. There are many other collections containing photographs of 19th- and 20th-century Latin American living conditions and architecture, the Spanish-American War, canal construction, the Cuban missile crisis, etc. In addition, several intriguing collections described in a 1955 catalog are either lost or scattered. They include a collection of portraits of Haitian presidents and government officials, 1805-1922; a "Jackson collection" of Mexican (1883-1884) and Caribbean (1900-1905) general scenes; and a "U.S.S. *Maine* collection." Consult the staff for further information.

The Prints and Photographs Division also houses several separate special collections, including:

Archive of Hispanic Culture. Some 19,000 photographs, 3,200 slides, and 2,500 negatives, from the 1880s to the 1940s, focusing on Latin American architecture (ecclesiastical and civil, particularly Mexico and Brazil), painting (photocopies of colonial religious paintings, *santos,* portraits, and modern Mexican murals), sculpture (some pre-Columbian and modern, mostly Ecuadorean colonial religious sculpture), graphic arts (photos of 16th-century codex illustrations, 19th-century engravings, lithographs, and genre prints, modern etchings, woodcuts, and posters), minor arts (textiles, furniture, jewelry, ceramics, etc.), and general scenes of Latin American culture. Materials in each category are arranged by country. There is also a large postcard collection containing excellent scenes of late 19th/early 20th-century daily life, by country.

Mexican Indian Pictorial Documents Collection. Three drawers of photographs related to archeology and indian artifacts.

Portrait Collection. Photographs of a wide range of major figures in Latin American history and inter-American relations, arranged alphabetically by name of individual.

Historical Prints Collection. Pre-20th-century lithographs, engravings, and other illustrations, with region and country files for Latin America, as well as subject files for "Columbus," "Discovery and Exploration," "Indians," "Mexican War," "Spanish-American War," and "Punitive Expedition Against Villa."

Stereoptic Collection. A fascinating collection of 1875-ca. 1920 stereographic views of Latin American daily life and rural conditions, arranged by country.

Poster Collection. Miscellaneous (primarily tourism) posters from every Latin American nation, with some political items from Argentina, Cuba, and Chile.

Historic American Buildings Survey. Photos and architectural drawings of Spanish houses, missions, forts, and monuments in the southwestern U.S.

Motion Pictures: The Motion Picture Section has miscellaneous, and rather limited, Latin American holdings. The following categories of Latin American materials are discernible, based on a survey of the section's card catalogs (which are arranged for the most part by film title, producer, or director):

Latin American films. Included is scattered documentary footage of living conditions and news events (from 1890s scenes of Mexico, Porfirio Díaz, and the Spanish-American War to footage of Juan Perón). Also included are copies of a few feature motion pictures by major Latin American directors (six Luís Bunuel films, for example) and a sizable number of commercial films produced by Latin American subsidiaries of U.S. motion-picture studios (particularly Columbia and RKO) for distribution in Latin America.

U.S.-produced films on Latin America. A substantial collection of U.S. television and motion-picture documentaries, post-1940 newsreels (Universal, "News-of-the-Day"), educational films, travelogues, tapes of commercial television interview programs, and some feature movies on Latin American topics.

A few special collections also contain material of interest to Latin Americanists. They include:

Theodore Roosevelt collection. A unique collection of rare footage of TR in Latin America, including the Spanish-American War and later trips to the Panama Canal, the Amazon, and Colombia.

George Kleine collection. One reel of 1907 Panama Canal scenes.

Films seized during World War II. German documentaries (including ethnographic films on Peru and the Amazon Basin) and Axis newsreels distributed in Latin America during the 1930s and 1940s.

4. a-c. Several 16mm and 35mm motion-picture screening machines are available for use by serious researchers. There is no charge. Reservations are required.

   d. Reproduction services are available for still photographs and motion pictures which are not subject to copyright or other restrictions.

5. No comprehensive published catalog or inventory of either still pictures or motion pictures is available. The only published reference tool for still pictures, Phil Vanderbilt, *Guide to the Special Collections of Prints and Photographs in the Library of Congress* (1955), is badly outdated and unreliable. Beyond the various card catalogs mentioned above, researchers must rely on the assistance of the staff in identifying and retrieving materials. (Some collections and acquisitions are occasionally described in the *Quarterly Journal of the Library of Congress*.)

Marine Corps Historical Center—Still Photo Archive See entry B5

F12 National Anthropological Film Center (Smithsonian Institution)

1. a. *Room 3210, North Building*
      955 L'Enfant Plaza, SW
      Washington, D.C. 20560
      381-6537

   b. 8:45 A.M.-5:15 P.M. Monday-Friday

   c. Open to serious researchers, by appointment. Researchers are requested to provide the staff with a description of their research project prior to their arrival.

   d. E. Richard Sorenson, Director

2-3. The Smithsonian's newly established National Anthropological Film Center is designed to be a national center for the preparation, preservation, and analysis of "visual information on human behavioral and cultural variation and on culturally unique expressions of human existence." Special attention is given to "the few remaining small, isolated cultural groups of the world which have evolved independently over thousands of years, and to other small social enclaves which represent vanishing unique expressions of human behavior and social organization."

Within the center's rapidly growing "National Anthropological Research Film Collection" of approximately 700,000 feet of uncut, unedited raw footage (some of which has been privately donated, some shot by Smithsonian anthropologists and the center's staff ethnocinematographers) are the following Latin American anthropological materials:

Canela indians of northeastern Brazil, 86,000 feet (1975)

Aymara indians of Bolivia, 36,800 feet (ca. 1973)

Bororo indians of Matto Grosso, Brazil, 4,000 feet (1930-1931, by Aloha Baker)

Huichol indians of northern Mexico, 42,000 feet (1974)

Yucatán, 180,000 feet (being processed)

Cross-cultural comparison of dance styles in Georgia, Haiti, and Nigeria (1930s, by Melville J. Herskovits).

Field notes, camera logs, and/or annotations by the respective filmmakers are available for most of the above.

4.   Some work-prints are available for on-site viewing. High-speed, slow-motion, and stop-frame viewers are available. No photoreproduction services are available.

5.   A computer index is planned. The center is described in E. Richard Sorenson, "To Further Phenomenological Inquiry: The National Anthropological Film Center," *Current Anthropology,* Vol. 16, No. 2 (June, 1975), pp. 267-269.

F13   National Archives and Records Service—Audiovisual Archives Division

1.   a.   *8th Street and Pennsylvania Avenue, NW*
       Washington, D.C. 20408
       523-3088 (Division)
       523-3267 (Motion Picture Branch)
       523-3236 (Still Picture Branch)

    b.   8:45 A.M.-5 P.M. Monday-Friday

    c.   Open to researchers with a National Archives research pass, obtainable from the Central Reference Division, Room 200-B.

    d.   James Moore, Director
       William Murphy, Chief—Motion Picture and Sound Recording Branch
       Joe Thomas, Chief—Still Picture Branch

2-3.   The National Archives' Audiovisual Archives contain more than 60,000 reels of film and well over five million still photographs, an audiovisual collection second only to that of the Library of Congress in the Washington area. Materials are arranged according to National Archives "record group" (RG). Record groups containing Latin American-related items include the following:

Motion pictures:

RG 18: Records of the Army Air Forces. A 1912 film on the raising of the battleship *Maine,* and World War II Air Transport Command briefing films of terrain, flight routes, and landing facilities in South America, the Caribbean, and the Canal Zone.

RG 24: Records of the Bureau of Naval Personnel. A ca.-1918 film about the newly acquired Virgin Islands.

RG 33: Records of the Federal Extension Service. Several 1930 films on general conditions in Latin America, by country; 1920s films dealing with inter-American meetings and U.S.-Mexican customs activities.

RG 59: General Records of the Department of State. Films depicting State Department activities and the U.S. role in world affairs—including 1911-1913 footage of the construction of the Panama Canal; a 1929 film on Bolivia; 1938 films on the "Good Neighbor" policy and Nazi infiltration of South America; and 1951 films on the "Point Four" program in Mexico and South America.

RG 106: Records of the Smithsonian Institution. Films from the Bureau of American Ethnology showing archeological explorations in Honduras and Yucatán, 1931-1941; and a 1927 newsreel on Charles Lindbergh's visit to Mexico City.

RG 111: Records of the Office of the Chief Signal Officer. Pre-World War I films on the construction of the Panama Canal, and 1916 footage of the Mexican Punitive Expedition.

RG 174: General Records of the Department of Labor. Television interview programs, panel discussions, and documentaries on current-events topics, 1960-1968.

RG 200: National Archives Gift Collection. A large and extremely noteworthy collection of commercial newsreels produced by Movietone, Pathé, Fox, International, Paramount, and Universal, 1919-1967. Holdings consist of released newsreels and outtakes of world news events. There is a substantial amount of Latin American coverage. RG 200 also features Time-Life's 1939-1951 documentary series "The March of Time," the Ford Film Collection of general-interest materials, 1914-1956, and the 1930-1951 Harmon Foundation film collection—each of which contains material on Latin America.

RG 207: General Records of the Department of Housing and Urban Development. Limited footage of Latin American housing conditions.

RG 208: Records of the Office of War Information. World War II newsreels on aspects of hemispheric defense and inter-American affairs.

RG 229: Records of the Office of Inter-American Affairs. Forty-five reels of informational and propaganda material on inter-American cooperation and the peoples of Latin America.

RG 234: Records of the Reconstruction Finance Corporation. Films dealing with U.S. Commercial Company development of sources of quinine in Guatemala and Rubber Development Corporation activities in Brazil, 1943-1944.

RG 286: Records of the Agency for International Development. Two 1955 reels on Rio Pact military cooperation and U.S. technical-assistance programs in Ecuador and Paraguay.

RG 291: Records of the Property Management and Disposal Service (General Services Administration). One 1957 reel on the processing of nickel in Cuba.

RG 306: Records of the United States Information Agency. Documentary footage on life in South America, visits of Latin American leaders to the United States, John F. Kennedy's 1962 trip to Mexico, and Lyndon Johnson's 1968 trip to Central America.

RG 362: Records of the Peace Corps. Film material on Peace Corps activities throughout Latin America.

Still photographs:

RG 11: General Records of the United States Government. Five photographs related to the 1909 U.S.-Paraguayan naturalization convention.

RG 18: Records of the Army Air Forces. Aerial photographs of the countries of the Caribbean basin.

RG 22: Records of the Fish and Wildlife Service. More than 100 photographs made by the U.S. Fish Commission steamer *Albatross* during an 1887-1889 voyage around South America.

RG 24: Records of the Bureau of Naval Personnel. Photographs of the Spanish Navy and damage to Spanish ships, 1895-1898.

RG 26: Records of the United States Coast Guard. Pictures illustrating Coast Guard participation in the Mexican and Spanish-American Wars.

RG 28: Records of the Post Office Department. Photos of the Pan American Airline Service, 1927-1935.

RG 30: Records of the Bureau of Public Roads. Nearly 1,000 scenes of Latin American transportation and the Pan-American Highway, 1900-1963.

RG 38: Records of the Office of the Chief of Naval Operations. Photographs of the defenses of Valparaiso, Chile, 1897, and of Veracruz and Tampico, Mexico, 1914.

RG 43: Records of International Conferences, Commissions, and Expositions. Photos of 1890-1899 Intercontinental Railway Commission surveys of Central and South America.

RG 54: Records of the Bureau of Plant Industry, Soils, and Agricultural Engineering. Photographs of rubber production and general conditions in 14 Central and South American nations, 1942-1948; and stereoscopic slides of the Panama Pacific Exposition

RG 59: General Records of the Department of State. Photographs of international conferences (including the 1909 U.S.-Venezuela Arbitration Protocol) and ceremonies; foreign diplomats and visiting dignitaries; State Department officials; and photographs received from U.S. diplomatic posts in Latin America, dating from the second half of the 19th century.

RG 66: Records of the Commission of Fine Arts. Lantern slides and film negatives of Latin American art and architecture.

RG 76: Records of Boundary and Claims Commissions and Arbitrations. Photos made by the Commission of Engineers for the Costa Rica-Panama Boundary Arbitration, 1910-1912.

RG 77: Records of the Office of the Chief of Engineers. Stereoscopic prints of an 1870-1874 expedition to locate a canal route across the Isthmus of Darien; International Boundary Commission photographs of monuments marking the U.S.-Mexican border, 1892-1894; glass negatives of Spanish engineering and defense works in Cuba and Puerto Rico, 1898; photos of the raising of the battleship *Maine*; and a photograph collection relating to a 1943 survey of the Orinoco-Casiquiare-Negro waterway.

RG 83: Records of the Bureau of Agricultural Economics. Pictures of farming operations in Argentina, Chile, and Peru, 1921-1923.

RG 90: Records of the Public Health Service. One hundred prints showing yellow-fever conditions in Central America, 1906.

RG 92: Records of the Office of the Quartermaster General. An album showing U.S. military installations in Cuba, 1899.

RG 94: Records of the Adjutant General's Office, 1780s-1917. Miscellaneous photos of the Spanish-American War and the 1916 Mexican Punitive Expedition.

RG 95: Records of the Forest Service. Photographs of Mexican rubber production, 1941-1945.

RG 106: Records of the Smithsonian Institution. Canal Zone photographs, 1900-1914.

RG 111: Records of the Office of the Chief Signal Officer. Illustrations of the Mexican War; an extensive photograph collection of the Spanish-American War; some 800 photos of the Mexican Punitive Expedition, and miscellaneous Caribbean and Central American scenes.

RG 115: Records of the Bureau of Reclamation. Photos of irrigation projects in Haiti, the Dominican Republic, and along the Rio Grande.

RG 127: Records of the United States Marine Corps. Photos relating to Marine Corps activities in the Caribbean basin.

RG 151: Records of the Bureau of Foreign and Domestic Commerce. Large collection of prints showing Latin American industry and commerce in the 1920s and 1930s.

RG 165: Records of the War Department General and Special Staffs. An extensive photographic collection focusing on the Spanish-American War, the U.S. occupation of Veracruz, the Mexican Punitive Expedition, and military affairs in Mexico, 1902-1910.

RG 168: Records of the National Guard Bureau. Spanish-American War photos.

RG 169: Records of the Foreign Economic Administration. Photographs related to the production of Latin American agricultural and mineral commodities during World War II.

RG 200: National Archives Gift Collection. Spanish-American War photos.

RG 208: Records of the Office of War Information. Some 200 prints and negatives of the 1945 Mexico City and United Nations conferences, and visits of Latin American leaders to the United States, 1947-1948.

RG 229: Records of the Office of Inter-American Affairs. Seventy-nine paintings and drawings pertaining to inter-American cooperation during World War II.

RG 234: Records of the Reconstruction Finance Corporation. Photos of Rubber Development Corporation activities in Brazil, 1942-1944.

RG 306: Records of the United States Information Agency. Includes the photographic file of the *New York Times* Paris bureau, 1900-1950, containing miscellaneous coverage of Latin American news events.

RG 350: Records of the Bureau of Insular Affairs. Photographs of people and places in Haiti, Santo Domingo, the Canal Zone, Cuba, and the Virgin Islands, 1898-1935.

4. a-b.   Motion-picture screening equipment is available on a reservation basis.

    c-d.   Subject to copyright and other restrictions, the staff will reproduce motion pictures (16mm and 35mm, black-and-white only) and still photographs for a fee.

5.   Two mimeographed surveys are available upon request: Mayfield S. Bray and William Murphy, *Motion Pictures in the Audiovisual Archives Division of the National Archives* (1972), and Mayfield S. Bray, *Still Pictures in the Audiovisual Archives Division of the National Archives* (1972). In addition, there are card catalogs for both the motion-picture and still-photo general

collections, as well as special card catalogs for several of the more extensive individual collections (notably the Universal Newsreel and Ford Film collections in the Motion Pictures Branch, and the Chief Signal Officer and *New York Times* Paris Bureau photograph collections in the Still Pictures Branch).

F14 National Gallery of Art—Photographic Archives

1. a. *Constitution Avenue at 6th Street, NW*
Washington, D.C. 20565
737-4215 (extension 231)

   b-c. The archives are open to serious researchers by appointment.

   d. Ruth Philbrick, Curator

2-3. The collection includes 15,000 black-and-white photographs of Mexican architecture. The staff indicates that there may also be a small number of photographs of Latin American paintings scattered throughout the collection.

F15 National Geographic Society Photograph Collection

1. a. *Illustrations Library*
17th and M Streets, NW
Washington, D.C. 20036
857-7492

   b. 8:30 A.M.-5 P.M. Monday-Friday

   c. Permission to examine the collection must be obtained in advance from Thomas R. Smith, Illustrations Editor (857-7194).

   d. Fern Dame, Illustrations Librarian

2-3. The total collection consists of 100,000 photographs (black-and-white and color) which have been published in the *National Geographic* magazine, as well as some 620,000 unpublished photographs (both color and black-and-white) relating to *National Geographic* articles, and several million slides. Latin American coverage is indeterminable but extensive.

4. Photoreproduction services are available.

5. The collection is organized geographically.

F16 National Museum of Natural History (Smithsonian Institution) —Anthropological Archives Photograph Collection

1. a. *Natural History Building, Room 60-A*
Constitution Avenue at 10th Street, NW
Washington, D.C. 20560
381-5225

   b. 9 A.M.-5 P.M. Monday-Friday

    c.   Open to the public. Visitors are requested to notify the staff prior to their arrival.

    d.   Herman Viola, Archivist

2.   The archives contains, within its total collection of 90,000 black-and-white photographs, several thousand pertaining to Latin America.

3.   Coverage includes archeological sites and artifacts, indians, workers, rural living conditions, and general scenes. The majority of the photographs date from the 1860s to the 1930s, with some later coverage.

4.   Photoduplication services are available.

5.   A card index is maintained.

F17   Naval Historical Center (Navy Department)—Photographic Section

1.   a.   *Washington Navy Yard, Building 76*
9th and M Streets, SE
Washington, D.C. 20374
433-2765

    b.   9 A.M.-4 P.M. Monday-Friday

    c.   Open to the public. Researchers are requested to call in advance for an appointment.

    d.   Charles Haberlein, Jr., Head

2.   The collection contains an estimated 1,200 photographs (primarily black-and-white) pertaining to Latin America.

3.   The core of the collection consists of photographs of Latin American naval vessels, from the mid-19th century to the present. The 19th-century holdings are particularly impressive, and include—in addition to Latin American ships dating back to the 1860s—photographs of 19th-century naval paintings, engravings, and illustrations. Mexican War materials (illustrations, war art, photos of participating U.S. officers) and Spanish-American War photographs are well represented. There is also coverage of early 20th-century U.S. naval interventions in the Caribbean basin, Franklin D. Roosevelt's 1936 South American cruise, the *Graf Spee* episode, and the Cuban missile crisis, as well as 20th-century Latin American naval vessels, officers, crews, and operations.

4.   Commercial photoreproduction services are available.

5.   There is a card index, with a geographic section arranged by country and a chronological section arranged by war or event. A vertical file contains some Latin American prints which have not as yet been referenced in the card index.

F18   Naval Photographic Center (Navy Department)

1.   a.   *U.S. Naval Station, Building 168*
Anacostia Naval District
Washington, D.C.
433-2168 (Still Picture Department)

Mail: Headquarters, Naval District
Washington, D.C. 20374

b. 7:15 A.M.-3:45 P.M. Monday-Friday

c. Open to the public. Researchers are requested to call in advance for an appointment.

d. Jack Carter, Head—Still Picture Department
Chris Eckard, Head—Still Library Reference Branch

2. Within the total collection of some 750,000 unclassified still photographs (color and black-and-white), there are approximately 2,500 photos of Latin American subjects.

3. Coverage includes Latin American naval officers and personnel, naval vessels and installations, visits by U.S. vessels and officials, U.S. military-assistance activities, joint U.S.-Latin American "Operation Unitas" naval maneuvers, and general scenes (including considerable coverage of 1970 Peruvian earthquake-relief activities). The photographs date predominantly from the mid-1950s to the present, and are of varying quality.

4. Commercial reproduction services are available.

5. There are two card indexes: a "Ships" file and a "Geographic" file. Each is arranged alphabetically by country.

F19 Oliveira Lima Collection (Catholic University)

1. a. *620 Michigan Avenue, NE*
Washington, D.C. 20017
635-5059

b. 1 P.M.-8 P.M. Tuesday
Noon-7 P.M. Wednesday-Friday
9 A.M.-5 P.M. Saturday
Closed, Sunday-Monday

c. Open to the public, appointments recommended.

d. Manoel Cardozo, Curator

2-5. The Oliveira Lima Library includes among its varied holdings a photograph collection numbering more than 1,500 black-and-white prints. Subjects include important members of the late 19th-early 20th century Brazilian elite, and Luzo-Brazilian art and architecture. Reproduction services are available for a fee.

F20 Organization of American States Photograph Collection

1. a. *Premier Building, Room 1109-A*
1725 Eye Street, NW
Washington, D.C. 20006
381-8700

b. 9 A.M.-5 P.M. Monday-Friday

    c. Open to researchers.

    d. Carl L. Headen, Archivist

2.   The collection consists of some 40,000 black-and-white prints, and is growing at a rate of approximately 100 prints per month.

3.   The main collection of the OAS photo archive is organized by country, with each country-file subdivided into categories for agriculture, antiquities, art, cities and towns, education, history, industry, minerals, native activities, native types, natural history, politics, public welfare, recreation, topography, and transportation. The photographs date from the very early 20th century to the present. Unfortunately, precise dates for many of the early prints are not recorded.

        The photo archive also includes a 3,500-print, alphabetically arranged, portrait collection of Latin American political and cultural figures, a Pan American conferences file, and a Columbiana file containing photographs of illustrations, statues, and other materials relating to Christopher Columbus.

4.   Prints are reproduced by the OAS Graphic Services Unit for a fee. For researchers outside of Washington, D.C., the archivist will supply photo copies of available prints on specific topics; reproductions of desired prints may then be ordered by mail.

Note: The Visual Arts unit of the OAS Department of Cultural Affairs, which produces slides, films, and video cassettes on Latin American art and general culture, possesses large collections of prints, negatives, and slides on Latin American art-works and artists (see entry L10). In addition, the OAS Columbus Memorial Library (see entry A43) has, within its rare-book collection, nine albums of 1925 photographs of Mexican colonial churches, an 1892 El Salvador photo album, and a portrait album of delegates to the First (1889-1890) Inter-American Conference.

Panama Canal Company Photograph Collection See entry A46

F21 Pan American Health Organization (PAHO) Photograph Collection

1.   a. *Room 212*
2121 Virginia Avenue, NW
Washington, D.C. 20037
331-5438

    b. 8:30 A.M.-5:30 P.M. Monday-Friday

    c. Open to the public. Appointment recommended.

    d. Roger Hamilton, Public Information Officer

2.   The collection consists of approximately 5,000 black-and-white prints.

3.   The majority of the photographs relate to Latin American public health services in the fields of nutrition, contagious diseases, maternal and child care, nursing, dental health, and sanitation. Additional subjects include inter-American health conferences and the effects of natural disasters, disease, and starvation on the peoples of Latin America. Coverage dates generally from the 1950s to the present.

4. There is no reproduction service. Prints might be loaned to researchers for outside commercial reproduction, although the staff is reluctant to loan its prints to individuals who are not affiliated with a press service or publishing firm.

5. The collection is arranged by medically related subject, and therein by country.

F22 Peace Corps (ACTION) Photograph Collection

1. a. *Paramount Building, Room 305*
        1735 Eye Street, NW
        Washington, D.C. 20525
        254-7524

    b. 8:30 A.M.-5 P.M. Monday-Friday

    c. Open to researchers. Appointment recommended.

    d. Anne Bringsjord, Director of Photo Services

2-3.   The collection contains some 8,000 color slides and 30,000 black-and-white negatives, with coverage concentrated predominantly on the living and working conditions of Peace Corps volunteers around the world. Approximately one-third of the collection focuses on Peace Corps activities in Latin America, from the organization's inception to the present. Holdings are arranged by country.

4. Limited numbers of prints will be supplied to researchers without charge.

F23 State Department Photograph Collection

1. a. *Bureau of Public Affairs*
        State Department Building, Room 4827A
        2201 C Street, NW
        Washington, D.C. 20520
        632-2352/53

    b. 8:45 A.M.-5:30 P.M. Monday-Friday

    c. Open to researchers, by appointment. Call ahead for clearance.

    d. Toni Marwitz, Films and Broadcasting Officer

2-3.   The collection contains an estimated 400-500 recent color slides of Latin American subjects and a small number of black-and-white prints (World War II-era to the present) of inter-American ceremonies, treaty signings, and State Department officials (including ambassadors) active in Latin American affairs. Also available is a four-part color film, "The History of U.S. Foreign Relations."

4. Reproduction services are available. There is no charge for prints.

Note: The State Department's Audio-Visual Services Division (Room B-258) possesses an indeterminate but apparently substantial collection of negatives and mounted prints focusing on departmental activities, ceremonies, conferences, and visits by foreign dignitaries, World War II-present. Visitors may browse. Staff-member Iris Worsley (632-1634) can provide detailed information.

The State Department's Foreign Service Institute (1400 Key Boulevard, Arlington, Virginia) has 13 commercial documentaries on Latin American topics, which occasionally are available for loan. The Foreign Service Institute also videotapes the lectures delivered to its training classes by guest lecturers. These videotapes, however, are restricted.

Textile Museum Photograph Collection See entry C11

United Nations Information Centre Film Collection See entry A52

Note: The commercial Ontario Theater (332-1807), located at 1700 Columbia Road, NW, presents popular Spanish American feature motion-pictures (in Spanish) on Saturdays and Sundays, noon-7 p.m.

In addition, the commercial Key Theater (333-5100), located at 1222 Wisconsin Avenue, NW, periodically presents a Latin American film series (the most recent of which focused on contemporary Cuban films).

G. Data Banks

Data Bank Entry Format (G)

1.   General Information
   a. *address; telephone number(s)*
   b. hours of service
   c. conditions of access (including fees charged for information retrieval)
   d. name/title of director and key staff members

2.   Description of data files (hard-data and bibliographic-reference) pertaining to Latin America

3.   Bibliographic aids facilitating use of storage media

G1   Agency for International Development (AID)—Development Information System

1.   a. *Office of Development Information*
         AID Bureau for Development Support
         Room 570, Pomponio Plaza
         1735 North Lynn Street
         Arlington, Virginia 22209
         235-9207

      b. 8:45 A.M.-5:30 P.M. Monday-Friday

      c. The system is primarily for the use of AID project designers, field project managers, and contract researchers, but terminals may be used by private scholars engaged in development research.

      d. Maury D. Brown, Deputy Director

2-3.   AID's Development Information System contains computerized technical and financial data on some 1,000 AID development projects active in 1974 or after. (There are plans to program data on selected earlier projects as well.) Data have been abstracted from AID project reports, feasibility studies, end-of-tour reports, project evaluations, contract research studies, and World Bank development-project evaluations. Each project is indexed by 20-40 project-subcomponent descriptors.

Note: Also see entries A3, G2, and J1.

G2 Agency for International Development (AID)—Economic and Social Data Bank

1. a. *Economic and Social Data Division*
        Office of Program Information and Analysis Services
        Bureau for Program and Policy Coordination
        Room 633, Pomponio Plaza
        1735 North Lynn Street
        Arlington, Virginia 22209
        235-9161

    b. 8:45 A.M.-5:30 P.M. Monday-Friday

    c. The data bank is primarily for the use of AID personnel, but the Economic and Social Division's terminals may be utilized by private scholars to the extent that such activities do not disrupt the staff's regular work schedule. Within such limits, the staff will also conduct data searches on specific topics for researchers.

    d. H. Patrick Peterson, Division Chief

2. AID's Economic and Social Data Bank contains some 450 worldwide country-level data elements obtained from the World Bank/IMF, United Nations, U.S. Department of Agriculture, Bureau of the Census, and other U.S. government agencies. Included are major social indicators (population, birth/death rates, life expectancy, literacy, etc.) and economic indicators (national accounts, central-government expenditures, international trade [by commodity and trading partners], agricultural and food production, etc.) for each Latin American country. Time series date back 30 years in many categories. The data bank also contains AID-generated Latin American statistics (population figures, loans and grants from the United States and international organizations, military expenditures, import/export figures), 1946 to the present. In addition, the staff is developing a computer file of field data collected as part of AID-funded development projects overseas. Included will be a substantial number of Latin American data-sets, largely in the form of urban and rural household surveys providing demographic (fertility, migration, etc.) and social/economic (income, manpower, occupation, family attitudes, opinions, etc.) data.

3. Many of the data bank's statistics are available in printed, hard-copy form in the publications of the AID Statistics and Reports Division (Bureau for Program and Policy Coordination, Office of Program Information and Analysis Services). See entry J1.

Note: Also see entries A3, G1, and J1.

G3 Agriculture Department—Data Services Center

1. a. *500 12th Street, SW*
        Washington, D.C. 20250

    b. 8:30 A.M.-5 P.M. Monday-Friday

    c. The facility is open to researchers. Tapes may be copied without charge.

    d.   Roger Strickland, Acting Director 447-8824
         Marge Bever, Special Assistant for International Data 447-8904

2.   Data files include a USDA-generated index of world agricultural production, 1950-present; a USDA grain-crop data base of international production-area and yield data, 1950-present; United Nations international trade data, 1967-present, UN Food and Agriculture Organization trade and production data, 1961-1974; and U.S. Agency for International Development population data, by country, 1950-present.

Note: In addition, the Agriculture Department's Foreign Agricultural Service (see entry J2) contains a Data Systems Division which stores USDA-generated machine-readable data on Latin American agricultural production, supply, and distribution, 1960-present, as well as detailed U.S. Census Bureau data on U.S. trade with the countries of Latin America back to 1965. For information, contact director Eldon Hildenbrandt (447-5255).

Agriculture Department, AGRICOLA See National Agricultural Library, entry A35

Alcohol, Drug Abuse, and Mental Health Administration (HEW) Data Bases See entry J14

G4   Commerce Department Data Bases

1. a. *Main Commerce Building*
       14th Street between Constitution Avenue and E Street, NW
       Washington, D.C. 20230
       377-2000 (Information)

2.   There is no single, centralized facility which stores all of the machine-readable data bases generated within the Commerce Department. Latin American data files are scattered throughout several of the department's bureaus and other subunits. Some individual offices will sell, or otherwise make available to private researchers, copies of tapes containing Latin American statistical data which they have compiled and programmed for their own use.

       Census Bureau. The Foreign Trade Division regularly sells tapes containing U.S.-Latin American trade statistics, on an individual basis or by subscription. Its Trade Information Office (763-5140) can provide order-forms and further details. Special tapes of import and export statistics designed to meet individual researchers' specifications can be ordered through the Foreign Trade Divison's Special Reports Branch (763-7700). Contact Charles C. Alexander.

      The Population Division's International Demographic Programs office (763-2870) maintains tapes of Latin American census statistics, mid-1950s to early-1970s. Copies might be made available to researchers. Jim Spitler (763-5577) can provide a list of data files on hand. In addition, the unit's International Demographic Data Center (763-2834) stores Latin American demographic data on discs, and will supply private researchers with microform and hard-copy output.

      Bureau of Economic Analysis. The International Investment Division (523-0660/0661) compiles data on U.S. private investment in Latin America, late-1940s to the present. Tapes of such data are available on a commercial basis from the division's Data Retrieval and Analysis Branch (523-0981).

The Balance of Payments Division (523-0620) programs U.S.-Latin American balance-of-payments data. Copies of tapes might be made available to private researchers at the discretion of division chief Louis J. Moczar.

Bureau of Export Development (Industry and Trade Administration). The Office of Export Development's "Foreign Traders Index" contains data on non-U.S. foreign business firms and products in Latin America. The office's Export Information Division (377-4992) supplies copies of tapes on a fee basis.

Note: Also see entry J5.

G5   Defense Documentation Center (Defense Department)

1.   a.   *Cameron Station, Building 5*
          Alexandria, Virginia 22314
          274-7633 (Document Information)
          274-6881 (Public Affairs)

     b.   7:30 A.M.-4 P.M. Monday-Friday

     c.   Open only to Department of Defense (DOD) personnel and staff members of private research firms under DOD research contract, subcontract, or grant.

     d.   Hubert E. Sauter, Administrator

2.   The Defense Documentation Center is a computerized repository of some 1.2 million technical research reports (both classified and unclassified) produced or funded by the Department of Defense. The focus of the collection is on the physical sciences, technology, and engineering as they pertain to national defense and military matters, although some social-science research on international relations is included. The bibliographic data base is on computer tape; full reports are available on microfiche. Nonclassified reports in the data base are frequently available to the public through the National Technical Information Service (see Appendix II-entry 11).

3.   A confidential, biweekly *Technical Abstracts Bulletin* of recent acquisitions is distributed to user organizations.

Educational Resources Information Center (ERIC) See entry J14

Energy Department Data Bases See entry J9

Housing and Urban Development Department (HUD)—International Information System See entry J15

G6   International Bank for Reconstruction and Development (World Bank)—Data Systems

1.   a.   *1818 H Street, NW*
          Washington, D.C. 20433
          477-3951

c. The World Bank maintains a variety of data systems for internal use. Copies of magnetic tapes are exchanged with U.S. government agencies and other international organizations, and will be made available to private users (universities, research centers, individual scholars) upon request, at little or no charge.

d. Helen Hughes, Director—Economic Analysis and Projections Department
Robert A. McPheeters, Jr., Adviser—Data Systems

2-3. The World Bank's Economic Analysis and Projections Department transfers a broad spectrum of statistical data into machine-readable format. Data systems of particular interest to Latin Americanists are:
Socio-Economic Data Bank, containing time series on a wide range of macro-level social and economic indicators, by country (the data also appear in published form in the World Bank's *Trade Tables, World Economic and Social Indicators,* and *World Bank Atlas).*
External-Debt (or Debtor-Reporting) Data System, containing data on public borrowing, external indebtedness, and balance of payments, by country (largely data published in the bank's *World Debt Tables* and some restricted information).
Capital Markets Data System, containing data on transactions in international capital markets, primarily western Europe, Japan, and the United States (data which appear in the bank's quarterly publication *Borrowing in International Capital Markets).*
Commodities and *Commodity Prices Data Systems,* comprising time series of data published in the annual *Commodity Trade and Price Trends.*
Metals and Minerals Data Base, containing data drawn from a variety of international and governmental sources.

International Communication Agency—Documents Index System
See entry J17

G7 International Monetary Fund—Data Bank

1. a. *700 19th Street, NW*
Washington, D.C. 20431
477-3207

c. The IMF programs data from four of its statistical publications into machine-readable form. Copies of magnetic tapes are made available on a commercial subscription basis. Each subscription consists of 12 monthly tapes, the corresponding IMF book publication, which serves as a guide to the contents of the tape, and documentation and instructions on how to use the data and programs contained on the tape. The cost is $1000 per year for each subscription ($300 for universities).

d. Earl Hicks, Director—IMF Bureau of Statistics
Robert L. Kline, Chief—Data Fund Division

2-3. *International Finance Statistics* tape subscriptions contain approximately 16,000 time series, including series appearing in the IMF's published *International Finance Statistics* country pages and world tables, exchange-rate series and international liquidity series for all countries, and 14 major series on countries' relationships with the IMF. Annual entries begin in 1948, quarterly and monthly entries at later dates.

Direction of Trade tape subscriptions contain approximately 42,000 time series reported in the IMF's published *Direction of Trade* country pages. Data include sources of imports and destination of exports for some 150 countries. Annual entries begin in 1948 and quarterly entries in 1969. All series are expressed in millions of U.S. dollars.

Balance of Payments tape subscriptions consist of about 35,000 time series on balance of payments components and aggregates covering 116 countries. Of these time series, some 33,000 correspond to data in the IMF's published *Balance of Payments Yearbook,* with annual data beginning in 1965 or later. The other 2,000 time series are long-term data series often extending back to the mid-1950s. All data are expressed in millions of SDRs.

Government Finance Statistics tape subscriptions contain approximately 13,000 annual time series of data reported in the IMF's published *Government Finance Statistics Yearbook.* Included are data on revenues, expenditures, lending, financing, debts, and social-security funds.

Library of Congress—MARC and SCORPIO Data Bases See entry A33

National Archives and Records Service—Machine-Readable Archives Division See entry B6

National Library of Medicine Data Bases See entry A39

G8 New York Times Information Bank, Inc.—Washington Office

1. a. *Suite 207*
      1909 K Street, NW
      Washington, D.C. 20036
      833-3291

   b. 9 A.M.-5 P.M. Monday-Friday

   c. Open to the public. Substantial fees charged for search and retrieval services.

   d. David Cearnel, Regional Manager
      Allen Eastlake, Retail Service Coordinator

2. The New York Times Information Bank is a commercial, computerized data base containing abstracts of news stories and articles from more than 60 U.S. and foreign publications, including the *New York Times* (1969-present); Washington *Post,* Miami *Herald,* Los Angeles *Times, Times of London, Foreign Affairs, Foreign Policy, Latin America,* and *Latin America Economic Report* (1972-present). Content of the Information Bank includes coverage of Latin American affairs and U.S.-Latin American political, economic, and military relations. No foreign-language publications are abstracted.

Smithsonian Science Information Exchange See entry J27

State Department—Foreign Affairs Document and Reference Center (FADRC) System See entry J28

Transportation Department, TRISNET See entry J29

G9 Treasury Department Data Systems

1. a. *Office of Data Services*
Office of the Assistant Secretary for Economic Policy
Department of the Treasury
15th Street and Pennsylvania Avenue, NW
Washington, D.C. 20220
566-5473

   b. 9 A.M.-5:30 P.M. Monday-Friday

   c. Access to scholars is on an individual basis at the discretion of the director. Copies of tapes will be supplied.

   d. Robert Brown, Director—Office of Data Services

2. One of the Treasury Department's data files contains data on the current status of U.S. Government loans and credits to Latin America, by country and transaction. Private researchers probably would not gain access to the department's computer terminals, but they can obtain copies of the data tapes.

Note: Also see entry J30.

ORGANIZATIONS

H. Associations (Academic, Professional, Cultural)

Association Entry Format (H)

1. *Address; telephone number(s)*
2. Chief official and titles
3. Programs and activities pertaining to Latin America
4. Library/reference collection
5. Publications

H1 American Anthropological Association (AAA)

1. *1703 New Hampshire Avenue, NW*
   Washington, D.C. 20009
   232-8800

2. E.J. Lehman, Executive Director

3. A professional association of anthropologists, the AAA holds an annual meeting each November at a varying site in the United States. In Washington, the organization sponsors a Congressional Fellowship Program which provides four-to-five-month internships on Congressional staffs for recent Ph.D.s in anthropology.

   The AAA's Washington office also serves as the administrative headquarters (handling memberships and publication subscriptions) for a number of affiliated professional associations:

   American Association of Physical Anthropologists
   American Ethnological Society
   American Folklore Society
   Anthropological Society of Washington
   Central States Anthropological Society
   Council on Anthropology and Education
   Latin American Anthropology Group
   Northeastern Anthropological Association
   Society for American Archeology
   Society for the Anthropology of Visual Communication
   Society for Applied Anthropology
   Society for Historical Archeology
   Society for Medical Anthropology
   Southwestern Anthropological Association

Of these, the Anthropological Society of Washington offers an annual program of monthly lectures, October through May, organized around a unifying theme, and usually held at the Smithsonian Institution. Past themes have included anthropological archeology in the Americas, new approaches to prehistoric cultural dynamics in the New World, urban anthropology, and language in society. The organization publishes a newsletter and anthologies of lecture papers.

The Latin American Anthropology Group is a national association founded "to provide a forum for discussion of controversial issues related to Latin America." It holds an annual meeting concurrently with that of the American Anthropological Association. The proceedings are published.

5. The American Anthropological Association publishes two quarterly journals, *American Anthropologist* and *American Ethnologist;* a monthly (except July and August) *Newsletter of the American Anthropological Association;* and various special publications—including B. L. Margolies, *Princes of the Earth: Subcultural Diversity in a Mexican Municipality* (1975), R. Bolton and E. Mayer (eds.), *Andean Kinship and Marriage* (1977), K. G. Heider, *Films for Anthropological Teaching* (6th ed., 1977), and *Federal Job Opportunities for Anthropologists* (1975).

The organization's Membership Department also handles the sale of publications of affiliated professional associations: the bimonthly *American Journal of Physical Anthropology* of the American Association of Physical Anthropologists; the *Newsletter* of the American Ethnological Society; the quarterly *Journal of American Folklore* of the American Folklore Society; the semiannual *CSAS Bulletin* of the Central States Anthropological Society; the quarterly *CAE Newsletter* of the Council on Anthropology and Education; the published proceedings of the Anthropological Society of Washington and the Latin American Anthropology Group; the semiannual *Studies in the Anthropology of Visual Communication* of the Society for the Anthropology of Visual Communication; the quarterly journal *American Antiquity* of the Society for American Archeology; the quarterly journal *Human Organization* of the Society for Applied Anthropology; the annual journal *Historical Archeology* and quarterly newsletter of the Society for Historical Archeology; the quarterly *Medical Anthropology Newsletter* of the Society for Medical Anthropology; and the quarterly *SWAA Newsletter* of the Southwestern Anthropological Association

Publications lists are available on request.

H2 American Association for the Advancement of Science (AAAS)

1. *1776 Massachusetts Avenue, NW*
    Washington, D.C. 20036
    467-4400

2. William D. Carey, Executive Officer
    James Rowe, Director—Western Hemisphere Cooperation, and Executive Secretary—*Interciencia* Association

3. The American Association for the Advancement of Science is the world's largest interdisciplinary scientific society. It has sections on anthropology, psychology, social and economic science, the history and philosophy of science, and each of the physical sciences. Each section sponsors symposia at the AAAS annual meeting, which is held in January at a varying site in North America. Among the symposia held recently, several have focused on

Latin American or less-developed-country topics—e.g., nutrition, agriculture, fertility, development policies.

The AAAS Office of International Science has developed a consortium of affiliated organizations through which contact between AAAS members and scientists abroad is facilitated. The Office of International Science serves as the executive secretariat of the *Interciencia* Association, a federation of scientific associations in the Western Hemisphere. The *Interciencia* Association sponsors several symposia each year at various hemispheric sites. Recent symposia have dealt with nontraditional science education, use of blood types in tracing the origins of native Americans, international cooperation in science and technology, marine sciences in the Americas, and nutrition and agriculture in Latin America.

5.   AAAS publishes a weekly magazine, *Science.* Abstracts of papers presented at the annual meeting, as well as the proceedings of selected symposia, are also published.

The *Interciencia* Association publishes the bimonthly *Interciencia: A Journal of Science and Technology for Development* (edited and published in Caracas).

American Association of Colleges for Teacher Education See entry I3

H3   American Association of Community and Junior Colleges—Office of International Services

1.   *1 Dupont Circle, NW*
Washington, D.C. 20036
293-7050

2.   Seymour Fersh, Director—Office of International Services

3.   The association's Office of International Services has arranged international conferences and exchange projects focusing on new forms of post-secondary education and short-cycle training, with participants from Latin America.

American Association of State Colleges and Universities See entry 14

H4   American Association of University Women (AAUW)—Program for International Relations

1.   *2401 Virginia Avenue, NW*
Washington, D.C. 20037
785-7700

2.   J. David Edwards, Assistant Director—Program for International Relations

3.   AAUW's International Relations office monitors, and keeps AAUW members informed on, U.S. foreign-policy matters, United Nations programs, and other international activities involving women's issues. The association maintains contact with national women's organizations in Latin America through the International Federation of University Women

(IFUW) (headquarters: Geneva, Switzerland). Through the IFUW's "pairing" program, local AAUW branches in the United States develop exchange and assistance projects with IFUW branches in other countries. The AAUW International Relations office coordinates and monitors U.S.-Latin American pairings.

AAUW provides doctoral and post-doctoral fellowships for U.S. women; international fellowships for advanced study in the United States for women from other countries; and "research and project" grants for AAUW members.

4. The association is building a library on women in development.

5. Program reports are available.

H5 American Bar Association (ABA)—Washington Office

1. *1800 M Street, NW*
Washington, D.C. 20036
331-2200

2. Herbert E. Hoffman, Director

3. The American Bar Association's Section of International Law is located at the ABA main office in Chicago. The Section of International Law holds its annual meeting in Washington, D.C. each spring in conjunction with the American Society of International Law (see entry H13).

   The Washington office administers the ABA's International Legal Exchange Program (described in entry 15).

5. ABA publications of potential interest to Latin Americanists include the monthly *American Bar Association Journal;* a quarterly newsletter, *International Law News;* and a quarterly journal, *International Lawyer.* All are available from the Chicago office.

H6 American Council on Education (ACE)—Overseas Liaison Committee (OLC)

.1. *Suite 210*
11 Dupont Circle, NW
Washington, D.C. 20036
833-4674

2. Charles H. Lyons, Director—Overseas Liaison Committee

3. The American Council on Education, which includes among its membership most U.S. colleges, universities, and professional educational organizations, serves as the chief point of contact between U.S. higher education and the U.S. government. The organization's Overseas Liaison Committee maintains close contact with post-secondary educational institutions in Africa, the Caribbean, and the South Pacific, arranging for the loan of academic experts and educational administrators from ACE member institutions to assist in the development and improvement of facilities of higher education in those regions. OLC has developed strong linkages with the Association of Caribbean Universities and Research Institutes and with individual universities throughout that region. It has also had a major interest in rural development programs, especially in Africa.

4. The Overseas Liaison Committee's reading room, which is open to the public, contains a variety of periodicals, bulletins, and newsletters from the Caribbean.

5. Program literature, and copies of OLC's irregularly issued *Rural Development Network Bulletin*, are available without charge on request.

Note: The American Council on Education also administers the Council for International Exchange of Scholars, which is discussed in entry 114.

American Federation of Labor and Congress of Industrial Organizations (AFL-CIO) See American Institute for Free Labor Development, entry 19

H7 American Foreign Service Association (AFSA)

1. *2101 E Street, NW*
   Washington, D.C. 20037
   338-4045

2. Allen B. Moreland, Executive Director

3. AFSA is a professional association of active U.S. foreign-service officers. It holds an annual meeting each June in Washington.

5. The organization publishes the monthly *Foreign Service Journal* and a monthly newsletter.

H8 American Historical Association (AHA)

1. *400 A Street, SE*
   Washington, D.C. 20003
   544-2422

2. Mack Thompson, Executive Director

3. A national association of historians, the AHA holds an annual convention in late December at a differing location in the United States. Each convention features several sessions on topics in Latin American history.

   Affiliated with the AHA is the Conference on Latin American History (CLAH), a national membership organization which holds an annual meeting concurrently with that of the AHA. CLAH, whose secretariat has recently been located at the University of Wisconsin—Milwaukee, is divided into regional-studies committees (Mexican, Brazilian, Gran Colombian, Andean, Caribe-Centro America, Chile-Rio de la Plata) and a historical-statistics committee, among others.

   Also affiliated with the AHA is the Society for Historians of American Foreign Relations (SHAFR), which sponsors its own annual conference as well as numerous activities at the AHA convention. Inter-American diplomatic history falls within the purview of the organization's interests and activities.

5. AHA publications include the *American Historical Review,* a journal with

five issues per year; the *AHA Newsletter* (nine issues per year); a biblio-graphy of *Recently Published Articles* (three issues per year); a quarterly *Employment Information Bulletin;* periodic lists of history doctoral disserta-tions in progress or recently completed at U.S. universities; and periodically updated *Guide to Departments of History* and *Fellowships and Grants of Interest to Historians.*

American Home Economics Association See entry I8

H9 American Political Science Association (APSA)

1. *1527 New Hampshire Avenue, NW*
   Washington, D.C. 20036
   483-2512

2. Evron Kirkpatrick, Executive Director

3. A national association of political scientists, APSA holds an annual convention, usually around Labor Day weekend, at a varying site in the United States. Sessions on Latin American and/or inter-American topics are frequently included.

   The association administers the Congressional Fellowship Program, a professional-level internship program that places political scientists, anthro-pologists, lawyers, journalists, and U.S. federal government officials on the staffs of senators, congressmen, and congressional committees.

5. APSA publications include a quarterly journal, the *American Political Science Review;* a quarterly news journal, *PS;* a quarterly newspaper on political-science teaching, *DEA News;* the proceedings of the annual meeting; directories of political scientists and department chairpersons; and various special publications for example, *Guide to Graduate Study in Political Science; Careers and the Study of Political Science: A Guide for Undergraduates; Career Alternatives for Political Scientists: A Guide for Faculty and Graduate Students; Research Support for Political Scientists: A Guide to Sources of Funds for Research Fellowships, Grants and Contracts;* and *Storming Washington: An Intern's Guide to National Government.*

H10 American Psychological Association (APA)

1. *1200 17th Street, NW*
   Washington, D.C. 20036
   833-7600

2. Charles A. Kiesler, Executive Officer

3. A national professional association of psychologists, the APA holds an annual convention, usually around Labor Day, at a varying site in North America. Occasional sessions focus on foreign and international psychology. The association's Committee on International Relations in Psychology maintains contact with Latin American national psychological societies and the Inter-American Society of Psychology through the International Union of Psychological Science and other channels. The Washington office has an

International Affairs department (833-7638) which responds to inquiries concerning international organizations and activities, and which assists foreign psychologists in the United States.

4. The APA's research library receives approximately 15 psychological journals from Latin America. These are abstracted by the APA's Psychological Information Services ("PsychINFO"). Abstracts are entered into a computerized PsychINFO data base, and published in the journal *Psychological Abstracts*. The library is open to researchers for on-site use. Contact Lois Granick (833-7624) for data-base information.

5. The association publishes numerous journals: *American Psychologist* (monthly), *Contemporary Psychology* (monthly), *Developmental Psychology* (bimonthly), *Journal of Abnormal Psychology* (bimonthly). *Journal of Applied Psychology* (bimonthly), *Journal of Comparative and Physiological Psychology* (bimonthly), *Journal of Consulting and Clinical Psychology* (bimonthly), *Journal of Counseling Psychology* (bimonthly) *Journal of Educational Psychology* (bimonthly), *Journal of Experimental Psychology* (quarterly), *Journal of Personality and Social Psychology* (monthly), *Professional Psychology* (quarterly), *Psychological Abstracts* (monthly), *Psychological Bulletin* (bimonthly), and *Psychological Review* (bimonthly). Other publications include a monthly newspaper, *APA Monitor;* a monthly *Employment Bulletin;* a biographical directory; and a survey of U.S. and Canadian graduate programs in psychology.

H11 American Public Health Association (APHA)

1. *1015 18th Street, NW*
Washington, D.C. 20036
467-5092/5084

2. William H. McBeath, Executive Director
Susi Kessler, Director of International Health Programs

3. APHA is an association of health-care professionals and other persons interested in the field of public health. Its International Health Programs office provides technical assistance and consultation services related to the development of integrated health delivery systems in developing countries. Fields of interest include health care, nutrition, family planning, environmental sanitation, health education, and the impact of health-care activities on other development programs.

   The association serves as the secretariat for the World Federation of Public Health Associations.

4. APHA's Resource Center (467-5492) maintains a vertical file of miscellaneous materials on health-care delivery systems, worldwide. Contents include articles from foreign health journals, along with feasibility studies, program evaluations, and other field reports prepared by APHA consultants sent to Latin America. The file is arranged by country. The Resource Center is open to researchers, 8:30 A.M.-5 P.M., Monday-Friday. Sally Coghlan is its manager.

5. APHA publications include the monthly *American Journal of Public Health; Salúbritas,* a quarterly newsletter (in English, Spanish, and French) focusing on the developing countries; and a monograph, *The State of the Art of Delivering Low Cost Health Services in Developing Countries* (1977).

H12 American Society for Public Administration (ASPA)

1.   *1225 Connecticut Avenue, NW*
        Washington, D.C. 20036
        785-3255

2.   Keith Mulrooncy, Exccutivc Dircctor

3.   ASPA is a national association of persons interested in public administration
        at the local, state, national, or international levels. Membership includes
        government administrators, teachers, researchers, consultants, students, and
        civic leaders. Within the society's Section on International and Comparative
        Administration (SICA) is a Latin American Development Administration
        Committee, which holds workshops at ASPA national meetings and which
        maintains liaison with Latin American institutes of public administration.

5.   ASPA publishes a bimonthly journal, *Public Administration Review,* and a
        monthly newspaper, *Public Administration Times.* The society's Section on
        International and Comparative Administration publishes a newsletter and an
        occasional-paper series.

H13 American Society of International Law

1.   *2223 Massachusetts Avenue, NW*
        Washington, D.C. 20008
        265-4313

2.   Seymour J. Rubin, Executive Director
        John Lawrence Hargrove, Director of Studies

3.   The American Society of International Law is a professional association
        which promotes study of the role of law in international relations. An annual
        meeting is held each April in Washington.
        The organization conducts a "research and study" program which brings
        together interdisciplinary panels and working groups (composed of members
        and nonmembers) to examine policy issues in international law. Current
        projects include an examination of the future of the inter-American system
        (the status of and prospects for the Organization of American States, Latin
        America's options in North-South relationships, hemispheric economic
        relations in a global context, human rights, the inter-American military
        system, Brazil within the inter-American system, the system as seen from
        Caracas, etc.), and a study of the role of law (legal aid, public interest law,
        law reform, etc.) in Latin American and Caribbean social change. Other
        current or recent projects have focused on law-of-the-sea issues; the
        accountability of the state in international law; and legal aspects of terrorism,
        human rights, international economic and mineral resources, international
        environmental problems, foreign investment, international trade, and the
        international monetary system.
        The organization also serves as the headquarters for the Association of
        Student International Law Societies.

4.   The society's library contains an estimated 22,000 items on all aspects of
        public international law. Latin American holdings include several Latin

American law reviews and textbooks on international law; works and briefs on foreign investment, multinational corporations, expropriations, boundary disputes, and law of the sea in Latin America; and documents and publications from the Organization of American States, Inter-American Development Bank, and Andean Pact. The library is open to the public, 9:30 A.M.-5:30 P.M., Monday-Friday. The librarian is Helen Philos.

5.   Publications include the quarterly *American Journal of International Law;* a quarterly *Newsletter;* a bimonthly *International Legal Materials* periodical containing treaties, legislation, and other primary source documents; the proceedings of the annual conference; a "Studies in Transnational Legal Policy" series of books and occasional papers (including a forthcoming report, "Beyond the Inter-American System," by Tom J. Farer); a book series on "International Crises and the Role of Law" (including a forthcoming anthology of papers resulting from the research project on the future of the inter-American system, edited by Tom J. Farer); and a "Foreign Investment" monograph series (which includes volumes on Mexico and Colombia). A biennial *Research and Study* report summarizing the organization's research projects is available on request.

H14   American Sociological Association (ASA)

1.   *1722 N Street, NW*
      Washington, D.C. 20036
      833-3410

2.   Russell Dynes, Executive Officer

3.   A national association of sociologists, the ASA holds an annual meeting, traditionally around Labor Day, at a differing site in the United States. Within ASA's Committee on World Sociology is an informal liaison group for Latin American studies, which convenes at the ASA annual meeting.

5.   The association publishes several journals, including the bimonthly *American Sociological Review*, bimonthly *Contemporary Sociology: A Journal of Reviews*, quarterly *The American Sociologist*, quarterly *Sociometry*, quarterly *Sociology of Education: A Journal of Research in Socialization and Social Structure*, and quarterly *The Journal of Health and Social Behavior*. Other publications are a newsletter, *ASA Footnotes* (nine issues per year); a monthly *Employment Bulletin;* and an annual *Guide to Graduate Departments of Sociology.*

H15   American Statistical Association (ASA)

1.   *806 15th Street, NW*
      Washington, D.C. 20005
      393-3253

2.   Fred Leone, Executive Director

3.   A "professional society for persons in statistics and related quantitative endeavors," the ASA holds an annual meeting in August at a varying site in the United States. The organization is divided into several sections, including a Business and Economic Statistics section, a Social Statistics section (with

interests in the fields of anthropology, education, demography, sociology, political science, public health, and social psychology), and a Survey Research Methods section. Each section meets in conjunction with the ASA annual meeting.

During 1975-1976, the association carried out a program entitled "Closer Communication, Interchange and Joint Development of Statistics and the Statistical Profession in Latin America and the United States," in which teams of ASA representatives visited Argentina, Brazil, Chile, Colombia, Mexico, and Venezuela to make contacts and participate in symposia. Program reports are available. As a result of this program, the ASA has arranged professional visits to the United States for a number of Latin American statisticians.

5. ASA publications include the quarterly *Journal of the American Statistical Association;* a second quarterly journal, *The American Statistician;* a newsletter, *Amstat News,* issued ten times per year; and *Current Index to Statistics,* an annual, computerized, keyword index to articles from over 3,000 statistical publications worldwide.

H16 Amnesty International USA—Washington Office

1. *6 E Street, SE*
Washington, D.C. 20003
544-0200

2. Stephanie Grant, Director—Washington Office

3. Amnesty International is a worldwide, human-rights organization which works for the release of "prisoners of conscience"—individuals imprisoned anywhere because of their political beliefs, religion, race, color, or ethnic origin. The organization works through "adoption groups" of members who come together to work (through letters and appeals to the imprisoning government) for the release of individual prisoners of conscience assigned to them by the Research Department of Amnesty International's International Secretariat in London. The organization also sends fact-finding missions to countries where human-rights violations are believed to be occurring. It currently has some 140,000 members in 78 countries, with national branches in 38 countries.

The Washington office is principally an information office. Staff member Francesca Jessup monitors Latin American developments.

5. Amnesty International publishes an annual survey of human-rights violations around the world (by country); special reports and background briefing papers on individual countries (including Argentina, Brazil, Chile, Guatemala, Nicaragua, Paraguay, and Uruguay); a monthly newsletter, *Amnesty Action;* and a quarterly bulletin, *Matchbox.*

H17 Association of American Chambers of Commerce in Latin America (AACCLA)

1. *1615 H Street, NW*
Washington, D.C. 20062
659-4637

2.   Patrick Hughson, President
        Keith Miceli, Executive Secretary

3.   AACCLA membership consists of local U.S. chambers of commerce in 15 Latin American nations. The association develops policy positions on inter-American economic issues. An annual meeting is held in Washington during April or May. Among the programs at the annual meeting is a "corporate briefing session" at which executives from U.S. chambers of commerce in Latin America present off-the-record analyses and forecasts of what their respective host-countries' current economic, political, and social conditions signify for U.S. business interests. The association also holds an annual "mid-year meeting" in October or November at a varying site in Latin America.

5.   A semiannual *AACCLA Report* describes the association's activities and includes country reports from U.S. chambers of commerce in Latin America.

H18   Association of American Geographers (AAG)

1.   *1710 16th Street, NW*
        Washington, D.C. 20009
        234-1450

2.   J. Warren Nystrom, Executive Director

3.   A national professional association of geographers, the AAG holds an annual meeting every April at a differing site in the United States. Affiliated with the association is the Conference of Latin Americanist Geographers (CLAG), a group which holds its own separate annual meetings at varying sites throughout the hemisphere, as well as special sessions at AAG annual meetings. The AAG maintains contact with Latin American geographic organizations through the Pan American Institute of Geography and History. There is a possibility that the association may sponsor seminar programs in conjunction with geographic institutes in Latin America.
        The AAG provides small grants to members for research and field work.

5.   Publications include two quarterly journals, the *Annals* and *The Professional Geographer;* the *AAG Newsletter* (monthly, except during summer months); an annual *Guide to Graduate Departments of Geography in the United States and Canada;* and an annual publication containing abstracts of all papers presented at the AAG annual meeting.

H19   Association of Former Intelligence Officers (AFIO)

1.   *6723 Whittier Avenue*
        McLean, Virginia
        790-0320

2.   John J. Coakley, Executive Director

3.   AFIO is a private association of persons who have previously served in a professional capacity with any U.S. intelligence or counterintelligence organization. It supports programs "that will permit effective and secure methods of gathering intelligence information necessary for the formulation

of national policy." The organization monitors media coverage of intelligence matters, and disseminates its views to civic groups, Congress, and the media. AFIO also provides information- and reference-services relating to issues involving the U.S. intelligence community, and will assist scholars in contacting former U.S. intelligence officers who served in Latin America.

AFIO holds an annual convention, during the fall, at a varying site in the United States. A monthly luncheon is held in Washington.

4. A library of materials on U.S. national-security matters is being developed. It will be open to researchers.

5. A bimonthly newsletter, *Periscope,* is published.

H20   Association on Third World Affairs, Inc.

1. *3114 Rodman Street, NW*
    Washington, D.C. 20008
    966-9326

2. Lorna Hahn, Executive Director

3. Members of the Association on Third World Affairs include individuals (diplomats, scholars, lawyers, engineers, etc.) and organizations interested in Third World political and economic affairs. The organization sponsors *ad hoc* lectures and panel discussions, with guest speakers, at various sites throughout Washington, including foreign embassies.

5. The association's bimonthly newsletter, *Third World Forum,* contains a Latin American section.

H21   Caribbean American Intercultural Organization (CAIO)

1. *Suite 114*
    1629 Columbia Road, NW
    Washington, D.C. 20009
    387-5115

2. Vincent McDonald, President

2. The Caribbean American Intercultural Organization serves as a cultural association and information service for the local Caribbean and West Indian communities. The organization holds five or six regular meetings each year at varying sites throughout the District of Columbia. It also sponsors *ad hoc* conferences on Caribbean topics, numerous social events, and an annual (late August) "Caribbean Heritage Week" of social, artistic, religious, athletic, and musical activities.

5. A quarterly newsletter is sent to anyone on the organization's mailing list. Other publications include the proceedings of CAIO conferences on: Caribbean women; ownership and control of assets in the Caribbean; the triangular interchange of ideas between Africa, the Caribbean, and the United States; and the English-speaking Caribbean in the 1970s; as well as a brief history of Caribbean immigrant organizations in the Washington, D.C. area, 1940-1976.

H22 Coalition for a New Foreign and Military Policy

1. *120 Maryland Avenue, NE*
   Washington, D.C. 20002
   546-8400

2. Brewster Rhoads, Associate Director
   Cynthia M. Buhl, Human Rights Coordinator

3. The Coalition for a New Foreign and Military Policy serves as a coordinating organization for some 40 national religious, political, social-action, labor, peace, and educational groups. It works, through lobbying efforts and the dissemination of information, "to develop a peaceful, non-interventionist, humanitarian, and open U.S. foreign and military policy." The coalition's Human Rights Working Group has as its goals "the extension and implementation of the human rights provisions of the bilateral U.S. military and economic assistance laws; the extension of effective human rights provisions to the replenishment bills for international financial institutions," and "ratification of pending UN human rights convenants." The Human Rights Working Group meets monthly.

5. Publications include periodic *Action Alerts* to member organizations, a periodically updated *Human Rights Action Guide,* and the minutes of the Human Rights Working Group's monthly meeting.

H23 Council of the Americas, Washington Office

1. *Mills Building, Suite 680*
   1700 Pennsylvania Avenue, NW
   Washington, D.C. 20006
   298-9016

2. Otto J. Reich, Director—Washington Operations

3. The Council of the Americas is a private, nonprofit business association composed of a membership of some 250 major U.S. corporations with business interests in Latin America. The organization, which has its headquarters in New York City, seeks "to further understanding and acceptance of the role of private enterprise as a positive force for the development of the Americas." Its Washington office monitors legislation in Congress, and represents the council's private-sector interests and viewpoints in conferences at U.S. government agencies and international/inter-American organizations, and in meetings with Latin American embassy officials. The Washington staff also arranges for representatives of member corporations to meet with officials of U.S. government agencies and international organizations, and with visiting Latin American policy-makers and businessmen.

   Staff members can provide researchers with information on numerous aspects of inter-American economic relations, including the activities of the council's member-corporations in Latin America, and Latin America's business climate, by country. Developments in Cuba are observed closely.

   Each year the council's New York headquarters sponsors, at various sites throughout the hemisphere, conferences, seminars, and workshops for corporation executives and invited guests on such topics as the trade and investment climate in Latin America, economic development in individual nations, technology transfer, guidelines for multinational corporations, management planning in changing environments, labor relations and arbitration, and investment analysis and negotiation. The Washington office organizes a biannual one-day conference for representatives of member corporations, U.S. government agencies, and international organizations. It also hosts various small meetings for Washington liaison representatives of member corporations.

4.   The Washington office maintains a reference collection of materials on investments and business conditions in Latin America. Included are council publications, business newsletters, and periodical reports on Latin American central banks, regional-integration organizations, and business groups. The office also maintains a large vertical file of miscellaneous materials relating to topics of interest to the council (trade, investment, expropriation, technology transfer, codes of conduct, the U.S. Generalized System of Preferences, multinational corporations, etc.), arranged by subject and by country. Both the reference collection and the office files will be made available to serious researchers on an individual basis, as space permits. Researchers are requested to call in advance for an appointment.

5.   The council's New York headquarters has produced numerous inter-American economic studies and collections of conference papers. A publications list can be obtained by writing:

> Council of the Americas
> 680 Park Avenue
> New York, New York 10021

The Washington office occasionally prepares educational information booklets, the most recent of which is *The United States, Panama, and the Panama Canal: A Guide to the Issues* (1976). This booklet, and the Council of the Americas' *Annual Report,* may be obtained without charge from the Washington office.

H24   Diplomatic and Consular Officers, Retired (DACOR, Inc.)

1.   *1718 H Street, NW*
Washington, D.C. 20006
298-7848

2.   Theodore J. Hadraba, Executive Director

3.   DACOR, Inc. is an association of retired U.S. foreign service officers, former ambassadors, and other public officials involved in the field of foreign affairs. An annual meeting is held in Washington every April. The organization can be a useful source of information for scholars interested in contacting former U.S. diplomats involved in inter-American affairs.

5.   A monthly bulletin is published.

H25   Foreign Policy Discussion Group

1.   *815 Connecticut Avenue, NW*
Washington, D.C. 20006
298-8290

2.   Charles T. Mayer, President

3.   The Foreign Policy Discussion Group consists of approximately 80 U.S. government officials, academicians, attorneys, etc. Meetings featuring distinguished speakers are held monthly (except summer) at varying local sites. Meetings are off-the-record and closed to nonmembers.
Membership is by invitation only.

H26 Inter-American Bar Association (IABA)

1.   *Suite 315*
1730 K Street, NW
Washington, D.C. 20006
293-1340

2.   John O. Dahlgren, Secretary General—Inter-American Bar Association
Charles R. Norberg, President—Inter-American Bar Foundation

3.   IABA is a professional organization of bar associations and individual lawyers from throughout the Western Hemisphere. Its principal activity is a biennial conference, held at varying sites throughout the hemisphere. The organization operates the Inter-American Academy of International and Comparative Law, in Rio de Janeiro.
    The Inter-American Bar Foundation functions as a companion organization to the Association. Its purpose is "to receive and disburse funds donated for the support of educational, literary, scientific, and charitable projects designed to promote the study of law and improve the administration of justice in the Western Hemisphere." The foundation has organized workshops and seminars in Latin American countries and in the United States on hemispheric subjects of contemporary legal interest (e.g., law and population, computers and the law, legal protection of human rights, legal status of women). It also provides occasional international travel grants for law students. The foundation's office is located at:

      310 Federal Bar Building West
      1819 H Street, NW
      Washington, D.C. 20006
      293-1455

5.   The Inter-American Bar Association publishes a newsletter (approximately three issues per year). The proceedings of the association's biennial conference are available for purchase from the Washington, D.C. executive headquarters. Reports from the Inter-American Bar Foundation's seminars on population and human rights are also available.

H27 Inter-American Council of Washington, D.C.

1.   The organization does not maintain a formal office. Written communications should be addressed:

      c/o Hispanic Division
      Library of Congress
      10 1st Street, SE
      Washington, D.C. 20540

Staff members of the Library of Congress' Hispanic Division (426-5397) can provide information on the organization's activities.

2. Presidency rotates annually

3. The Inter-American Council is a professional association of Washington-area Latin Americanists. Its primary activity is a monthly luncheon with a guest speaker (approximately nine luncheons per year, at varying locations). Speakers include former Latin American presidents, representatives of international organizations and Latin American embassies, and area academicians. These luncheons offer non-Washingtonians an excellent opportunity to make contact with local Latin Americanists.

    In addition to its monthly luncheons, the Inter-American Council sponsors an annual spring symposium on a selected topic in Latin American/inter-American affairs. Special social events are also held periodically.

5. Members receive a monthly newsletter.

H28 International Association of Chiefs of Police (IACP)

1. *11 Firstfield Road*
    Gaithersburg, Maryland 20760
    948-0922

2. Glen D. King, Executive Director

3. An international association of police and security officials, IACP has members in some 20 Latin American and Caribbean nations. The organization holds an annual conference in October at a varying site in North America. IACP staff specialists have provided a variety of technical-assistance field services to Latin American police and security organizations —including preparation of in-depth surveys of organization, administration and management procedures, manpower deployment, field operations, communications, records-management, etc.

4. The IACP library contains scattered publications of Latin American police departments, including the Brazilian police review.

5. Publications include a monthly magazine, *The Police Chief;* a quarterly *Journal of Police Science and Administration;* and the *Police Yearbook,* which contains the proceedings of the annual conference. The organization also publishes numerous technical "training aids," many of which have been translated into Spanish or Portuguese.

H29 International Development Conference

1. *Suite 550*
    1120 19th Street, NW
    Washington, D.C. 20036
    659-1234

2. Lawrence Kegan, Chairman
    Barbara Huddleston, President

3. The International Development Conference is a forum for discussion of

U.S.-Third World relations and development issues facing underdeveloped countries. The conferences, which are held irregularly (e.g., 1970, 1972, 1973, 1978) in Washington, D.C., are sponsored by a broad spectrum of U.S. organizations, including farm, labor, and business associations; religious and women's organizations; youth groups; educational and civic interests. Conference participants include representatives of the U.S. government, international organizations, business, the academic community, and non-governmental organizations. All sessions are open to the public. Anyone interested in attending may request to be placed on the conference's mailing list.

5. Summary reports from recent conferences are available.

International Economic Policy Association See entry M25

H30 International Road Federation (IRF)

1. *Washington Building, Suite 1023*
    15th Street and New York Avenue, NW
    Washington, D.C. 20005
    783-6722

2. W. Gerald Wilson, President

3. IRF is an international federation of more than 60 national road associations, including those of almost every Latin American nation. Private businesses and associations from throughout the world are also members. The organization acts as a clearinghouse for information on highway systems and highway transport worldwide. It holds a world meeting (every four years) and regional seminars, and provides a variety of services—including technical-assistance and consultation services, technical-exchange programs, and graduate fellowships for foreign engineering students.

5. The federation publishes a monthly newsletter and an annual *World Survey of Current Research and Development on Roads and Road Transport.* Other publications include international *Road and Motor Vehicle Statistics* (by country), *Limits of Motor Vehicle Sizes and Weights* (by country), a map-book of the *Pan American Highway System, by Countries,* and a directory of world road administrators and national highway associations.

Latin American Studies Association (LASA)—Washington Office

[As this volume went to press, preliminary plans were underway to establish a LASA liaison office in Washington.]

H31 National Academy of Sciences (NAS)

1. *2101 Constitution Avenue, NW*
    Washington, D.C. 20418
    393-8100

2. Philip Handler, President
Murray Todd, Executive Director—Commission on International Relations
Victor Rabinowitz, Staff Director—Board on Science and Technology for
International Development

3. The National Academy of Sciences is a private, nonprofit organization of
scientists and engineers. Through its National Research Council, NAS serves
as an official adviser to the U.S. government on matters of science and
technology. The National Research Council is composed of eight assemblies
and commissions, among which are the following:

   Commission on International Relations (CIR). CIR, in turn, is divided
into various boards, including a Board on Science and Technology for
International Development (BOSTID). BOSTID has conducted studies and
sponsored workshops on the role of science and technology in the social and
economic development of Latin America, Asia, and Africa. Workshops have
been held in several Latin American nations, bringing U.S. technical
specialists together with their Latin American counterparts to consider
development problems relating to education, industrial research, energy,
agriculture, natural resources, and appropriate technologies. BOSTID also
has advisory panels or commissions on technology innovation, international
health, natural resources, industrialization, and technological education.

   Assembly of Social and Behavioral Sciences. Within this division is a
Committee on Population and Demography, which is developing a panel on
Latin America.

5. Numerous Latin American reports and studies produced by the Board on
Science and Technology for International Development are available from
the BOSTID office. A publications list will be provided on request.

   The Fellowship Office of the National Research Council's Commission on
Human Resources has prepared two useful booklets, *A Selected List of
Major Fellowship Opportunities and Aids to Advanced Education for
United States Citizens* and *A Selected List of Major Fellowship Opportuni-
ties and Aids to Advanced Education for Foreign Nationals,* both available
free on request.

National Association of Manufacturers See entry M28

H32 National Association of State Universities and Land-Grant Colleges —Office of International Programs and Studies

1. *Suite 710*
1 Dupont Circle, NW
Washington, D.C. 20036
293-7120

2. James W. Cowan, Director—Office of International Programs and Studies

3. The association's Office of International Programs and Studies coordinates
the educational, research, and training programs which association member-
institutions conduct in developing countries, with particular emphasis on
development assistance and agricultural education. The office also monitors
the international food and agricultural development activities of the U.S.
government.

National Conference of Catholic Bishops—Committee for the Church of Latin America See entry 125

National Education Association See entry 126

H33 Pan American Liaison Committee of Women's Organizations

1. *Box 13-G, Thunderbird Drive*
   Lusby, Maryland 20657
   (301) 326-3962

2. Stella Boudrias, President

3. The Pan American Liaison Committee of Women's Organizations is an association of women and women's groups in the United States and Latin America. The majority of its members are in the Washington, D.C. area. The organization sponsors charitable, educational, and cultural projects. A monthly meeting is held at a varying site in the Washington area. The presidency rotates biennially. The organization can be reached locally through former president Rita Johnston (469-6691).

5. A newsletter (monthly except summer) is disseminated.

H34 Population Association of America (PAA)

1. *P.O. Box 14182*
   Benjamin Franklin Station
   Washington, D.C. 20044
   393-3253

2. Edgar M. Bisgyer, Business Manager

3. PAA is a scientific and professional society for persons interested in all aspects of population, demography, family planning, migration, vital statistics, and related subjects, worldwide. An annual meeting on population issues is held during April at a varying site in the United States.

5. PAA publications include a quarterly journal *Demography;* a quarterly newsletter, *PAA Affairs; Population Index,* a quarterly bibliographic index to international literature on population topics; and a brochure, *Careers in Demography.*

H35 Population Crisis Committee (PCC)

1. *Suite 550*
   1120 19th Street, NW
   Washington, D.C. 20036
   659-1833

2. Phyllis T. Piotrow, Executive Director

3.   The Population Crisis Committee is a nonprofit educational organization consisting of approximately 35 distinguished U.S. citizens and a staff of some 20-25. It "works as a catalyst with national and international organizations to promote population awareness among policymakers and to encourage high-level support for a wide range of population policies and programs, particularly in the developing countries." The committee's principal activity is fund-raising for the International Planned Parenthood Federation (headquarters: London), the United Nations Fund for Population Activities, and the Draper World Population Fund.

4.   The organization's library contains various materials on Latin American population, family planning, and women, including newsletters and bulletins from Latin American population and family-planning agencies. The collection is open to researchers. The librarian is Janet L. Stanley.

5.   Publications include periodically issued briefing papers on global population topics, and an annual or semiannual *Draper World Population Fund Report.*

H36   San Martín Society of Washington, D.C.

1.   *P.O. Box 33*
McLean, Virginia 22101

2.   Christian Garcia-Godoy, President

3.   The San Martín Society of Washington, D.C. is an association of individuals interested in the study of the Argentine general José de San Martín and the South American liberation movements which he led. The organization sponsors periodic commemorative ceremonies and other events.

4.   President Christian Garcia-Godoy possesses a large personal collection of books and archival documents pertaining to San Martín and the revolutions of independence in southern South America.

5.   A quarterly newsletter, *San Martín News*, is disseminated to members.

H37   Society for International Development (SID)—Washington Office

1.   *1346 Connecticut Avenue, NW*
Washington, D.C. 20036
296-3810

2.   W. P. J. Boichel, Director—Washington Office

3.   The Society for International Development is an international educational and scientific association which serves as a forum for the exchange of ideas and experiences among persons who are concerned with problems of global social and economic development. Membership consists primarily of development specialists—administrators, economists, engineers, educators, health officers, lawyers, technicians, etc.—from some 130 countries. There are six chapters in Latin America. The organization sponsors a world conference (every two or three years at varying international sites) and

periodic Latin American regional conferences. SID's international headquarters are in Rome. An information and reference service on any subject related to economic and social development is maintained in Paris. The Washington office also provides reference services.

SID's local Washington, D.C., chapter features "work groups" on agriculture and rural development, women in development, development finance, development technology, development training, and alternative development strategies. Each work group holds a regular (usually monthly) luncheon meeting. The Washington chapter also sponsors dinners, conferences, seminars, and other special events, including briefings by senior officials from Washington-based development institutions.

5.   SID publications include the quarterly *International Development Review,* a bimonthly *Survey of International Development,* and an *International Roster on Development Skills.* The Washington, D.C. chapter also disseminates a newsletter.

H38   United States Catholic Conference (USCC)

1.   *1312 Massachusetts Avenue, NW*
Washington, D.C. 20005
659-6000

2.   Francis J. Lally, Secretary—Department of Social Development and World Peace
J. Bryan Hehir, Associate Secretary—Office of International Justice and Peace
Thomas Quigley, Adviser on Latin American Affairs—Office of International Justice and Peace

3.   The United States Catholic Conference, a civil corporation of the U.S. Catholic bishops, describes itself as "the national-level action agency for the Catholic Church in the United States." Within its Department of Social Development and World Peace, staff members of the Office of International Justice and Peace (659-6812) advise the U.S. bishops on Latin American affairs, draft policy proposals, and conduct research. The office is active in Latin American-oriented human-rights activities in the Washington area. Adviser on Latin American Affairs Thomas Quigley maintains contact with episcopal conferences and other church groups and research centers throughout Latin America.

4.   The Office of International Justice and Peace reference library contains a collection of books, documents, and periodicals relating to church-state relations in Latin America. Some 20-30 Latin American church periodicals (*Mensaje,* ecclesiastical reviews, diocesan publications) and a large number of religious and political newsletters are received. Materials range back to the 1960s in date. The collection is open to researchers, 9 A.M.-5 P.M., Monday-Friday.

The office's Adviser on Latin American Affairs, Thomas Quigley, also maintains a large collection of Latin American church documents, correspondence, human-rights case files, etc.

5.   The Office of International Justice and Peace publishes *LADOC* ("Latin

American Documentation"), a bimonthly collection of Latin American Catholic Church documents (pastoral letters, episcopal statements, etc.) translated into English.

Note: Also see National Conference of Catholic Bishops, entry I25.

H39 Washington Institute of Foreign Affairs

1. *613 15th Street, NW*
Washington, D.C. 20005
737-5932

2. Lyman L. Lemnitzer, President

3. The Washington Institute of Foreign Affairs is an association of some 250 distinguished public officials, academicians, lawyers, and businessmen. Its principal activity is a meeting (approximately weekly) at which prominent speakers discuss problems in international affairs. These sessions are off-the-record, and members may not bring guests.

    Membership is by invitation only. Several former U.S. ambassadors to Latin America are members.

5. A membership list is available on request.

H40 World Population Society (WPS)

1. *Suite 200*
1337 Connecticut Avenue, NW
Washington, D.C. 20036
833-2440

2. Philander P. Claxton, Jr., President
Frank H. Oram, Associate Director

3. WPS is an international, interdisciplinary association of scientific and professional "populationists." The organization has members in some 60 countries. It promotes population planning, research, and education in less developed countries, and sponsors an annual or biannual conference at varying international sites.

5. Publications include a newsletter and the proceedings of WPS international conferences. A worldwide directory of populationists is planned.

    The World Population Society's Washington, D.C. chapter has compiled a useful *Directory of the Population-Related Community of the Washington, D.C. Area* (3rd ed., 1978).

I. Cultural-Exchange and Technical-Assistance Organizations

Cultural-Exchange and Technical-Assistance Organization Entry Format (I)

1. *Address; telephone number(s)*
2. Chief official and title
3. Programs and activities pertaining to Latin America
4. Publications

I 1 Academy for Educational Development, Inc.—International Operations Division

1. *1414 22nd Street, NW*
   Washington, D.C. 20037
   862-1900

2. Stephen F. Mosely, Director—International Operations Division

3. The Academy for Educational Development is a private, nonprofit, research and technical-assistance organization which aids developing nations in the development of education programs, both formal and nontraditional. Fields of specialization include educational technology; instructional communications systems (radio, television, satellite); educational planning, administration, and finance; content and curriculum development; testing and evaluation; teacher training; and specialized education (vocational, agricultural, nutritional, etc.). Activities in Latin America and the Caribbean have included assessments of national education systems (in the Dominican Republic, Guatemala, Honduras, Nicaragua, Panama, and Paraguay); evaluations of educational development programs (El Salvador, Guatemala, Honduras); preparation of feasibility, policy, and project-planning studies; operational project advisory assistance; and specialized consulting and training services. The organization works closely with the U.S. Agency for International Development.
   The academy's Clearinghouse on Development Communication (CDC) provides information and reference services relating to educational development, instructional technology, and the application of communications technology to development problems. Among the facility's 9,000 books, documents, and research reports are substantial quantities of unpublished, country-specific material from Latin America—including in-depth material on educational television in Colombia, El Salvador, and Mexico; rural radio

programs and schools in Colombia and Guatemala; educational radio in Mexico; and the use of communications satellites generally. Some nonprint materials (films, audio- and video-tapes) are also available. The Clearinghouse is open to serious researchers, 9 A.M.-5 P.M. Monday-Friday.

4. The international projects of the Academy for Educational Development are described in the report "International Operations Division: An Overview" (March, 1978), available on request. The Clearinghouse on Development Communication publishes a quarterly newsletter, *CDC Reports,* containing information on recent international activities relating to the use of communications media in development programs. Other publications are "project profiles" of individual projects, and "information bulletins" dealing—usually on a comparative basis—with the application of communications media to major sectoral and multi-sectoral development problems.

I 2 Agricultural Cooperative Development International (ACDI)

1. *1430 K Street, NW*
    Washington, D.C. 20005
    638-4661

2. Donald H. Thomas, President

3. ACDI is a nonprofit organization which provides assistance to developing nations in the development of agricultural cooperatives. Activities include advisory and training services, and preparation of feasibility studies and project designs. Fields of specialization include agricultural credit, agricultural and cooperative banking, marketing, processing, farm supply, education, and policy planning. The organization has worked in several Latin American and Caribbean countries. It works closely with the U.S. Agency for International Development.

4. Publications include an annual report and a bimonthly newsletter.

I 3 American Association of Colleges for Teacher Education (AACTE) —International Section

1. *Suite 610*
    1 Dupont Circle, NW
    Washington, D.C. 20036
    293-2450

2. Frank Klassen, Director—International Section

3. AACTE's International Section conducts educational-exchange and technical-assistance programs in Latin America and the Caribbean. Its internship program brings foreign educators and administrators (ranging from university professors to government ministers of education) to the United States to work with U.S. counterparts. A "study-abroad" program provides training for U.S. teachers in Mexico, Costa Rica, and elsewhere. In cooperation with the U.S. Agency for International Development, the unit provides technical assistance (advisers, training services, material) to foreign teacher-training programs (a project is currently under way in Jamaica). The unit also

conducts research and evaluation studies on foreign systems of teacher education (including a recent Chilean study for the Organization of American States).

International Section staff members are also in contact with Latin American educational specialists through their participation in the International Council on Education for Teaching.

I 4 American Association of State Colleges and Universities (AASCU) —Office of International Programs

1. *Suite 700*
   1 Dupont Circle, NW
   Washington, D.C. 20036
   293-7070

2. Maurice Harari, Director—Office of International Programs

3. AASCU's Office of International Programs is conducting an exchange program with Argentina, in which Argentine elementary and secondary school teachers and education administrators visit schools in the United States, and U.S. professors of education travel to Argentina.

I 5 American Bar Association (ABA)—International Legal Exchange Program

1. *1800 M Street, NW*
   Washington, D.C. 20036
   331-2258

2. Kathrine Lee Ebert, Staff Director

3. The ABA's Washington office administers one- to six-month training exchanges and internship programs for lawyers, law professors, judges, and other members of the legal profession in the United States and foreign countries. It also arranges seminar programs for foreign legal groups visiting the United States. Numerous U.S.-Latin American exchanges have taken place.

4. Program literature is available.

I 6 American Council of Young Political Leaders

1. *Suite 300*
   1616 H Street, NW
   Washington, D.C. 20006
   347-7806

2. H. Joseph Farmer, Executive Director

3. The American Council of Young Political Leaders arranges bilateral international exchange programs and study tours for delegations of young political leaders and government officials from the United States and foreign countries. Recent exchanges have included a study tour of the United States for young officials of Mexico's PRI, and a study tour to Jamaica by a U.S. delegation.

4.   Program literature is available.

American Council on Education See entry H6

I 7 American Council on International Sports (ACIS)

1.   *817 23rd Street, NW*
        Washington, D.C. 20052
        676-7246

2.   Carl A. Troester, Jr., Executive Director

3.   The American Council on International Sports is a private, nonprofit organization which administers international sports-exchange programs in cooperation with the State Department, the U.S. Olympic Committee, and numerous foreign and international sports federations. It arranges tours for U.S. and foreign athletes, coaches, teams, and instructors; provides technical and advisory assistance to foreign governments (especially those of developing countries) to assist them in planning national sports and physical-education programs; and sponsors international coaching clinics and sports symposia. The organization has handled numerous U.S.-Latin American athletic, training, and advisory exchanges.

        ACIS maintains a reference collection of literature on sports and physical education around the world.

4.   A monthly newsletter (*News Briefs*) and an information brochure are available on request.

I 8 American Home Economics Association—International Family Planning Project

1.   *2010 Massachusetts Avenue, NW*
        Washington, D.C. 20036
        862-8300

2.   Betty Brabble, Director—International Family Planning Project

3.   The American Home Economics Association's International Family Planning Project provides educational materials and in-country training services to foreign home-economics educational systems to assist them in integrating family planning and population information into their programs. The project, which is funded by the U.S. Agency for International Development, has worked in several Caribbean and Central American nations.

4.   Publications include resource and training materials for field personnel, and a quarterly newsletter, *The Link*.

I 9 American Institute for Free Labor Development (AIFLD)

1.   *1015 20th Street, NW*
        Washington, D.C. 20036
        659-6300

2.   George Meany, President
William C. Doherty, Jr., Executive Director

3.   The American Institute for Free Labor Development is a private, nonprofit organization founded by the American Federation of Labor and Congress of Industrial Organizations to provide training in "the principles of democratic trade unionism" for Latin American labor leaders. With funding from the U.S. Agency for International Development, instructors operating out of AIFLD field offices in 19 Latin American and Caribbean countries conduct local and regional courses in labor-union philosophy, labor history, organizing, and collective-bargaining methods. The organization also has an advanced-study center in Front Royal, Virginia. In addition, through the Washington, D.C. Consortium of Universities' Consortium Committee on Latin American Studies, AIFLD sponsors an "inter-American labor economics program" designed to provide Latin American and Caribbean labor movements with university-trained economists. The organization also provides technical assistance (including interest-free loans and grants) and advisory services to Latin American and Caribbean trade unions in the fields of organization, administration, collective-bargaining, workers' housing, agricultural and consumer cooperatives, and community development.

        AIFLD has close ties with the Inter-American Regional Organization of Workers (ORIT) and the Caribbean Congress of Labour. In 1974, it established Central American and Caribbean Labor Economics Research Centers which have published technical reports dealing with statistics, cost-of-living, productivity, social security, salaries, fringe benefits, etc. An annual Western Hemisphère Economic Conference is sponsored.

4.   Publications include a bimonthly newsletter, *AIFLD Reports* (available in English and Spanish); an annual progress report; and various program brochures.

American Public Health Association—International Health Programs See entry H11

I 10   American Red Cross—Office of International Service

1.   *17th and D Streets, NW*
Washington, D.C. 20006
857-3591

2.   Dorothy Taaffe, Director—Office of International Service

3.   The American Red Cross is a humanitarian disaster-relief and health-education organization. It is affiliated with national Red Cross organizations in every Latin American nation through the League of Red Cross Societies, based in Geneva, Switzerland. The Office of International Service supervises the donation of supplies, funds, and technical assistance for relief in major foreign disaster and refugee situations. It has also provided technical assistance and training services to Red Cross organizations in many Latin American and Caribbean countries in such fields as primary health care, paramedical education, first aid, disaster preparedness, cardiopulmonary resuscitation, and the development of blood centers. (Red Cross services on behalf of victims of human-rights violations in Latin America are handled by the international League office in Switzerland.)

The American Red Cross' National Headquarters Library (857-3491) maintains a large vertical file of miscellaneous publications (annual reports, periodicals, manuals, disaster reports, etc.) from Latin American national Red Cross organizations, by country. The library also has the proceedings of international Red Cross conferences (from the 1860s to the present), reports and publications of the International Committee of the Red Cross and the League of Red Cross Societies, and reports by the American Red Cross on disaster-relief activities in Latin America. The library is open to researchers, 8:30 A.M.-4:45 P.M., Monday-Friday. Interlibrary loan and photoduplication facilities are available.

4. International Red Cross programs and activities (including those of the American Red Cross' Office of International Service) are described in the *Annual Report* of the League of Red Cross Societies, and in that organization's bimonthly periodical *Panorama*.

Note: Also see entries B1 and F4.

I 11   Baptist World Relief

1. *1628 16th Street, NW*
    Washington, D.C. 20009
    265-5027

2. C. Ronald Goulding, Staff Executive

3. Baptist World Relief administers the Baptist World Alliance's Relief Fund program. It provides funds to Baptist groups in the Third World for the purchase of equipment needed in local development projects (schools, clinics, irrigation projects, etc.). It has also been active in Latin American disaster relief.

4. Activities are described in the monthly *Baptist World* magazine.

I 12   Brazilian-American Cultural Institute (BACI)

1. *Suite 211*
    4201 Connecticut Avenue, NW
    Washington, D.C. 20008
    362-8334

2. José Neistein, Director

3. The Brazilian-American Cultural Institute, which is operated by the Brazilian Embassy, offers a variety of educational and cultural programs, including courses in Portuguese language and Brazilian literature; an annual lecture series on Brazilian history and civilization; concerts, recitals, and poetry readings by visiting Brazilian artists; and showings of Brazilian films (at the Brazilian Embassy's screening room). Participation is open to individuals who, for a moderate fee, become members of the institute.

    BACI also operates an art gallery, which presents temporary exhibits of contemporary Brazilian art. The gallery is open to the public, 9 A.M.-7 P.M., Monday-Friday.

    A scholarship for travel or study in Brazil is awarded each year to the best student in BACI's language courses.

4.   An annual list of program events is available on request. BACI also offers a publications series, which includes language learning materials; Haydée S. Magro and Paulo DePaula, *Leituras Brasileiras Contemporâneas* (also available on cassette); José Neistein and Manoel Cardozo, *Poesia Brasileira Moderna* (a bilingual anthology); Henry Keith and Raymond Sayers, *Cecília Meireles* (poems in translation); Manuel Bandeira, *Brief History of Brazilian Literature;* Dias Gomes, *Journey to Bahia;* Bettencourt Machado, *Machado of Brazil;* Vasco Mariz, *Villa-Lobos; Life and Work;* and Margarette de Andrade, *The Expansion of Brazilian Language Instruction in the U.S.* A publications list is available.

Note: Also see entries A10 and D1.

I 13 CARE (Cooperative for American Relief Everywhere), Inc.— Washington Office

1.   *1028 Connecticut Avenue, NW*
Washington, D.C. 20036
296-5696

2.   Ronwyn Ingraham, Director—Washington Office

3.   CARE, Inc. is a private, nonprofit, technical-assistance and disaster-relief organization. It currently has "Partnership Development" assistance programs in 13 Latin American countries. Activities include food programs, nutrition and health-care training, adult education and vocational training, rural development projects, and community self-help projects. The organization's world headquarters and international programming staff are located in New York City. The Washington field office is a public-information and fund-raising unit.

4.   An annual report and information pamphlets are available on request.

I 14 Council for International Exchange of Scholars (American Council on Education)

1.   *Suite 300*
11 Dupont Circle, NW
Washington, D.C. 20036
833-4950

2.   Adolph Y. Wilburn, Director
Anne Carpenter, Executive Associate (Latin American programs)

3.   The Council for International Exchange of Scholars, a component of the American Council on Education, administers on behalf of the U.S. government the postdoctoral and professorial division of the Fulbright-Hays Mutual Educational and Cultural Exchange program for senior scholars. The council publicizes opportunities for U.S. scholars to lecture and/or conduct research in foreign—including Latin American—countries. It receives and screens applications and selects candidates for awards. It also provides placement and support services to foreign scholars spending time in the United States under the Fulbright-Hays program.

The council maintains a register of U.S. scholars interested in appointments abroad. Registrants receive an annual spring announcement of program opportunities.

4.   Several information brochures are available free on request. They include: *General Information: Fulbright-Hays Awards to Americans for University Lecturing and Advanced Research Abroad; Fulbright-Hays Awards Abroad for Americans: University Lecturing and Advanced Research; Fulbright-Hays Scholars: Awards to Americans for University Lecturing and Advanced Research Abroad; Mutual Educational Exchange Program: Scholars from Abroad; Directory of Visiting Lecturers and Research Scholars;* and *CIES Activities, Programs, Organization.*

I 15   Credit Union National Association (CUNA)—Global Projects Division

1.   *Suite 404*
      1120 19th Street, NW
      Washington, D.C. 20036
      659-4571

2.   Paul Hebert, Director

3.   CUNA's Global Projects Division provides technical assistance (grants and advisory services) to aid in the development of credit unions abroad. It is currently engaged in projects in Panama, Paraguay, and Haiti. It maintains close ties with the World Council of Credit Unions, the Latin American Confederation of Savings and Credit Cooperatives, and the Confederation of Caribbean Credit Unions.

4.   The division's activities are summarized in the World Council of Credit Unions' annual report.

I 16   Experiment in International Living—Washington Office

1.   *Suite 802*
      1346 Connecticut Avenue, NW
      Washington, D.C. 20036
      872-1330

2.   Todd Hunt, Director—Washington Office

3.   The Experiment in International Living is a private, nonprofit educational organization which sponsors international "homestay" exchange programs and cross-cultural education programs for high school students, college students, and adults from the United States and foreign countries. Programs for U.S. students have been established in Argentina, Bolivia, Brazil, Chile, Costa Rica, Guadeloupe, Mexico, and Peru. Some scholarships are awarded.
      The organization's headquarters are in Brattleboro, Vermont.

4.   Publications include a quarterly newsletter, *Odyssey,* and numerous program brochures.

I 17 Foundation for Cooperative Housing (FCH) International

1. *Suite 409*
   2101 L Street, NW
   Washington, D.C. 20037
   857-4100

2. Charles Dean, President—International Division

3. FCH International provides technical assistance to foreign governments and community organizations in the development of cooperative and nonprofit housing projects for low and moderate income families. Activities include advisory and training services in the areas of project planning, construction, land use, finance, and management; and preparation of feasibility studies, shelter sector-analyses, and housing policy studies. The organization has assisted local projects throughout Latin America and the Caribbean.

4. A quarterly newsletter and miscellaneous technical reports are available.

I 18 Goodwill Industries of America, Inc.—International Operations

1. *9200 Wisconsin Avenue, NW*
   Washington, D.C. 20014
   530-6500

2. George Soloyanis, Director—International Operations

3. Goodwill Industries' international office supplies advisory personnel and information in the field of vocational rehabilitation to the organization's autonomous affiliates in some 12 Latin American and Caribbean nations.

4. Activities are described in the Goodwill Industries annual report.

I 19 Institute of International Education (IIE)—Washington Office

1. *Suite 200*
   11 Dupont Circle, NW
   Washington, D.C. 20036
   438-0001

2. Peter D. Pelham, Director of Washington Office

3. The New York City-based Institute of International Education is a private nonprofit organization which administers—on behalf of the U.S. government, private U.S. foundations, foreign governments and institutes, etc.—large number of educational and cultural exchange programs, including the Fulbright-Hays Mutual Educational Exchange Program predoctoral research and study awards for U.S. and foreign graduate students; UNESCO Fellowships; Ford Foundation Latin American Graduate Fellowships; ITT International Fellowships; University of North Carolina Population Center Internships; Harvard University Institute for International Development projects in economic planning and development; the Venezuelan government's Gran Mariscal de Ayacucho scholarship program; and the Mexican Technical Exchange Program. Two special IIE programs—the Program of Educational and Technical Exchange with Central America and the

Caribbean (PETECA), and the Program of Educational and Technical Exchange with the South Americans (PETESA)—enable students from Latin America and the Caribbean to study in the United States. The organization also provides a variety of technical-assistance services, including financial and administrative support to U.S. specialists working in agricultural and economic development, population studies, urban planning, and other fields in the less developed countries, as well as supply and purchasing services to International Institutes of Agriculture and foreign development agencies. The IIE maintains Latin American branch offices in Mexico City, Lima, and Santiago, Chile. The Washington office provides information and counseling services on all aspects of international educational exchange, and assists in the U.S. government's International Visitors Program.

4. The organization publishes a long list of reference materials and information brochures, including: *Basic Facts on Foreign Study* (1976); *Scholarships and Fellowships for Foreign Study: A Selected Bibliography* (1975); Dr. Daniel Marien, *Guide to Foreign Medical Schools* (4th ed., 1975); Janet Lowenstein and Mary Louise Taylor (eds.), *Handbook on International Study for U.S. Nationals—Volume II: Study in the American Republics Area* (1976); Gail A. Cohen (ed.), *Summer Study Abroad* (1977), *Teaching Abroad* (1976), and *U.S. College-Sponsored Programs Abroad* (1977); Robert Spencer and Ruth Awe, *International Educational Exchange: A Bibliography* (1970); and numerous guides to U.S. educational programs for foreign students. Also see IIE's report series *Issues in International Education,* particularly No. 2—Reynold E. Carlson, *The Andean Common Market* (1975); No. 6—E. Croft Long, *Alternatives to Traditional Medical Training in Latin America* (1976); and No. 7—*Latin American Studies: New Roles, New Constraints* (1976).

A publications list, an annual report, a summary of sponsored projects, and a quarterly newsletter (*IIE Reports*) are available on request.

I 20 Institutional Development and Economic Affairs Service, Inc. (IDEAS)

1. *11800 Sunrise Valley Drive*
   Reston, Virginia 22091
   860-2500

2. Brian Beun, President

3. IDEAS is a nonprofit technical-assistance and research organization with headquarters in Nederland, Colorado. It is currently conducting an experimental rural-development management-training project in Mexico aimed at developing a model agricultural-development program financed by private investment capital.

4. Program literature is available.

I 21 Inter-American Development Institute (IDI)

1. *Suite 803*
   11 Dupont Circle, NW
   Washington, D.C. 20036
   332-0822

2. Marina Fanning, Director

3. Formerly known as the Inter-American Literacy Foundation, the Inter-American Development Institute is a private, nonprofit, technical-assistance organization which uses the tools of basic, nonformal education to develop and implement field training projects in literacy, health, nutrition, sanitation, agriculture, family life education, crafts and basic-skills training, and community development throughout Latin America. Recent projects have included the design of a community-development program among Panama's Guaymi indians, rural Latin American nutritional studies, and the development of a Latin American educational radio network.

I 22 Inter-American Foundation

1. *1515 Wilson Boulevard*
    Rosslyn, Virginia 22209
    841-3800

2. William M. Dyal, Jr., President

3. The Inter-American Foundation is a nonprofit, U.S. government-financed development-assistance corporation which provides funding to local, non-governmental Latin American groups and community organizations for small-scale social and economic development projects. Since the inception of its programs in 1971, the foundation has provided over $65 million in grants to nearly 600 projects in 27 Latin American and Caribbean nations. Individual grants have ranged from $400 to $2 million, with average grants falling within the $100,000-$200,000 range. Activities funded include a wide variety of "social-change" projects, such as workers' self-managed enterprises and labor unions, credit and production cooperatives, self-help housing, legal-aid clinics, agricultural extension services, cultural-awareness programs and projects of peasant associations, women's movements, and indian community organizations.

    The Inter-American Foundation offers Masters-level, doctoral, and postdoctoral "Learning Fellowships" (of three- to 12-months duration) for field research on social-change processes in Latin America and the Caribbean. A Graduate Student Intern Program is also available.

4. The organization publishes an *Annual Report* and a *Journal of the Inter-American Foundation* (three issues per year), both free on request. A five-year program summary, *They Know How: An Experiment in Development Assistance* (1977) can be purchased from the U.S. Government Printing Office.

International Association of Chiefs of Police See entry H28

I 23 International Voluntary Services, Inc.

1. *Suite 605*
    1717 Massachusetts Avenue, NW
    Washington, D.C. 20036
    387-5533

2.   John T. Rigby, Executive Director

3.   International Voluntary Services, Inc. is a private, nonprofit organization which recruits international volunteer specialists in agriculture, health and nutrition, education, engineering, and cooperative/small-business development to provide technical assistance for rural development projects in developing countries. The organization has assisted in several Latin American development projects. It works closely with the U.S. Agency for International Development.

4.   The organization publishes annual and quarterly reports.

I 24 League of Women Voters—Overseas Education Fund

1.   *2101 L Street, NW*
Washington, D.C. 20037
466-3430

2.   Elise Smith, Executive Director
Louise Montgomery, Director of Field Programs

3.   The League of Women Voters' Overseas Education Fund provides technical assistance (consultation and training services) to women's organizations in Latin America. Emphasis is on aiding women's groups to strengthen themselves institutionally and to improve their capability for increasing the participation of women in national development. Areas of Latin American program-development in which the fund has been particularly active include job-training and income-generation, child care, nutrition, health, and education.

The staff's Resource Center contains a miscellaneous collection of reports by the fund's field representative, as well as unpublished studies prepared by women's organizations in Latin America. The collection constitutes a unique resource for research on the changing roles of women in Latin American society. The facility is open to researchers, 9 A.M.-5 P.M., Monday-Friday.

4.   Publications include an *Annual Report,* pamphlets entitled "Overseas Education Fund: Programs in Brief" and "The Women of Latin America," and numerous Spanish-language educational manuals and pamphlets. A publications list is available on request.

I 25 National Conference of Catholic Bishops—U.S. Bishops' Fund for Latin America

1.   *1312 Massachusetts Avenue, NW*
Washington, D.C. 20005
659-6828

2.   Frances L. Neason, Executive Director—Secretariat for Latin America

3.   Within the National Conference of Catholic Bishops is a committee for the Church of Latin America, consisting of seven U.S. Catholic bishops. The committee, through its secretariat in Washington, administers the U.S. Bishops' Fund for Latin America, which channels financial aid to Latin American Catholic Church elements and to U.S. Catholic missionary groups

working in Latin America. Activities funded include pastoral, educational, and training programs, evangelization, "human promotion," and research, including socio-religious studies. Not funded are Church construction or maintenance projects, land purchases, or purchases of equipment.

4.   A set of guidelines for aid requests is available. Copies of some funded research studies are housed in the United States Catholic Conference's Office of International Justice and Peace library (see entry H38).

I 26   National Education Association (NEA)—Office of International Relations

1.   *1201 16th Street, NW*
Washington, D.C. 20036
833-4105

2.   Braulio Alonso, Director—Office of International Relations

3.   NEA's Office of International Relations provides information, consultants, and training to elementary- and secondary-school teacher organizations in Latin America and the Caribbean.

I 27   National 4-H Council

1.   *7100 Connecticut Avenue, NW*
Washington, D.C. 20015
656-9000

2.   Grant A. Shrum, Executive Director
Melvin J. Thompson, Director—International Programs

3.   The National 4-H Council is a private, nonprofit youth branch of the Cooperative Extension Service of the U.S. Department of Agriculture and state land-grant universities. The council sponsors "International 4-H Youth Exchange" travel and study programs for young leaders from rural areas in the United States and foreign (including Latin American) countries. It has also provided technical assistance and training services to Central American and Caribbean governmental agencies seeking to establish rural youth development programs.

4.   Program information is available on request.

I 28   National Rural Electric Cooperative Association—International Programs Division

1.   *2000 Florida Avenue, NW*
Washington, D.C. 20009
265-7400

2.   Thomas Venables, Coordinator of International Programs

3.   The National Rural Electric Cooperative Association's International Programs Division provides technical assistance to foreign government agencies,

utility companies, and cooperatives in developing and operating rural electric systems and electricity cooperatives. Activities include the preparation of country surveys and feasibility studies, as well as on-site advisory, consulting, and training services. In Latin America, assistance projects have been carried out in Argentina, Bolivia, Brazil, Chile, Colombia, Costa Rica, Ecuador, Nicaragua, Peru, and Venezuela. The organization works closely with the U.S. Agency for International Development.

4.   A newsletter, *Rural Electric Co-ops Overseas,* is published three to four times per year.

I 29   Pan American Development Foundation (PADF)

1.   *Cafritz Building, Suite 622*
1625 Eye Street, NW
Washington, D.C. 20006
381-8651/8652

2.   Michael D. Miller, Executive Vice President

3.   PADF is a private, nonprofit technical-assistance organization closely affiliated with the Organization of American States. It raises tax-deductible contributions of money and materials from U.S. corporations, foundations, and other private-sector organizations, and uses those contributions to support the development activities of low-income groups in Latin America. The organization has two main programs. Its Revolving Loan Fund Program channels long-term, low-interest financial loans, largely through Latin American national development foundations, to marginal community groups for the development of cooperatives, potable water systems, and other small-scale, local self-help projects. A Material Services Program provides donations of technical equipment and supplies to Latin American medical facilities, vocational schools, and small business enterprises.

PADF sponsors, in cooperation with the OAS, the Inter-American Society, membership in which is open to all interested Latin Americanists. The Inter-American Society holds a monthly Lecture Series, featuring presentations by resident ambassadors of Latin American and Caribbean nations.

4.   An *Annual Report,* a quarterly newsletter, and various descriptive brochures are available upon request.

I 30   Partners of the Americas

1.   *2001 S Street, NW*
Washington, D.C. 20009
332-7332

2.   Alan A. Rubin, President

3.   Partners of the Americas is a private, nonprofit organization which coordinates bilateral technical-assistance and cultural-exchange "partnership" programs between 43 U.S. states and 20 Latin American nations. A committee of private, voluntary, citizens' groups in a U.S. state is matched with a similar committee in a selected Latin American country. Subcommit-

tees are established to develop bilateral development and exchange projects in education, health services, rehabilitation of the physically and mentally handicapped, agricultural and rural development, business investment, sports, and the cultural arts. Projects link "partner" schools and universities, state agencies, health facilities, cities, professional associations, 4-H clubs, etc., and concentrate on the exchange of specialists, training instructors, and material. Washington staff-members provide training workshops and advisory services to program participants in project development, committee organization, promotion, and fund-raising.

A National Association of the Partners of the Alliance, Inc. (NAPA, Inc.) was established in 1966 to function as the servicing, administrative, and advisory agency for Partners of the Americas in the United States.

4.   Publications include an annual *Activities Report,* a quarterly newsletter (*Partners*), an annual *Statistical Highlights of the Partners Program,* a periodically-updated *Directory of Partner Committee Officers,* and numerous brochures describing specific programs.

I 31   Project HOPE (People-to-People Health Foundation, Inc.)

1.   *2233 Wisconsin Avenue, NW*
      Washington, D.C. 20007
      338-6110

2.   William B. Walsh, President

3.   The People-to-People Health Foundation is a nonprofit corporation which provides educational and training programs in the health sciences (medicine, dentistry, nursing, nutrition, family planning, hospital- and health-care planning) to national ministries of health, medical schools, hospitals, and clinics in developing countries. It currently has programs in Brazil, Colombia, Guatemala, Peru, and the Caribbean.

4.   Publications include a quarterly newsletter, country-program reports, and an "Educational Monographs" series featuring titles relating to disease and the development of specialized medical-education programs in Latin America and the Caribbean.

I 32   Public Welfare Foundation, Inc.

1.   *Suite 505*
      2600 Virginia Avenue, NW
      Washington, D.C. 20037
      965-1800

2.   Davis Haines, President

3.   The Public Welfare Foundation, Inc. is a private, nonprofit, charitable organization which provides grants (usually less than $20,000) to private, nonprofit groups (schools, clinics, missionaries, development groups, etc.) for health, welfare, and educational projects that "alleviate human suffering" anywhere in the world. The foundation has supported numerous projects in Latin America and the Caribbean (examples: immunization and potable-water projects in Haiti; a program of handicapped rehabilitation and

education in Peru; a pre-school education project in Dominica, West Indies; a Maryknoll Sisters health-care program in El Salvador; a project to develop a vocational center in Trinidad).

4. An annual report is available on request.

I 33 Seventh-Day Adventist World Service (SAWS)

1. *6840 Eastern Avenue, NW*
   Washington, D.C. 20012
   723-0800

2. Howard D. Burbank, Executive Secretary and Manager

3. The Seventh-Day Adventist World Service operates a number of humanitarian and development-assistance programs in Latin American and Caribbean countries. Activities, which are under the direction of country-program managers in the field, include food, health-care, educational, and rehabilitation programs, and construction projects (schools, roads, water systems, and other community projects). The organization has also been active in Latin American disaster relief.

4. Overseas programs are described in an annual report, *The SAWS Reporter.*

I 34 Sister Cities International (Town Affiliation Association of the U.S., Inc.)

1. *1625 Eye Street, NW*
   Washington, D.C. 20006
   293-5504

2. Thomas Gittins, Executive Vice President

3. Sister Cities International coordinates exchange programs (educational, cultural, professional, and technical) linking cities in the United States with cities in foreign countries. Some 250 Latin American cities are currently participating as affiliated "partners" of individual U.S. cities.

4. A bimonthly newsletter, *Sister City News,* and various informational materials are available.

I 35 Volunteer Development Corps

1. *1629 K Street, NW*
   Washington, D.C. 20006
   223-3349

2. David W. Angevine, President

3. The Volunteer Development Corps is a private, nonprofit organization which recruits specialists—primarily from U.S. agricultural, industrial, and commercial cooperatives—to provide short-term voluntary technical assistance (planning, advisory, and training services) to cooperatives and government agencies in developing countries. The organization has worked with

numerous cooperatives and federations in Latin America and the Caribbean. It is funded mainly by the U.S. Agency for International Development.

4.   Project summaries are available to researchers at the organization's office.

I 36   Volunteers in Technical Assistance, Inc. (VITA, Inc.)

1.   *3706 Rhode Island Avenue*
       Mt. Rainier, Maryland 20822
       277-7000

2.   Thomas Fox, Executive Director
       Sandra Atkins, Program Officer for Latin America

3.   VITA, Inc. recruits volunteer consultants to advise on matters of appropriate technology in overseas development projects. Latin American activities have focused primarily on the Caribbean basin. The organization is partially funded by the U.S. Agency for International Development, and has worked under contract with the Peace Corps.

4.   Publications include a quarterly newsletter, *VITA News,* and some 50 project handbooks and technical manuals.

I 37   World Wildlife Fund—U.S.

1.   *Suite 800*
       1601 Connecticut Avenue, NW
       Washington, D.C. 20009
       387-0800

2.   Russell Train, President

3.   The World Wildlife Fund is a private, international conservation organization committed to preserving endangered animals and the wilderness areas on which they depend for survival. It provides grants for habitat surveys, projects to develop or expand national parks and preserves, anti-poaching programs, and other wildlife-conservation, research, and education programs throughout the world. Projects have been funded in almost every Latin American nation. The organization's international headquarters are in Switzerland.

       A triennial international congress is held at varying sites throughout the world. The World Wildlife Fund works closely with other organizations involved in international and Latin American conservation activities, including the International Union for Conservation of Nature and Natural Resources, the Natural Resources Defense Council-International Program, the Nature Conservancy-International Program, the Caribbean Conservation Association, and the International Council for Bird Preservation. Staff scientist Tom Lovejoy has considerable Latin American experience.

4.   Program literature is available on request.

J. United States Government Agencies

United States Government Agency Entry Format* (J)

1. General Information
    a. *address; telephone number(s)*
    b. conditions of access
    c. name/title of director and heads of relevant divisions

2. Agency functions, programs, and research activities (including in-house research, contract research, research grants, and employment of outside consultants)

3. Agency libraries and reference facilities

4. Internal agency records (including unpublished research products)

5. Publications
    a. published reports, periodicals, and series
    b. bibliographies

*In the case of large, structurally-complex agencies, each relevant division/bureau will be described separately in accordance with the above entry format.

Introductory Note

The agencies and departments of the United States government constitute a vast reservoir of information on Latin America. Perhaps the government's foremost resource for researchers is its personnel. Almost invariably, the officials with whom the author spoke proved receptive to consultations with serious researchers and were willing to provide information within the limits imposed by their work schedules and security regulations.

The Latin Americanist will also, of course, find significant research material in government reports and internal documents. In attempting to gain access to the written records of government agencies (those records which are not directly obtainable from the agency or openly available at the National Archives), researchers will wish to familiarize themselves with Freedom-of-Information Act processes. The Freedom-of-Information Act (Public Law 89-487 of 1966, as amended by Public Law 93-502 of 1974) provides that any citizen has the right of access to, and can obtain copies of, any document, file, or other record in the possession of any federal agency or department, with certain exemptions (including certain personnel records, and classified documents whose classification can be justified as essential to national security). Most government agencies have a Freedom-of-Information office or officer available to process requests for internal agency documents. In contacting them (in writing or via telephone), researchers should cite the Freedom-of-Information Act, and should make their requests as detailed and specific as possible. Researchers are not required to explain or justify their requests. Denials of requests may be appealed to the director of the agency. (Such appeals are often successful.) Rejected appeals may be challenged through court litigation. By law, agencies have 10 working days in which to respond to an initial Freedom-of-Information Act request, and 20 days in which to respond to an appeal. Researchers should note that agencies are permitted to charge rather substantial fees for document searches and photoreproduction of released documents. Information on such fees should be requested when filing an initial Freedom-of-Information Act request. In most cases, researchers are permitted to examine released records in person at the agency.

There are several organizations in Washington which can assist researchers in using Freedom-of-Information Act processes. They include the Freedom of Information Clearinghouse, P.O. Box 19367 (2000 P Street, NW, Suite 700), Washington, D.C. 20036 (telephone: 785-3704), which is a project of Ralph Nader's Center for the Study of Responsive Law; and the Project on National Security and Civil Liberties, 122 Maryland Avenue, NE, Washington, D.C. 20002 (telephone: 544-5380), an organization sponsored by the American Civil Liberties Union and the Center for National Security Studies. Both organizations distribute, without charge, guides to Freedom-of-Information Act processes. Another useful guide can be found in the October 1975 issue of the American Historical Association *Newsletter.* A particularly useful source of information on declassified government documents, Carrollton Press, is described in Appendix II-entry 13.

A final note: Researchers should be forewarned that the government's bureaucratic structures are labyrinthine and subject to frequent reorganization. (Indeed, as this volume went to press the Agency for International Development and Energy Department were in the process of major reorganizations. In addition, various agencies within the "national intelligence community" regularly reorganize their internal structures precisely in order to disguise their functional activities and confuse foreign observers.) As a result, many of the office names and telephone numbers listed in the entries which follow are highly subject to change and must be considered somewhat transitory.

J1   Agency for International Development (AID)

1. a. *State Department Building*
        320 21st Street, NW
        Washington, D.C. 20523
        655-4000 (Information)
        632-1850 (Freedom-of-Information and Public Inquiries)

    b. Not open to the public. Visitors are admitted on an appointment basis.

2.   An agency of the State Department, AID directs the foreign economic assistance programs of the United States. Development assistance—largely in the form of loans, grants, and technical training services—focuses on agriculture, nutrition, population planning, health care, education, housing, and development planning. Recipients are primarily the poorest of the less-developed countries (those with average annual per capita incomes below $520).

        The vast bulk of AID's research is produced under contract and research grant by universities and research centers. The Bureau for Latin America, Bureau for Development Support, and Bureau for Program and Policy Coordination (discussed below) each contract for Latin American-related research and periodically engage academic specialists as consultants in the fields listed above.

3.   See "Libraries" section, entry A3.

4.   The internal records and unpublished reports in the files of AID bureaus and offices are periodically turned over to the agency's Communications and Records Management Division for transfer to storage facilities in the Washington National Records Center (Suitland, Maryland) where they will eventually be made available to researchers by the National Archives and Records Service. Both the AID Records Management staff (632-8518) and the originating agency offices maintain shelflist-indexes of retired documents. Researchers may be able to gain access to these shelflists by contacting AID Freedom of Information officer Arnold H. Dadian in the Office of Public Affairs.

AID's small Freedom of Information office (632-1850) is most cooperative in helping outside researchers gain access to classified AID documents. The staff works aggressively for public disclosure of records in declassification-review decisions within the agency. An estimated 95 percent of materials requested under FOI are released to the researcher. Released materials may be inspected by the researcher in the staff's office.

A large number of agency research studies (published and unpublished, classified and unclassified), program reports, and project files are available in the AID Reference Center (see entry A3).

5. a-b. Summaries of agency-sponsored research studies are published in the quarterly *A.I.D. Research and Development Abstracts,* which contains information on how to purchase a full paper- or microfiche copy of any study listed therein. A projected multivolume series, *Research Literature for Development,* will provide similar abstracts of cumulative AID-sponsored research produced since 1962, by subject. Volume 1, *Food Production and Nutrition* (1976), has been published. AID-funded research projects are listed in a semiannual index, *Current Technical Service Contracts and Grants.* Copies of these publications can be obtained from the Bureau for Development Support (235-8936).

The *A.I.D. Bibliography Series* consists, to date, of 28 subject bibliographies on specialized aspects of agriculture, education, health, industrial development, development administration, technical-assistance methodology, and civic participation. Copies are available in the AID Reference Center (632-9345).

Copies of the agency's annual budget presentation and program review to Congress, *Fiscal Year Submission to the Congress* (including a volume on Latin American programs), can be obtained from the Office of Public Affairs (632-8628), which also distributes two periodicals: *War on Hunger,* a monthly bulletin containing short articles, transcripts of speeches, news notes, and reviews on topics in international development; and *Front Lines,* an internal agency newsletter issued every three weeks. *Development Digest,* a quarterly journal of excerpts, summaries, and reprints of current materials on social and economic development, is available by subscription. A descriptive brochure, *AID's Challenge in an Interdependent World* (1977), is available on request.

Other publications are described below, under their originating office.

BUREAU FOR LATIN AMERICA (LA)   632-8246

AID country-desk officers in the Office of Central American Affairs (632-0156) and Office of South American Affairs (632-0181) are a primary source of country-specific information on U.S. aid programs, the operations of USAID field missions, current economic conditions, and development activities in their countries of responsibility. They can provide researchers with unclassified agency materials, including "working documents," "program evaluation studies," and *Development Assistance Program* ("DAP") field reports from USAID missions surveying development activities and general conditions in their host countries. The desk-officer can also place researchers in contact with appropriate sectoral specialists within the agency.

Office of Development Resources (LA/DR) 632-9148

The various functional units of this office—the Development Finance Division (632-3620), Education/Human Resources Division (632-9394), Rural Development Division (632-8128), Health/Nutrition/Population Coordination Division (632-9146), and Multisectoral Activities Division (632-1205)—monitor and evaluate AID development projects in Latin America from a broad sectoral perspective. They review project proposals received from field missions and prepare 50-300-page "issues papers" (usually unclassified) analyzing the proposed projects. The office also produces "inter-country studies" evaluating projects within a single sector of development activity in three or four countries. In addition, staff members can provide researchers with field-produced "sectoral assessments" of single categories of development activity in individual countries (e.g., "Health: El Salvador").

Office of Development Programs (LA/DP) 632-3362

The budget and program-management unit of the Bureau for Latin America, this office prepares the Latin American section of AID's annual *Fiscal Year Submission to the Congress*. It also studies loan terms and other operational aspects of regional policy issues, and has primary responsibility within the bureau for liaison with the Inter-American Development Bank, the World Bank/IMF, and other organizations (including CARE and the AFL-CIO).

BUREAU FOR DEVELOPMENT SUPPORT (DSB) 632-8558

This functional bureau provides technical expertise and support to USAID field missions throughout the world. Its offices are structured in accordance with the sectors of development-assistance in which the agency is active. Each office designs, coordinates, and manages AID contract-research studies in its sector of specialization. Within each office there can usually be found one or more staff members with technical expertise in Latin American aspects of their field of specialization. (All offices, unless otherwise noted, are in the Rosslyn Plaza building, 1601 Kent Street, Arlington, Virginia 22209.)

Office of Urban Development (DSB/UD) 235-8902

Interested in city planning, urban finance and tax-revenue programs, credit facilities, employment, regional village patterns and migration trends, and the development of agricultural marketing centers and commercial and public enterprises.

Office of Rural Development (DSB/RD) 235-8918

Studies components of integrated rural-development programs: agricultural production, financial markets, rural credit facilities, income-generation, social services, transportation, health care, education, and nongovernmental forms of local participation.

Office of Agriculture (DSB/AGR) 235-8945

Concerned with agricultural economics, soil and water management (e.g., fertilizer, irrigation) food crop production, livestock production (including animal husbandry, disease, and range management), and commercial development of fisheries (both inland and coastal) in poor regions.

Office of Education and Human Resources (DSB/EHR) 235-9015

Deals with all aspects of "outreach" training (farmers, paramedics, teachers, etc.), nonformal education programs, radio/television education systems, and educational technology.

Office of Development Administration (DSB/DA) 235-9027

Focuses on improving the inter-sectoral development-planning and management capabilities of government ministries, and the training of public administrators and managers.

Office of Nutrition (DSB/N) 235-8927

Interested in malnutrition levels, food fortification, vitamin deficiencies and their alleviation, and food technology, particularly the development of weaning-foods.

Office of Health (DSB/H) 235-8929

Concerned with environmental sanitation, water-supply systems, and other health-related development projects.

Office of Science and Technology (DSB/OST) 235-9046

Involved with development technologies and engineering: agricultural mechanization, solar energy development, etc.

Office of Population (DSB/POP) 235-9677

Latin American Divison
Room 316, Rosslyn Plaza "E"
1621 North Kent Street
Arlington, Virginia 22209

The Latin American Division of the Office of Population assists AID missions in Latin America in the design and development of family-planning projects, public-awareness educational programs, training programs for community health leaders, health administrators, physicians, nurses, midwives, etc., and clinic-development programs. It can provide researchers with current Latin American demographic data, as can the Office of Population's Demographic Data and Analysis Division (235-9692), which produces AID population studies and participates in the designing of world fertility surveys.

Office of Development Information (DSB/DI) 235-9207
Room 570, Pomponio Plaza
1735 North Lynn Street
Arlington, Virginia 22209

This office constitutes a "memory bank" for AID missions and project designers. It administers the AID Reference Center and Technical Information Center (see entry A3), and manages the computerized Development

Information System data base for AID project materials (see entry G1). The office can assist researchers in identifying and obtaining project papers (feasibility studies, evaluations, etc.), AID contract research studies, and development-assistance data, by country or development activity. It produces the quarterly *A.I.D. Research and Development Abstracts* and the *Research Literature for Development* series. It also plans to prepare a series of "project histories" summarizing and evaluating the performance of individual AID field missions, as well as a series of "information packages" analyzing AID development programs by subject-area (with bibliographies).

BUREAU FOR PROGRAM AND POLICY COORDINATION (PPC) 632-0482

Charles Montrie, Latin American Regional Coordinator   632-8952

Functional offices within this bureau—notably the Office of Policy Development and Analysis (632-8382) and Office of Development Program Review and Evaluation (632-8594)—provide macro-level policy recommendations, administrative studies, foreign-aid effectiveness analyses, and program reviews for the AID Administrator. A Latin American Regional Coordinator serves as a channel of liaison between the global policy perspectives of this bureau and the regional policy interests of the Bureau for Latin America.

Office of Program Information and Analysis Services (PPC/PIAS)
Statistics and Reports Division   235-9836
Room 669, Pomponio Plaza
1735 North Lynn Street
Arlington, Virginia 22209

The Statistics and Reports Division of the Office of Program Information and Analysis Services produces several unclassified statistical publications of interest to Latin Americanists. An annually updated *U.S. Overseas Loans and Grants, and Assistance from International Organizations: Obligations and Loan Authorizations, July 1, 1945-*   contains statistical tables for Latin America (by region and country) itemizing U.S. economic and military assistance for the periods 1946-1948, 1949-1952, 1953-1961, 1962-1969, and annually beginning in 1970, with a supplement listing assistance received from the major international lending institutions during equivalent time periods. A periodically updated, looseleaf *A.I.D. Economic Data Book: Latin America* contains statistical series of social and economic indicators (including population trends, national product, agricultural production, foreign trade, commodity exports, international reserves, student enrollment, and consumer prices) by region and country, with time series extending back to 1960 and earlier for many categories. Selected statistics from this publication are provided in *Latin American Economic Growth Trends* (1977) and the annual *Selected Economic Data for the Less Developed Countries* (the latter containing regional comparisons for Latin America, Africa, and Asia). A periodically updated *Food and Total Agricultural Production in Less Developed Countries, 1950-*   provides statistical indexes of food and other agricultural production (gross and per capita) for Latin America, by country. *Operations Report,* a periodical which terminated publication in 1973, contained extensive, detailed statistical data on U.S. economic-aid programs in Latin America (loans, technical assistance, disaster relief, etc.), by country, for the period 1948-1973.

The staff will assist researchers in obtaining statistical information on Latin America.

OFFICE OF REIMBURSABLE DEVELOPMENT PROGRAMS (AA/RDP)

Michael L. Dilegge, Regional Program Officer for Latin America   632-7937

AID's Reimbursable Development Program arranges for former U.S. aid-recipient nations in Latin America which have advanced into "middle-income" status (and are consequently ineligible for further U.S. aid funds) to purchase continued technical and training services from the United States. Venezuela is currently the leading Latin American customer.

OFFICE OF WOMEN IN DEVELOPMENT (AA/WID)   632-3992

This unit conducts, and contracts for, research on women in the development process, primarily from a regional-level and broader comparative perspective. Recent research has centered on the measurement of women's contributions to household and community economies in the developing world. The office is developing a roster of private academic specialists available for service as technical consultants to AID field missions for women-in-development projects.

OFFICE OF FOOD-FOR-PEACE (FFP)   235-9220

Room 549, Pomponio Plaza
1735 North Lynn Street
Arlington, Virginia 22209

This office administers U.S. food-aid programs, under funding from the Agriculture Department. Food aid is supplied to Latin America both on a bilateral, government-to-government basis (Bolivia, Peru), and through U.S. voluntary assistance organizations (CARE, Catholic Relief Services, Seventh Day Adventists, etc.) primarily in Central America and the Caribbean. Programs include preschool feeding, school lunch programs, "food-for-work" programs (food as payment to unskilled laborers on development projects), and disaster relief.

OFFICE OF UNITED STATES FOREIGN DISASTER ASSISTANCE (OFDA) 632-8924

The U.S national coordinating center for public and private relief efforts during natural disasters in Latin America and elsewhere. The office prepares an annual report, *Foreign Disaster Emergency Relief*.

OFFICE OF LABOR AFFAIRS (OLAB)   632-3662

The principal AID/State Department unit for liaison with the AFL-CIO and its Latin American activities (see entry I 9).

Note: Also see entries A3, F1, G1, and G2.

J2   Agriculture Department (USDA)

1.   a.   *Independence Avenue between 12th and 14th Streets, SW*
         Washington, D.C. 20250
         447-2791 (Public Affairs)

   b.   Open to the public. Appointments recommended.

2.   USDA participates in U.S. food-aid, commodity-sales, and agricultural-development programs in Latin America. Several of its divisions (discussed below) collect information and conduct research on Latin American agricultural conditions. Virtually all research is produced in-house.

3.   See National Agricultural Library, entry A35.

4.   There is no centralized USDA records-management facility. The internal records of each departmental subunit remain in that unit's files until they ultimately reach the National Archives.

5.   USDA publications are described below.

FOREIGN AGRICULTURAL SERVICE (FAS)   447-3448 (Information)
USDA South Building
14th Street and Independence Avenue, SW

John McDonald, Western Hemisphere Area Officer—Attaché Service
    447-2688/2690

The Foreign Agricultural Service maintains agricultural attachés in U.S. embassies and consulates throughout Latin America. These attachés serve as sources of current information on agricultural production, market conditions, trade, and host-government policies. Their reports, almost all of which are unclassified, can be obtained by private researchers from the FAS Communications, Reports, and Records office (447-6135). The FAS Western Hemisphere Area Officer can place researchers in contact with attachés in Latin America.

Foreign Commodity Analysis
Brice Meeker, Director   447-7233

Agricultural economists of this FAS unit analyze world agricultural commodities from the standpoint of production, trade, competition, marketing, prices, consumption, etc. The unit is organized into divisions for individual commodity groups, and includes a Cotton division (447-6271), Dairy, Livestock, and Poultry division (447-7217), Fruit and Vegetable division (447-5330), Grain and Feed division (447-6219), Oilseeds and Products division (447-7037), Sugar and Tropical Products division (447-3423), and Tobacco division (447-3000). Although each division's focus is worldwide, there are usually individual staff members with special expertise on Latin American commodities.

FAS publications, all of which are available to researchers without charge, include:
    Foreign Agriculture, a weekly magazine containing articles on world food topics.
    Weekly Roundup of World Food Production and Trade, a regular news-release summarizing international agricultural developments.
    Foreign Agricultural Circulars, an irregularly issued series of reports containing data on the principal commodities in world trade (including coffee, sugar, cocoa, fruits, and livestock).
    Miscellaneous *Special Reports*—including studies of cotton production in Mexico, Central America, Brazil, and Colombia, the South American tobacco industry, Brazilian citrus processing, Mexican horticultural exports, and the Peruvian fishmeal industry.

Recent issues of each publication can be obtained from the FAS Information Division (447-3448). The FAS Foreign Information Publications section (447-7937) maintains file copies of every FAS report published since 1951.

ECONOMICS, STATISTICS, AND COOPERATIVES SERVICE (ESCS)

500 12th Street, SW   447-8038 (Information)

Foreign Demand and Competition Division   447-8219
Developing Countries Program Area
Howard Hall, Latin American Project Leader   447-8133

Within the Economics, Statistics, and Cooperatives Service (ESCS), which absorbed the former Economic Research Service and several other USDA units, the Foreign Demand and Competition Division has primary responsibility for foreign economic research. Within the Foreign Demand and Competition Division's Developing Countries Program Area, a small Latin American group conducts research on Latin American agricultural and general economic conditions, market developments, monetary and trade conditions, and governmental policies affecting the export of U.S. farm products. Staff economists (one each for Mexico/Central America, Caribbean/north coast of South America, Brazil/Andean republics, and the southern cone) will provide information and open their files to researchers.

The Latin American unit produces: *Western Hemisphere Agricultural Situation,* an annual review and forecast of Latin American economic conditions and policy changes, by country and agricultural sector; an annual *Indices of Agricultural Production for the Western Hemisphere, Excluding the United States and Cuba,* containing 10-year series of annual agricultural-production data, by commodity and country; and miscellaneous research reports, including *Agricultural Trade of the Western Hemisphere, A Statistical Review, 1963-1973* (1975), and various country studies, agricultural sector analyses, and trade projections. The unit also contributes regional data to several other ESCS periodical publications, including: the monthly *Foreign Agricultural Trade of the United States,* containing import and export statistics by commodity group and country; *World Economic Conditions in Relation to Agricultural Trade,* a semiannual review of economic conditions in both the developed and developing countries; the quarterly *Outlook for U.S. Agricultural Exports,* by commodity and world region; the annual *Handbook of Agricultural Charts;* and trimestral *World Agricultural Situation* reports. No comprehensive research bibliography is maintained, but copies of recent publications can be obtained from the unit itself or from the ESCS Publications Unit (447-7255). The Publications Unit maintains a comprehensive card index of ESCS foreign economic research publications. A fairly complete collection of such publications is available in the National Agricultural Library.

National Economic Analysis Division
Agricultural History Branch
Wayne Rasmussen, Supervisory Historian   447-8183

The "Ag. History" Branch maintains two major reference aids of potential significance to Latin Americanists. The first is a bibliographic card index of books and articles on agricultural history, foreign as well as domestic, with Latin American country-divisions. The second is an extensive vertical file of policy documents relating to the agricultural programs of USDA and other

U.S. government agencies since World War II, with substantial material on U.S. food-aid and agricultural-development programs overseas. Both reference aids are available to outside researchers.

Within the "Ag. History" Branch is a Documentation Center (447-2474), which maintains a computerized bibliographic data base on agricultural economic topics. The data base is a component part of the National Agricultural Library's AGRICOLA system (see entry A35), and can be accessed without charge through the library's terminals.

INTERNATIONAL DEVELOPMENT STAFF (IDS) 447-7393

USDA South Building
14th Street and Independence Avenue, SW

Kenneth Laurent, Technical Assistance Program Leader for Latin America 235-2294

USDA's International Development Staff supplies technical-assistance advisers for Latin American agricultural-development projects sponsored by the U.S. Agency for International Development, OAS, Inter-American Development Bank, World Bank, and United Nations' Food and Agriculture Organization. It also coordinates agricultural training programs for foreign nationals in the United States.

Sector Analysis
Robert House, Director 447-5925

This unit of IDS produces Latin American agricultural and farm-policy assessments, under contract with AID. The staff's agricultural economists have designed and evaluated detailed, farm-level field surveys of Guatemala and the Dominican Republic. The survey data-sets—covering agricultural practices, labor and crop-production patterns, farm income, rural household composition, land use and tenancy, marketing, credit, etc.—are available to private researchers, as are most of the unit's other "working documents," including agricultural assessments of Bolivia, Haiti, and Jamaica. The staff has also produced bibliographies of data sources pertaining to agricultural development in Bolivia, Haiti, and Jamaica (also available on request). Much of the unit's data has been collected in the field from Latin American government sources.

USDA/USAID Reports and Technical Inquiries Group 447-2893

This unit provides technical-information support to U.S. field missions engaged in agricultural-assistance projects overseas. Its reference collection —consisting of monographs, IDS studies, a vertical file of U.S. technical-assistance field-mission reports by country, and a separate country-file of miscellaneous reports from U.S. and Latin American government agencies and international organizations—is open to private researchers. Holdings date from the early 1960s.

OFFICE OF THE GENERAL SALES MANAGER (OGSM) 447-2612

USDA South Building
14th Street and Independence Avenue, SW

Charles Delaplane, Coordinator for Latin America 447-7797

USDA's Office of the General Sales Manager administers, in collaboration with the Agency for International Development, U.S. food-aid and food-sales programs in Latin America. It also monitors the foreign sales of private U.S. agricultural exporters. The office publishes an annual report, *Food for Peace,* containing descriptive and statistical data on U.S. food aid to Latin America, by country. It also produces *U.S. Export Sales,* a weekly statistical bulletin of information on the commercial sales of private U.S. food exporters.

Note: Also see entry G3.

Air Force Department See entry J8

J3   Arms Control and Disarmament Agency (ACDA)

1.   a.   *State Department Building*
320 21st Street, NW
Washington, D.C. 20451
632-9504/9505 (Public Affairs)

b.   The agency's offices are not open to the public. Visits should be arranged in advance.

2.   Although the U.S. Arms Control and Disarmament Agency's primary function centers on the negotiation of arms-limitation agreements with the Soviet Union, the agency also monitors weapons buildups and the flow of arms trade in the Third World. ACDA's Latin American specialist is Lorna Watson (632-8651), who works jointly in the agency's Weapons Evaluation and Control Branch and its Non-Proliferation Branch. Her fields of specialization include arms transfers to Latin America, multilateral hemispheric arms-control treaties, and regional nuclear nonproliferation. She will confer with private researchers, and can refer them to other pertinent specialists in the State Department and Defense Department.

ACDA's "external research program" has occasionally funded contract-research studies on Third World arms control, weapons transfers, and relationships between domestic economies and levels of national military spending. Latin American external research studies include *Arms Control and Local Conflict: Volume VII—Some Relationships Between U.S. Military Training in Latin America and Weapons Acquisition Patterns* (M.I.T., 1970); *The Control of Local Conflict: Volume II—Latin American Studies* (Browne and Shaw, 1969); and *Possibilities for Arms Control in Latin America: The Armament Policies and National Security Perceptions of Argentina* (Department of Commerce, 1970). Unsolicited research proposals on topics of interest to the agency will be considered. Contact Evalyn Dexter (235-8248) for further information.

3.   The Arms Control and Disarmament Agency Library (in Room 804, 1700 North Lynn Street, Arlington, Virginia 22209) maintains a collection of ACDA publications and unclassified contract-research reports. In addition, within its 8,000-volume general-reference collection are a small number of titles on Third World arms trade, nuclear nonproliferation, and nuclear energy. Researchers should contact librarian Diane Ferguson (235-9550) for permission to use the collection. The library is open 9 A.M.-4:45 P.M., Monday-Friday.

4.   The agency's internal records, including classified research reports, are

controlled by the Office of Administration's Communications Services section (632-8666/0931). A documents index is maintained. Access to classified records, or to the documents index, is possible only through Freedom-of-Information Act processes. Charles Oleszycki (632-0760) is ACDA's Freedom of Information officer.

5. a. Publications include an annual *World Military Expenditures and Arms Transfers* (which includes data for Latin America) and ACDA's annual *Arms Control Report* to Congress. Copies of both can be obtained from the Office of Public Affairs.

   b. The agency's unclassified contract-research reports are listed in an irregular-ly-issued *ACDA External Research Reports*. Also see the periodically-updated list of *Offical Publications of the United States Arms Control and Disarmament Agency.* Copies of each are available from the ACDA Library.

Army Department See entry J8

Canal Zone Government See Panama Canal Company, entry J25

Census Bureau See Commerce Department, entry J5

J4   Central Intelligence Agency (CIA)

1. a. *Langley, Virginia*
   351-1100 (Information)
   351-7676 (Public Affairs)

   Mail: Washington, D.C. 20505

   b. Closed to anyone without a security clearance. The agency occasionally provides tours for large groups (100-500 persons) from academic, business, and other private organizations. Contact the Public Affairs Office for further information.

2. Latin American specialists in the Office of Political Research and Analysis, the National Foreign Assessment Center, and other units monitor and analyze Latin American affairs. They are not regularly accessible to private researchers. Indeed, the main contact-points within CIA for outside researchers are public-affairs advisers (Herbert Hetu, Dale Peterson) in the Public Affairs Office.

   CIA occasionally funds contract research, primarily for technical studies and for research on aspects of methodology and model-building. The agency also utilizes foreign-area specialists as outside consultants for regional studies. Research- and consultant-contracts are administered by the Coordinator for Academic Relations and External Analytical Support, James King (351-5075).

3. The CIA Library (351-7701), which unquestionably contains an outstanding collection of Latin American-related publications and documents, is inaccessible to researchers except through institutional interlibrary-loan channels. The library's unclassified book holdings are indexed in the computerized Ohio College Library Catalog (OCLC), Columbus, Ohio.

4.   CIA internal records are accessible only through Freedom-of-Information Act processes. Information and Privacy Coordinator Gene Wilson (351-7486) handles FOI matters for the agency.

There is currently no centralized collection of CIA records which have been released through Freedom-of-Information Act requests. One useful collection of such documents can be found in the library of the Center for National Security Studies (see entry M10). Researchers should also note that many CIA documents are listed in the *Declassified Documents Quarterly Catalog* published by the commercial Carrollton Press, (see Appendix I-entry 13). Other potential sources of useful information are the staff members of Congressional committees (see entry J6) and of the Congressional Research Service's Foreign Affairs and National Defense Division (entry J7).

Although there are as yet no significant materials in the CIA record-group at the National Archives, the Military Archives Division—Modern Military Branch (entry B6) has assembled a small collection of copies of declassified CIA documents found in the branch's post-World War II military records.

5.   The Central Intelligence Agency produces a number of unclassified publications, including a semiannual *National Basic Intelligence Factbook* (containing political, economic, and military data on foreign countries), a monthly *Chiefs of State and Cabinet Members of Foreign Governments,* a weekly *Economic Indicators,* an *International Energy Biweekly Statistical Review,* a biweekly *International Oil Developments Statistical Survey,* an annual *Communist Aid to the Less Developed Countries of the Free World,* and special individual publications (e.g., a *Directory of the Cuban Government and Mass Organizations; The Cuban Economy: A Statistical Review, 1968-1976,* and a "Cuban Party and Government Leadership" wall chart). These publications are released to the public through the Library of Congress Exchange and Gift Division's "Documents Expediting Project" (426-5253), which makes them available, on an annual commercial-subscription basis, as a package called the "CIA Reference Aid series." For a subscription price of $225 per year, the Documents Expediting Project staff will send subscribers a copy of every publication received from CIA during the forthcoming year (plus a copy of any back issues still on hand). A list of titles included in the series during the past two years is available from the Documents Expediting Project staff, which also maintains a card index to all CIA publications received since the program's inception in 1973. A copy of each publication is also entered into the Library of Congress main collection. (Copies may be purchased through the library's Photoduplication Service [426-5640].) Local Washington-area subscribers to the "CIA Reference Aid series" include the libraries of the University of Maryland, American University, and George Mason University, as well as numerous foreign embassies.

U.S. Government Printing Office bookstores (see Appendix II-entry 13) sell the *National Basic Intelligence Factbook* as well as unclassified CIA-produced maps of foreign countries.

J5 Commerce Department

1. a.   *Main Commerce Building*
       14th Street between Constitution Avenue and E Street, NW
       Washington, D.C. 20230
       377-2000 (Information)

b. Open to the public.

2. Several of the department's subunits (described individually below) focus in part on Latin American commerce and economic conditions. Most research is conducted in-house, although various bureaus within the Industry and Trade Administration occasionally utilize outside contract research, usually employing private domestic or foreign research institutions.

3. The two departmental libraries of primary interest to Latin Americanists—the Commerce Department Library and the Census Bureau Library—are described in the "Libraries" section, entries A13 and A12, respectively. Several other smaller libraries and reference collections are discussed below.

4. Each major Commerce Department subunit has a records-management facility which stores internal records until they are transferred to the National Archives. Inventories of retired office files are maintained. The department's Records Management Division Chief, Ivy Parr (377-3630), can direct researchers to appropriate records-management offices and provide assistance in obtaining retired documents.

Most departmental subunits also maintain a Freedom-of-Information officer. Freedom-of-Information Act requests should be routed through Carolyn Wong, Head of the Central Reference and Records Inspection Facility (377-5659), Information Management Division, Office of Organization and Management Systems, under the Office of the Secretary of Commerce.

5. The Commerce Department's biweekly news magazine, *Commerce America,* contains reports on foreign and domestic business conditions. There is a semiannual issue devoted to the world trade outlook, with a section of Latin American country reports. An annual *Commerce Publications Catalog and Index* lists the department's major publication series. Contact the Office of Publications (377-3721) for copies.

Other publications and bibliographies are discussed below, under their originating offices.

INDUSTRY AND TRADE ADMINISTRATION (ITA)
377-5087/3808 (*Information*)

The primary mission of the Industry and Trade Administration (formerly the Domestic and International Business Administration) is "to provide both information and direct aid to U.S. businesses, especially in encouraging development of export markets."

Bureau of International Economic Policy and Research (BIEPR) 377-3022

This bureau is the primary center within the Commerce Department for the monitoring of Latin American economic affairs. It is also responsible for most of the department's international economic research, analysis, and policy-drafting.

Office of Country Affairs 377-4506

Country specialists in the newly-created Office of Country Affairs monitor trade and economic patterns in Latin America. The office should constitute the Latin Americanist's primary contact- and referral-point within the Commerce Department.

Office of International Economic Research   377-5638

This office assembles and analyzes U.S. and foreign trade and economic data. Subjects covered include broad, worldwide trade developments and trends, sector analyses, export projections, and international economic indicators. A "Staff Economic Report" series is published. It includes *U.S. Trade With Developing Economies: The Growing Importance of Manufactured Goods* (1975); a classified study, *Capital Requirements of the Non-OPEC Less Developed Countries* (1976); a bibliography of *Selected Basic References on Trade Barriers and International Trade Flows* (1976); and a periodically updated, annotated bibliography, *Survey of Current International Economic Research.* The office also publishes a monthly analysis of *Trends in U.S. Foreign Trade* containing Latin American data by country and commodity; an annual *Market Share Reports* series (by country) comparing U.S. performance in 900 manufactured products with that of 13 other major supplier nations; and a quarterly statistical report, *International Economic Indicators,* which provides comparative domestic data on the United States and its seven major northern-hemisphere trading competitors.

The unit has two reference facilities, both of which are open to the public. Its World Trade Reference Room (377-4855), located in room 5899-A, contains a collection of the official trade-statistics publications of every foreign government in the world, with holdings dating back four years. The U.S. Foreign Trade Reference Room (377-2185), located in room 5889, has detailed U.S. Census Bureau statistics (both published and unpublished) on U.S. foreign trade back to 1940.

Office of International Trade Policy   377-5327

The Office of International Trade Policy assists in the development of U.S. positions in international trade negotiations. It monitors and analyzes developments related to foreign tariffs, import-quota systems, and international commodity agreements. The office publishes progress reports on multilateral trade negotiations in the department's bi-weekly *Commerce America.*

Office of International Finance and Investment   377-4925

This office monitors and analyzes worldwide activity in the fields of international lending, debt problems, taxation, technology transfer, antitrust matters, expropriations, and other investment disputes. The office's two-volume report, *The Multinational Corporation: Studies on U.S. Foreign Investment* (1972-1973), is available on request.

Bureau of Export Development (BED)   377-5261

The Bureau of Export Development (formerly the Bureau of International Commerce) coordinates U.S. trade-promotion programs overseas and promotes increased export activity within the U.S. domestic economy.

Office of International Marketing   377-4231

Latin American "country marketing managers" (one each for Brazil/River Plate, Mexico/Central America, and the Andean Region/Caribbean) within the Office of International Marketing coordinate U.S. trade-promotion activities in Latin America (including the operation of a U.S. Trade Center in Sao Paulo, Brazil). The office produces, almost entirely through foreign contract research, in-depth foreign-country market-research surveys and studies. It also publishes an "International Marketing Information Series" of periodicals designed to assist U.S. businessmen in their overseas operations. Included in the series are:

Foreign Economic Trends and Their Implications for the United States —individual, annual or semiannual country-reports from U.S. embassies, containing statistical data (with time-series extending back 4-5 years) on income, production, employment, money and prices, balance of payments, and trade, plus a narrative summary of the current economic situation and trends as they affect prospects for U.S. business interests.

Overseas Business Reports—annually updated country-reports (with separate series on basic economic data, foreign trade regulations, marketing, and selling), plus a series on the world trade outlook by region (including Latin America), and miscellaneous reports (including *The Caribbean Free Trade Association* [1972], *The Andean Common Market: Implications for U.S. Business* [1973], and *The Caribbean Community and Common Market: The Implications for U.S. Business* [1975]).

Country Market Sectoral Surveys—individual analyses of the most promising U.S. industrial-export opportunities in various foreign countries (including Brazil and Venezuela).

Global Market Surveys—analyses of the 20-30 best foreign markets for a single U.S. industry or group of industries.

The office maintains an International Marketing Information Center (377-2470) containing recent copies of the unit's published and unpublished reports. This facility, located in room 4051, is open to researchers. Many of the Office of International Marketing's published and unpublished reports are also available for purchase from the National Technical Information Service (see Appendix II-entry 11).

Office of Export Development   377-5131

This office provides counseling and information services to U.S. businesses on foreign export markets and investment opportunities. Its *Foreign Market Reports* series contains data (received from U.S. State Department Foreign Service officers or from private foreign contract-research organizations) on foreign economic conditions, by country. A monthly index is sold by subscription. The office also prepares, on request, "World Traders Data Reports" describing the history, operations, sales, territories, business connections, and chief executives of individual foreign business firms.

The unit's Export Information Reference Room (377-2997), located in room 1063, contains, in addition to *Foreign Market Reports,* a variety of current World Bank and Inter-American Development Bank unpublished reports and papers which may not be available to private researchers elsewhere—including monthly operational summaries of loans under consideration by both banks, appraisal reports on bank-funded projects, and World Bank economic and country studies. The facility is open to the public.

Bureau of East-West Trade (BEWT)   377-5251

The Bureau of East-West Trade promotes increased U.S. trade links with the centrally planned economies of communist nations. Staff economist Larry Theriot (377-4422) monitors Cuban commerce, trade, market potential, and export capabilities. A bureau publication, *United States Commercial Relations with Cuba* (1975), is currently being updated.

BUREAU OF THE CENSUS   763-7662 (Information)
Suitland Road and Silver Hill Road
Suitland, Maryland
Mail: Department of Commerce
Washington, D.C. 20233

The Census Bureau generates a considerable quantity of Latin American demographic and foreign-trade statistics. A daily shuttle-service links the bureau's various offices with the Main Commerce Building in downtown Washington.

Foreign Trade Division   763-5342
Federal Office Building 3
Suitland, Maryland

This unit compiles detailed statistical data (primarily from shippers' export declarations and U.S. customs entries) on the quantity and value of U.S. exports and imports, by commodity and country of destination or origin. The results appear in a series of monthly publications: *U.S. Exports, U.S. General Imports, Highlights of U.S. Export and Import Trade, U.S. Waterborne Exports and General Imports,* and *U.S. Airborne Exports and General Imports.* A periodically updated *Guide to Foreign Trade Statistics* describes the contents of these publications. Most of the division's published statistical tabulations are also available on both microform and computer tape. The *Guide to Foreign Trade Statistics* has commercial ordering instructions.

The unit's Trade Information Office (763-5140) can provide reference information on U.S.-Latin American trade for the latest five-year period. The Trade Information Office also handles computer-tape and microform sales.

Population Division
International Demographic Statistics Staff   763-2870
Scuderi Building
4235 28th Avenue
Marlow Heights, Maryland 20031

The Population Division's International Demographic Statistics country-analysts compile (from Latin American censuses and other official statistical publications) in-depth current data on a broad range of Latin American socioeconomic and demographic indicators. The unit's annual publication *World Population* presents figures for total population and vital rates (births, deaths, growth rates), by country, 1950-present. A "Country Demographic Profiles" series provides more detailed statistics (for total population, age-sex distribution, projections of women of child-bearing age, urban population, marital status, migration, fertility, mortality, family planning, number and size of households, education, land use, labor force by industry and occupation, and other selected indicators) for individual nations, including—thus far—Costa Rica, Jamaica, Guatemala, Panama, Honduras, Chile, Mexico, and Brazil. The unit also publishes occasional "International Research Documents," among them *Demographic Estimates Based on the 1970 Population Census of Brazil* and *Projections of the Rural and Urban Populations of Colombia, 1965-2000.* Staff analysts maintain country-notebooks and files of background data, and will provide reference and research assistance to scholars.

The unit's International Demographic Data Center (763-2834) stores data on microfilm, and can supply researchers with hard-copy Latin American demographic statistics (often in considerably greater depth than those produced in the unit's publications) dating back to roughly 1955.

BUREAU OF ECONOMIC ANALYSIS (BEA)   523-0777 (Information)
Tower Building
14th and K Streets, NW
Washington, D.C. 20230

The Bureau of Economic Analysis monitors the state of the U.S. domestic economy, including the nation's international transactions (trade, private capital flows, changes in official reserve assets, foreign aid, transportation, travel, etc.). Its monthly *Survey of Current Business* periodically contains economic data relating to Latin America. The bureau's small Reference Room (523-0595), located in room B-7, contains a full collection of BEA periodicals and staff papers.

International Investment Divison   523-0660/0661

The International Investment Division measures U.S. direct investments overseas and analyzes the economic impact of multinational corporations. Its primary data consist of confidential quarterly reports from U.S. corporations with foreign investments. The division publishes aggregated annual statistics (with Latin American investment figures broken down by country or subregion) in the bureau's *Survey of Current Business.* In addition, it has produced "benchmark censuses" entitled *U.S. Direct Investment Abroad* for the years 1966 and 1977, containing data—by industry and world area—on the value of U.S. overseas investment, the directly measurable balance-of-payments transactions between U.S. companies and their foreign affiliates, foreign affiliates' shares of U.S. companies' earnings, the portion of that share reinvested in foreign affiliates, and foreign affiliates' finances and operations. Also see the division's *Revised Data Series on U.S. Direct Investment Abroad, 1966-1974* (1976), containing data on net capital outflows, reinvestment earnings, balance-of-payment income, earnings, fees and royalties. A *Special Survey of U.S. Multinational Companies, 1970* (1972) presents balance-sheet, income-account, employment, and trade data, for 1966 and 1970, on U.S. multinationals and their foreign affiliates.

The staff can provide researchers with aggregate data on U.S. private investments in Latin America, by country and industry, back to the late 1940s. It cannot, however, compromise the confidentiality of its reporting corporations by providing information on the investments of individual companies.

The unit's raw data are transferred to computer tapes for storage. Private researchers are permitted limited access to the tapes, on a commercial basis. Contact the division's Data Retrieval and Analysis Branch (523-0981) for further information.

Balance of Payments Division   523-0620

This division prepares current statistics and analyses of the United States' balance of international payments and the nation's international investment position. Results are published quarterly in issues of the *Survey of Current Business.* Included are regional totals for Latin America, with country totals only for Venezuela.

MARITIME ADMINISTRATION
Main Commerce Building

Office of Trade Studies and Statistics   377-4758

The Maritime Administration's Office of Trade Studies and Statistics compiles statistical data—from private U.S. commercial shippers' reports and other sources—on U.S. ocean-borne trade with Latin America and on Latin American merchant shipping, by country. Data are available to researchers in hard copy or computer files. The office produces several annual publications which contain Latin American data, including: *Merchant Fleets of the World, A Statistical Analysis of the World's Merchant Fleets, New Ship Construction,* and *Essential U.S. Trade Routes.*

Office of International Activities   377-5685

This office is responsible for maintaining U.S. maritime relations with Latin American governments. It administers an "equal-access" agreement with Brazil.

NATIONAL OCEANIC AND ATMOSPHERIC ADMINISTRATION (NOAA)
Washington Science Center
Rockville, Maryland 20852

International Relations   443-8761

The International Relations staff can refer researchers to NOAA's extensive technical climatological, meteorological, oceanographic, and marine-resources data-gathering activities relating to Latin America.

Library and Information Services Divison   443-8330 (Reference)

NOAA possesses large library holdings pertaining to the atmospheric and earth sciences, oceanography, hydrology, fisheries, etc. The collection is dispersed among several library centers throughout the metropolitan area. Library and Information Services Division personnel answer inquiries regarding collection contents and center locations. ·

National Marine Fisheries Service
Office of the Assistant Director for International Fisheries
International Analysis and Services Division 634-7267/7307
Page Building No. 2, 3300 Whitehaven Street, NW
Washington, D.C. 20235

The International Analysis and Services Division of NOAA's National Marine Fisheries Service collects extensive data on Latin American and Caribbean fishing. Subjects covered include the economics of fishing, trade, marketing, government policies and agencies, and international disputes. The unit's information sources are Latin American government publications and foreign trade journals, as well as U.S. government data. Its files are arranged by country and subject, and include photographs and maps.

PATENT AND TRADEMARK OFFICE
2021 Jefferson Davis Highway
Arlington, Virginia 22202

Office of Legislation and International Affairs   557-3065
Crystal Plaza, Building 6

This office collects published materials on foreign patent and trademark laws and regulations. Staff members can provide reference information relating to Latin America.

Patent Office Scientific Library   557-2957 (Reference)
Crystal Plaza, Building 3

The library collects the published patents and/or periodicals containing abstracts of patents from every Latin American nation which publishes such materials. (Mexican holdings date back to 1891; Argentine holdings begin in 1921.) The collection constitutes a significant resource for research on Latin American science and technology. The staff has compiled an inventory of its foreign holdings, by country. Card catalogs are also available. Contact Barrington Balthrop, Chief of the library's Foreign Patent Services and Records Section (557-2970) for further information.

J6   Congress

1. a. *The Capitol*
        Washington, D.C. 20510
        224-3121

    b. The Senate and House of Representatives galleries, as well as most committee hearings, are open to the public.

2. Both houses of Congress are normally in session throughout the year, with periodic recesses intervening. Congressional committees and subcommittees seldom adhere to a formal fixed schedule in holding meetings and hearings. Those committees and subcommittees with jurisdiction over inter-American matters are listed below. Committee staff members are usually willing to confer with private researchers. Announcements of forthcoming committee activities—including locations and subject matter—appear in the "Daily Digest" section of the *Congressional Record*. In addition, the *Washington Post* newspaper each morning publishes a schedule of that day's Congressional activities.

    The Congressional Research Service (see entry J7) serves as the principal research arm of the Congress. Latin American specialists in its Foreign Affairs and National Defense Division can provide information on recent or forthcoming Congressional activities pertaining to inter-American affairs. Another useful source of information on Latin American-related Congressional matters is the Washington Office on Latin America (see entry M39).

3. The Library of Congress is described in the "Libraries" section, entry A33.

5. The proceedings of the Senate and House of Representatives appear in the *Congressional Record,* which is published daily when Congress is in session. Committee publications—including transcripts of hearings, special reports, and other documents—are available from the office of the individual committee's staff. To receive publications issued by a committee, researchers may request to be placed on the committee's mailing list. Committee publications are also available commercially at Government Printing Office bookstores (see Appendix II—entry 13). The Government Printing Office regularly prepares subject-bibliographies of Congressional publications on foreign affairs, U.S. intelligence activities, and other topics of interest to

Latin Americanists. Lists of these bibliographies, as well as the bibliographies themselves, are available without charge.

STANDING COMMITTEES OF THE SENATE

Foreign Relations Committee   224-4651
Dirksen Senate Office Building, Room 4229

Has Subcommittees on Western Hemisphere Affairs, Foreign Assistance, Foreign Economic Policy, International Operations, and Arms Control, Oceans, and International Environment.

Agriculture, Nutrition, and Forestry Committee   224-2035
Russell State Office Building, Room 322

Includes a Subcommittee on Foreign Agricultural Policy.

Appropriations Committee   224-3471
Dirksen Senate Office Building, Room 1235

Has a Subcommittee on Foreign Operations.

Armed Services Committee   224-3871
Russell Senate Office Building, Room 212

Includes a Subcommittee on Intelligence.

Banking, Housing, and Urban Affairs Committee   224-7391
Dirksen Senate Office Building, Room 5300

Has a Subcommittee on International Finance.

Finance Committee   224-4515
Dirksen Senate Office Building, Room 2227

Includes a Subcommittee on International Trade.

STANDING COMMITTEES OF THE HOUSE OF REPRESENTATIVES

International Relations Committee   225-5021
Rayburn House Office Building, Room 2170

Has Subcommittees on Inter-American Affairs, International Development, International Economic Policy and Trade, International Operations, International Organizations, and International Security and Scientific Affairs.

Agriculture Committee   225-2171
Longworth House Office Building, Room 1301

Deals with sugar import quotas, and other inter-American agricultural issues.

Appropriations Committee   225-2771
The Capitol, Room H-218

Includes a Subcommittee on Foreign Operations.

Armed Services Committee   225-4151
Rayburn House Office Building, Room 2120

Has a Subcommittee on Intelligence and Military Application of Nuclear Energy.

Banking, Currency, and Housing Committee   225-4247
Rayburn House Office Building, Room 2129

Includes a Subcommittee on International Development Institutions and Finance and a Subcommittee on International Trade, Investment, and Monetary Policy.

Merchant Marine and Fisheries Committee   225-4047
Longworth House Office Building, Room 1334

Has a Subcommittee on the Panama Canal.

Ways and Means Committee   225-3625
Longworth House Office Building, Room 1102

Includes a Subcommittee on Trade.

JOINT COMMITTEES OF THE CONGRESS

Joint Economic Committee   224-5171
Dirksen Senate Office Building, Room G-133

Has a Subcommittee on International Economics.

Note: In addition, various Select and Special Committees of the Senate or House—notably the Senate's Select Committee on Intelligence (224-1700), the House Permanent Select Committee on Intelligence (225-4121), and the House Select Committee on Population (225-0570)—periodically focus on Latin American-related issues.

J7   Congressional Research Service (CRS)

1.   a.   *Library of Congress, Main Building*
10 1st Street, SE
Washington, D.C. 20540
426-5700

b.   Not open to the public.

2.   The Congressional Research Service provides reference and research assistance to members of Congress and to Congressional committees. Latin American specialists—Barry Sklar (426-5057), Larry Storrs (426-5050), and Roslyn Roberts (426-6003)—in the Foreign Affairs and National Defense Division prepare research reports, background studies, and other materials on Latin American policy issues of current concern in Congress. Their reference and research services are not available to the public.

3.   See Library of Congress, entry A33

4.   CRS research products are considered to be the property of the Congressional member or committee which requested them. They are normally available to private researchers only from the office of a member or committee of Congress. Periodically, CRS research studies are read into the *Congressional Record* or published in a Congressional committee report.

5.   CRS *Issue Briefs* review major policy topics (e.g., Panama Canal, Cuba), summarize the pertinent legislative history, and provide bibliographies for further reading. They are distributed only to members of Congress. A monthly digest of CRS studies, the *CRS Review,* is also sent to members of

Congress. For copies of these publications, researchers should contact the office of one of their Congressional representatives.

In addition, the Congressional Research Service indexes recent periodical articles on public policy issues (including foreign affairs, by country) from some 1,500 journals (primarily U.S.). This "Bibliographic Citation" file is accessible to researchers in machine-readable format through the Library of Congress' SCORPIO automated data base (see entry A33).

J8   Defense Department (DOD)

1. a. *The Pentagon*
   Washington, D.C. 20301
   545-6700 (Information)
   697-9312 (Public Affairs)

   b. Closed to those without a security clearance or an appointment arranged in advance.

2. The Department of Defense (DOD) and its major affiliated components—the Departments of the Army, Navy, and Air Force—conduct little international-affairs research. Most of their activities relating to Latin America are of an operational and classified nature.

3. See Army Library (entry A7) and Navy Department Library (entry A41).

4. Each major subunit of DOD controls its own internal records until they are retired to the jurisdiction of the National Archives. DOD's Records Management Branch (695-0970), under the Office of the Secretary of Defense, can refer researchers to individual records-control facilities within the department.

   A Directorate for Freedom of Information and Security Review (697-4325), in the Office of the Assistant Secretary of Defense for Public Affairs, processes FOI requests for the records of the Office of the Secretary of Defense and the Joint Chiefs of Staff; it can direct researchers to appropriate FOI officers in other DOD subunits, agencies, and services.

5. No unclassified Defense Department publications of primary interest to Latin Americanists were discerned, other than the few mentioned below. Researchers should note, however, that DOD-generated data on Latin American armed forces and U.S. military assistance to Latin America appear in the State Department's *Country Fact Sheets* (see entry J28) and the Agency for International Development's *U.S. Overseas Loans and Grants, and Assistance from International Organizations: Obligations and Loan Authorizations, July 1, 1945-* (entry J1), respectively. The DOD-funded Foreign Area Handbook series, which is prepared by American University's Foreign Area Studies staff, is discussed in entry M4.

OFFICE OF THE ASSISTANT SECRETARY OF DEFENSE FOR INTERNATIONAL SECURITY AFFAIRS (ISA)

Directorate, Inter-American Region
David W. Quant, Deputy Director   697-9301

Inter-American Region "country directors" in ISA are the researcher's best contact-point in the Defense Department. They monitor political-military and economic affairs in Latin America and draft policy-papers for the Secretary of Defense on inter-American relations, including U.S. military assistance and sales. Staff members confer with researchers and will provide them with access to unclassified U.S. military assistance program (MAP) data.

Virtually all of the unit's internal policy papers remain classified. ISA's "external research program," however, contracts defense studies through private research centers. Inter-American studies have not figured significantly in recent contract research, but unsolicited proposals focusing on U.S. defense and national-security topics of particular current concern to the Defense Department will be considered. Unclassified ISA contract-research studies will be made available to researchers. Contact the ISA Director of Policy Research, Jerrold Milsted (697-2682), for further information.

DEFENSE INTELLIGENCE AGENCY (DIA) 697-7072 (Information)
692-5766 (Freedom of Information Service)

Deputy Director for Intelligence Research
Western Division—Latin American Branch 692-5400

DIA coordinates the foreign military intelligence-gathering activities of the U.S. armed forces' three intelligence services: the Army's Assistant Chief of Staff for Intelligence (ACSI), the Office of Naval Intelligence (ONI), and the Air Force Intelligence Service (AFIS). From U.S. embassies throughout Latin America, defense attaches from the three services provide DIA analysts with information on Latin America's armed forces, including their military capabilities, numbers of personnel, deployments, equipment, and political roles, as well as biographic data on leading members of the officer corps. Attache reports remain classified. Analysts in DIA's Latin American Military Capabilities Section (692-6618) might be willing to confer with private researchers within the extremely narrow limits imposed by the agency's stringent security regulations.

A Latin American Section (695-0542) in DIA's Current Intelligence Production Division monitors daily military developments in Latin America, including international tensions, political interventions, and arms purchases.

The DIA Reference Library (962-5311) is closed to outside researchers.

NATIONAL SECURITY AGENCY (NSA) 688-6524 (Information)
Fort George G. Meade, Maryland 20755

One of the "big three" of the U.S. intelligence community (along with CIA and DIA), NSA is perhaps the most secretive. The agency conducts highly technical, communications intelligence-gathering activities worldwide. Its organizational structure remains classified.

DEFENSE SECURITY ASSISTANCE AGENCY 695-3291

Directorate for Operations
Latin American Division 697-0704

The Latin American Division of the Defense Security Assistance Agency implements U.S. military assistance (MAP) programs in Latin America. The agency produces an unclassified *Facts Book* (annual), containing tabular data on U.S. military assistance programs and foreign military sales, by country, for the latest two-year period. The publication may be obtained, without charge, from Stanley Stack, director of the agency's Data Management Division (697-3574).

OFFICE OF THE SECRETARY OF DEFENSE (OSD)

Historian's Office
Alfred Goldberg, Historian 697-4216/4217

The OSD Historian's Office prepares historical studies of the Department of Defense. It maintains a small archive of retired DOD documents and a reference file of unclassified materials (legislative records, DOD publications, press clippings, etc.) relating to the structural evolution of the department, its subagencies, and related military services. The office may be visited by outside researchers on an appointment basis. The staff can provide a variety of reference- and research-assistance services.

The Historian's Office is preparing for publication several historical studies, including a multivolume history of the Office of the Secretary of Defense, a documentary volume on the organizational evolution of the Department of Defense since 1947, a study of the origins of the U.S. military assistance program and NATO, 1948-1951, and a two-volume history of U.S. prisoners of war in southeast Asia.

JOINT CHIEFS OF STAFF (JCS) 695-3241

Plans and Policy Directorate (J-5)
Western Hemisphere Division—Latin American Branch 697-5416

The Latin American branch prepares policy papers and estimates for the Joint Chiefs of Staff relating to U.S. security interests in Latin America—Panama Canal defense, security assistance, military relations, etc. Its products are all classified.

Office of the Secretary of the Joint Chiefs of Staff
Historical Division 697-3088
Documents Division 695-5363

The JCS Historical Division prepares JCS histories and special background studies. Most of its products are classified, although several volumes dealing with the JCS during the 1940s have been declassified and released to the Military Archives Division—Modern Military Branch at the National Archives (see entry B6). In addition to providing reference assistance on the history of the Joint Chiefs of Staff, Chief Historian Robert J. Watson and his staff can assist researchers in identifying and locating JCS documents.

The Historical Division's "archival" materials consist of JCS records held by the JCS Documents Division. This unit reviews internal records for release through the National Archives and handles Freedom-of-Information Act requests involving JCS documents.

ARMY DEPARTMENT 697-2352 (Public Information)

Deputy Chief of Staff for Operations and Plans
Politico-Military Division—Western Hemisphere Regional Branch 695-3852

Latin American desk officers in the Western Hemisphere Regional Branch prepare memoranda and position papers (some unclassified) that contribute to the formulation of Army policy on the full range of issues affecting U.S. security interests in Latin America.

Deputy Chief of Staff for Operations and Plans
Security Assistance Division 697-5293

The Security Assistance Division has administrative authority over the U.S. Army's School of the Americas in the Canal Zone. The division's officer-personnel can assist researchers in obtaining information about the school from the Canal Zone.

Assistant Chief of Staff for Intelligence (ACSI)
Foreign Intelligence Directorate
Western Branch—Latin American Desk   695-9870

ACSI, the Army's intelligence service, has a single Latin American desk officer who monitors developments in Latin America and prepares information papers and Army contributions to national intelligence estimates.

U.S. Army Center of Military History   693-5002
Forrestal Building, Room 6A015
1000 Independence Avenue, SW
Washington, D.C. 20314

Maurice Matloff, Chief Historian

The Center of Military History produces several on-going multivolume series of U.S. Army historical studies, including *United States Army in World War II, United States Army in the Korean War,* and an *Army Lineage* series. A list of *Publications of the U.S. Army Center of Military History* is obtainable from the center.

The center does not maintain any archival collection of military records. It does, however, house a substantial collection of unpublished historical studies (three-fourths of which are unclassified) produced by U.S. Army unit historians. Included are some 70 studies, by Caribbean Defense Command historians, of Latin American wartime affairs and U.S. Army administrative and operational activities in Latin America during World War II.

Staff historians can assist researchers in verifying historical information, compiling bibliographies, and locating military source materials in the National Archives and other depositories, including the extensive Army Military History Research Collection at Carlisle Barracks, Pennsylvania 17013.

The Center of Military History's 25,000-volume reference library contains a large collection of Army publications, regulations, and directories, but very little on Latin America.

NAVY DEPARTMENT   697-4627 (Public Information)

Deputy Chief of Naval Operations (Plans, Policy, and Operations)
Politico-Military Policy Division—Western Hemisphere Branch   695-2492

Latin American desk officers in this unit monitor political/military developments in Latin America and prepare policy papers on issues of particular concern to the U.S. Navy, including arms transfers and security assistance.

Office of Naval Intelligence (ONI)
Plans, Policy, and Estimates Division
Latin America Desk   695-3974

A single Latin American desk officer maintains data on Latin American naval affairs and Soviet naval activities in Latin America.

Naval Historical Center   433-2210/2364
Washington Navy Yard, Building 220
9th and M Streets, SE
Washington, D.C. 20374

William J. Morgan, Head—Historical Research Branch

The Naval Historical Center has produced several publications of potential interest to Latin Americanists, including the multivolume *Dictionary of American Naval Fighting Ships;* a periodically updated *United States Naval History: A Bibliography;* Dean C. Allard and Betty Bern (comps.), *U.S. Naval History Sources in the Washington Area and Suggested Research Subjects* (1970); and Admiral H. G. Rickover's *How the Battleship Maine Was Destroyed* (1976). A list of *Naval Historical Publications in Print* is available on request.

The Historical Research Branch holds a large collection of photocopied naval and maritime documents dating back to the American Revolution. Staff historians can provide reference assistance and research consultation.

[Note: Also see Naval Historical Center-Operational Archives (entry B9) and Naval Historical Center-Photographic Section (entry F17).]

Marine Corps Historical Center   433-3534 (Information)
Washington Navy Yard, Building 58   433-3483 (Reference)
9th and M Streets, SE
Washington, D.C. 20374

Henry J. Shaw, Jr., Historian   433-3839

The Historical Branch of the Marine Corps Historical Center has published several studies of Marine Corps activities overseas, including *The United States Marines in the War With Spain, Marines in the Dominican Republic, 1916-1924, The United States Marines in Nicaragua,* and *One Hundred and Eighty Landings of the United States Marines, 1800-1934.* A *Marine Corps Historical Publications Catalog* is available on request. Staff members of the Histories Section and Reference Section consult with private researchers.

[Note: The Marine Corps Historical Center's Archives, personal-papers and oral-history collections, Still Photo Archive, and reference library are described in the "Archives" section, entry B5.]

AIR FORCE DEPARTMENT   695-5554 (Public Information)

Deputy Chief of Staff (Plans and Operations)
Deputy Director for Plans and Policy—Western Hemisphere Division   695-4152

Latin American desk officers in this unit assist in the formulation of U.S. Air Force policies on inter-American politico-military issues of concern to the Air Force, such as U.S. foreign military sales.

Air Force Intelligence Service (AFIS)
Directorate of Threat Applications
Latin American Desk   694-5261

Two Latin American analysts monitor current events and maintain technical data (on Latin American aircraft, airfields, etc.) on topics of interest to the U.S. Air Force.

Office of Air Force History   693-7399
Forrestal Building, Room 8E082
1000 Independence Avenue, SW
Washington, D.C. 20374

Stanley L. Falk, Chief Historian

Staff historians of this office prepare Air Force historical studies (largely classified). They will provide reference services and can assist researchers in locating Air Force records.

[Note: The Office of Air Force History's archival holdings are described in the Archives section, entry B10.]

NATIONAL DEFENSE UNIVERSITY (National War College)

Fort Lesley J. McNair
Fourth and P Streets, SW
Washington, D.C. 20319

Lt. Col. Frank M. Wright, Director of Latin American Studies   693-8385

The National War College conducts an annual 10-month course of study on national-security policy formulation for some 140 senior-level U.S. military officers and civilian government officials. Issues-oriented Latin American area seminars and lectures form part of the core course (focusing on the international environment, global issues, regional politics, military strategy, security issues, etc.). Students may in addition focus on Latin American area studies as a specialized elective. Most lectures and seminars are presented by governmental and academic specialists invited by the College. The annual Latin American course guide and syllabus may be obtained from the National War College Chief of Staff (693-8318) or from the Director of Latin American Studies. Interested outsiders are permitted to attend selected lectures and seminars.

National Defense University Library
J. Thomas Russell, Director   693-8437

The National Defense University Library—which consists of the collections of the National War College Library and the Industrial College of the Armed Forces Library—has a small (approximately 2,000 titles) but excellent collection of English-language secondary literature on Latin American history, economics, politics, and international (largely inter-American) relations. Holdings consist almost entirely of post-1960 imprints. Included are a substantial number of studies by the Rand Corporation, Brookings Institution, and University of Miami's Center for Advanced International Studies. There are no Latin American armed forces journals.

The library is not open to the public, but private researchers may use its facilities after obtaining the permission of the director. Interlibrary loan service is available.

J9   Energy Department (DOE)

1.   a.   *Forrestal Building*
1000 Independence Avenue, SW
Washington, D.C. 20545
252-5000 (Information)

[Note: Those offices of the newly created Department of Energy (DOE) which are of primary interest to Latin Americanists are scheduled to be consolidated at the department's Forrestal Building headquarters in the near future. Thus, their present locations (at sites throughout the Washington area) and telephone numbers will shortly be out-of-date, and have not been included in this guide. Contact the departmental information operator (252-5000) for specific addresses and phone numbers.]

b. Access to some offices is restricted. Visitors should arrange appointments in advance.

2. See below.

4. Some DOE materials are restricted. Contact the department's Freedom of Information Office (under the Office of Administration) for problems relating to access.

ENERGY INFORMATION ADMINISTRATION (EIA)

The Energy Information Administration is responsible for all data collection and data processing within the Department of Energy. It is the primary Latin American data-gathering element in DOE.

Assistant Administrator for Energy Data
Office of Energy Data and Interpretation
Division of Interfuel, Nuclear, and Other Energy Sources Statistics
International Statistics Branch

Nathaniel Guyol, Chief of the International Statistics Branch, has some 40 years of personal experience in Latin American energy matters. He maintains an extensive and growing collection of Spanish- and Portuguese-language publications on virtually all aspects of energy in Latin America, including government statistics and energy accounts, the reports of power companies and commissions, development corporation reports, etc. This specialized collection, which may be one of the most comprehensive in existence, is filed—by country and energy commodity—in the International Statistics Branch's Documentation Center, and may be consulted by private researchers.
   The branch supplies Latin American energy data (production, consumption, capacity, trade, etc.) to other DOE units, and prepares energy-statistics surveys of foreign countries (including one on Brazil).

Assistant Administrator for Applied Analysis
Office of Integrative Analysis
Division of International Analysis

The Division of International Analysis is involved in econometric forecasting and modeling. Its computer files include United Nations data on world energy consumption 1950-1975 and DOE nuclear-facility profiles (both broken down by country). Computer printouts will be supplied to researchers upon request.

Energy Information Administration Clearinghouse

The clearinghouse disseminates several EIA publications of potential interest to Latin Americanists, including an *International Petroleum Annual* report containing data on oil production, trade, consumption, and prices, by country; a *World Natural Gas Production and Consumption* annual report; an annual *World Petroleum Production* report focusing on OPEC member nations; and a *Monthly Energy Review* with international statistics based on published CIA data.

ASSISTANT SECRETARY FOR INTERNATIONAL AFFAIRS

The International Affairs component of the Department of Energy consists primarily of offices drawn from the former Energy Research and Development Administration (ERDA) and Federal Energy Administration (FEA). Staff members are largely policy analysts and program managers.

Deputy Assistant Secretary for International Programs

A single Latin American desk officer (Bill Carter) in the Office of International Programs monitors Latin American energy research and development activities and technology interchange, including nuclear matters. His data sources include the reports of DOE field representatives in Mexico City and Brasilia, as well as State Department reporting. His files contain both classified and unclassified materials interspersed together, and are not normally accessible to private researchers. He will confer with researchers, however.

The Office of Nuclear Affairs is concerned with issues of nuclear proliferation in the Third World. Staff member Edward Milenky is a Latin Americanist.

The Office of LDC Programs (also under the Deputy Assistant Secretary for International Programs) has developed a computerized "World Energy Data System" (WENDS) which contains generalized data on Latin American energy production and consumption. Contact Mat Worthington for further information.

Deputy Assistant Secretary for International Policy Development

The Office of Special Regions Policy is involved in the formulation of DOE energy policies relating to developing countries (both energy importers and exporters).

Deputy Assistant Secretary for International Trade and Resources

Analysts in the Office of Resource Trade and the Office of Industry Operations monitor, respectively, Latin American oil flows and the activities of U.S. oil companies in Latin America.

Deputy Assistant Secretary for International Energy Research

Staff members of the Office of Current Assessments monitor, primarily from U.S. intelligence sources, Latin American developments relating to hydrocarbons and nuclear energy. The unit disseminates an unclassified and periodically updated report on *The Role of Foreign Governments in the Energy Industries,* which contains a section on Latin America. Staff energy editor Elizabeth Bauer has prepared unclassified energy profiles of Mexico, Argentina, and Brazil.

J10 Environmental Protection Agency (EPA)

1. a. *Waterside Mall*
      401 M Street, SW
      Washington, D.C. 20460
      755-2673

   b. Open to researchers. Appointments recommended.

2.   EPA's Office of International Activities (755-2780) coordinates various bilateral U.S.-Latin American environmental programs and agreements. Conrad Kleveno (755-0430), in the Office of International Activities' International Organizations and Western Hemisphere Division, maintains a collection of information on Latin American environmental conditions, including reports from EPA's counterpart agencies in Latin America, national environmental legislation, and materials from the Pan American Health Organization and international conferences. His files, which are arranged by country, will be made available to private researchers.

Another EPA unit, the U.S. International Environmental Referral Center (755-1836/38), has a collection of miscellaneous foreign environmental documents acquired by EPA between 1972 and 1976 through bilateral information-exchange programs. This collection, which is also arranged by country, may be examined by outside researchers on an appointment basis. A country-index is available. The U.S. International Environmental Referral Center can also provide researchers with an international directory of sources of environmental information in every nation which is participating in the United Nations Environment Program—International Referral System (headquarters: Nairobi, Kenya). Referral services relating to sources of Latin American environmental information, by country, will be provided without charge.

J11   Export-Import Bank of the United States

1.   a.   *811 Vermont Avenue, NW*
          Washington, D.C. 20571
          566-2117

     b.   Open to the public. Internal records restricted.

2.   "Eximbank" extends loans and credits to foreign borrowers to assist them in financing purchases of U.S. goods and services. Country loan officers and international economists in the Latin American Division (566-8943) maintain loan-project files and prepare country and regional studies of Latin American "credit-worthiness" and economic conditions. Although their loan records and country assessments are confidential, staff members will gladly discuss general questions with scholars.

In addition, the bank's Policy Analysis staff (566-8861) prepares research studies—from a global rather than a regional perspective—on international economic developments which may impact upon Eximbank and its programs. Research areas include methodologies for country analysis and review of bank programs, export-financing patterns and programs in the U.S. and other industrialized nations, trends in individual industries and commodities worldwide, international and domestic capital market development, and fluctuations in interest rates, prices, and other economic indicators. These studies are also considered confidential. A bibliography is maintained.

3.   The Export-Import Bank Library is discussed in the "Libraries" section, entry A16.

4.   Virtually all of the bank's loan-project files, research reports, and other internal records are considered privileged and confidential. Researchers may gain access to them only through Freedom-of-Information Act processes.

(To date, such efforts have been largely unsuccessful.) Senior Vice President for Research and Communications Donald A. Furtado (566-8873) serves as the bank's Freedom of Information officer.

Most of Eximbank's internal records, from its inception in 1934 to the present, are under the jurisdiction of the Organization and Information Division (566-8901). Records for the period 1934-1967 are being microfiched (after which the originals will be transferred to the National Archives). A computerized index is being developed for records relating to the bank's active loan projects. Contact Helene Wall, Manager of Records and Central Files (566-8815), for further information.

5.   Bank publications include an *Annual Report* and more detailed *Supplement to the Annual Report* (which together provide data on Eximbank transactions, by loan project); a semiannual *Report to the U.S. Congress on Export Credit Competition and the Export-Import Bank of the United States;* and a quarterly newsletter, *Eximbank Record.* Copies are available from the Public Affairs office (566-8990).

J12   Federal Reserve Board

1.   a.   *20th Street and Constitution Avenue, NW*
          Washington, D.C. 20551
          452-3000 (Information)
          452-3684 (Public Information Office)

     b.   Open to the public. Appointment recommended.

2.   The Federal Reserve Board manages the central bank of the United States. Its Division of International Finance (452-3614) monitors international economic matters—including foreign exchange operations, changes in the structure of U.S. international transactions, economic and financial developments abroad, etc.—which may affect U.S. monetary policy. Staff economists in the division's seven sections compile data (largely from other U.S. government sources and foreign central banks), and prepare policy analyses and research reports, some of which are distributed to the public (see point 5 below) and some of which are for internal use only (see point 4 below).

          The International Development Section (452-3771), which focuses on economic/financial problems and policies in the developing countries, is the only section of the Division of International Finance with a specifically designated Latin American staff specialist (Yves Maroni, 452-3784). This is probably the Latin Americanist's best contact-point within the division, although other sections may periodically focus on Latin American or inter-American economic affairs from a broader global perspective. The International Banking Section (452-3768) monitors the foreign activities of U.S. banks, and analyzes international banking flows and their impact on money and credit markets. The U.S. International Transactions Section (452-3728) deals with international trade and capital movements, and their influences on the U.S. economy. The Financial Markets Section (452-3796) analyzes the behavior of exchange markets and international money and capital markets. The World Payments and Economic Activity Section (452-3712) examines economic trends and policies in the industrial nations (primarily the "Group of Ten"). The International Trade and Financial Studies Section (452-3708) conducts long-range theoretical research on international economic problems. The Quantitative Studies Section (452-3540) has responsibility for the development and maintenance of econometric models of the interdependence of the U.S. economy and foreign economies.

The Division of International Finance employs private economists in various consulting roles. Scholars are frequently invited to lead or participate in staff seminars.

3.   The Federal Reserve Board Library is discussed in the "Libraries" section, entry A17.

4.   Division of International Finance research reports, briefing papers, and other internal studies are filed in the division's Information Center (452-3411), which is closed to private researchers. Copies of these and all other Federal Reserve Board internal records are also filed in the Board's Records Section (452-3277). Access to unpublished reports and other internal records, many of which are considered confidential, is possible only through Freedom-of-Information Act processes. Helen Wolcott (452-3684), in the Public Information Office, is the Board's Freedom of Information officer.

5.   Some Division of International Finance reports and briefing papers are periodically selected for outside circulation and are made available as "International Finance Discussion Papers." A bibliography, and copies of individual papers, may be obtained from the division. To be placed on the mailing list, call 452-3725.

Statistical releases and articles by division staff members occasionally appear in the Federal Reserve Board's monthly *Federal Reserve Bulletin*.

Foreign Broadcast Information Service (FBIS)
See Appendix I-entry 27

J13   Foreign Claims Settlement Commission of the United States

1.   a.   *1111 20th Street, NW*
Washington, D.C. 20579
653-6166

b.   Open to the public.

2.   The Foreign Claims Settlement Commission of the United States processes claims by U.S. nationals against foreign governments in cases arising from major foreign nationalizations involving numerous U.S. claimants. (Claims involving a single U.S. claimant in a foreign country—an expropriated corporation in Peru or Chile, for example—remain under the jurisdiction of the State Department.) The Commission presently administers the claims filed by some 10,000 U.S. nationals (individuals and corporations) against the Cuban government. These Cuban claims-files—which include individual claims, supporting background documentation, and the commission's rulings regarding the legitimacy of the evidence presented by the claimants—are stored in the Washington National Records Center (Suitland, Maryland), but they will be retrieved for researchers to examine in the Commission's library.

3.   A small library (653-6152) contains bound volumes of the Commission's claims decisions since 1950. Included is material relating to Panama.

5.   The Commission publishes an *Annual Report* to Congress.

J14 Health, Education, and Welfare Department (HEW)

1. a. *330 Independence Avenue, SW*
   Washington, D.C. 20201
   245-6296

   a. Open to the public.

2. See below.

3. See National Institute of Education—Educational Research Library (entry A38) and National Library of Medicine (entry A39).

EDUCATION DIVISION

Office of Education—Division of International Education 245-9692
Regional Building 3
7th and D Streets, SW
Washington, D.C. 20202

The Division of International Education administers a variety of international research, exchange, and training programs. The division's Clearinghouse (245-7804) serves as a reference center for information on research and study opportunities overseas. Two informative pamphlets, *Selected Programs and Services of the Division of International Education* and *Selected U.S. Office of Education Publications to Further International Education,* are available without charge from the clearinghouse.

The division's International Services and Research Branch (245-7401) produces surveys of the education systems of foreign—including Latin American—countries. The staff's reference files, which include the reports of Latin American national ministries of education, U.S. embassy reports, Latin American university publications, and special UNESCO materials, may be used by private researchers. Contact Charles Hauch (245-9425), chief of the Branch's Comparative Education Section and the staff's Latin American specialist, for further information. A list of the unit's country surveys, and individual surveys of the Cuban, Ecuadorean, Mexican, Peruvian, and Venezuelan education systems, are available without charge. The unit has a limited contract-research program.

The division's International Studies Branch (245-2356) administers NDEA Title VI and Fulbright-Hays programs for foreign language and area studies. Information brochures are available.

National Institute of Education (NIE)
Information and Communications Systems Division—Central ERIC
    Branch 254-5555
1200 19th Street, NW
Washington, D.C. 20208

The National Institute of Education's Information and Communications Systems Division administers the computerized Educational Resources Information Center (ERIC) data bases. The ERIC system contains bibliographic information on international—including Latin American—education. Researchers can access the system through computer terminals at numerous institutions, usually on a fee basis. For access to the system in the Washington area, see two useful NIE publications, *Survey of ERIC Data*

Base Search Services and *Directory of ERIC Collections in the Washington, D.C. Area,* both obtainable without charge from the Educational Reference Center (254-7934) of NIE's Educational Resources Division.

The following publications will also be of assistance to researchers in working with ERIC data bases:

Resources in Education (a monthly index)

Current Index to Journals in Education (a monthly index)

Thesaurus of ERIC Descriptors

ERIC Identifiers: Term Posting and Statistics for Research in Education

PUBLIC HEALTH SERVICE

Office of the Assistant Secretary for Health
Office of International Health—Office for the Americas   443-4560

Parklawn Building
5600 Fishers Lane
Rockville, Maryland 20852

The Office of International Health administers bilateral U.S. international health agreements and maintains liaison with the Pan American Health Organization and other international organizations. Marlyn Kefauver, director of the Office for the Americas, is a good contact- and referral-point for information on Latin American-related medical research within the U.S. government or for questions relating to inter-American health programs.

Elsewhere within the Office of International Health, the Division of Program Analysis (443-4550) has prepared Latin American background papers, as well as health sector assessments of Bolivia, Colombia, the Dominican Republic, El Salvador, Guatemala, Nicaragua, and Panama for the U.S. Agency for International Development. Copies are available to private researchers. Contact Karen Lashman or Julie Weisman.

National Institutes of Health (NIH)
John E. Fogarty International Center for Advanced Study in the Health
  Sciences   496-1415
9000 Rockville Pike
Bethesda, Maryland 20014

The Fogarty International Center conducts international exchange programs and provides postdoctoral fellowships and grants for technical research in the biomedical sciences.

The center's International Cooperation and Geographic Studies Branch (496-5903) publishes studies of foreign health systems. An anthology of articles on the status of biomedical research in Latin America and the Caribbean is being prepared. The unit also prepares the *National Institutes of Health Annual Report of International Activities,* which provides a useful survey of international scientific programs and technical projects carried out within the multipartite NIH research complex.

Alcohol, Drug Abuse, and Mental Health Administration (ADAMHA)
International Activities Office   443-2600
Parklawn Building
5600 Fishers Lane
Rockville, Maryland 20852

The three major components of the Alcohol, Drug Abuse, and Mental Health Administration—the National Institute of Mental Health, National

Institute on Drug Abuse, and National Institute on Alcohol Abuse and Alcoholism—fund Latin American-related contract-research in the biological, epidemiological, behavioral, psychosocial, and social sciences (including anthropology and sociology). ADAMHA's International Activities Office maintains contract-research project files, and can refer researchers to pertinent sources of information within each of the three institutes.

Each of the three institutes operates its own information clearinghouse. Each clearinghouse maintains a computerized bibliographic data base containing translated abstracts of foreign-language books, periodical literature, and research reports on its particular field of interest. Clearinghouse staff-members will conduct computer searches for researchers without charge, and can assist researchers in locating and obtaining full copies of items indexed in their respective data bases. Contact:

National Clearinghouse for Mental Health Information   443-4517
National Clearinghouse for Drug Abuse Information   443-6500
National Clearinghouse for Alcohol Information   948-4450

SOCIAL SECURITY ADMINISTRATION

Office of Research and Statistics—Comparative International Studies Staff
673-5714
Universal North Building, Room 322-B
1875 Connecticut Avenue, NW
Washington, D.C. 20009

Within the Social Security Administration of HEW, the Comparative International Studies Staff of the Office of Research and Statistics studies the social security programs (old-age and survivors' disability, health-care systems, unemployment insurance, workmen's compensation, family allowances, etc.) of foreign nations. A survey, *Social Security Programs Throughout the World,* is updated biennially. In addition, comparative international studies prepared by the staff appear in the monthly *Social Security Bulletin* and in special reports. The staff's Latin American specialists—Robert Weise and Frank McArdle—will confer with researchers. Their data sources include publications and reports received through information-exchange programs from Latin American social security agencies.

The unit's Foreign Language Reference Room (673-5713) contains books, periodicals, and country-files of documents from Latin America. It is open to the public.

J15   Housing and Urban Development Department (HUD)

1. a. *451 7th Street, SW*
        Washington, D.C. 20410
        755-5111

    b. Open to the public.

2.   Within HUD's Office of International Affairs, the Information and Technology division (755-5770) maintains an extensive collection of documents and reports on foreign—including Latin American—housing, urbanization, community development, urban and regional planning, urban finance and social services, housing construction, and engineering technology. Holdings include the reports of foreign government ministries and agencies, foreign legislation, United Nations housing studies and statistical reports, studies by

research organizations and individual specialists, and bibliographies. The collection was begun in 1944, although many older holdings have been eliminated. Copies of individual items within the collection will be supplied to researchers without charge. A quarterly *International Cumulative Accessions* list is produced.

The collection is cataloged in the division's "international information system," a computerized bibliographic data base. Entries in the system are indexed by country, subject, and corporate author. The staff will run searches of the data base for researchers without charge. Contact information specialist Susan Judd for further information.

3.   The HUD Library, located in room 8141 (telephone: 755-6370), contains a modest number of works—almost exclusively post-1960 imprints—on Latin American housing, city growth, urban planning and development, urban finance, economic planning, and building construction. Included are sporadic government reports on housing, slum eradication, and social welfare, along with some housing censuses and reports from national housing and mortgage banks. The library is open to the public, 8:30 A.M.-5:15 P.M., Monday-Friday.

5. a. The Office of International Affairs publishes:

HUD International Newsletter (approximately monthly), containing short articles, abstracts of periodical literature, news of HUD's international activities, and a calendar of international events.

HUD International Information Sources, an irregularly produced series of bibliographies and lists of information sources on foreign housing and urban affairs.

HUD International Special Reports, an occasional series of in-depth studies and summaries.

HUD International Country Profiles on housing and urban affairs in individual nations. Several Latin American country profiles have been produced.

Copies of these publications are available without charge from the Information and Technology division (755-5770).

    b. A periodically revised "Selected Documents Checklist" is available.

J16 Interior Department

1. a. *18th and C Streets, NW*
Washington, D.C. 20240
343-3171 (Public Affairs)

    b. Most offices are open to the public.

2.   See below.

3.   See Interior Department—Natural Resources Library (entry A27) and Geological Survey Library (entry A20).

BUREAU OF MINES

Office of International Data and Analysis
Central and South America Area Office   634-1278/632-9352
Columbia Plaza
2401 E Street, NW
Washington, D.C. 20241

Four area specialists in the Central and South America Area Office of the Bureau of Mines' Office of International Data and Analysis collect information on Latin American minerals and mining (production, trade, legislation, technology, etc.). The unit's data sources include Latin American mining-statistics and trade publications, and the reports of technical and trade associations. Contact with private researchers is welcomed.

   Country reports reviewing the yearly performance of the mining industry in each Latin American nation are published in an annual "International" volume of the Bureau of Mines' three-volume *Minerals Yearbook*.

U.S. GEOLOGICAL SURVEY (USGS)   860-6118

National Center
12201 Sunrise Valley Drive
Reston, Virginia 22092

The U.S. Geological Survey provides technical and training assistance to Latin American geological, hydrological, and cartographic services. Three international units—the Geologic Division's Office of International Geology (860-6418), the Water Resources Division's Office of International Activities (860-6548), and the Topographic Division's Branch of International Activities (860-6241)—can refer researchers to individual staff specialists with expertise in Latin American earth sciences (including earthquake studies), mineral and water resources, and cartography.

   The U.S. Geological Survey has published numerous technical studies on the geology, hydrology, and mineral resources of Latin American countries. These are indexed in three reference publications: a *Bibliography of Reports Resulting from U.S. Geological Survey Participation in the United States Technical Assistance Program, 1940-1967* (USGS Bulletin 1263); a supplement covering the years 1967-1974 (USGS Bulletin 1426); and an "open-file report" supplement covering the years 1975-1977. Copies of the first two publications can be obtained, for a small fee, from the USGS Publications Division's Branch of Distribution (751-6777). The third is available from the Geologic Division's Office of International Geology (860-6551).

J17   International Communication Agency (ICA)

1.   a.   *1750 Pennsylvania Avenue, NW*
         Washington, D.C. 20547
         724-9103 (Public Information)

     b.   Agency offices (with the exception of the Library) are open to the public. Contact individual divisions for working hours.

2.   The International Communication Agency—which was formed by a recent merger of the former United States Information Agency (USIA) and the

State Department's Bureau of Educational and Cultural Affairs—disseminates cultural information about the United States to foreign audiences and administers the major cultural-exchange programs of the U.S. government. The agency funds both in-house and contract research, primarily on international public-opinion and media-affairs topics. Outside consultants are utilized on occasion.

3. The ICA Library is discussed in the "Libraries" section, entry A28.

4. The ICA Documents Index System (DIS), a computerized list of all classified, declassified, and unclassified ICA and former USIA records, is maintained by Agency Archivist Raymond Harvey (Room 532—see ICA Archive, below). DIS, which was inaugurated in 1973, can itemize message communications, internal memoranda, country assessments, and research studies by date, subject, or geographic area of the world. Each April, a computer print-out of documents declassified by the agency during the previous year is forwarded to the National Security Council. Researchers wishing to gain access to this print-out and/or the documents listed on it should contact the Office of Congressional and Public Liaison (724-9103).

5. The agency produces a wide variety of publications, research reports, films, and tapes, described below. Almost all of these products are unclassified. Catalogs of materials, and access to specific items, can be obtained by contacting the respective functional offices.

OFFICE OF AMERICAN REPUBLICS AFFFAIRS   724-9091

The key Latin American unit of ICA, this office oversees the agency's programs in Latin America and serves as the coordinating point between ICA field offices and the agency's Washington-based media-production elements (described below). Country-desk (officially "program") officers are accessible and willing to discuss ICA activities in their respective countries of responsibility.

DIRECTORATE FOR PROGRAMS (PGM)

Office of Research and Evaluation   724-9545

The Office of Research and Evaluation conducts sociological and demographic research on Latin American audiences (their attitudes, opinions, media habits, and reactions to ICA programs), and generally evaluates the psychological environment for U.S. cultural-information programs in Latin America. Field data are usually obtained through contract research—primarily employing Latin American survey- and market-research firms within the country under study, or U.S. firms and private scholars where no Latin American organizations are available. Consultants are occasionally employed for advice on methodological matters. Staff member Charles Spencer (724-9226) is particularly knowledgeable regarding the office's Latin American research activities.

Three divisions within the Office of Research and Evaluation analyze Latin American field data. A Media Research Division (724-9106) produces an on-going series of "program evaluation studies" which assess the impact of ICA information programs (periodicals, films, radio broadcasts, etc.) on Latin American audiences, by region and country. An Attitude and Audience Research Division (724-9036) produces public-opinion surveys of Latin Americans' attitudes toward various domestic and international issues, and publishes country-studies and multi-year trend comparisons dating back some 20 years. (Survey data-sets are supplied to the Roper Public Opinion Research Center at Williams College, and to the University of Michigan Inter-University Consortium for Political Research.) The Attitude and Audience Research Division also produces "influence-structure studies" which analyze changes in the political power structures of Latin American nations. A Foreign Information Research Division (724-9289) studies Communist activities on a world-wide basis.

The Office of Research and Evaluation disseminates its research reports to some 45 depository libraries in the United States (including the Library of Congress, the New York Public Library, U.S. military service academies, and selected university libraries). A list of these depositories is available. Office of Research and Evaluation reports are indexed in the ICA Documents Index System (see point 4, above).

Press and Publications Service   724-9712
1776 Pennsylvania Avenue, NW
Washington, D.C. 20547

The Publications Division (724-9718) of this unit produces four periodicals for dissemination in Latin America. *Perspectivas Económicas* (Spanish-language only) is a quarterly journal containing articles on United States domestic and international economic affairs. *Horizontes* (Spanish and Portuguese editions) is a bi-monthly general-interest magazine focusing on American life and culture. *Facetas* (*Diálogo* in Brazil) is a quarterly journal which reprints articles on intellectual and cultural themes taken from U.S. periodicals. *Problems of Communism,* a bi-monthly journal, is distributed to Latin America in English only.

The Press Division's Latin American branch (724-9479) produces a daily teletype news-service which is made available to Latin American news media. Coverage—totaling some 15,000 words per day—centers on White House press briefings, texts of addresses by U.S. leaders, and background stories on U.S. domestic and foreign policies. Outside scholars are occasionally commissioned to write specialized pieces on current issues in U.S.-Latin American relations.

A regularly updated *Text Catalog* indexes the contents of the Press Division's teletype news coverage. Recent copies of Press Division teletype texts and Publications Division periodicals are available in the Press and Publications Service reading room (Room 402).

Television and Film Service   376-7792
Patrick Henry Building
601 D Street, NW
Washington, D.C. 20547

This unit produces ICA information films on aspects of American life thought to be of interest to Latin American audiences. Recent films have focused on earthquake recovery techniques, solar energy, and Puerto Rico. The unit also video-tapes television interviews with U.S. governmental and diplomatic officials on topical issues in U.S.-Latin American relations for distribution by ICA field representatives in Latin America. Motion pictures and video-tapes in current use by ICA may be viewed in the unit's two screening rooms. An *Active USIA/IMV Films and Television Program Master Catalog* is available, and is updated biennially. Copies of inactive and outdated items are stored in ICA's New York City film archive, and may be ordered for screening in Washington. Contact the Latin American Programs Affairs officer for additional information.

ICA Archive   724-9372
Room 532
1750 Pennsylvania Avenue, NW
Washington, D.C. 20547

The ICA Archive holds an extensive collection of historical records (Congressional documents, agency records, biographical registers, etc.) related to ICA, USIA, and predecessor agencies, dating from 1933 to the present. Included are a large number of documents—including minutes of inter-agency meetings and cultural-exchange grant records—pertaining to the 1938-1978 operations of the State Department's former Bureau of Educational and Cultural Affairs. In addition, the archive contains a comprehensive collection of publications produced for dissemination overseas by ICA and its various predecessors. Here, for example, can be found complete sets of the Coordinator of Inter-American Affairs' World War II propaganda publication *En Guardia,* as well as subsequent USIA and ICA Spanish- and Portuguese-language periodicals disseminated in Latin America. Through ICA's Documents Index System, Archivist Raymond Harvey can also provide the researcher with access to declassified ICA internal records.

ICA Foreign Press Center   724-1640
202 National Press Building
529 14th Street, NW
Washington, D.C. 20045

ICA's Foreign Press Center provides a variety of information services—ICA and commercial wire-service teletype outlets, radio tie-lines to State Department and Defense Department press briefings, etc.—for use by foreign radio, television, and print journalists stationed in Washington. Director Henry Grady has detailed knowledge of the resident Latin American press corps. The center also maintains a regularly updated directory of foreign correspondents assigned to Washington, which is available on request.

VOICE OF AMERICA (VOA)

American Republics Division   755-1961
HEW Building
330 Independence Avenue, SW
Washington, D.C. 20201

Melvin Niswander, Chief—American Republics Division

The American Republics Division produces Voice of America shortwave radio broadcasts to Latin America, currently transmitting five and one-half hours per day in Spanish and two hours per day in Portuguese. It also supplies tapes of newscasts and commentaries to Latin American radio stations through ICA field offices. The staff—some 70 writers, editors, translators, and broadcasters—is largely composed of Latin American emigrants with long experience in radio broadcasting in their former home countries. The American Republics Division periodically contracts private specialists to prepare feature reports on specialized scientific and cultural topics.

A considerable quantity of "raw material" accumulated for potential inclusion in VOA news broadcasts (including tapes of historically significant ceremonies, public addresses, and interviews related to inter-American affairs) is retained in VOA's Program Documentation Staff Tape Library, Room 2218 (755-4643). VOA scripts and broadcast tapes, however, are seldom retained for longer than four months. Information about the content of VOA programming is published in a daily *Content Report,* which lists program titles, newscast subject-matter, and VOA's sources of information. Since 1973, similar broadcast-content information has also been entered into a VOA computer storage facility. A brief quarterly brochure, *Broadcast Schedule,* describes examples of VOA broadcasting. Guy Farmer, Spanish language branch chief of the American Republics Division, is more than happy to provide scholars with access to VOA materials and facilities.

The News and Current Affairs unit of VOA maintains a Latin American news-desk (755-4444), whose four staff members keep abreast of Latin American current events on a 20-hour-per-day basis.

DIRECTORATE FOR EDUCATIONAL AND CULTURAL AFFAIRS (ECA)

1776 Pennsylvania Avenue, NW
Washington, D.C. 20547
724-9032

This directorate administers and coordinates a wide variety of U.S. cultural-exchange programs, including: the Fulbright-Hays educational-exchange programs (one consisting of grants for pre-doctoral study and research in Latin America, and the other providing postdoctoral Latin American teaching and research fellowships for U.S. scholars); the Latin American Scholars program (which brings 12 Latin American scholars to the United States for a year of university teaching); the Regional Seminars program (which brings selected Latin American specialists to the United States to participate in seminars on special themes, such as U.S. foreign-policy formulation, law/human rights, education, museum management, administration of the arts, etc.); the International Visitors program (providing 30-day familiarization trips in the United States for invited Latin American visitors); and the American Speakers program (under which U.S. specialists are sent to Latin America to lecture on recent developments within their fields of expertise).

In addition, the directorate provides seed money and other partial funding for numerous private exchange programs. These include: the Fletcher School of Law and Diplomacy (Tufts University) Teaching Fellowships in Latin America (for young U.S. scholars); the Latin American Scholarship Program of American Universities (through which Latin American educators improve their professional teaching skills at some 300 U.S. host universities); Partners of the Americas (which coordinates athletic, artistic, medical, and other exchange programs between U.S. states and Latin American countries); the Tufts University/Harvard University Fulbright-Fletcher Visiting Fellows Program and the University of Texas LBJ-Fulbright Mid-Career Program (in which mid-career Latin American government, business, and professional leaders study in Boston and Austin respectively); the University of Arizona Speakers Program (in which Latin American professors lecture in southwestern states); the University of Illinois Legal Exchange Program (providing Latin American legal specialists with opportunities for advanced study in aspects of international law); the Phelps-Stokes Fund (which sponsors, primarily at predominantly black southern colleges and universities, multinational seminars on peoples of the Caribbean); and annual Latin American writers conferences at selected U.S. universities.

Information pamphlets describing individual programs are available on request.

Office of Cultural Centers and Resources
1717 H Street, NW
Washington, D.C. 20547
632-6700

This office provides support for ICA information centers in Latin America, supplying books, language instructors, and speakers.

J18   International Trade Commisstion

1.   a.   *701 E Street, NW*
         Washington, D.C. 20436
         523-0173

     b.   Open to the public.

2.   The U.S. International Trade Commission (formerly the Tariff Commission) monitors the importation of foreign goods into the United States in terms of their impact on domestic U.S. agriculture and industry. A Latin American analyst (Janet Whisler, 724-0100) in the Commission's Office of Economic Research compiles Latin American economic data (primarily from U.S. government and international-organization sources) and forecasts changes in trade trends as they relate to Latin American exports to the United States. Her files, which are broken down by country, are accessible to outside researchers. She can also refer researchers to other International Trade Commission staff analysts who monitor international flows of individual commodities (sugar, coffee, etc.) from a worldwide perspective. (Note: The Office of Economic Research is located in the Bicentennial Building, 600 E Street, NW.)

3.   The International Trade Commission Library is described in the "Libraries" section, entry A30.

4.   The Director of Administration (523-0287) maintains control of retired internal records. The Commission Secretary, Kenneth Mason (523-0161), serves as the Commission's Freedom of Information officer.

5.   The Commission's annual report, *Operation of the Trade Agreement Program,* contains data on U.S.-Latin American trade by country and commodity, changes in Latin American foreign-investment policies, and recent developments in Latin American regional economic groupings. Copies may be obtained from the Office of the Secretary (523-0161). Publication of a bimonthly or quarterly statistical report on U.S. imports of Latin American commodities is contemplated.

Joint Publications Research Service (JPRS) See Appendix I-entry 38

J19 Justice Department

1. a. *Constitution Avenue and 10th Street, NW*
      Washington, D.C. 20530
      737-8200

   a. Some departmental agencies, such as the FBI, are not normally open to the public. Contact individual offices for their policies on accessibility.

2. See below.

4. For access to restricted Justice Department internal records, contact the department's Freedom of Information office (739-3184). Several subagencies of the Justice Department have their own separate FOI offices. These, where relevant to Latin Americanists, are noted below.

CRIMINAL DIVISION

Foreign Agents Registration Unit   739-3154

"Political or quasi-political" representatives of foreign governments (including lobbyists, but excluding diplomats and commercial agents) as well as representatives of foreign political parties are required to register with this unit and provide it with a detailed description of their activities in the United States. They must also file a copy of any materials they disseminate in this country. All of these records, which date from 1938 to the present, may be examined by researchers at the:

> Public Office   739-2332
> Federal Triangle Building
> 315 9th Street (at D Street), NW
> Washington, D.C. 20530

The *Annual Report of the Attorney General* provides a listing of foreign agents registered with this unit. The Public Office will photocopy its records for researchers, at cost.

Also on file at the Public Office are some 120 case histories, 1956-present, of foreign espionage agents—including former Cuban intelligence operatives—now residing in the United States. These, too, are open to researchers.

FEDERAL BUREAU OF INVESTIGATION (FBI)   324-5352 (Public Affairs)

J. Edgar Hoover Building   324-5520 (Freedom of Information Office)
Pennsylvania Avenue between 9th and 10th Streets, NW
Washington, D.C. 20535

FBI legal attachés assigned to U.S. embassies throughout Latin America maintain liaison with local law-enforcement agencies. The Bureau's Intelligence Division and Criminal Investigation Division coordinate the counterespionage and counterintelligence activities of FBI field offices throughout the United States. Internal records are classified, and accessible only via Freedom-of-Information Act channels.

The FBI's Public Affairs Office (324-5352) answers inquiries and provides reference and research assistance to scholars. Staff member David Cassens is knowledgeable regarding FBI espionage activities in Latin America during World War II.

IMMIGRATION AND NATURALIZATION SERVICE

Information Services Division—Statistical Branch   376-8377
425 Eye Street, NW
Washington, D.C. 20536

The Statistical Branch of the Immigration and Naturalization Service's Information Services Division monitors Latin American emigration to the United States. The unit can provide detailed U.S. immigration figures by quarter or year, country of origin, age, sex, and occupation, dating back to 1820 in some categories. The branch's library, which contains a substantial collection of historical literature and statistical data, is open to the public.

The *Annual Report* of the Commissioner of Immigration and Naturalization contains a considerable quantity of data—both current and historical —on foreign immigration.

DRUG ENFORCEMENT ADMINISTRATION (DEA)

1405 Eye Street, NW
Washington, D.C. 20537
633-1249 (Public Affairs)
633-1380/1396 (Freedom of Information Office)

A Latin American Section (633-1213/1345) within the Office of Enforcement receives information on narcotics production and trafficking from Drug Enforcement Administration field agents in Latin America and from Latin American law-enforcement agencies. A Latin American Section (633-1505) within the Office of Intelligence has a data-analysis function. Most of the data files of these units are classified, but there are indications that much restricted information will be released in response to Freedom-of-Information Act requests. Initial inquiries should be directed to the Office of Public Affairs (633-1249).

The DEA's quarterly magazine *Drug Enforcement* contains articles on international activities.

J20   Labor Department

1.   a.   *200 Constitution Avenue, NW*
Washington, D.C. 20210
523-8165

b.   Department offices are open to the public.

2.   The Latin American-related functions of the Bureau of International Labor Affairs and Bureau of Labor Statistics are outlined below.

3.   The Labor Department Library is described in the "Libraries" section, entry A32.

4.   Many internal records on inter-American labor relations are classified, and

are available only through Freedom-of-Information Act processes. Sofia Petters (523-8065) is the department's Freedom of Information officer.

BUREAU OF INTERNATIONAL LABOR AFFAIRS

Office of Foreign Labor Affairs
Dan Lazorchick, Director   523-7571

A Latin American Area Adviser and an Assistant Labor Adviser for Latin America in the Office of Foreign Labor Affairs are the Labor Department's primary specialists on U.S.-Latin American labor relations and Latin American trade-unionism. They serve as the department's contact-point with labor attachés in U.S. embassies throughout Latin America and are also responsible for liaison with private U.S. labor organizations involved in Latin American labor development. They are accessible to private researchers and will make available unclassified labor-attaché reports.

Office of Foreign Economic Research
Harry Grubert, Director   523-7597

Trade and labor economists in the Office of Foreign Economic Research analyze the impact of U.S. foreign-trade, foreign-investment, and tariff policies on the U.S. domestic labor force. Their research studies have included evaluations of the effects of U.S. investments and technology transfer in Latin America on wages and employment in the United States. Much of the unit's research is performed under contract by academic institutions and private scholars. Lists of research reports, and copies of reports, will be made available to researchers on request.

BUREAU OF LABOR STATISTICS

Division of Foreign Labor Statistics and Trade
John Chandler, Chief   523-9291

The Division of Foreign Labor Statistics and Trade collects data and conducts research on foreign labor conditions—employment and wage levels, labor force, costs, benefits, productivity, etc. Although its primary focus is on the Western industrial nations, the unit receives Latin American government publications containing industrial and labor statistics. Current holdings are available to the public. Older materials are sent to the Labor Department Library. Division staff-members will confer with researchers.

   The division publishes foreign labor figures in the Bureau of Labor Statistics' *Monthly Labor Review* and annual *Handbook of Labor Statistics*.

Division of International Price Indexes
Edward E. Murphy, Chief   523-9724

This unit measures and analyzes price trends for U.S. imports and exports, by commodity.

Maritime Administration See entry J5

J21   National Endowment for the Humanities (NEH)

1.   a.   *806 15th Street, NW*
Washington, D.C. 20506
724-0386 (Public Information)

b. Open to the public.

2. The National Endowment for the Humanities provides postdoctoral fellowships and grants for research in a wide variety of disciplines, including languages, linguistics, literature, history, jurisprudence, philosophy, archeology, comparative religion, the history, criticism, theory, and practice of the arts, and "those aspects of the social sciences which have humanistic content and apply humanistic methods."

The Division of Fellowships (724-0376) provides stipends to individual scholars and teachers.

The Division of Research Grants (724-0341) provides support to group projects and research centers, and for projects relating to the preparation of research tools and the editing of humanistic texts.

5. An annually updated booklet, *Program Announcement,* describes NEH activities and provides information on application procedures and deadlines.

The Endowment's *Annual Report* contains detailed information about NEH programs, as well as lists of grant recipients and amounts awarded.

These publications, and other brochures describing specific programs, are available without charge from the Office of Public Information.

National Oceanic and Atmospheric Administration (NOAA)
See entry J5

J22 National Science Foundation (NSF)

1. a. *1800 G Street, NW*
Washington, D.C. 20550
632-7970

b. Open to the public.

2. The National Science Foundation provides grants and fellowships for research, primarily but not exclusively in the fields of physical science and technology.

NSF's Division of International Programs has a Latin American Section (632-5806) which constitutes a useful initial contact-point for Latin Americanists with inquiries relating to NSF research-funding activities. The Division of International Programs coordinates a variety of cooperative NSF bilateral research and exchange programs linking scientific researchers in the United States and Latin America. This division also administers a Scientists and Engineers in Economic Development (SEED) program which provides grants to U.S. development specialists working or teaching in developing nations.

NSF's Division of Social Sciences (632-4234) supports some foreign-area research (both dissertation-level and post-doctoral) in economics, political science, sociology, demography, economic and social geography, and the history and philosophy of science.

The Division of Behavioral and Neural Sciences (634-4230) supports research (in anthropology, linguistics, and social psychology) relating to the cultural determinants of human behavior.

5. An NSF *Guide to Programs,* a monthly *NSF Bulletin,* and the organization's *Annual Report* are available from the Public Information Branch (632-

5722). Information brochures describing the specific programs of individual divisions may be obtained by contacting the respective divisions.

J23 National Security Council (NSC)

1. a. *Old Executive Office Building*
   17th Street and Pennsylvania Avenue, NW
   Washington, D.C. 20506
   395-3440

   b. No public access.

2. National Security Council staff members—including the Council's Latin American specialist (395-6961) in the North-South section—do not regularly make themselves available to private researchers, although individual exceptions might be made. The NSC has, in the past, occasionally engaged private academic specialists as consultants.

4. Access to most National Security Council internal documents is possible, if at all, only through Freedom-of-Information Act processes. Gary Barron (395-4970) administers FOI matters for the Council. The NSC periodically provides the Military Archives Division—Modern Military Branch of the National Archives (see entry B6) with an updated, computer-printout list of those policy-papers, intelligence directives, and other internal records which have been wholly or partially declassified by NSC. Copies of many of these declassified NSC records, which date from 1947 to present, are available in the Modern Military Branch, although no formal NSC record-group has been established. The Modern Military Branch also has a complete index to NSC numbered policy papers 1-177 (1947-1953), which is a useful source of information for the preparation of Freedom-of-Information Act requests. Contact William Cunliffe (523-3340), Assistant Chief of the Modern Military Branch, for further information.

Navy Department See entry J8

J24 Overseas Private Investment Corporation (OPIC)

1. a. *Board of Trade Building*
   1129 20th Street, NW
   Washington, D.C. 20527
   632-1804

   b. Open to the public. Appointment recommended.

2. The Overseas Private Investment Corporation "assists United States investors to make profitable investments in about 80 developing countries." The agency provides discounted insurance policies to U.S. multinational corporations to protect them against the political risks of expropriation, inconvertibility of foreign currency holdings, and damage from war, revolution, or insurrection. It also protects U.S. lending institutions against both commercial and political risks by guaranteeing payment of principal and interest on loans made to private investors. In addition, OPIC offers investment

information and counseling, and shares in the costs of finding, developing, and financing investment projects overseas.

Latin American specialists in OPIC's Insurance Department (632-9634) and Finance Department (254-3416) monitor business conditions and the investment environment in Latin America. Periodically they travel to Latin America to identify new investment projects and assist U.S. investors. They will confer with researchers.

3. OPIC's library (632-9329) has diverse holdings relating to international business and investment. Included are reports from several private U.S. corporations with investments in Latin America, publications of U.S. government agencies (Departments of State, Commerce, Treasury, Agriculture), confidential World Bank/International Monetary Fund country- and project-assessments, an alphabetically arranged vertical file of miscellaneous foreign-country data, and legislation pertaining to OPIC. There are also separate volumes of records relating to OPIC involvement in overseas investment disputes and settlements, including one on I.T.T./Chile which contains a variety of legal papers and communications. The library is open to the public, 8:45 A.M.-5:30 P.M., Monday-Friday. A card index of holdings is maintained.

4. The corporation's internal records—which include claims-settlement files as well as information submitted by private U.S. companies in Latin America (their agreements with host governments, business- and project-forecasts, etc.)—are considered confidential and are inaccessible to private researchers except via Freedom-of-Information Act processes. Director of Public Affairs Robert Jordan (632-1854) serves as OPIC's Freedom of Information officer.

5. OPIC publishes an *Annual Report,* and *Topics,* a bimonthly newsletter which regularly includes a supplement featuring information on a country or region of investor interest. There have been supplements on Bolivia and Central America.

J25 Panama Canal Company (and Canal Zone Government)— Washington Office

1. a. *Pennsylvania Building, Room 312*
      425 13th Street, NW
      Washington, D.C. 20004
      724-0104

   b. Open to researchers. Appointment recommended.

   c. Thomas M. Constant, Secretary of the Panama Canal Company and Assistant to the Governor of the Canal Zone.

2. The head of the Washington office acts as a liaison between the U.S. Panama Canal Company/Canal Zone Government (both of which are headquartered in the Canal Zone) and various governmental agencies and Congressional committees in Washington. He and his small staff can provide extensive data on the history and operation of the Canal and of civil government in the Canal Zone. Information which they do not have on hand will be obtained from the Canal Zone.

3. The Panama Canal Company's reference collection is described in the "Libraries" section, entry A46.

4.   The office's internal records include correspondence with officials in the Canal Zone, and Panama Canal administrative records pertaining to ship transits, tolls, etc. Some materials are restricted.

5.   Both the Panama Canal Company and the Canal Zone Government produce annual reports.

J26   Peace Corps (ACTION)

1.   a.   *806 Connecticut Avenue, NW*
      Washington, D.C. 20525
      254-7526 (Public Affairs)

    b.   Open to the public. Appointment recommended.

2.   Peace Corps programs overseas are administered through ACTION's Office of International Operations. Within the Office of International Operations, country-desk officers in the Latin America-Caribbean Regional Office (254-9714) provide liaison between field volunteers and the Washington headquarters. They can provide information on past and present Peace Corps programs in Latin America (frequently having served as field volunteers themselves). They are accessible to researchers.

    The Evaluation Division (254-7983) of ACTION's Office of Policy and Planning prepares assessments of Peace Corps programs and projects in Latin America. An annually updated bibliography of evaluations produced since 1961 is maintained by Peace Corps Evaluation Coordinator Rick Williams. The Evaluation Division utilizes geographic, linguistic, and programmatic consultants, and, on occasion, private research contractors.

3.   The ACTION Library (formerly the Peace Corps Library) is discussed in the "Libraries" section, entry A2.

4.   The Peace Corps does not appear to have a centralized internal records-filing system. Miscellaneous program documents, country reports, and all program evaluations prepared by the Evaluation Division are available at the ACTION Library (254-3307); pre-1970 evaluations may be classified "limited official use," but can be obtained through a Freedom-of-Information Act request. Operational field communications and internal Peace Corps memoranda may be retained in the working files of Latin America-Caribbean Regional Office country-desk officers, or may have been retired to the Washington National Records Center (Suitland, Maryland). The Director of ACTION's Administrative Services Division (under the Office of Administration and Finance), John Nolan (254-8105), who serves as the Peace Corps' Freedom of Information officer, is a good source of information on retired records.

5.   a.   An irregularly issued *Program and Training Journal* contains background and country-training information for Peace Corps volunteers. Copies may be obtained through ACTION's Office of Multilateral and Special Programs (254-7386).

    b.   See point 2, above.

Note: Also see entry F22.

J27   Smithsonian Institution

1. a. *Headquarters:*
        Smithsonian Institution ("Castle") Building
        1000 Jefferson Drive, SW
        Washington, D.C. 20560
        628-4422 (Information)
        737-8811 ("Dial-A-Museum" [*recorded information on current museum activities and events*]*)*

    b. The main Smithsonian Institution Building and the numerous museums, galleries, and other Smithsonian facilities scattered throughout Washington, D.C., are open to the public.

2. See below. Other Smithsonian Institution entities are described in entries A36, A40, B2, B8, B12, C4, C5, C7, C8, F12, F16, M16, M34, and M40.

3. See entries A36 and A40.

4. The Smithsonian Institution Archives and the Smithsonian's National Anthropological Archives are described in entries B12 and B8, respectively.

5. The monthly *Smithsonian* magazine is available on a commercial subscription basis. For information, call 381-6311.

Office of Fellowships and Grants
381-5071

The Office of Fellowships and Grants administers several pre- and postdoctoral research fellowship programs designed to enable private researchers to work with Smithsonian staff experts and research collections. Awards range in length from a few weeks to 12 months. The various programs will be of greatest potential interest to Latin Americanists in the fields of archeology, ethnology, physical anthropology, art history, cultural history, ethnic studies, and museum management. Fellowships are also offered for biological and zoogeographical research at the Smithsonian Tropical Research Institute in the Canal Zone. A brochure, *Smithsonian Opportunities for Research and Study in History, Art, Science,* is available upon request.

Smithsonian Resident Associates Program
381-5157

Through membership in the Smithsonian Associates, any member of the public can participate in a variety of special Smithsonian educational and cultural programs, including periodic lectures and lecture series on Latin American archeology, art, general culture, or natural history. (Some lectures are open to the public, and are advertised in local newspapers; others are announced only in the members' monthly *Associate* newsletter.) The Resident Associate Program also conducts culturally oriented educational tours of foreign countries ("Foreign Study Tours" [381-5520] and "Foreign Charter Tours" [381-5635]). Past foreign-tour groups have travelled to Mexico and Central America.

Smithsonian Science Information Exchange (SSIE), Inc.
1730 M Street, NW
Washington, D.C. 20036
381-4211

The Smithsonian Science Information Exchange serves as a computerized
clearinghouse of information on research projects currently in progress,
primarily in the physical and life sciences, but also in the social and
behavioral sciences (including research projects in Latin American agricultural and rural economic development; anthropology and archeology; education; family planning; medicine, health, and health-care administration;
migration; and inter-American political and economic relations). Research
projects funded by U.S. government agencies constitute some 80 to 90 per
cent of the data base's holdings; the remainder are projects of universities,
research centers, and private foundations. The data base can be accessed
geographically or by subject.

For a fee, the SSIE staff will conduct computer searches for private
researchers. An *SSIE Science Newsletter* (ten issues per year) contains recent
additions to the data base.

J28 State Department

1. a. *2201 C Street, NW*
        Washington, D.C. 20520
        655-4000 (Information)
        632-9606 (Bureau of Public Affairs)
        632-0772 (Freedom-of-Information Staff)

    b. The building is not open to the public. Appointments with department
        personnel should be made in advance to ensure admittance.

2. Various State Department offices (described individually below) monitor
    conditions in Latin America, conduct research, and prepare policy papers on
    Latin American/inter-American topics. Personnel are usually willing to talk
    with researchers, within the limits imposed by security regulations. Both the
    Bureau of Inter-American Affairs and the Bureau of Intelligence and
    Research utilize Latin American-oriented contract research and employ
    Latin Americanist scholars as consultants.

3. The State Department Library is described in the "Libraries" section, entry
    A49.

4. State Department internal classified records (dispatches, telegrams, and
    other message-communications between Washington and the department's
    diplomatic posts overseas; inter- and intra-office memoranda, research
    studies, policy papers, etc.) are filed in the Bureau of Administration's For-
    eign Affairs Document and Reference Center (FADRC) (described below),
    which eventually forwards them to the National Archives (Civil Archives Di-
    vision, Diplomatic Branch—see entry B6). There they become accessible to
    private researchers on a gradual chronological basis determined by the latest
    year for which the State Department's official *Foreign Relations of the
    United States* documentary series has been published. Currently, most rec-
    ords are open at the National Archives through 1949 (access to post-1949
    records is possible only via Freedom-of-Information Act processes). A

computerized index exists for all internal records processed by FADRC since July, 1973.

Within the Bureau of Public Affairs, a Freedom of Information staff (632-0772) receives Freedom-of-Information Act declassification-review requests for restricted State Department records and coordinates the subsequent records-search and review process with the Foreign Affairs Document and Reference Center (FADRC) and the department's geographic bureaus, respectively. Of the nearly 500,000 pages of documents reviewed in 1976, 353,000 pages were released to the public. Researchers may examine documents which have been released to them in the unit's public-access reading room. The staff cooperates with researchers throughout the review process, and can be of assistance in appealing release-denials. The director is Barbara Ennis.

5. a. State Department publications include the weekly *Department of State Bulletin* (containing statements, addresses, and excerpts from news conferences of the President, Secretary of State, and other officials; State Department press releases; texts of treaties and international agreements; articles on international affairs; and lists of Congressional documents relating to foreign policy); a *Background Notes* series of general-information fact-sheets, by country (updated biannually); *Gist,* a series of one-page reference-aids on current international issues; and a monthly *Department of State Newsletter.*

Useful directories include the regularly updated *Biographic Register* of State Department officials (classified since 1974, unfortunately); a trimestral *Key Officers of Foreign Service Posts—Guide for Business Representatives* (formerly *Foreign Service List*); *Diplomatic List* and *Employees of Diplomatic Missions* (quarterly lists of the names and addresses of foreign diplomatic personnel in Washington); an annual *Foreign Consular Officers in the United States;* and periodically revised *Lists of Visits of Presidents of the United States to Foreign Countries, 1789-1976* and *Lists of Visits of Foreign Chiefs of State and Heads of Government, 1789-1976.*

In addition, the department issues a large number of special public releases, including discussion papers (a recent example: "The United States and the Third World" [1976]), special reports (primarily on economic topics, such as "Latin America and the Trade Act of 1974" [1977]), information pamphlets (e.g., "Panama Canal: The New Treaties" [1977]), policy statements, speeches, addresses, news conferences, and other selected documents. To be placed on the department's mailing list (a special mailing-list for Latin American materials is available), contact the Bureau of Public Affairs' Office of Plans and Management (632-9859). Other department publications are discussed below, under their originating office.

b. Bibliographies include *Major Publications of the Department of State: An Annotated Bibliography* (revised edition, 1977), and three successive issues of *Publications of the Department of State* covering the periods 1929-1952, 1953-1957, and 1958-1960 respectively.

BUREAU OF INTER-AMERICAN AFFAIRS (ARA)   632-9210

The Bureau of Inter-American Affairs coordinates and supervises U.S. diplomatic activities in Latin America. The bureau places a high priority on cooperation with private scholars. Country-desk officers in the Office of Andean Affairs (632-1715), Office of East Coast Affairs (632-0913), Office of Caribbean Affairs (632-2621), Office of Central American Affairs (632-9469), Office of Mexican Affairs (632-9894), Office of Panamanian Affairs (632-

1112), and Office of the Coordinator of Cuban Affairs (632-9272) will provide information on current conditions in, and U.S. policy toward, their nations of responsibility. They will also make relevant unclassified documents available to scholars.

[It should be noted that fields of expertise and responsibility within the State Department's various geographic and functional bureaus and their respective subunits frequently overlap, with the result that the scholar interested, for example, in Venezuelan oil-export policy, U.S.-Peruvian fishing disputes, or Mexican gas pipelines might glean useful information not only from the appropriate country-desk officer in ARA but from specialists in ARA's Office of Regional Economic Policy, the Bureau of Intelligence and Research's Office of Research and Analysis for American Republics and Office of Economic Research and Analysis, and specialized functional offices in the Bureau of Economic and Business Affairs or the Bureau of Oceans and International Environmental and Scientific Affairs (discussed below). As a general rule, however, the ARA country-desk officer should serve as the scholar's initial contact- and referral-point in the department.]

Office of Policy Planning, Public and Congressional Affairs (ARA/ PPC) 632-9492

The office prepares policy recommendations, background papers, and public policy-statements for State Department officials on broad Latin American policy issues. Its Public and Congressional Affairs branch (632-9286) assists scholars in identifying and contacting appropriate departmental specialists.

Office of Regional Economic Policy (ARA/ECP) 632-2079

This operational and planning office carries out functions similar to those of ARA-PPC mentioned above, but with a specialized functional focus on inter-American economic affairs. The office is composed of a Finance, Development and Analysis branch (632-9460), an Investment, Technology and Energy branch (632-0465), and a Trade, Commodities and Resources branch (632-2345).

Office of Regional Political Programs (ARA/RPP) 632-9362

RPP also carries out functions similar to those of ARA/PPC, but with a specialized (and primarily multilateral) focus on military assistance, narcotics control, labor affairs, maritime problems, and the United Nations.

Permanent Mission of the United States of America to the Organization of American States (USOAS) 632-9376

Staff members of the U.S. delegation to the OAS attend OAS meetings and prepare briefing papers and other reports (often classified) relating to their assigned areas of responsibility, which include OAS political affairs, economic affairs, educational, scientific and cultural affairs, budget affairs, and OAS specialized agencies. A collection of recent OAS documents is maintained.

POLICY PLANNING STAFF (S/P) 632-2372

The Policy Planning Staff provides the Office of the Secretary of State with broad, global policy recommendations and viewpoints independent from the more "parochial" policy lines of the Bureau of Inter-American Affairs and other geographic bureaus. The staff includes specialists in Latin American and North-South economics. They are accessible to scholars.

The Policy Planning Staff sponsors a regular series of "Open Forum" luncheon discussions (open only to State Department personnel), which serve as a mechanism for internal departmental debate on policy issues. A classified magazine, *Open Forum,* is published.

BUREAU OF INTELLIGENCE AND RESEARCH (INR)   632-0342

Office of Research and Analysis for American Republics (INR/DDR/RAR)
Hunter L. Estep, Director   632-2229

The principal Latin American research arm of the State Department, this office prepares some 800-1,200 "pieces" of research each year, ranging from one-page current-intelligence "spot" analyses to 20-30-page research memoranda. Its primary "clientele" are high-level officers and the Bureau of Inter-American Affairs. Research subject areas encompass the full range of Latin American policy issues, and are primarily short- and mid-term in scope. Virtually all of the office's work is classified.

Office of External Research (INR/XR)
E. Raymond Platig, Director   632-1342
Daniel Fendrick, Senior Program Officer for Latin America 632-2758

The Office of External Research serves as the State Department's primary contact-point with private scholars. The office manages the department's contract-research program and arranges for the use of outside consultants. It also periodically invites selected Latin Americanist scholars to participate with State Department and other government officials in conferences, colloquia, roundtable discussions, and ambassadorial briefings. Staff members do not engage in research activities of their own, but they can provide researchers with copies of unclassified State Department in-house and contract-research studies and research bibliographies.

The unit also serves as the staff secretariat for the government-wide Inter-Agency Committee on Foreign Affairs Research (IC/FAR), which formerly was known as the Foreign Affairs Research Coordination Group and subsequently as the National Security Council Under Secretaries Committee's Subcommittee on Foreign Affairs Research (USC/FAR). In this capacity, the Office of External Research serves as a coordinating point and information clearinghouse for U.S. government-produced and government-funded research on foreign areas and international relations, endeavoring to minimize duplication of research and to maximize inter-agency exchange of information.

The office publishes a quarterly and annual computerized inventory of *Government-Supported Research Projects on Foreign Affairs* (unclassified). In addition, its useful and previously unclassified *Foreign Affairs Research: A Directory of Governmental Resources* (1969) was updated in 1977, but is now for internal use only. A quarterly newsletter, *FAR Horizons,* has terminated publication.

In addition, the Office of External Research administers the:

Foreign Affairs Research Documentation Center
Room 4111, Pomponio Plaza East
1800 North Kent Street
Arlington, Virginia 22209
235-9420

This facility, which is open to the public, collects and disseminates both reports produced under government research contracts and relevant unpublished research papers produced by individual scholars, academic and other research centers, and foundations. Its collection consists of some 15,000 recently completed research studies on foreign areas and international affairs. Subject fields include anthropology, communications, demography, economics, geography, history, international relations, law, linguistics, philosophy, political science, psychology, social statistics, and sociology. Items are held for five years and are then discarded. Private researchers may borrow from the center only studies funded by the State Department; other papers must be obtained from the individual author or sponsoring government agency. Both dictionary and geographic card catalogs are maintained.

The FAR Documentation Center publishes a monthly acquisitions list, *Foreign Affairs Research Papers Available.* Contact the center for a free sample copy or for information on subscriptions. In addition, a *Special Papers Available* series includes an annual volume on Latin American-related holdings. A five-year (1971-1976) cumulative index of Latin American acquisitions is also available.

Office of Economic Research and Analysis (INR/DDR/REC) 632-2186

This office studies international economic issues, including U.S.-Latin American economic relations. The Commodity and Developing Country Division (632-0453) produces research on the North-South dialogue, trade, and commodities. The Trade Investment and Payments Division (632-0090) studies Latin American balance-of-payments, foreign-exchange, and debt problems, and investment disputes involving private U.S. companies in Latin America. Researchers can obtain copies of the CIA's unclassified annual publication *Communist Aid to the Less Developed Countries of the Free World* through the Communist Economic Relations Division (632-9128).

The Office of Economic Research and Analysis also produces occasional *Intelligence Reports* for inter-agency dissemination. A small number of these reports are unclassified.

Office of Political-Military Affairs and Theatre Forces (INR/DDR/PMT) 632-2043

This office conducts research (some relating to Latin America) on international arms sales, national military production and military capabilities, nuclear capabilities, and potential international military confrontations.

Office of Strategic Affairs 632-2086

The research interests of the Office of Strategic Affairs include Latin American nuclear nonproliferation.

Office of the Geographer (INR/DDR/RGE)
Robert D. Hodgson, The Geographer 632-1428

This unit monitors international politico-geographic patterns, and issues three series of publications (all unclassified): *International Boundary Studies* (irregular); *Limits of the Sea* (irregular); and *Geographic Notes* (issued each time there occurs a significant change in international sovereignty—such as the emergence of a new state, name change of a country, or modification of the major civil divisions within a country). An annually updated general-reference booklet, *Status of the World's Nations,* is also produced.

BUREAU OF ECONOMIC AND BUSINESS AFFAIRS (EB) 632-0396

The functionally structured Bureau of Economic and Business Affairs has primary responsibility within the State Department for the formulation and implementation of U.S. foreign economic policy. It monitors the economic policies of foreign nations, coordinates the Latin American regional economic policies of the United States with the Bureau of Inter-American Affairs and with other U.S. government agencies, conducts bilateral and multilateral negotiations on economic matters, and represents the U.S. at international conferences. Latin Americanists engaged in research on technical economic topics may find the most knowledgeable State Department expertise within this bureau rather than the Bureau of Inter-American Affairs.

Office of Business Practices (EB/IFD/BP) 632-9452

Concerned with legal aspects of technology transfer, including Latin American industrial-property legislation (patents, trademarks), copyright laws, and antitrust matters.

Office of Monetary Affairs (EB/IFD/OMA) 632-1114

Interested in Latin American monetary conditions, financial loans, balance-of-payments problems, debt policies, re-scheduling policies, and the collection of debts and claims. Has primary responsibility for State Department relations with the International Monetary Fund. Maintains liaison with the Treasury Department.

Office of Development Finance (EB/IFD/ODF) 632-9426

Represents the State Department in interagency decisions on U.S. loan policies and contributions to. international financial institutions, and has primary responsibility for the State Department's relations with the Inter-American Development Bank, the World Bank, and other international lending institutions.

Office of Investment Affairs (EB/IFD/OIA) 632-1128

Formulates investment policy; handles investment disputes, expropriation cases, and problems involving multinational corporations in Latin America and elsewhere.

Office of International Trade (EB/ITP/OT) 632-2534

Drafts commercial policy, conducts bilateral and multilateral international trade negotiations, has primary responsibility within the State Department for the Generalized System of Preferences, and monitors Latin American participation in UNCTAD, GATT, and other international economic forums.

Office of East-West Trade (EB/ITP/EWT) 632-0964

Deals with U.S. export-control and embargo policies toward Cuba. Maintains liaison with the Commerce Department on export-licensing of U.S. strategic (particularly nuclear) materials to Latin America.

Office of Fuels and Energy (EB/ORF/FSE) 632-1420

Formulates energy policy, represents the United States at international conferences, and conducts negotiations with Venezuela, Mexico, and other key Latin American producers of oil and gas.

Office of International Commodities (EB/ORF/ICD)   632-7952

Involved in the negotiation of multilateral commodities agreements. Latin American focus centers on tropical products (coffee, sugar, bananas, cotton), strategic materials (rubber, tin, bauxite, iron ore, and other minerals), and fibers.

Office of Food Policy and Programs (EB/ORF/OFP)   632-3090
Handles questions relating to Latin American meat exports. Coordinates U.S. food-aid programs with the Agriculture Department.

Office of Aviation (EB/TCA/OA)   632-0316
Conducts bilateral commercial-aviation negotiations with Latin American governments.

Office of International Communications Policy (EB/TCA/TD)   632-3405
Concerned with telecommunications problems: radio, telephone, telegraph, undersea cable, satellite/space systems.

Office of Maritime Affairs (EB/TCA/MA)   632-0704

Involved in questions relating to maritime trade and commerce. Monitors Latin American shipping regulations and cargo preference laws, and endeavors to discourage discrimination against U.S. commercial shipping.

Office of Commercial Affairs (EB/TCA/OCA)   632-8097

Concerned with the management of U.S. trade-promotion activities and trade centers in Latin America. Works closely with the Commerce Department to assure that U.S. embassies provide the economic information and services required by the U.S. business community. In coordination with the Commerce Department, establishes commercial task-forces to identify major commercial opportunities for U.S. firms in Latin America and to publicize those opportunities in the United States.

BUREAU OF POLITICO-MILITARY AFFAIRS (P/M)   632-9022

This bureau develops policy recommendations in the areas of security policy, military assistance, nuclear policy, and arms control. Its primary focus is functional rather than geographic. Virtually all of its work is classified.

Office of International Security Policy (PM/ISP)   632-2056

Analyzes broad regional problems from a long-range strategic perspective. Examples of recent Latin American interests: arms build-ups, border tensions, Cuban military activities overseas, naval control of the South Atlantic.

Office of Non-Proliferation Policy (PM/NPP)   632-1835
Monitors nuclear development in Argentina and Brazil.

Office of Security Assistance and Sales (PM/SAS)   632-3882
Monitors U.S. and other international arms-transfers to Latin America.

Office of Munitions Control (Rosslyn, Virginia) (PM/MC)   235-9755
Administers the licensing of private U.S. arms exporters.

Office of International Security Operations (PM/ISO) 632-1616

Concerned with visits of Latin American military officers to the United States, as well as U.S. military aircraft and ship movements in Latin America.

Office of Disarmament and Arms Control (PM/DCA) 632-1862

Focus is on SALT and other arms-control negotiations. Little current activity involving Latin America.

BUREAU OF HUMAN RIGHTS AND HUMANITARIAN AFFAIRS (HA) 632-0334

This small bureau monitors human-rights conditions in Latin American nations as reported by U.S. embassies, and prepares policy recommendations concerning U.S. military and economic-development assistance programs to Latin America. It also coordinates the preparation of annual (since 1976) State Department unclassified reports to Congress on the human-rights situation in every Latin American country receiving U.S. military or economic aid. The staff's Latin American specialist (currently Michele Bova [632-2126]) maintains close contact with private organizations and individuals interested in Latin American human-rights issues.

BUREAU OF INTERNATIONAL ORGANIZATIONS AFFAIRS (IO) 632-9600

This bureau coordinates United States participation in the United Nations. Selected staff members in the bureau's various functional offices monitor the activities of Latin American delegations, and Latin American repercussions of U.S. policy positions, within the UN General Assembly and Security Council, and in the many specialized UN commissions and conferences (ECLA, UNCTAD, etc.). There are functional offices concentrating on UN political affairs (632-2392), international economic affairs (632-2506), labor affairs (632-1121), human-rights affairs (632-0572), development and humanitarian programs (632-1544), agriculture (632-2525), transportation and communications (632-7930), health and narcotics (632-0590), international women's programs (632-6906), UNESCO (632-3619), and science and technology (632-3511).

BUREAU OF OCEANS AND INTERNATIONAL ENVIRONMENTAL AND SCIENTIFIC AFFAIRS (OES) 632-1554

This functional bureau focuses on foreign-policy questions relating to oceans, fisheries, environmental and population issues, and nuclear, space, and energy technology. It represents the United States in international negotiations and conferences, and directs the State Department's Scientific/ Technological and Fisheries Attaché programs.

Office of Ocean Affairs (OES/OFA/OCA) 632-3262

Concerned with maritime boundaries, law-of-the-sea issues, marine pollution, and Antarctic resources.

Office of Fisheries Affairs (OES/OFA/FA) 632-1727

Monitors U.S.-Latin American fishing disputes. Represents the United States in the International Fisheries Commission, and negotiates bilateral and multilateral fishing agreements.

Office of Marine Science and Technology (OES/OFA/MST)   632-0853
Represents the U.S. in specialized international scientific forums and handles
clearances for U.S. research vessels working in Latin American waters.

Office of Environmental Affairs (OES/ENP/EN)   632-9278

Concerned with a broad range of global environmental issues, including
natural-resource depletion, land and sea pollution, endangered species, and
weather modification.

Office of Population Affairs (OES/ENP/PD)   632-2232

Monitors demographic trends and U.S.-supported family-planning programs in Latin America, with a particular focus on Mexico, Brazil, and
Colombia.

OFFICE OF THE LEGAL ADVISER

Michael Kozak, Assistant Legal Adviser for Inter-American Affairs
632-0734

Staff lawyers in the office of the Assistant Legal Adviser for Inter-American
Affairs will provide researchers with information on inter-American legal
issues, including the status of treaties and other international agreements.
Other sections of the Office of the Legal Adviser also occasionally work on
Latin American topics. The Assistant Legal Adviser for Ocean, Environ-
ment, and Scientific Affairs (632-1700) handles questions involving maritime
and fisheries boundaries. The Assistant Legal Adviser for Politico-Military
Affairs (632-7838) works on legal aspects of U.S. arms sales to Latin
America.
   Scholars may make arrangements to use the law library of the Office of the
Legal Adviser (632-2628). Latin American holdings are not extensive,
however.
   Publications of the Office of the Legal Adviser include the annual *Digest
of United States Practice in International Law,* containing policy statements
of the official U.S. position on every major question of international law,
including human rights and law of the sea; and *Treaties in Force,* an annual
list of all U.S. international agreements in force on January 1 of the year of
publication. Full texts of U.S. treaties and international agreements are
found in the 13-volume *Treaties and Other International Agreements of the
United States of America, 1776-1949* and annual *United States Treaties and
Other International Agreements* (1950-present).

BUREAU OF PUBLIC AFFAIRS (PA)   632-9606

Office of the Historian (PA/HO)
Columbia Plaza, Room 3100
2401 E St., NW
Washington, D.C. 20520

David F. Trask, Historian   632-8888
William Z. Slany, Associate Historian for Western Hemisphere and Eu-
   rope   632-8767
Stephen Kane, Inter-American Group Chief   632-2033

The primary activity of the Historical Office is preparation of the State
Department's *Foreign Relations of the United States* documentary series.
The staff maintains close contact with the department's Foreign Affairs

Document and Reference Center (FADRC) records facility, the Diplomatic Branch of the National Archives, and presidential libraries throughout the United States. Staff members are outstanding sources of information on the State Department's past and present records-filing systems, and the location, content, and accessibility of U.S. diplomatic records and source materials generally. They are available for consultation and research guidance.

The office provides internships for graduate students, and regularly employs a small number of young professional historians on a temporary, short-term (ca. 6-12 months) basis. It has also sponsored discussion sessions and conducted guided tours of State Department records facilities, usually in conjunction with the annual conventions which national historical associations such as the American Historical Association and the Society for Historians of American Foreign Relations periodically hold in Washington, D.C.

In addition to *Foreign Relations,* the Historical Office prepares *Major Publications of the Department of State: An Annotated Bibliography,* as well as a pamphlet on the public availability of diplomatic records in foreign archives, and occasional "Historical Studies," including *U.S. Policy Toward Latin America: Recognition and Non-Recognition of Governments and Interruptions in Diplomatic Relations, 1933-1974* (1975) and *Treaty Rights Acquired by the United States to Construct the Panama Canal* (1975).

Office of Public Programs (PA/PP)
James M. Montgomery, Director   632-1433

The Office of Public Programs organizes the State Department's Scholar-Diplomat Seminars, which bring scholars (usually younger Ph.Ds) into the department for one week of discussion-sessions and participation in the work of a departmental bureau. There are usually two Latin American seminars per year, as well as single annual seminars relating to State Department functional interests (economic and business affairs, politico-military affairs, legal affairs, international organizations, population, educational and cultural affairs, science and technology). Media-Diplomat Seminars and Executive-Diplomat Seminars are also held. Information pamphlets are available from the Office of Public Programs.

In addition, this unit sponsors conferences and special briefings on U.S. foreign policy for private organizations, and supplies State Department speakers to universities, business, and other groups (on request).

BUREAU OF ADMINISTRATION (A)   632-1492

Foreign Affairs Document and Reference Center (FADRC)
John S. Pruden, Director   632-0394

FADRC administers the official centralized file of internal State Department records (including cable traffic, overseas-post records, and Washington office "lot" files) until such time as they are forwarded to the National Archives. Records received by FADRC since July, 1973 have been computer-indexed. Neither FADRC's records-files nor its computerized index are open to outside researchers. (A research area formerly open to the public is no longer in existence.)

The unit publishes the extremely informative, unclassified *Country Fact Sheets* (see volume 4: *Inter-American Affairs*), a regularly updated compendium of data from the State Department, Defense Department, Agency for International Development, International Communication Agency, and

Arms Control and Disarmament Agency. Included in the Latin American volume are sections of data for each country on: basic facts, treaties and international agreements, military forces, the status of foreign military purchases and military assistance programs, economic indicators, trade, principal foreign-aid donors and external aid obtained, U.S. assistance commitments, AID projects, cultural and information programs being carried out by the U.S. and other foreign nations, foreign investments (by investor country), U.S. private-investment levels (including total earnings and reinvested earnings), an evaluation of the domestic climate for foreign investment, major governmental officials, U.S. citizen presence, United Nations participation, and an annotated bibliography of the State Department Library's periodical holdings on the country in question. Data time-series for most categories of information begin in the early 1970s. *Country Fact Sheets* is distributed to the libraries of several U.S. government agencies.

FADRC also prepares a *Monthly Highlights Report*—a 12-15-page documents-index of major items selected from incoming State Department message traffic, organized by geographic region of the world and subdivided by type of reporting (political, economic, military, sociological, and technological). This publication, which has been in existence only since 1977, is for internal use only. It is possible, however, that access to copies might be obtained through staff members of the State Department Historical Office.

FOREIGN SERVICE INSTITUTE   235-8750
1400 Key Boulevard
Arlington, Virginia 22209

W. Lawrence Dutton, Dean—School of Area Studies   235-8839
David Scott Palmer, Chairman—Latin American Studies   235-8726

The State Department's Foreign Service Institute provides language and area training programs for U.S. government personnel. Included within the six-month general program of studies is a Latin American seminar program covering history, politics, economics, society and culture, general policy issues, and special problems (e.g., economic development, delayed industrialization, migration and urbanization, the role of women, etc.). Courses are taught for the most part by guest lecturers from the academic community. Interested outsiders may receive permission to attend lectures. A general bibliography and general syllabus for Latin American studies are available, as are individual course syllabi.

In addition, several specialized Foreign Service Institute programs focus in part on Latin America. These include: Executive Seminar in National and International Affairs, a 10-month orientation to contemporary trends in domestic and foreign issues for senior officials of U.S. government agencies; Foreign Affairs Interdepartmental Seminar, providing mid-level officials with two weeks of training on major policy issues as perceived by various government agencies; a Post Professional Development Program providing scholarly books, articles, lectures, seminars, and discussions for foreign-service officers in Latin America; and training programs focusing on international narcotics control and terrorism.

Note: Also see entry F23.

J29 Transportation Department (DOT)

1. a. *400 7th Street, SW*
        Washington, D.C. 20590
        426-4000

    b. Open to the public.

2. Within DOT's Office of International Transportation Programs (426-4368), the International Transportation Division (755-7684) maintains geographic files of foreign transportation data, most of which is supplied by U.S. embassies overseas. Unclassified materials, which constitute the vast majority of the holdings, will be made available to researchers.

    The Information Management Branch (426-0975) of DOT's Research and Special Programs Directorate is attempting to develop, in conjunction with the Transportation Research Board of the National Academy of Science's National Research Council and numerous other organizations, a computerized bibliographic data base known as TRISNET (Transportation Research Information Services Network). The system currently contains a small number of references to literature on Latin American railroads, highways, bridges, tunnels, air transport, maritime topics, etc., indexed by country and transportation mode. The system is accessible to private researchers, for a fee, through the Transportation Research Board's computer terminal. Contact the board's Special Projects office (389-6611) for further information. A guide, *TRISNET: Directory to Transportation Research Information Services* (1976), is available.

    The Foreign Projects Division (426-0380) of DOT's Federal Highway Administration has field advisers monitoring and overseeing construction of the Panama-Colombia segment of the Pan American Highway.

3. The Transportation Department Library is described in the "Libraries" section, entry A50.

J30 Treasury Department

1. a. *15th Street and Pennsylvania Avenue, NW*
        Washington, D.C. 20220
        566-2000

    b. Visitors should arrange appointments in advance.

2. Staff economists in the Office of the Assistant Secretary for International Affairs (OASIA) (566-5363) and its various sub-units analyze international monetary and financial issues. Of primary significance to Latin Americanists is OASIA's Office of the Deputy Assistant Secretary for Developing Nations (566-8243), which is further divided into an Office of Developing Nations Finance (566-2373) and an Office of International Development Banks (566-8171). Within the Office of Developing Nations Finance, a Latin American Regional Coordinator (John Sweeney, 566-2896) and four country-desk analysts monitor Latin American monetary and financial conditions. These specialists are the primary contact-point within the Treasury Department —and probably within the U.S. Government—for information relating to U.S.-Latin American debt levels, balance-of-payments conditions, and

general monetary relations. Their data sources include U.S. financial-attaché reports and Latin American banking reports. Most of the unit's internal products, which consist primarily of operational policy papers, are for internal use only, but staff members will confer with private scholars.

Within the Office of International Development Banks, two analysts monitor the operations of the Inter-American Development Bank and contribute to the formulation of U.S. policy toward the bank.

Three other units under OASIA—the Office of the Deputy Assistant Secretary for Trade and Raw Materials Policy (566-2748), Office of the Deputy Assistant Secretary for Energy and Investment Policy (566-5881), and Office of the Deputy Assistant Secretary for International Monetary Affairs (566-5232)—focus on Latin American issues from broader global and topical perspectives.

Elsewhere within the Treasury Department, the Internal Revenue Service's Tax Administration Advisory Services Division (566-4163) conducts a "tax administration assistance program" of technical assistance and training services for governmental tax administrators and finance managers in developing countries. The program, which was quite active in Latin America during the 1960s, currently is in operation in only one Latin American country (El Salvador). The division's data files on Latin American national tax systems are not accessible to private researchers.

3. The Treasury Department Library is discussed in the "Libraries" section, entry A51.

4. Retired Treasury Department internal records are controlled by the Office of Administration's Records Management Branch (566-2010). Access to most documents is possible only through Freedom-of-Information Act processes. The Treasury Department's Freedom of Information officer is Katherine Jordan (566-5573).

5. a. Two annual reports published by the Office of the Assistant Secretary for International Affairs contain Latin American data: the *Report on Developing Countries External Debt and Debt Relief Provided by the United States,* and the *Annual Report of the National Advisory Council on International Monetary and Financial Policies.* Also see the quarterly *Foreign Credits of the United States Government—Status of Active Foreign Credits of the United States Government,* prepared by the Office of Data Services (566-5127).

In addition, the *Annual Report of the Secretary of the Treasury on the State of the Finances* (with a separate *Statistical Appendix*) and the monthly *Treasury Bulletin* contain international financial statistics.

b. A *Select List of Treasury Publications* is available from the Office of Public Affairs (566-2041).

K. Latin American and Caribbean Embassies

Latin American and Caribbean Embassies Entry Format (K)

1. General information
    a. *address; telephone*
    b. hours

2. Reference facilities

3. Publications

4. Sponsored events and programs

Introductory Note

Each of the Latin American and Caribbean embassies listed below answers general-reference inquiries. Press/public-affairs officers or political secretaries can obtain recent social and economic statistics, provide information on political and legal matters, and answer questions about their nation's participation in international agreements and its position on international issues. Commercial, military, and cultural attachés are usually available to answer inquiries on matters which fall within their specialized areas of responsibility.

In addition, nearly every Latin American and Caribbean nation with an embassy in Washington is also represented by a diplomatic mission to the Organization of American States and by a military delegation to the Inter-American Defense Board. These missions and delegations are frequently located at addresses separate from the embassy, but they can invariably be reached through the embassy's telephone number. For further information on their specific activities see entries L4 and L10.

K1 Embassy of Argentina

1. a. *1600 New Hampshire Avenue, NW*
        Washington, D.C. 20009
        332-7100

    b. 9 A.M.-5 P.M. Monday-Friday

2. A small reference collection of general-information literature and government statistical publications is maintained for public use. A small number of documentary films and music recordings are also available.

3. A monthly current-events newsletter, *Argentina,* and an irregularly issued magazine, *Argentina,* are distributed.

4. The embassy sponsors occasional concerts, art exhibits, and lecture series (on politics, literature, etc.) at the OAS, the Inter-American Development Bank, and other locations in the city. Persons wishing to attend such programs will be placed on the embassy's mailing list.

K2 Embassy of the Bahamas

1. a. *Suite 865*
        600 New Hampshire Avenue, NW
        Washington, D.C. 20037
        338-3940

    b. 9 A.M.-5 P.M. Monday-Friday
        Reading Room: 2 P.M.-5 P.M. Monday-Friday

2. The embassy maintains a reading room with a small but expanding reference collection of government publications, including legal codes and the official gazette.

K3 Embassy of Barbados

1. a. *2144 Wyoming Avenue, NW*
        Washington, D.C. 20008
        387-7373

    b. 9 A.M.-5 P.M. Monday-Friday

2. A small reference collection of economic and other materials is available in the embassy's reading room. Approximately four films are available for loan.

3. A current-events newsletter, *Barbados News Bulletin* (irregular), is distributed.

K4 Embassy of Bolivia

1. a. *3012 Massachusetts Avenue, NW*
        Washington, D.C. 20036
        483-4410

    b. 9:30 A.M.-5 P.M. Monday-Friday

2. Included in the embassy's extremely small public reference collection are periodicals relating to Bolivian foreign relations and mining.

4. Occasional concerts and art exhibits are held at the OAS and the Inter-American Development Bank.

K5 Embassy of Brazil

1. a. *3006 Massachusetts Avenue, NW*
        Washington, D.C. 20008
        797-0100

b. 9 A.M.-1 P.M. and 2 P.M.-5 P.M. Monday-Friday

2. The Brazilian Embassy maintains a well-stocked, 3,000-volume, public reference library specializing in Brazilian social-science materials. Nearly 300 serial titles, including government publications and private periodicals, are currently received. The library possesses a complete collection of Brazilian decree-laws, as well as the official Brazilian statistical yearbook, 1908-present. The library ranks within the "B" range for research on Brazil. In addition, the Embassy's Information Section (797-0213) answers general-reference inquiries.

The library maintains a collection of 2,000 slides on Brazilian art and general culture, while the Embassy's Cultural Section has eight general-interest film documentaries and a handful of Brazilian-produced feature motion pictures. These materials are available for loan without charge.

3. An embassy newsletter, *Brazil Today* (irregular), and *Boletím,* a news digest of Brazilian current events (irregular), are distributed without charge.

4. The Cultural Section presents a variety of free public programs, including a bimonthly film series featuring Brazilian commercial motion pictures, as well as occasional concerts, art exhibits, and conferences on Brazilian history, literature, and culture. Anyone interested in attending should request to be placed on the embassy mailing-list in order to receive announcements of forthcoming events. In addition, the Brazilian-American Cultural Institute, an embassy-subsidized, cultural center, conducts an extensive range of educational and cultural programs. For further information, see entry 112.

K6 Embassy of Chile

1. a. *1736 Massachusetts Avenue, NW*
   Washington, D.C. 20036
   785-1746

   b. 9 A.M.-5 P.M. Monday-Friday

2. A 2,000-volume public reference library is maintained. It receives the major Chilean serials publications, including government *decretos,* statistical yearbooks, and central-bank publications, as well as Chilean academic periodicals. Five Chilean newspapers are also currently received. The library falls between the "A" and "B" ranges for research on Chile. The librarian answers general-information inquiries.

   The embassy's Cultural Section has small film, slide, and music collections available for loan, without charge.

3. The embassy disseminates a quarterly newsletter, *Chile Today,* and a monthly economic bulletin prepared by the Chilean development corporation, *Chile Economic News.*

4. Cultural programs are presented on occasion.

K7 Embassy of Colombia

1. a. *2118 Leroy Place, NW*
   Washington, D.C. 20008
   387-5828

b. 9:30 A.M.-5:30 P.M. Monday-Friday

2. The embassy is attempting to update and reorganize its small reference library. Current holdings include a variety of government ministerial reports and statistical publications dating back some two decades, and a rather extensive collection of materials relating to Colombian literature.

3. A monthly general-information and economics newsletter, *Colombia Today* (prepared by the Colombian Information Office in New York City), is distributed.

4. Sporadic concerts and arts/crafts exhibitions are held at various local sites. Those wishing to attend will, upon request, be placed on the embassy's mailing list.

K8 Embassy of Costa Rica

1. a. *2112 S Street, NW*
   Washington, D.C. 20008
   234-2945

   b. 9:30 A.M.-1 P.M. and 2:30 P.M.-4 P.M. Monday-Friday

2. No reference library is maintained, but the embassy staff will attempt to answer all inquiries.

K9 Cuban Interest Section

1. a. *2630 16th Street, NW*
   Washington, D.C. 20009
   797-8518

   b. 9 A.M.-5 P.M. Monday-Friday. Visitors are received by appointment only.

2. Some form of reference facility will be established. The Second Secretary for Cultural Affairs assists scholars in obtaining research data from Havana.

K10 Embassy of the Dominican Republic

1. a. *1715 22nd Street, NW*
   Washington, D.C. 20008
   332-6280

   b. 9 A.M.-4 P.M. Monday-Friday

2. No public reference collection is maintained. The staff will obtain information for researchers, but requests that inquiries be submitted in writing.

K11 Embassy of Ecuador

1. a. *2535 15th Street, NW*
   Washington, D.C. 20009
   234-7200

b. 9:15 A.M.-1 P.M. and 2:30 P.M.-5:30 P.M. Monday-Friday

2. A small, uncataloged reference collection exists, but contains primarily tourist information and dated government publications.

3. A monthly Spanish-language newsletter, *Boletín de noticias,* is distributed.

K12 Embassy of El Salvador

1. a. *2308 California Street, NW*
    Washington, D.C. 20008
    265-3480

    b. 9:30 A.M.-4:30 P.M. Monday-Friday

2. Materials from the embassy staff's private reference collection will be made available to researchers upon request. The collection contains a large number of government statistical publications—including central-bank, government-ministry, commodities, and CACM reports—dating back many years.

4. Cultural events are presented on an ad hoc basis. Anyone interested in attending may request to be placed on the embassy's mailing list.

K13 Embassy of Grenada

1. a. *Suite 612*
    927 15th Street, NW
    Washington, D.C. 20005
    347-3198

    b. 9:30 A.M.-4:30 P.M. Monday-Friday

2. No public reference collection is maintained, but the official gazette and other government materials might be made available to researchers on an individual basis.

K14 Embassy of Guatemala

1. a. *2220 R Street, NW*
    Washington, D.C. 20008
    332-2865

    b. 9:30 A.M.-1 P.M. and 2 P.M.-5 P.M. Monday-Friday

2. A small reference collection of legal codes and government serials covering the past five years will be made available to researchers.

K15 Embassy of Guyana

1. a. *2490 Tracy Place, NW*
    Washington, D.C. 20008
    265-6900

    b. 9 A.M.-5 P.M. Monday-Friday

2.   No public reference facility is maintained, but the staff will attempt to obtain information for researchers. The embassy has available a collection of some 15 general-information films.

3.   A bimonthly newsletter, *Embassy News,* is distributed.

K16 Embassy of Haiti

1. a. *4400 17th Street, NW*
        Washington, D.C. 20011
        723-7000

    b. 10 A.M.-3 P.M. Monday-Friday

2.   A small general-information reference collection is available for public use.

4.   Local concerts and arts/crafts exhibitions are presented. Anyone interested in learning of such events in advance may ask to be placed on the embassy's mailing list.

K17 Embassy of Honduras

1. a. *Suite 408*
        4301 Connecticut Avenue, NW
        Washington, D.C. 20008
        966-7700

    b. 10 A.M.-4 P.M. Monday-Friday

2.   No public reference facility is maintained, but the staff will attempt to obtain requested information.

3.   A monthly Spanish-language newsletter, *Carta mensual,* is distributed.

4.   The embassy sponsors occasional events in collaboration with the OAS.

K18 Embassy of Jamaica

1. a. *1666 Connecticut Avenue, NW*
        Washington, D.C. 20009
        387-1010

    b. 9 A.M.-5 P.M. Monday-Friday

2.   A small reference collection of recent government publications and statistical serials is maintained for public use. A few films, music-tapes, and art pieces are available for loan.

3.   A current-events newsletter, *Jamaica Newsletter* (monthly), is distributed.

K19 Embassy of Mexico

1. a. *2829 16th Street, NW*
        Washington, D.C. 20009
        234-6000

b.   10 A.M.-6 P.M. Monday-Friday

2.   No library or public reference collection is maintained. The Cultural Section (234-8636) responds to general inquiries.

K20   Embassy of Nicaragua

1.   a.   *1627 New Hampshire Avenue, NW*
Washington, D.C. 20009
387-4371

b.   9:30 A.M.-1 P.M. and 3 P.M.-5 P.M. Monday-Friday

2.   No public reference facility is maintained. The staff attempts to answer inquiries.

K21   Embassy of Panama

1.   a.   *2862 McGill Terrace, NW*
Washington, D.C. 20008
483-1407

b.   9 A.M.-1 P.M. and 3 P.M.-5 P.M. Monday-Friday

2.   Materials from the staff's small reference collection of government publications are made available to researchers. The embassy's small film collection contains a few recent political films related to the Canal. A small (5-10-piece) collection of native art is available for lending.

K22   Embassy of Paraguay

1.   a.   *2400 Massachusetts Avenue, NW*
Washington, D.C. 20008
483-6960

b.   9:30 A.M.-1 P.M. and 2 P.M.-4 P.M. Monday-Friday

2.   No reference collection is maintained. The staff will attempt to respond to information requests.

K23   Embassy of Peru

1.   a.   *1700 Massachusetts Avenue, NW*
Washington, D.C. 20036
833-9860

b.   9 A.M.-5 P.M. Monday-Friday

2.   No formal reference facility is maintained, but staff members will respond to inquiries. The embassy has an art collection of some 100 pieces available for lending.

3.   A monthly newsletter, the *Peruvian Embassy Bulletin,* is distributed.

4. A variety of cultural events are sponsored each year. Anyone wishing to receive announcements may request to be placed on the embassy's mailing list.

K24 Embassy of Surinam

1. a. *Suite 711*
2600 Virginia Avenue, NW
Washington, D.C. 20037
338-6980

  b. 9 A.M.-1 P.M. and 2:30 P.M.-5:30 P.M. Monday-Friday

2. No public reference facilities are maintained, but the staff will attempt to provide information. It prefers that inquiries be submitted in writing.

3. A current-events newsletter, *News in Brief* (irregular), is distributed.

K25 Embassy of Trinidad and Tobago

1. a. *1708 Massachusetts Avenue, NW*
Washington, D.C. 20036
467-6490

  b. 9 A.M.-5 P.M. Monday-Friday

2. The embassy reading room contains a small reference collection, including several government economic and statistical serials.

K26 Embassy of Uruguay

1. a. *1918 F Street, NW*
Washington, D.C. 20006
331-1313

  b. 9:30 A.M.-5:30 P.M. Monday-Friday

2. No public reference facilities are available. The staff will draw upon the embassy's internal materials and communicate with government agencies in Montevideo in an effort to provide information for researchers.

K27 Embassy of Venezuela

1. a. *2445 Massachusetts Avenue, NW*
Washington, D.C. 20008
265-9600

  b. 9 A.M.-1 P.M. and 2 P.M.-5 P.M. Monday-Friday

2. The Venezuelan Embassy maintains an Information Service, located adjacent to the embassy at 2437 California Street. Within the Information Service is a 4,000-volume reference library containing Venezuelan monographs on history, geography, politics, petroleum, etc., and a good collection

of government serials (*gacetas,* petroleum and other statistical bulletins, annual ministerial reports, etc.) dating back some ten years in coverage. The library ranks within the "A" range for research on Venezuela. The Information Service also has a small film collection which includes several rather dated documentaries from the 1950s which may be of significance for coverage of Venezuelan political history. In addition, a small music collection and a collection of some 300 slides (50 on art) are available.

3. The embassy distributes two general-interest monthly newsletters, *Venezuela Today* and *Venezuela ahora,* and a magazine, *Venezuela Up-To-Date* (irregular).

4. Concerts and exhibits are occasionally presented at the OAS.

Note: The interests in Belize, the British West Indies Associated States, and the other British dependencies in the Caribbean are represented in Washington by the British Embassy, located at 3100 Massachusetts Avenue, NW (462-1340). The interests of French Guiana and French territories in the Caribbean are represented in Washington by the Embassy of France, 2535 Belmont Road, NW (234-0990). The interests of the six Caribbean islands comprising the Netherlands Antilles are represented in Washington by the Embassy of the Netherlands, 4200 Linnean Avenue, NW (244-5300).

L. International Organizations

International Organization Entry Format* (L)

1. General information
   a. *address; telephone numbers*
   b. conditions of access
   c. name/title of director and heads of relevant divisions

2. Organization functions, programs, and research activities (including in-house research, contract research, research grants, and employment of outside consultants)

3. Libraries and reference facilities

4. Internal records (including unpublished research products)

5. Publications
   a. published reports, periodicals, and series
   b. bibliographies

   *Note: In the case of large, structurally complex organizations, each relevant division or sub-unit will be described separately in accordance with the above entry format.

L1 Inter-American Commercial Arbitration Commission (IACAC)

1. a. *310 Federal Bar Building West*
      1819 H Street, NW
      Washington, D.C. 20006
      293-1455

   b. Open to the public.

   c. Charles R. Norberg, Treasurer and General Counsel

2. The Inter-American Commercial Arbitration Commission is a quasi-governmental international body which promotes arbitration and conciliation of international commercial disputes. The commission is composed of delegates from National Sections in 18 Latin American nations and the United States. The National Sections consist of representatives of chambers of commerce and other commercial or legal groups in each member nation. (The United States' National Section is the American Arbitration Association in New York City.) When called upon to assist in the settlement of an international commercial dispute, IACAC provides advice and consultation

and, when necessary, works through its appropriate National Sections to appoint arbitrators and establish arbitration rules and procedures.

The commission meets biennially in an Inter-American Conference on Commercial Arbitration, held at varying sites throughout the hemisphere. It also sponsors seminars in the United States and Latin America on an ad hoc basis.

It maintains an Academy of International Arbitration in Mexico City.

3. The General Counsel's collection of documents and research materials on Latin American arbitration laws is open to researchers.

4. Arbitration case-files remain confidential.

5. A quarterly newsletter, *Inter-American Arbitration,* is disseminated.

L2 Inter-American Commission of Women

1. a. *Paramount Building, Room 730*
   1735 Eye Street, NW
   Washington, D.C. 20006
   381-8847/8440

   Mail: OAS General Secretariat
   Washington, D.C. 20006

   b. Open to visitors.

   c. Gabriela Touchard López, President
   Gabriela A. Fernández-Dávila, Executive Secretary
   Marijane E. Peplow, Assistant Executive Secretary

2. The Inter-American Commission of Women is a specialized advisory organ of the Organization of American States composed of one delegate from each OAS member nation and a support staff of three professionals. The commission promotes women's rights in Latin America by lobbying against discriminatory laws and by endeavoring to mobilize, organize, and train Latin American women for fuller participation in their nations' political and economic life. It holds a biennial assembly; sponsors international conferences on women's issues; conducts national and regional training seminars and leadership courses at its Multinational Women's Center in Córdoba, Argentina, and at numerous other sites throughout Latin America; and actively promotes the creation of official Women's Bureaus within the structures of Latin American national governments. In addition, it maintains liaison with the United States Commission on the Status of Women and with national women's-rights organizations throughout the hemisphere. The commission's Washington headquarters sponsors an annual student-internship program (primarily for college undergraduates).

3. A reference collection of commission documents, assembly and conference proceedings, and publications, as well as a small number of legal studies and other books on women in Latin America, is currently being developed.

4-5. The commission staff prepares reports on the political, educational, legal, and medical status of women in Latin America for distribution to the OAS and to Latin American governments. Publications include *Inter-American*

Conventions on Women (1972); *Inter-American Commission of Women, 1928-1973* (1974); the proceedings and resolutions of commission assemblies and conferences; manuals on leadership, education, etc.; and a monthly *Informational Bulletin.* (Two other periodicals, *Noticiero* and *Enlace,* apparently suspended publication in 1975 and 1976 respectively.)

L3 Inter-American Commission on Human Rights

1. a. *Premier Building, Room 1003*
       1725 Eye Street, NW
       Washington, D.C. 20006
       381-8765/8766

       Mail: OAS General Secretariat
       Washington, D.C. 20006

    b. Open to visitors

    c. Andrés Aguilar, Chairman
       Edmundo Vargas Carreño, Executive Secretary

2. The Inter-American Commission on Human Rights is a consultative organ of the Organization of American States. It is composed of seven official delegates elected by the OAS Permanent Council and a support staff of five lawyers. The commission receives complaints from individuals and organizations (political parties, trade unions, etc.) in Latin America regarding alleged violations of human rights and infringements of individual liberties. It then examines the charges—occasionally by means of on-site investigations—and, when warranted, addresses official inquiries on behalf of the victims to the national governments involved.

3. An extremely limited reference collection of human-rights documents is maintained.

4-5. Owing to the inherent sensitivities and potential dangers involved, the commission's case-files are not open to researchers. The commission's annual report to the OAS General Assembly and its special reports on the status of human rights in individual countries (recent studies focus on Chile and Cuba) are, however, available to researchers as OAS official documents (see entry L10). Publications include the acts and resolutions of inter-American conferences on human rights; *The Organization of American States and Human Rights, 1960-1967* (1972) and inter-American yearbooks on human rights for 1968 through 1970; a *Handbook of Existing Rules Pertaining to Human Rights* (1975); and two pamphlets, *American Declaration of the Rights and Duties of Man* and *La Comisión Interamericana de Derechos Humanos: ¿Qué Es y Cómo Funciona?*

L4 Inter-American Defense Board

1. a. *2600 16th Street, NW*
       Washington, D.C. 20441
       387-7860

    b. Not open to the public, but visitors will be received by appointment.

2.	The Inter-American Defense Board is an autonomous, multinational military organization funded through the Organization of American States. Its staff of delegates—comprised of high-level armed forces officers from 21 member nations—prepares hemispheric defense plans, develops procedures for the standardization of inter-American military organizations and operations, and produces studies on strategic and military affairs. A Council of Delegates meets regularly at closed, biweekly general assemblies. The Inter-American Defense Board also operates the Inter-American Defense College (see entries A25 and L5).

3.	A small reference library is maintained for staff use. It contains some 700 works on military history, a growing collection of official Latin American military documents, and transcripts of inter-American military conferences and the proceedings of Inter-American Defense Board delegate assemblies. Six Latin American armed-forces *revistas* are currently received. The collection ranks within the "A" range for research on selected aspects of military affairs.

4-5.	The staff of officer-delegates produces a variety of research publications, all classified. They include "Strategic Defense Plans," "Strategic Evaluations," "Guerrilla and Counterguerrilla Warfare," "Contribution of the Armed Forces in Economic-Social Development of Countries," "Military Civic Action," "Dictionaries of Military Terms," and others. These, along with the board's internal documents and working papers (including, presumably, materials relating to IADB peace-keeping activities in the Dominican Republic in 1965 and the Honduras-El Salvador border incidents of 1969 and 1976) are maintained in the board's Conferences and Documents section. Although all such resources are "for official use only," there are indications that outside scholars working on research projects of particular interest to the board might be provided with at least limited access. Inquiries should be directed to the Secretary, Inter-American Defense Board.

## L5	Inter-American Defense College

1.	a.	*Fort Lesley J. McNair*
Washington, D.C. 20319
693-8068

	b.	Not open to the public, but visitors will be received on an appointment basis.

2.	The Inter-American Defense College is an international military institution for advanced studies, operated by the Inter-American Defense Board. The student body consists of approximately 50 military officers (usually with the rank of colonel, lieutenant colonel, or the equivalent) and civilian governmental officials selected by the various American republics for a nine-month period of instruction at the college. The curriculum emphasizes international politics, economics, the psycho-social sciences, and military affairs—with equal periods of study devoted to theoretical considerations, the global situation, and inter-American/Latin American affairs. The faculty consists of a small number of nonteaching advisers and approximately 175 guest speakers.

3.	The Inter-American Defense College Library is discussed in the "Libraries" section, entry A25.

4. During the course of their studies, students prepare individual research papers on selected geopolitical, economic, and military topics. These papers are filed in the Inter-American Defense College Library, and, although presently restricted from outside use, could reveal valuable insights into the philosophies of influential members of the Latin American officer corps, many of whom have gone on to assume positions of importance in their national governments.

L6   Inter-American Development Bank

1. a. *808 17th Street, NW*
      Washington, D.C. 20577
      634-8000

   b. Bank offices are open to visitors, by appointment.

   c. Antonio Ortiz Mena, President

2. The Inter-American Development Bank is an international financial institution representing 37 member nations. Its stated function is "to foster socioeconomic development in Latin America on a multilateral basis." Bank operations are centered around a series of "lending sectors:" agricultural and rural development; physical infrastructure (highways, ports, electric power, telecommunications, and gas pipelines); industrial development; urban development (primarily housing and sanitation); education; tourism; and technical cooperation to promote regional economic integration. The bank conducts in-house research on socioeconomic and financial conditions in Latin America (see below). The bank periodically commissions outside research on socioeconomic topics and employs consultants in specialized areas of sectorial analysis.

3. The Inter-American Development Bank Library is discussed in the "Libraries" section, entry A26.

4. The bank's unpublished internal reports and records are filed in two separate collections. Both are officially closed to outsiders, but private scholars might gain limited access by contacting appropriate officials. The Secretariat Department maintains a depository of formal policy-studies, position papers, and other documents prepared, or utilized, by the bank's Board of Directors. Deputy Secretary Arturo Calventi (634-8909) can be of assistance. The Administrative Department operates a Records Center which contains staff-level working papers (communications, memoranda, reports) and bank correspondence with field officers and borrowers. Contact Kenneth Cole (634-8800) for further information. In addition, the bank's Law Library maintains a complete collection of documents and working papers related to each of the bank's loan projects, including project proposals and bank appraisals. Although this collection is for the private use of the bank's legal staff alone, researchers might gain access by securing the permission of the appropriate loan officer in the bank's Operations Department (634-8170).

5. a. The bank's *Annual Report* describes the bank's operations, capital resources, and loan projects, by country. It contains a wealth of statistical data on Latin America. Other publications are the bank's annual survey of *Economic and Social Progress in Latin America,* the *Proceedings* of the annual meeting of

the Board of Governors, summaries of yearly roundtables on selected economic and social themes, a monthly newsletter, *IDB News,* and miscellaneous studies on development issues affecting Latin America. Free copies of these publications can be obtained from the Office of Information.

b. A bibliography, "Publications of the Inter-American Development Bank," is also available without charge

---

Economic and Social Development Department
Cecilio J. Morales, Manager
634-8374

The Economic and Social Development Department, with a staff of some 80 professional economists (three-fourths of whom are Latin Americans), is the bank's primary research division. Its research studies are designed to provide bank officials with current data on the economic environment in Latin America. A series of "country studies" (some six each year) surveys general economic conditions in the bank's Latin American member nations. A series of "general studies" (approximately eight per year) analyzes structural aspects of Latin American economic sectors (agriculture, industry, finance, etc.) on a regional and subregional basis. Other studies deal with questions of technical assistance and regional integration. Some of the department's research products are published, while others are for internal bank use only. A research bibliography is available upon request.

A Technical-Information Documentation Center (634-8385) supports the department staff's research activities with a large reference collection of current serials, statistical bulletins, and annual reports from international organizations and from Latin American governmental and financial institutions. The Economic and Social Development Department's research products, restricted and non-restricted, are filed here. The center also produces a periodical "Calendar to Future International, Regional Meetings and Seminars Concerned with Economic and Social Development." Scholars may gain access to the center's materials by contacting the department manager (634-8374) or the bank librarian (634-8382/83/84).

Operations Department
Norman Marques Jones, Manager
634-8170

The Operations Department, the key "functional" division within the bank structure, administers and supervises bank loans to Latin American borrowers. Country-desk loan officers can provide information regarding the nature and progress of bank-funded development projects.

Project Analysis Department
Guillermo Moore, Manager
634-8528

The Project Analysis Department conducts feasibility studies of loan requests, evaluating the technical viability of proposed development projects. Its "sectorially" structured divisions (Social Projects, Infrastructure-Development Projects, Development Finance Institutions, Agricultural Development Projects, Industrial Development Projects) conduct what might best be described as "applied research."

Plans and Programs Department
José D. Epstein, Manager
634-8116

This department conducts broader studies to support the formulation of bank policy and lending strategy—how bank funds are to be allocated, which types of development projects are to be financed, etc.

L7 Inter-American Nuclear Energy Commission

1. a. *Paramount Building, Room 1134*
      1735 Eye Street, NW
      Washington, D.C. 20006
      381-8733/8734

   Mail: OAS General Secretariat
      Washington, D.C. 20006

   b. Open to visitors

   c. Marcelo Alonso, Executive Secretary

2. The Inter-American Nuclear Energy Commission is a consultative organ of the Organization of American States composed of delegates appointed by OAS member nations. The commission endeavors to promote and coordinate the exchange of technical information and research specialists in fields related to the peaceful application of nuclear energy to Latin American industry, agriculture, and medicine. Topics of particular current interest are nucleo-electric power and exploration for deposits of radioactive ores. The commission compiles information on the nuclear-energy programs of hemispheric nations. It also drafts recommendations and assists in the formulation of inter-American conventions on technical matters such as radiation safety, civil liability for nuclear damages, and legal aspects of the transportation of nuclear material.

3. The commission collects documents and reports from the nuclear-energy commissions, agencies, and related institutes of OAS member nations, the International Atomic Energy Agency, and other international organizations.

5. a. The *Informe Final* of the executive secretary describes the proceedings of the commission's biennial meeting. A recent *Plan of Action Proposed for the Biennium, 1978-1979* (1977) discusses the commission's current programs and contains substantial data on Latin American nuclear-energy programs, installations, resources, and development plans, by country. These and other commission reports are included among the OAS' official documents (see entry L10).

Inter-American Statistical Institute See entries A45 and L10

L8 International Bank for Reconstruction and Development (World Bank)

1. a. *1818 H Street, NW*
      Washington, D.C. 20433
      477-1234

b. Not open to the public. Visitors received by appointment.

c. Robert S. McNamara, President

2. The IBRD, or World Bank, is an intergovernmental lending institution composed of 129 member nations. The bank provides capital and technical assistance for long-term economic development projects in the less-developed nations. Major sectors of lending activity are agriculture and smallholder development; education; industrialization (with increasing emphasis on support for local development-finance companies); population planning (research and facilities); urban development (housing and sanitation); and tourism. Bank departments conduct extensive research on international economic affairs (Latin American research activities are described below). The bank funds contract research, utilizes individual professional and academic consultants (technical specialists, notably engineers, agronomists, and fiscal experts), and supports research projects in Latin American academic and research institutes. (Two pamphlets, "Use of Consultants by the World Bank and Its Borrowers," and "World Bank Research Program: Abstracts of Current Studies," are available from the Publications Unit.)

Latin America and the Caribbean Regional Office   477-5901
Adalbert Krieger, Regional Vice-President
John A. Holsen, Chief Economist
Louis V. Perez, Program Coordinator

This office plans and administers the 40-50 development-assistance projects (totaling some $2 billion) which the World Bank finances in Latin America each year. The staff—approximately 200 economists, financial analysts, technical specialists (agronomists, etc.), and lawyers, half of whom are from Latin America—is in daily contact with Latin American governmental and banking officials, and spends two to three months of each year on data-gathering field missions. A large number of confidential economic reports and special studies are produced, including assessments of Latin American development requirements and priorities, policy recommendations, project appraisals, and loan evaluations. Many of the office's research products are disseminated to selected international organizations and U.S. government agencies—including the U.S. Department of Commerce—where periodically they inadvertently become accessible to private researchers in departmental libraries. Scholars have also gained access to office research materials through personal contact with individual staff members.

The office's research activities are supported by the bank's Latin American Regional Information and Documents Center (477-5446), which maintains a reference collection of internally and externally produced materials.

International Finance Corporation   477-3424
1809 G Street, NW
Gordon F. McClure, Vice-President, Operations—Latin America, Caribbean, and Europe

The International Finance Corporation, a World Bank affiliate, uses its capital resources to encourage the growth of private enterprise and the private sector in developing nations. In Latin America, IFC investment loans assist in the financing of local and multinational business ventures in the fields of manufacturing, mining, agribusiness, and tourism. The IFC also supports the development of mortgage banks, savings and loan associations, stock exchanges, and other capital-markets institutions which channel domestic savings into productive private enterprises. Washington staff members function primarily as investment bankers.

3.   See "Joint Bank-Fund Library" in the "Libraries" section, entry A31.

4.   All bank research reports and other internal working papers are ultimately filed in the Records Center (477-4536) of the Administrative Services Department, which maintains an index of "Documentation Available to Staff."

5. a. The bank issues a variety of periodical publications. The *World Bank Annual Report* reviews bank projects, economic trends in developing countries, capital flows, and the external public debts of 86 developing countries. *Summary Proceedings of the Annual Meeting* contains texts of addresses and resolutions. *Finance and Development,* a quarterly review produced jointly with the International Monetary Fund, contains nontechnical articles dealing with problems of money, economic growth and development, national and international monetary policies, trade and exchange systems, and the nature of World Bank/IMF assistance to the developing nations. A bimonthly newspaper, *Report,* features news on economic development and World Bank activities.

Several periodical statistical reports will be of particular interest to Latin Americanists. The irregularly published *World Tables* contains long-range time series of statistical data on a wide range of social and economic indicators, by country. An annual *World Bank Atlas* provides data on population, per capita product, and growth rates. The monthly *Economic and Social Indicators* presents global indicators by income group of population, GNP, national savings, and investment. Included are statistical tables on external public debt, energy production and consumption, agricultural and industrial production, external trade, commodity prices and price forecasts, consumer prices by areas and selected countries, and international reserves by income groups. The annual *World Debt Tables* contains historical data on the external public debt situation for 86 developing countries, with additional statistical tables showing commitments, new flows, grant disbursements, debt-service time-profile ratios, and information on creditor-country distribution of loans to 26 major debtor countries. An annual *Commodity Trade and Price Trends* contains a variety of data on the import and export trade of developing countries, by country and region. Included are market price quotations on 42 commodities which figure importantly in world trade. *Borrowing in International Capital Markets,* issued quarterly, provides detailed descriptive lists of individual transactions as well as summary statistics of amounts by borrowing country.

The bank also publishes a book series (including recent country-studies on Peru, Ecuador, and Colombia), bibliographies on development topics, and a series of staff research reports, "Sector Working Papers and Policy Papers," many of which deal specifically with Latin American development topics.

b. A full *Catalog of Publications* is available from the bank's Publications Unit.

L9 International Monetary Fund

1. a. *700 19th Street, NW*
Washington, D.C. 20431
477-7000

b. Not open to public. Visitors received by appointment.

c. Jacques De La Rosière, Managing Director

2. The IMF works to promote international currency stability by seeking to eliminate restrictive exchange practices among its 126 member nations and by allocating the fund's monetary reserves to assist members in meeting temporary balance-of-payments disequilibria. The fund's departments compile and analyze statistics on international financial and economic conditions. Latin American activities are discussed below. Little contract research is funded, but the IMF maintains a pool of private international fiscal and central-banking specialists to act as advisers to foreign governments.

Western Hemisphere Department
E. Walter Robichek, Director
477-2988

The principal operational element of the IMF for Latin American affairs, the Western Hemisphere Department has a staff of some 50 professional economists (approximately half from Latin America) assigned as country specialists in seven geographic divisions. The department analyzes trends in Latin American fiscal and monetary affairs. Staff teams make periodic trips to Latin American capitals to collect data, analyze financial policies and trends, and hold policy consultations with national finance ministers and central-bank officials. Frequently, the staff's private information on the level of Latin American monetary reserves is considerably more accurate than public data which appear in the IMF's statistical publications.

The department prepares an annual report on "recent economic developments" in each country of the hemisphere. It also produces highly confidential "staff reports" appraising Latin American fiscal conditions based on field consultations. These materials are not presently available to outside researchers. Western Hemisphere Department staff members, however, are accessible to scholars.

3. See "Joint Bank-Fund Library" in the "Libraries" section, entry A31.

4. Fund documents, reports, and other working papers—virtually all confidential—are filed in the Records Division of the IMF's Secretary Department, which maintains a cumulative list of internal fund materials.

5. a. The IMF issues a broad range of periodical publications. The *Annual Report of the Executive Director* reviews the fund's activities and surveys the world economy, with emphasis on balance-of-payments problems, exchange rates, international liquidity, and world trade. The *Annual Report on Exchange Restrictions* reviews developments in the field of exchange controls and restrictions, by country. *Summary Proceedings* is a record of the fund's annual meeting. The biweekly *IMF Survey* reports fund activities (including press releases, texts of communiques and major statements, SDR valuations, and exchange rates) within the context of developments in national economies and international finance. *Finance and Development,* a joint quarterly review of IMF/World Bank activities, is directed primarily toward a nontechnical audience. It contains articles dealing with problems of money and economic growth, national and international monetary policies, trade and exchange systems, economic development, and Bank/Fund development assistance. *Staff Papers* (three issues per year) contains studies on monetary and financial problems prepared by members of the IMF staff.

Four major statistical periodicals are produced. The monthly *International Financial Statistics* contains data on exchange rates, international liquidity, money and banking, international trade, prices, production, government finance, interest rates, etc., by country and region. The monthly *Direction of Trade* provides data on imports and exports, by country, with comparative data for the corresponding period of the previous year. The *Government Finance Statistics Yearbook* provides data on revenues, expenditures, lending, financing, and debt of central governments, and also indicates amounts represented by social security funds and extrabudgetary operations. The *Balance of Payments Yearbook* provides relevant statistics on member nations.

The IMF also publishes a book series (which includes a three-volume history, *The International Monetary Fund, 1945-1965: Twenty Years of International Monetary Cooperation* and a two-volume sequel, *The International Monetary Fund, 1966-1971: The System Under Stress)*, a pamphlet series (including "The International Monetary Fund and Latin America"), and miscellaneous special reports.

b. A *Catalogue of Publications, 1946-1971* and a "Publications" brochure are available. Contact the IMF Publications Office or the Office of Information.

L10 Organization of American States

1. a. *Pan American Union Building*
        17th Street and Constitution Avenue, NW
        Washington, D.C. 20006
        331-1010

    Additional Offices:

    Premier Building
    1725 Eye Street, NW
    Washington, D.C. 20006

    Paramount Building
    1735 Eye Street, NW
    Washington, D.C. 20006

    Mail: OAS General Secretariat
    Washington, D.C. 20006

    b. Open to the public, 9 A.M.-5:30 P.M. Monday-Friday.

2. The world's oldest international regional organization, the Organization of American States serves as a forum for the negotiation of inter-American agreements and provides technical assistance to Latin American member-governments in the areas of economic, social, educational, scientific, and technological development. The OAS Permanent Council, composed of delegations from some 25 member nations, meets in regular deliberative sessions in Washington on the first and third Wednesdays of each month, September through June. Its meetings are open to the public. Other major OAS deliberative bodies—the General Assembly, the Inter-American Social and Economic Council, the Inter-American Council for Education, Science, and Culture, and numerous specialized conferences—convene on an annual basis at rotating sites throughout the hemisphere (including, periodically, Washington).

The OAS General Secretariat, the organization's permanent support staff in Washington, carries out OAS technical-assistance programs (primarily advisory services and training), conducts research, and produces a multiplicity of publications and unpublished reports. The activities of the various units of the General Secretariat are described below. Many of these units periodically contract outside research in specialized scientific and economic areas. The OAS offers a wide range of pre- and postdoctoral fellowships and travel grants (some 1,800 annually) for research and study in virtually every field of the humanities, social sciences, and physical sciences. Fellowship programs are administered by the Trainee Selection Unit (381-8591) of the General Secretariat's Office of Direct Services Operations.

3. The Organization of American States Columbus Memorial Library is discussed in the "Libraries" section, entry A43. Specialized OAS office libraries on education and statistics are discussed in entries A44 and A45, respectively.

4. Unpublished OAS research reports remain in the files of the originating offices described below. A partial bibliography has been prepared (see section 5.b., below).

    All OAS internal records are eventually housed in the Organization of American States Records Management Center, which is described in the "Archives" section, entry B11.

5. a. The OAS issues an enormous quantity of publications. Its "official records" series includes the *Annual Report of the Secretary General;* the texts of multilateral treaties, conventions, and agreements; and the resolutions and proceedings of the General Assembly, Permanent Council, Inter-American Economic and Social Council, Inter-American Council for Education, Science, and Culture, Inter-American Juridical Committee, Inter-American Commission on Human Rights, Inter-American Nuclear Energy Commission, hemispheric foreign-ministers' meetings, and a host of other specialized conferences and commissions. These records are available on microform.

    "Technical and informational publications" include specialized studies in the fields of economics, regional development, statistics, social affairs, science, law, philosophy, education, fine arts, bibliography and library science, youth affairs, and tourism. Among the legal publications are a "Constitutions" series, a series of "Statements of the Laws of the American Republics in Matters Affecting Business," and specialized works in international law (private investment, copyright, etc., and a yearbook: *Anuario Jurídico Interamericano*). A large quantity of general-information material on the inter-American system and the Latin American nations is also produced. Researchers may find the following regularly updated, general-information publications useful: *Organization of American States: A Handbook, OAS Directory* (listing the delegations of member nations), *Chiefs of State and Cabinet Ministers of the American Republics, OAS in the Americas* (which summarizes OAS programs in each member nation), a *Quarterly List of Conferences,* a *Weekly Schedule of Meetings at Headquarters,* and a *Quarterly Report on Conferences.*

    OAS periodicals include the illustrated, monthly, general-interest magazine *Américas,* and the *OAS Chronicle,* a monthly newsletter containing current information on major inter-American events and the texts of important official documents. Several other specialized periodicals are discussed below.

b. OAS official documents are indexed in the annual *Documentos Oficiales de la Organización de los Estados Americanos.* OAS publications are listed in the *Catalog of Publications.* Both are available from the General Secretariat's Department of Publications.

In addition, in an initial attempt to identify and register the many valuable unpublished research studies produced each year within the OAS, the Department of Publications compiled a *Catálogo de Informes Técnicos y Documentos de la OEA: 1974-1975.* Included are reference data (author, title, producing office, date, and number of pages) on unpublished OAS technical reports, contract-research studies, reports of seminars and workshops, papers presented by OAS staff members at outside conferences, and studies produced by OAS fellowship-holders. An expanded version covering the years 1974-1976 is in preparation. Nonrestricted reports and documents listed in the catalog are available on microfiche.

ECONOMIC AND SOCIAL AREA   381-8250/8335

Development Programming
Room 402, Premier Building
381-8725/8726

The staff economists of this unit maintain up-to-date information on economic conditions in Latin America. The unit produces periodic country-reviews and short-term economic-forecasting studies analyzing the general economic situation and economic development programs of OAS member nations. Those research studies which have been cleared for release by the respective member nation are available to scholars as OAS official documents.

Also within the Development Programming unit is the OAS' former Department of Statistics (Tulio Montenegro, Director) (381-8207). The statistical office provides technical assistance and training to member nations in the development, improvement, and standardization of their national statistical systems. It also assists other units of the OAS General Secretariat in preparing statistical surveys and country-profiles. The statistical office serves as the secretariat of the Inter-American Statistical Institute, a technical professional organization comprised of hemispheric statistical experts and organizations, which operates the Inter-American Center for Statistical Training in Santiago, Chile, and which holds an Inter-American Statistical Conference every five years. The statistical office produces reports on problems in Latin American statistical methodology; a biennial, multi-volume publication, *America en Cifras,* containing socio-economic, demographic, and cultural statistical information; a trimestral journal, *Estadística;* and a semiannual *List of Publications Received,* a useful index of the recent statistical publications of Latin American governments and international organizations. Staff members can provide researchers with current statistical data, by country, for all major subject categories. They can also assist researchers in identifying sources of Latin American statistics and in contacting Latin American government statistical agencies. The office's Statistical Reference Collection is discussed in the "Libraries" section, entry A45.

The Development Programming unit also encompasses the former OAS Industrial Development Program, whose staff economists provide technical assistance to member nations in evaluating the potential of their natural resources for industrial development, in designing industrialization policies, and in creating systems to absorb and utilize available technology. Fishing and mining resources are areas of particular attention. This office's research activities focus on resource economics and on industrial planning and promotion. Its publications include case studies on the promotion of both private-sector industrial investment and manufactured export products. Unpublished research reports include analyses of the Latin American industrialization process.

Regional Development Program
Room 703, Premier Building
381-8767/8768

The Regional Development Program assists member nations in preparing strategies for the development of natural resources in undeveloped geographic regions. It provides technical experts to survey and evaluate the resources of underutilized areas, work out packages of specific development projects, and draw up comprehensive regional-development plans to attract investment, people, and services into the regions targeted for development. The unit has established a training and research center, the Inter-American Center for Regional Development, at Maracaibo, Venezuela. Several of the Regional Development Program's studies have been published, including the multivolume *Cuenca del Río de la Plata: Estudio para su Planificación y Desarrollo; Región Zuliana, República de Venezuela—Estudio para el Aprovechamiento Racional de los Recursos Naturales;* and *El Salvador, Zonificación Agrícola.* Among the unit's approximately 30-40 unpublished research reports on other Latin American regional-development projects are recent studies of the Darien region of Panama and Colombia, the Esmeraldas River basin of Ecuador, the Pilcomayo River basin of Argentina, Paraguay, and Bolivia, the Paraguay River basin of Brazil, and the Pacific coastal region of Nicaragua.

Rural Development Program
Room 905, Premier Building
381-8541

This unit provides technical assistance and training to member nations in the design and implementation of strategies and projects to raise the productivity, income, and general welfare of marginal populations in rural areas. Technical advisory field missions collaborate with national planning and development agencies to devise employment schemes which will help to reverse rural-urban imbalances, and to develop programs for integrated rural development and for the strengthening of small and intermediate urban centers which provide services and serve as support for rural development. Recently, the Rural Development Program has become increasingly active in assisting in the development of economic cooperatives and other community organizations. Publications include a series of manuals on cooperative- and community-development. In addition, numerous unpublished research reports on urban and rural development strategies and projects are listed in the *Catálogo de Informes Técnicos y Documentos de la OEA, 1974-1976.*

Social Development Program
Room 504, Premier Building
381-8515/8516

This unit provides technical advisory missions to member states to assist in formulating and carrying out policies and plans on manpower utilization, generation of employment, labor development, and the modernization of social-security systems. It also sponsors training programs in labor economics, human resources, and social development at the Inter-American Center for Integrated Social Development in Buenos Aires and at various other Latin American sites. The unit's published works include studies of personnel administration and public relations in Latin American social-security agencies. Among its unpublished research reports, most of which are of a confidential and restricted nature, are numerous studies on social and political aspects of the Latin American development process, and analyses of income redistribution, labor markets, and intra-Latin American migration. For a listing, see the OAS *Catálogo de Informes Técnicos y Documentos de la OEA, 1974-1976.*

International Trade Program
Room 719, Paramount Building
381-8813/8814

This unit works with member nations on problems related to international trade, transportation, communications, and finance, including the recording and controlling of external debts. Affiliated with the unit is the OAS Special Committee for Consultation and Negotiation (CECON), which works in coordination with GATT and UNCTAD to promote multilateral reductions in inter-American tariffs and other trade restrictions and to secure greater access in United States markets for Latin American primary and manufactured goods. The International Trade Program has published studies on transnational enterprises in Latin America and on the external financing of Latin American development programs. It also produces two monthly periodicals: *CECON Trade News,* a bulletin containing information on tariffs, customs duties, and trade legislation pending before the U.S. Congress, and *Boletín de Precios Internacionales de Productos Básicos,* a statistical summary of commodity prices.

The program operates the Inter-American Center for Export Promotion in Bogotá, and the Inter-American Center for Training in National and International Marketing in Rio de Janeiro.

Public Sector Program
Room 1920, Paramount Building
381-8547/8548

The Public Sector program office (formerly the Development Financing program office) works with member states and Latin American regional-integration organizations in the formulation and evaluation of public-revenue, public-expenditure, capital-markets, and private-investment policies. It also collaborates in setting up tax, budget, capital-market, and private-investment management and programming systems, and offers training courses and seminars at the Inter-American Centers for Training in Public Administration in Buenos Aires and Caracas, the Inter-American Center for Tax Studies in Buenos Aires, and other institutions in Latin America. The unit produces published studies and unpublished reports on Latin American tax and revenue systems, and publishes *Public Sector* (formerly *Development Financing*), a quarterly review of Latin American internal development-finance activities.

Development Projects Program
Room 710, Premier Building
381-8801/8569

Field missions from this unit work with the national planners, technical specialists, and training institutions of member nations to assist them in developing sound methodologies and institutional bases for formulating and evaluating their national development projects. The unit also prepares technical reports on specific Latin American development projects. Some 150 of these unpublished reports are listed in the *Catálogo de Informes Técnicos y Documentos de la OEA, 1974-1976.*

Tourism Development Program
Room 414, Premier Building
381-8467/8874

This unit assists member nations in planning, promoting, and financing national tourism programs. Training programs are carried out in Inter-American Centers for Training in Tourism throughout Latin America. The unit publishes guides to tourism and travel in Latin America, and prepares numerous unpublished reports and evaluations of national tourism-development plans.

DEVELOPMENT COOPERATION AREA   381-8471

Office of Analysis and Evaluation of Development Cooperation Programs
Room 820-C, Paramount Building
381-8103

This office receives the development-aid requests of member nations and evaluates them from the viewpoints of feasibility, funding, and availability of resources. It monitors those development projects which receive OAS assistance, and prepares unpublished technical reports and country-studies.

Office of International Cooperation
Room 822, Paramount Building
381-8746/8747

The Office of International Cooperation provides coordination and liaison between the development-assistance programs and resources of the OAS and those of nonmember states, international organizations, and nongovernmental organizations.

Office of Coordination and Support of Offices Away from Headquarters
Room 825, Paramount Building
381-8575

This office provides liaison with OAS field offices and agencies in Latin America. It also administers the Inter-American Emergency Aid Fund (FONDEM), which channels relief assistance to victims of earthquakes and other natural disasters in Latin America.

Office of Youth Affairs
Room 613, Paramount Building
381-8375

The Office of Youth Affairs provides technical assistance to youth councils, sports confederations, and voluntary-service organizations in member states.

It promotes youth activities and sports programs, provides training fellowships, internships, and exchange programs for athletes, youth leaders, and young artists, and organizes inter-American athletic events and competitions for young artists and musicians. The office also publishes a semiannual information bulletin, *Juventud.*

EDUCATION, SCIENCE, AND CULTURE AREA   381-8638/8639

Department of Educational Affairs
Room 924, Paramount Building
381-8661

The Department of Educational Affairs promotes uniform educational standards and improvements in school systems throughout Latin America. It conducts technical-assistance missions and specialized training programs (courses and fellowships), organizes technical conferences, and conducts research. The department's Administration and Planning Unit (381-8125) focuses on educational administration, evaluation, and school construction. The Curriculum and Educational Technology Unit (381-8444) develops textbooks, teachers-aids, and school curricula, and supplies materials and financial aid to Latin American educational centers. The Technical Education, Adult Education, and Educational·Research Unit (381-8305) assists member nations in the development of educational-television, vocational-, and adult-education programs. The Department of Educational Affairs publishes studies of Latin American education programs, as well as a quarterly journal, *La Educación.* In addition, the *Catálogo de Informes Técnicos y Documentos de la OEA, 1974-1976* lists nearly 200 unpublished research reports prepared by the department on specialized problems in Latin American education (largely by country). The department's library collection is discussed in the "Libraries" section, entry A44.

Department of Scientific Affairs
Room 1134, Paramount Building
381-8733

The Department of Scientific Affairs promotes the accelerated development of science and technology in Latin America. Its stated goals are institutional development, the upgrading of technically trained personnel, and the diffusion of scientific and technological information. The department supplies direct technical-assistance services to OAS member nations in the form of advisory missions, research and publications programs, advanced courses and specialized conferences, training fellowships and travel grants, modern equipment, and bibliographic materials. Specialized departmental units concentrate on basic sciences, applied sciences, scientific and technological policy and planning, technological development, and technology transfer. Publications include numerous surveys and country-studies; monograph series in biology, physics, chemistry, and mathematics; a quarterly journal, *Ciencia Interamericana;* and a newsletter, *Noticiero* (irregular). Recent examples of unpublished research reports prepared by the department are *Evaluación, Estado Actual, y Posibles Líneas de Acción Futura en el Campo del Desarrollo Tecnológico en América Latina y el Caribe,* studies of technology transfer in Bolivia, Chile, Colombia, Venezuela, and Central America, and diverse reports on recent developments in the basic and applied sciences.

Department of Cultural Affairs
Room 920, Paramount Building
381-8220

The Folklore and Handicrafts Unit (381-8353) assists member nations in developing facilities for the preservation, development, and promotion of the popular arts. In an effort to preserve folk arts by making them economically viable, the unit supports training programs at the Inter-American Institute of Ethnomusicology and Folklore in Caracas and at regional arts/crafts centers throughout Latin America, where artisans are taught techniques of improving traditional crafts so as to assure them of commercial markets. It also assists in the formation of artisan cooperatives, regional folk-art repositories, and information centers. The activities of the unit's field missions are described in unpublished reports.

The Technical Unit of Cultural Heritage (381-8717) provides technical assistance for the restoration, preservation, and display of historic artifacts, art works, buildings, and urban areas. It assists in organizing local museums, and supports the training of specialized personnel at the Inter-American Center for the Restoration of Cultural Property in Mexico City. The unit is also currently assisting in efforts to identify, locate, and register artifacts of significant cultural value that have been illegally removed from Latin America. Among its unpublished reports are field evaluations of the physical condition of colonial missions and other historic sites, and analyses of Latin American historic restoration and preservation programs.

The Technical Unit for the Development of Libraries and Archives (381-8293) provides advisory assistance, equipment, and bibliographic materials to libraries and archives in member states. Training courses in library and archival management, documents preservation and microfilming, and library cataloging are offered through the multinational Center for the Training of Archivists in Córdoba, Argentina, and numerous other Latin American institutions. The unit has published a series of *Estudios Bibliotecarios,* and has prepared recent unpublished reports evaluating libraries in Argentina, Bolivia, Costa Rica, El Salvador, Venezuela, and the Caribbean, as well as archives in Costa Rica and Colombia.

The Music Unit (381-8353) works closely with the Inter-American Institute of Musical Training in Santiago, Chile, and with national music academies and conservatories throughout Latin America to promote music education and the development of orchestras and ensembles. Fellowships are offered for the advanced training of Latin American composers, conductors, and performers, as well as specialists in musicology and music education. Each year in Washington, the Music Unit sponsors, in conjunction with the Washington Performing Arts Society and the Kennedy Center for the Performing Arts, a series of some 30 concerts by outstanding Latin American musical figures (presented at approximately biweekly intervals, October through April). It also sponsors an annual Inter-American Music Festival, as well as a special concert-series during the OAS' annual Pan American Week (held in April). The unit has recently begun production of an "Inter-American Musical Editions" series of records and tape cassettes featuring the music of major Latin American composers and performers. An active publications program includes the on-going multivolume series *Composers of the Americas,* which catalogs the works of major hemispheric composers; a sheet-music series, *Contemporary Music of the Americas; National Anthems of the American Nations;* and short studies of Latin American, Jamaican, and Honduran song. (A periodical, *Boletín Interamericano de*

Música, is no longer published.) The unit also maintains a tape collection of Inter-American Music Festivals (1954-present), scores and tapes relating to OAS music fellowships, and a heterogeneous collection of ca. World War II-era Latin American records.

The Visual Arts Unit (381-8261) serves as a clearinghouse for information on the visual and graphic arts of modern Latin America. It produces films, slide-sets, and video cassettes on Latin American art, artists, and general culture (a catalog, *Latin American Audio-Visual Materials,* is available). It also administers the Museum of Modern Art of Latin America (see entry C10), presents rotating exhibitions of Latin American art, and sponsors conferences and traveling exhibits in Latin America. Publications include numerous short works on Latin American art and architecture, and an irregular *Boletín de Artes Visuales.* The unit maintains a vertical file with some 100,000 catalogs, critical essays, news clippings, and other material, ranging in date from the 1920s to the present, on Latin American modern art and artists. Scattered throughout the unit's offices is a large and valuable, but completely uncataloged, reference collection of art books, encyclopedias, periodicals, catalogs, pamphlets, and clippings. Also available is a biographical card index of Latin American painters (up-to-date through the 1950s), separate collections of some 10,000 black-and-white photographs and 1,000 black-and-white negatives on Latin American arts, crafts, and artists, and some 5,000 color slides on Latin American art works, general scenes, and OAS events. Presently in storage within the unit are approximately 140 crated sets of color reproductions of the works of major Latin American modern artists, and extensive collections of original paintings, prints, and drawings left on consignment by Latin American artists.

The Technical Unit on Studies and Research (381-8668) sponsors conferences and supports research in Latin American literature, philosophy, history, and other areas of the humanities. It publishes the *Inter-American Review of Bibliography,* a quarterly "journal of humanistic studies."

Note: Also see entries A43, A44, A45, B11, D4, and F20.

L11   Pan American Health Organization (PAHO)

1. a. *525 23rd Street, NW*
      Washington, D.C. 20037
      223-4700

   b. Open to the public. Visitors required to register at entrance. Appointment recommended.

2.   The Pan American Health Organization (PAHO) is a specialized agency of the Organization of American States. It also serves as the U.N. World Health Organization's Regional Office for the Americas.

      PAHO provides technical assistance and training to Latin American national public-health services in such fields as disease eradication and control, health-program development and administration, and environmental sanitation. The organization sponsors seminars and conferences for health administrators, physicians, entomologists, etc., and provides training fellowships to health professionals in some 250 fields.

      Technical advisors in PAHO's Division of Family Health (331-5259), Division of Disease Control (331-5221), Division of Health Services (331-

5222), Division of Environmental Health (331-5351), and Division of Human Resources and Research (331-5236) can provide researchers with Latin American health statistics and data on public-health structures and programs. Although their primary focus is topical and regional, they can also refer researchers to sources of country data in health fields.

3. The PAHO Library is discussed in the "Libraries" section, entry A47.

4. Records and correspondence are filed in the PAHO Archives (331-5331).

5. a. PAHO periodical publications include three technical journals—a monthly *Boletín de la Oficina Sanitaria Panamericana* (Spanish only), a quarterly *Bulletin of the Pan American Health Organization* (English only), and a quarterly *Educación Médica y Salud* (Spanish only)—as well as a quarterly magazine, *Pan American Health* (English and Spanish), and a *Weekly Epidemiological Report* (English and Spanish). PAHO also publishes an "Official Documents" series (which includes an annual report, financial reports, and conference proceedings), and a "Scientific Publications" series of technical studies in the fields of biomedical research, disease control, health statistics, nutrition, health-service administration and planning, family health and population dynamics, human-resource development, laboratory services, zoonoses and veterinary public health, and vector control.

b. A *Catálogo de Publicaciones* and *Publications of PAHO: Short List of English Titles Available in the Scientific Publications Series* may be obtained from the Publications Office (331-5281/82).

L12 United Nations Development Programme—Washington Office

1. a. *2101 L Street, NW*
      Washington, D.C. 20037
      296-5074

   b. Open to researchers. Appointment recommended.

   c. Charles L. Perry, Liaison Officer

2-3. The Washington liaison office of the United Nations Development Programme maintains a small collection of country proposals and project records relating to U.N.-assisted development programs in Latin America. These documents are open to researchers, except in instances in which Latin American governments have placed restrictions on their release. The office staff will also obtain for researchers additional records on U.N. development programs in Latin America from U.N. headquarters in New York City.

L13 United Nations Economic Commission for Latin America (ECLA) —Washington Office

1. a. *1801 K Street, NW*
      Washington, D.C. 20006
      296-0822

   b. Open to the public. Appointment recommended.

    c. David H. Pollock, Director

2.   ECLA's Washington staff of three professional economists (four during the portion of each year which Raul Prebisch spends in Washington) conducts research, represents ECLA at conferences, and keeps other ECLA regional offices abreast of data produced by United States, international, and inter-American governmental and financial organizations located in Washington. The staff's research activities encompass a broad range of economic topics, with emphasis on the impact of global and regional trends on the Latin American economies. Recent studies, for example, have analyzed transnational enterprises (their effect on the Latin American balance-of-payments, etc.), the organization of the international commodity market, and problems affecting the Latin American external sector (the global energy crisis and its impact on international trade policy and international development assistance; U.S. trade trends, proposed reforms of the international monetary system, etc.).

3.   The Washington office maintains a small reference collection of ECLA documents and research materials for internal staff use. The staff is happy to assist researchers within the limits imposed by its heavy work schedule. The office, however, is not equipped to provide reference services, and it encourages researchers to utilize the full collections of ECLA publications available at the Library of Congress, Joint Bank-Fund Library, and other area depositories.

4-5.   Staff research products are forwarded to ECLA headquarters in Santiago, Chile, where they are incorporated within ECLA's various publications.

M. Research Centers and Information Offices

Research Center and Information Office Entry Format (M)

1. *Address, telephone numbers*
2. Chief official and title
3. Parental organization
4. Programs and research activities pertaining to Latin America
5. Library/research facilities
6. Publications

Academy for Educational Development, Inc. See entry I1

M1 Academy of American Franciscan History

1. *9901 Caritas Drive*
    Potomac, Maryland 20854
    365-1763

2. Antonine S. Tibesar, OFM, Director

4. The academy conducts research on the history of the Franciscan Order and the Catholic Church in Latin America. The staff is a major source of information on the religious history of colonial Latin America. Each staff member, a friar trained as a research historian, has a lifetime's accumulation of knowledge and an extensive personal library on his area of specialization in colonial religious history: Antonine Tibesar (Peru), Mathias Kiemen (Brazil), Lino Gómez Canedo (Venezuela, Mexico), Francisco Morales (Mexico), and Neal Kaveny (Mexico).

    The staff is particularly knowledgeable regarding Franciscan documentary source materials in Latin American and European archives. The academy also maintains contact with 437 "corresponding members," including a large percentage of Franciscan scholars in Latin America.

    At roughly three-year intervals, the academy holds an awards banquet at which it bestows its honorary Serra Award to "an outstanding scholar in the field of Ibero-American history."

5. For information on the Academy of American Franciscan History Library, see "Libraries" section, entry A1.

6.   The academy has an active publications program (nearly 40 volumes to date), including monographs, translations of Franciscan classics, and documents collections. Special efforts are being directed toward the compilation and publication of catalogs and calendars of Franciscan source documents in foreign archives. Recent programs have focused on the Mexican Museum of Anthropology's Fondo Franciscano, the Archivo Franciscano in the National Library of Mexico, and the Archivo de la Provincia de los Doce Apóstoles in Lima. A *Booklist* is available upon request.

The academy also publishes *The Americas: A Quarterly Review of Inter-American Cultural History.*

M2 Advanced International Studies Institute (University of Miami)

1.   *Suite 1122*
4330 East-West Highway
Bethesda, Maryland 20014
951-0818

2.   Mose L. Harvey, Director

3.   The Advanced International Studies Institute is a research arm of the University of Miami (Coral Gables, Florida). It was formerly known as the Center for Advanced International Studies (University of Miami)— Washington Research Division.

4.   The institute's 12-person research staff concentrates on Soviet studies. Mose L. Harvey and Morris Rothenberg have done work on Soviet involvement in Latin America. Future research interests may include Cuban overseas activities.

6.   Institute publications include an "Occasional Papers in International Affairs" series and a "Monographs in International Affairs" series. Among the monographs published are:
Susan Frutkin, *Aimé Césaire: Black Between Worlds* (1973)
Charles D. Corbett, *The Latin American Military as a Socio-Political Force: Case Studies of Bolivia and Argentina* (1972)
Irving B. Reed, Jaime Suchlicki, and Dodd L. Harvey, *The Latin American Scene of the Seventies: A Basic Fact Book* (1972)
Leon Gouré, Mose L. Harvey, and Morris Rothenberg, *Soviet Penetration of Latin America* (1975)
Alexis U. Floridi and Annette E. Stiefbold, *The Uncertain Alliance: The Catholic Church and Labor in Latin America* (1973)
The Center for Advanced International Studies' quarterly *Journal of Inter-American Studies and World Affairs* is published from Florida.

M3 American Enterprise Institute for Public Policy Research (AEI)

1.   *1150 17th Street, NW*
Washington, D.C. 20036
862-5800

2.   William J. Baroody, President
Robert J. Pranger, Director of Foreign and Defense Policy Studies

4. The American Enterprise Institute is a non-profit research organization which studies U.S. national policy issues, both domestic and international. Research on Latin American and inter-American topics falls within the purview of AEI's Foreign and Defense Policy Studies program. A small number of six- to 12-month fellowships are awarded to Visiting Scholars for research in international affairs and foreign policy. Academic specialists are frequently commissioned to prepare research studies on international topics.

The organization annually sponsors some 30 conferences, seminars, discussions, and debates on public policy issues. Events are by invitation only. Latin Americanists interested in attending may request to be placed on AEI's foreign-relations mailing list.

6. AEI has published numerous books and monographs on foreign affairs, international economics, energy, food, foreign aid, and military assistance. Among its recent publications on Latin America are:

James E. Boyce and François J. Lombard, *Colombia's Treatment of Foreign Banks* (1976)

Juergen B. Donges, *Brazil's Trotting Peg* (1971)

Roger W. Fontaine, *Brazil and the United States: Toward a Maturing Relationship* (1974)

Roger W. Fontaine, *On Negotiating With Cuba* (1975)

William E. Ratliff, *Castroism and Communism in Latin America, 1959-1976: The Varieties of Marxist-Leninist Experience* (1976)

Riordan Roett (ed.), *Brazil in the Seventies* (1976)

Frederick C. Turner, *Responsible Parenthood: The Politics of Mexico's New Population Policies* (1974)

Robert B. Williamson, *et al.* (eds.), *Latin American-U.S. Economic Interactions: Conflict, Accommodation, and Policies for the Future* (1974)

A publications list, the organization's annual report, and a quarterly *Memorandum* reporting AEI activities are available on request.

American Society of International Law See entry H13

M4 American University—Foreign Area Studies (FAS)

1. *5010 Wisconsin Avenue, NW*
Washington, D.C. 20016
686-2769

2. William Evans-Smith, Director

4. Operating under a U.S. Department of the Army contract, FAS has prepared a large series of handbooks (more than 100 titles in print) on the social, economic, political, and military institutions of foreign countries. The staff numbers approximately 30 persons, including 18 foreign-area research specialists.

5. The FAS library, numbering some 6,000 volumes, consists largely of English-language secondary literature. No Latin American newspapers or periodicals are currently received, although in the past the library has subscribed to the major newspapers and periodicals from individual Latin American countries during the period in which a related FAS country handbook was being prepared. The librarian is Gilda Nimer.

6.   Book-length country surveys—formerly known as *Area Handbooks*—have been published on some 23 Latin American and Caribbean nations.

M5   Battelle Memorial Institute—Washington Operations

1.   *2030 M Street, NW*
       Washington, D.C. 20036
       785-8400

2.   George B. Johnson, Director of Washington Operations
       William Paul McGreevey, Director—Population and Development Policy
          Program

4.   Battelle Memorial Institute is a nonprofit research organization with headquarters in Columbus, Ohio. Although its research has traditionally concentrated on science and technology, the organization in 1977 launched a Population and Development Policy Program (PDP) directed toward demographic research and technical-assistance activities in Latin America, Asia, and Africa. The PDP program focuses on several central issues—determinants of fertility, the changing status and roles of women, consequences of family size for personal and family welfare, population impact analysis, and bottlenecks to effective population/family-planning programs. Research is conducted under subcontract by local research institutions in the field, as well as by researchers at Battelle's Population Study Center in Seattle, Washington, and at the organization's Washington, D.C. office. Studies are currently under way in seven Latin American countries.
       An annual fellowship program is available for 12 Third World researchers engaged in demographic research on their home countries at U.S. universities.

5.   Program director William Paul McGreevey is in the process of developing a working library of population field data. The holdings will be made available to interested researchers.

6.   A pamphlet describing the Population and Development Policy Program's objectives is available on request. Publication of country-specific data and broader comparative studies is planned.

M6   Brookings Institution

1.   *1775 Massachusetts Avenue, NW*
       Washington, D.C. 20036
       797-6000

2.   Bruce K. MacLaury, President
       John D. Steinbruner, Director—Foreign Policy Studies
       Joseph Grunwald, Senior Fellow
       William R. Cline, Senior Fellow

4.   Brookings is a private, nonprofit institution devoted to public-policy research, with major research programs in Economic Studies, Governmental Studies, and Foreign Policy Studies. Latin American-related economic research, of which there has been considerable, falls within the purview of Foreign Policy Studies. Recent projects—many of which have been conduct-

ed in collaboration with Latin American economic research institutions through the Program on Joint Studies on Latin American Economic Integration (ECIEL)—have focused on Central American economic integration and development; income and spending of urban families in Latin America; consumption, income, and prices in the economic development of Latin America; wage structures in Latin American manufacturing industries; international price and real-income comparisons; and problems of labor-force absorption in Latin American industrialization. In addition, Brookings' Economic Studies program devotes much attention to research on international economics.

In addition to the resident staff's Senior Fellows, Staff Associates, Research Associates, and Research Assistants, Brookings offers the following temporary appointments and fellowship opportunities: dissertation-stage Research Fellowships, postdoctoral Economic Policy Fellowships, Federal Executive Fellowships (for senior U.S. government officials), a pre- and/or postdoctoral Guest Scholar Program, and postdoctoral Visiting Professor and Younger Scholar Programs in international economics and foreign policy studies.

The organization's Advanced Study Program sponsors conferences, seminars, roundtable discussions, and other activities for government officials, scholars, and business executives. All are by invitation only.

5. Within the 55,000-volume Brookings Institution Library collection are an estimated 900 volumes on Latin America, consisting largely of English-language secondary literature on economics and international relations. On-site use of the library is restricted to Brookings staff-members, and the collection is accessible to outside researchers only via inter-library loan. For reference and inter-library loan information, call 797-6234, 8:30 A.M.-5 P.M., Monday-Friday.

Brookings' Social Science Computation Center (797-6180) possesses some 20 data bases, including a file of International Monetary Fund financial data. The facility may be used by outside researchers who are affiliated with a nonprofit or governmental organization.

6. Brookings has published numerous Latin American economic studies over the years. Recent titles include:

Joseph Grunwald, Miguel S. Wionczek, and Martin Carnoy, *Latin American Economic Integration and U.S. Policy* (1972)

Martin Carnoy, *Industrialization in a Latin American Common Market* (1972)

William R. Cline, *International Monetary Reform and the Developing Countries* (1975)

Charles R. Frank, Jr., and Richard C. Webb (eds.), *Income Distribution and Growth in the Less-Developed Countries* (1977)

C. Fred Bergsten, Thomas Horst, and Theodore Moran, *American Multinationals and American Interests* (1978)

William R. Cline and Enrique Delgado (eds.), *Economic Integration in Central America* (1978)

Philip Musgrove, *Consumer Behavior in Latin America: Income and Spending of Families in Ten Andean Cities* (1978)

Also available are *Brookings Papers on Economic Activity* (three per year), a quarterly *Brookings Bulletin,* an annual report, and a publications list.

M7 Carnegie Endowment for International Peace—Washington Office

1. *11 Dupont Circle, NW*
   Washington, D.C. 20036
   797-6400

2. Thomas L. Hughes, President
   Ben Stephansky, Director—Latin American Program

4. The New York City-based Carnegie Endowment for International Peace is a private foundation which sponsors research in a variety of international-affairs fields, including arms control, human-rights policy, pre-crisis fact-finding, international law, and international organization. The Washington office's new Latin American program will conduct selected research projects of significance from a U.S. policy perspective. An initial project will track the transition to civilian government in Ecuador, Peru, and Bolivia, examining the policy implications for the United States and international lending institutions. Workshops, roundtables, and seminars are planned.

6. The organization assists in the publishing of the quarterly magazine *Foreign Policy.* Future Latin American research may appear in the Carnegie Endowment's monograph series.

M8 Center for Defense Information (CDI)

1. *122 Maryland Avenue, NE*
   Washington, D.C. 20002
   543-0400

2. Rear Admiral (ret.) Gene R. La Rocque, Director

3. The Fund for Peace

4. The Center for Defense Information conducts research on U.S. defense- and weapons-policy issues, attempting to present an alternative view to that of the Pentagon. Recent research interests have included the Panama Canal treaties, Latin American nuclear non-proliferation, and U.S. arms sales abroad. The organization disseminates its views through publications, media appearances, Congressional testimony, and other outlets. Public reference and briefing services are provided. The staff is made up of permanent researchers and special consultants. Staff members Jo Husbands and Johanna Mendelson are Latin Americanists, and director La Rocque is a former director of the Inter-American Defense College. CDI offers internships (for undergraduates and recent graduates), and Junior Fellowships (usually advanced doctoral candidates or recent Ph.D.s) for research or defense-related issues.

5. The Center's 1,500-volume library contains Defense Department documents, post-1960 Congressional committee hearing records, periodicals, and vertical-file materials—all bearing on military and foreign-affairs matters. Included is a full set of Defense Department maps pertaining to the Panama Canal treaty negotiations. The library is open to researchers, 9 A.M.-5 P.M. Monday-Friday.

6. CDI publishes a monthly newsletter, *The Defense Monitor,* which can be obtained without charge upon request. The August 1976, and January 1978 issues focused on the Panama Canal.

M9 Center for International Policy

1. *120 Maryland Avenue, NE*
    Washington, D.C. 20012
    544-4666

2. Donald L. Ranard, Director

3. The Fund for Peace

4. The Center for International Policy is a private, nonprofit research organization initiated to provide an independent, critical perspective on current U.S. foreign-policy issues. The center's primary focus is on U.S.-Third World relations, especially the links between U.S. economic and military aid and authoritarian repression in Latin America and East Asia.

6. The Center publishes an annual survey of *Human Rights and the U.S. Foreign Assistance Program,* which contains a considerable amount of U.S. government statistical data on aid programs in Latin America. In addition, a bimonthly *International Policy Reports* series occasionally focuses on Latin America—for example, "Chile's Chronic Economic Crisis" (September, 1976), and "Toward Detente in Cuba: Issues and Obstacles" (November, 1977).

M10 Center for National Security Studies

1. *122 Maryland Avenue, NE*
    Washington, D.C. 20002
    544-5380

2. Morton Halperin, Director

3. The Fund for Peace

4. The Center for National Security Studies monitors the activities of U.S. intelligence agencies and national security institutions, working to "expose secret policies to public debate." Recent research projects have included an investigation into covert CIA activities at home and abroad. The organization has obtained numerous documents from the CIA and other U.S. government agencies through the Freedom of Information Act, and it assists individual researchers in gaining access to government information through FOI.

    An internship program is open to undergraduate, graduate, and law students.

5. The center's library contains a variety of materials on the overseas activities of U.S. intelligence agencies, including Congressional committee-hearing records, and CIA documents obtained via FOI relating to CIA operations in Latin America. The library is open to researchers by appointment.

6. The organization's monthly newsletter, *First Principles,* is available on a subscription basis. The findings of the CIA research project mentioned above were published by the center in 1977 as *CIA's Covert Operations Versus Human Rights.*

M11   Committee for Economic Development (CED)

1.   *1700 K Street, NW*
     Washington, D.C. 20006
     296-5860

2.   Robert C. Holland

4.   The Committee for Economic Development is a nonprofit, business-related, research and educational organization with headquarters in New York City. Composed of some 200 trustees (mostly board chairmen, university and corporation presidents) and a research support staff (including six researchers in Washington), CED issues policy statements and recommendations on public policy issues. In the field of international economics, the organization has conducted research on Latin American economic development, regional integration and trade, and the role of multinational corporations in Latin America.

6.   Publications include: *Economic Development Issues: Latin America* (1967), *Regional Integration and the Trade of Latin America* (1968), and *The Role of International Companies in Latin American Regional Integration: Autos and Petrochemicals* (1972). A publications list is available.

M12   Council for Inter-American Security (CIS)

1.   *305 4th Street, NE*
     Washington, D.C. 20002
     543-2070

2.   Ronald F. Docksai, Chairman
     L. Francis Bouchey, Executive Vice President

4.   The Council for Inter-American Security is an independent research and education group which monitors hemispheric-defense issues and the Marxist "assault on personal liberty, political freedom, and the free economy" in the Americas, with a particular focus on the "Soviet-Cuban Axis." The organization's members "are committed to political liberty, limited government, economic freedom, and traditional moral values." CIS disseminates its views through publications, media presentations, and Congressional testimony and liaison. It sponsors periodic CIS Round Table discussions for young political leaders, businessmen, and press representatives, both in Washington and in cities throughout the United States. An annual Inter-American Symposium is also held, at varying hemispheric sites.

6.   Publications include a bimonthly newsletter, *West Watch,* and special reports and monographs on a variety of hemispheric political, economic, and strategic issues, including human rights, the Panama Canal, U.S.-Cuban relations, Cuban political prisoners, East-West trade, and Soviet/Cuban penetration of Nicaragua, Mexico, Jamaica, and other nations. The organization also conducts an annual survey of U.S. public opinion on selected hemispheric issues.

M13 Council on American Affairs

1. *1716 New Hampshire Avenue, NW*
   Washington, D.C. 20009
   232-1040

2. Roger Pearson, Director

4. The Council on American Affairs is a nonprofit educational organization which prepares and disseminates analyses of "economic, social, and political trends, both domestic and international." It is the U.S. member of the World Anti-Communist League (headquarters: Taiwan), and participates in the League's international conferences.

6. The Council on American Affairs publishes a quarterly *Journal of Social and Political Studies,* and a monograph series, which includes Belden Bell (ed.), *Nicaragua—an Ally Under Siege,* and Donald Dozer, *The Panama Canal in Perspective.*

M14 Council on Hemispheric Affairs (COHA)

1. *Suite 504*
   1735 New Hampshire Avenue, NW
   Washington, D.C. 20009
   332-8860

2. Laurence R. Birns, Director

4. The Council on Hemispheric Affairs is a "private, non-profit education and information body" formed in 1975 to increase U.S. "public and governmental understanding of Latin American realities." The council's small staff monitors inter-American political, economic, and military relations, and works to promote "democratic ideals, human rights, and freedom of thought and person" in Latin America. The organization disseminates its views through media releases, reports to foreign-policy organizations throughout the United States, petitions (to the State Department, the Inter-American Commission on Human Rights, and other agencies) on behalf of victims of human-rights violations in Latin America, and meetings with policy-makers in Washington and New York City (where the council also has an office).

   The organization will provide office facilities and research assistants to scholars coming to Washington, D.C. to conduct research on Latin American and inter-American affairs. A volunteer internship program is available to college students.

5. A reference file on patterns of human-rights violations in Latin America (containing case-histories of persecuted religious spokesmen and political dissidents, by country) is open to researchers. A clippings-file of U.S. and Latin American newspaper and periodical articles is also available.

M15 Dumbarton Oaks (Harvard University)—Center for Pre-Columbian Studies

1. *1703 32nd Street, NW*
   Washington, D.C. 20007
   232-3101

2.   Elizabeth Benson, Director

3.   Harvard University

4.   The center supports research and publications on pre-Columbian art, archeology, and cultural history, with a focus on the "high art of the high cultures." Approximately two fellowships for dissertation or postdoctoral research at Dumbarton Oaks are awarded each year.

       The center sponsors an annual conference and occasional public lectures on pre-Columbian topics. The conferences are increasingly attempting to focus· on cross-cultural themes (for example: feline cults, death and the afterlife in pre-Columbian cultures, the sea in the pre-Columbian world).

5.   The center's library is described in the "Libraries" section, entry A15.

6.   An active publishing program includes the "Studies in Pre-Columbian Art and Archeology" series (18 paperbound volumes to date), center conference proceedings, and other miscellaneous monographs.

Note: Also see entries A15, C2, and F6.

M16   Dwight D. Eisenhower Institute for Historical Research (Smithsonian Institution)

1.   *National Museum of History and Technology, Room 4027*
       12th Street and Constitution Avenue, NW
       Washington, D.C. 20560
       381-5458

2.   Forrest Pogue, Director

4.   The Eisenhower Institute provides predoctoral and postdoctoral fellowships for research in military history, U.S. and foreign. It also acts as an information center for scholars desiring access to documents pertaining to military history located in Washington, D.C., or in repositories elsewhere in the United States.

       Research topics in Latin American military history and the history of U.S.-Latin American military relations fall within the scope of the institute's fellowship program. Applications are administered by the Smithsonian Institution's Office of Fellowships and Grants (see entry J27).

5.   The institute has a library collection of more than 5,000 volumes on military history.

M17   EPICA (Ecumenical Program for Inter-American Communication and Action)

1.   *1470 Irving Street, NW*
       Washington, D.C. 20010
       332-0292

2.   Philip Wheaton and Mildred Mays, Co-Directors.

3.   Funded by the National Council of Churches.

4.   EPICA is "a Washington-based task force working on issues of justice and liberation for Latin America" from "an anti-imperialist perspective." The group's primary geographic focus is on Central America and the Caribbean basin. It issues reports, sponsors educational workshops, and coordinates forums, tours, media exposure, and Congressional contacts for Latin Americans visiting the United States. It also has organized programs highlighting abuses of human rights and the repression of labor unions, *campesino* groups, church leaders, and political parties. Volunteer interns are utilized.

5.   A small documentation library of research materials—much of which consists of field material from Central America and the Caribbean—is available to researchers.

6.   Publications include "country primers" on Panama, Jamaica, and Puerto Rico, and "special issue pamphlets" on Panama, the Dominican Republic, Haiti, and Puerto Rico. A list of "resource materials" is available on request.

M18   Georgetown University—Center for Strategic and International Studies (CSIS)

1.   *1800 K Street, NW*
Washington, D.C. 20006
833-8595

2.   David M. Abshire, Chairman
Roger W. Fontaine, Director of Latin American Studies

4.   Georgetown University's off-campus Center for Strategic and International Studies conducts policy-oriented research on international affairs. Separate rescarch divisions focus on various world regions (Europe, Canada, Soviet Union, Latin America, Africa, Middle East, Pacific Basin) and topical studies (natural resources, defense, international economics, etc.).

The small Latin American Studies staff analyzes current policy issues. Special seminars and roundtable discussions are conducted periodically (by invitation only).

CSIS also sponsors an annual conference on a selected international theme. In addition, the center conducts—on approximately a monthly basis—a "congressional staff seminar series" and an "international seminar series," both of which periodically feature Latin American presentations. To be placed on the mailing list for seminar announcements, contact Lyn Bickel.

6.   The center's *Washington Papers* publications series (published by SAGE Publications, Inc.) has included: Ernst Halperin, *Terrorism in Latin America* (1976), and Roger W. Fontaine, *The Andean Pact: A Political Analysis* (1977). An anthology of papers presented at the 1975 CSIS annual conference was published as Roger W. Fontaine and James Theberge (eds.), *Latin America's New Internationalism: The End of Hemispheric Isolation* (New York: Praeger, 1976). A publications list and the center's annual report are available on request.

The center also publishes *The Washington Review of Strategic and International Studies,* a quarterly journal.

M19 Georgetown University—Institute for International and Foreign Trade Law

1. *Georgetown University Law Center*
   600 New Jersey Avenue, NW
   Washington, D.C. 20001
   624-8330

2. Don Wallace, Jr., Director

4. The small research staff of Georgetown University's Institute for International and Foreign Trade Law studies legal aspects of international economic affairs, including legal problems related to economic development in less-developed countries (e.g., multinational foreign investment, procurement of basic goods and services by developing nations). The institute offers fellowships and training courses to foreign law students and officials.

   The institute's Investment Negotiation Center provides training courses and advisory services to assist officials from developing nations in negotiating with foreign investors and contractors.

   The institute has sponsored, at approximately two-year intervals, conferences on broad legal aspects of international affairs. It also presents, approximately every six weeks during the academic year, a luncheon-speaker series. Those interested in attending should request to be placed on the institute's mailing list.

6. The institute has published several studies on international investment and procurement, as well as a four-volume *Lawyer's Guide to International Business Transactions* (2nd ed., 1977). A publications list is available on request.

M20 Institute for Policy Studies

1. *1909 Q Street, NW*
   Washington, D.C. 20009
   234-9382

2. Robert Borosage, Director
   Richard J. Barnet and Marcus G. Raskin, Senior Distinguished Fellows
   Roberta Salper, Coordinator—Latin American Unit

3. The Institute for Policy Studies is an independent, nonprofit center for research on U.S. public policy problems, international and domestic. The institute's Latin American Unit "follows current developments throughout Latin America and the Caribbean, and seeks to aid in the formulation of policies that may lead to a more just and adequate relationship between the two regions of the hemisphere." The unit sponsors a monthly or bimonthly Latin American Round Table, featuring speakers from Latin American or Caribbean political and governmental organizations and from U.S. academic and governmental circles. These programs are by invitation only, but interested Latin Americanists will be placed on the unit's mailing list. Seminars and field conferences have also been held, on an ad hoc basis.

   The institute staff consists primarily of resident fellows. In addition, project directors and research associates affiliate with the organization on a temporary, contract basis. Positions as research assistants and volunteer interns are also available. In collaboration with the Union Graduate School of California, the Institute for Policy Studies also offers a multidisciplinary Ph.D. program within which students may concentrate on a Latin American or inter-American research project of their choosing.

6. The Latin American Unit's Latin American Round Table speaker presentations are published as *LART Papers: Studies on Latin America and the Caribbean.* A publications list is available. Latin American-related research also appears periodically in the Institute's *Transnational Institute Pamphlet Series,* and in its bimonthly bulletin *Communications.*

M21 Institute of American Relations (IAR)

1. *325 Constitution Avenue, NE*
    Washington, D.C. 20002
    543-5121

2. Victor Fediay, Director

4. The Institute of American Relations—which encompasses the moribund Committee on Latin America—is "a publicly supported, non-partisan educational institution dedicated to a better public understanding of the United States and its position in world affairs." The organization monitors the impact of international events on the national interests of the United States. It believes that the U.S. national interest "in the long run depends on political and economic stability in Asia, Africa, and Latin America," and it advocates "a sustained surveillance of communist designs." It conducts seminars and sponsors U.S. public-opinion surveys on major foreign-policy issues.

6. IAR publishes a semimonthly newsletter, *American Relations;* a pamphlet series on Latin America (including "American Public Opinion Toward the Panama Canal: A Nationwide Survey" and Hanson W. Baldwin, "The Panama Canal Treaties: Are They Salvageable?"), and a human-rights study series of pamphlets.

M22 Institute of International Law and Economic Development (IILED)

1. *Suite 345*
    1511 K Street, NW
    Washington, D.C. 20005
    347-0277

2. Arnold H. Leibowitz, President

4. The Institute of International Law and Economic Development is a nonprofit research organization which analyzes "contemporary international legal and economic problems resulting from the changes taking place in the international economic order." It has had a particular interest in the economic problems, political status, and constitutional rights of the citizens of small island areas of the Caribbean and the Pacific. The research staff consists of six attorneys and six economists. Volunteer interns are utilized.

6. IILED produced an *Annotated Bibliography on Transnational Enterprises With Emphasis on Latin America* for the Organization of American States in 1974. A report, *Legal Perspectives on Associated Statehood in the Eastern Caribbean,* will be published as part of the organization's "Occasional Papers" series.

M23 International Center for Research on Women (ICRW)

1. *2000 P Street, NW*
   Washington, D.C. 20036
   466-3544

2. Coralie Turbitt, President

4. The International Center for Research on Women is a nonprofit organization interested in the role of women in the development process. Its Latin American research has, to date, focused on Central America—e.g., the development of a methodology for the collection of data on rural women in Nicaragua; a study of women in the Guatemalan labor force. The staff's Latin American specialists are Mayra Buvinic and Nadia Youssef.

   The organization's occasional conferences and roundtables are by invitation only.

5. ICRW has a library of approximately 1,000 items, including a number of unpublished manuscripts and documents from Latin America. The library is open to researchers.

6. A quarterly *ICRW Newsletter* is available free on request.

M24 International Development Research Centre (IDRC)—Washington Office

1, *1028 Connecticut Avenue, NW*
   Washington, D.C. 20036
   659-9590

2. Star Solomon, Washington Representative

4. The International Development Research Centre is a nonprofit public corporation funded by the Canadian government. It "supports research projects that are identified, designed, conducted, and managed by developing-country researchers in their own countries." Funds for research in agriculture, food and nutrition sciences, health sciences, information sciences, and social sciences/human resources (studies on education, population, agrarian reform, etc.) are channeled to government agencies, universities, research centers, and other institutions in developing countries. Projects which apply science and technology "to improve the well-being of rural peoples" are favored. A variety of pre- and postdoctoral research awards are available.

   IDRC's headquarters and international staff are located in Ottawa, Canada. The organization maintains a Latin American regional office in Bogotá.

6. Publications include an annual report, a monthly newsletter (*IDRC Features*), a quarterly magazine (*IDRC Reports*), and numerous scientific and technical papers.

M25 International Economic Policy Association (IEPA)

1.   *Suite 908*
1625 Eye Street, NW
Washington, D.C. 20006
331-1974

2.   Timothy W. Stanley, President

4.   IEPA is a nonprofit association of some 15 U.S.-based multinational corporations. Its Washington staff conducts research for its members on U.S. and foreign government policies affecting international trade, investments, finance, taxation, and related economic and monetary developments. The organization advocates "policies and practices by business concerns and governments that will keep American trade and investments abroad in a state of good health and repute."

An IEPA affiliate, the Center for Multinational Studies (same address), conducts research on the effects of multinational corporations upon the U.S. and world economy.

6.   IEPA publications include a monograph series of appraisals of the U.S. balance of payments, and research reports on various issues relating to the foreign economic policy of the United States (natural resources, petroleum, international commercial aviation).

The Center for Multinational Studies publishes a series of occasional papers on MNCs.

M26 International Food Policy Research Institute (IFPRI)

1.   *1776 Massachusetts Avenue, NW*
Washington, D.C. 20036
862-5600

2.   John W. Miller, Director

4.   The International Food Policy Research Institute is a private, nonprofit research organization which studies world food problems and methods of increasing the availability of food in developing countries. Its research program analyzes: trends in the production, exchange, and consumption of food in developing countries; policies that affect agricultural production in developing countries; programs and policies to improve distribution of available foodstuffs; and policies to increase the effectiveness of international trade in alleviating food scarcities. Latin American research currently in progress includes studies of Latin American livestock production, minimum-price policies in northeast Brazil, trade liberalization, and national trade policies.

The institute sponsors a monthly "Food Policy Seminar" and occasional international conferences (including a 1978 conference on the "Question of Food Security in the Developing Countries" in Mexico). Interested researchers will be placed on the organization's mailing list.

5.   IFPRI is building a library collection of country-level field data from the developing countries. The library is open to researchers for on-site use, 9 A.M.-5:30 P.M., Monday-Friday. Interlibrary loan service is available.

6.　The following IFPRI published research reports focus in part on Latin America: *Meeting Food Needs in the Developing World* (1976), *The Commodity Trade Issue in International Negotiations* (1976), *Potential of Agricultural Exports to Finance Increased Food Imports* (1977), and *Food Needs of Developing Countries: Projections of Production and Consumption to 1990* (1977). An annual report and a publications list are also available, on request. In the future, the organization hopes to provide a bibliographic service on food-policy issues.

M27　International Institute for Environment and Development—Washington Office

1.　*1302 18th Street, NW*
Washington, D.C. 20036
462-0900

2.　Robert Stein, Director—Washington Office

4.　The London-based International Institute for Environment and Development studies the impact of development on the environment in Third World countries. Recent research projects have included an analysis of the impact of multilateral aid from international lending organizations (the Inter-American Development Bank, Caribbean Development Bank, Organization of American States, World Bank, and others) on the global environment, and a study of national development policies related to human settlements in several Latin American nations.

　　The Washington office consists of four research specialists and a number of outside consultants.

5.　The office's small library contains a collection of specialized United Nations conference documents relating to environmental issues. The collection may be used by researchers on an appointment basis.

6.　An annual report and a publications list are available on request.

M28　National Association of Manufacturers (NAM)—International Economic Affairs Department

1.　*1776 F Street, NW*
Washington, D.C. 20006
331-3769

2.　Lawrence A. Fox, Vice President for International Economic Affairs

4.　The International Economic Affairs Department conducts research on international trade, investment, and finance for NAM member companies.

6.　Publications include an annual year-end survey and projection of leading international economic issues, a monthly newsletter (*International Economic Report*), and special research reports (e.g., "LDC External Debt: Facts, Figures, Perspectives" [May 12, 1977]; "Competitiveness of U.S. Exports as Measured by Relative Exchange Rate Changes, 1960-1976" [March 22, 1977]).

M29 National Planning Association (NPA)

1.   *1606 New Hampshire Avenue, NW*
     Washington, D.C. 20009
     265-7685

2.   John Miller, President
     Theodore Geiger, Director of International Studies

4.   The National Planning Association is a private, nonprofit, research organization which produces policy studies and reports on domestic and international economic problems. Research projects (some of which are commissioned, some carried out in-house) are conducted under the direction of committees composed of leaders from business, labor, agriculture, and education. The International Department's four-person research staff has recently examined such topics as the external-debt problems of less-developed countries, and the challenge posed to the United States by the manufactured exports of advanced LDCs.

6.   NPA prepares, under contract for the U.S. Agency for International Development, the quarterly *Development Digest.* The organization also publishes a quarterly periodical, *New International Realities,* and individual research studies on national and international economic issues.

M30 Overseas Development Council (ODC)

1.   *1717 Massachusetts Avenue, NW*
     Washington, D.C. 20036
     234-8701

2.   James S. Grant, President
     Robert Ayres, Senior Fellow

4.   The Overseas Development Council is an independent, nonprofit research organization established in 1969 "to increase American understanding of the economic and social problems confronting the developing countries and of the importance of these countries to the United States in an increasingly interdependent world." The staff prepares research and policy papers analyzing major issues in North-South relations (usually from a global rather than a regional perspective). Subjects of recent interest have included Third World development strategies and their impact on the U.S. economy, the interrelationship of health and population strategies to Third World development, world energy trading systems, the impact of international capital flows and monetary reform on Third World development, policy issues related to world hunger and food scarcity, and alternative channels of resource transfer.

  In addition to the staff's resident Senior Fellows, ODC offers opportunities for development specialists from academia, government, and business to work at ODC as Visiting Fellows. Recent studies by Visiting Fellows have focused on the history of U.S. foreign policy toward developing nations, the ethics of technology transfer, private debt flows, and the impact of interdependence on minorities in the United States.

  ODC sponsors a wide range of activities, including conferences, seminars, and workshops on international issues related to development; "transnational dialogues" and other discussions bringing together participants from both developing and developed countries; briefings for the media and for local representatives of major U.S. nongovernmental organizations; and workshops to improve the development capabilities of private voluntary organizations. Participation is by invitation only.

6.   ODC publications include: *The U.S. and World Development: Agenda for Action,* an annual book-length assessment of major problems and decisions facing the United States in its relations with the developing nations; other books—e.g., Irene Tinker and Michele Bo Bramsen (eds.), *Women and World Development* (1976) and Mayra Buvinic, *Women and World Development: An Annotated Bibliography* (1976); a "development papers" series (including Roger D. Hansen, *U.S.-Latin American Economic Policy: Bilateral, Regional, or Global?* [No. 18, January, 1975]); a "communiques" series (including Helen C. Low, *The Panama Canal Treaty in Perspective* [No. 29, April, 1976]); a "monograph" series (including Colin I. Bradford, Jr., *Forces for Change in Latin America: U.S. Policy Implications* [1971]); and an "occasional papers" series. A publications list is available.

M31 Population Reference Bureau, Inc.

1.   1337 Connecticut Avenue, NW
Washington, D.C. 20036
785-4664

2.   Robert M. Avedon, President

4.   The Population Reference Bureau is a nonprofit educational organization which compiles and disseminates demographic information on national and international population issues. It relies primarily on United Nations publications for Latin American data. Public reference services are provided.

5.   A 15,000-volume research library is open to serious researchers, 8:30 A.M.-4:30 P.M., Monday-Friday.

6.   The organization publishes a monthly *Intercom* (International Newsletter on Population), bimonthly *Population Bulletins,* an annual "World Population Data Sheet" (wall chart), and special publications, including *World Population Growth and Response, 1965-1975: A Decade of Global Action* (1976), and *Sourcebook on Population, 1970-1976* (1976).

M32 Potomac Associates

1.   *1740 Massachusetts Avenue, NW*
Washington, D.C. 20036
785-6234

2.   William Watts, President

4.   Potomac Associates is a private, nonprofit research organization which examines U.S. public-policy issues, both domestic and international. In the field of foreign policy, the organization conducts analyses and U.S. public-opinion surveys relating to U.S. relations with other countries. Most of its

research is carried out on a contract basis. Little work has been done on Latin America thus far.

6. Potomac Associates periodically publishes reports entitled *Policy Perspectives.* A 1977 report on "The United States and Cuba: Old Issues and New Directions" is available on request. A monograph series includes a biennial volume on the *State of the Nation* and several studies of U.S. foreign policy. A publications list is available.

M33 Rand Corporation—Washington Office

1. *2100 M Street, NW*
Washington, D.C. 20037
296-5000

2. George K. Tanham, Vice President—Washington Operations
Frederic S. Nyland, Director—Washington Office National Security
Research

4. The Rand Corporation (whose headquarters are in Santa Monica, California) is a private, nonprofit research organization which analyzes domestic and international issues affecting the U.S. public welfare and national security. Rand's National Security research divisions have produced numerous analyses of Latin American politics, economics, sociology/demography, and international relations, including studies of U.S. security interests in Latin America. The Washington office's National Security Research staff numbers approximately 50 professionals.

5. The Washington office library—which contains several thousand volumes, mostly in the social sciences—is closed to non-Rand personnel. Nonclassified materials may be obtained through the library's interlibrary loan service.

6. Much of Rand's strategic research is produced under contract for U.S. government agencies, and is accordingly security-classified and unavailable to private researchers. Unclassified Rand publications are disseminated to some 320 U.S. libraries on a subscription basis. Local Washington-area subscribers include the Library of Congress, George Washington University Library, and the Army Library.

   Some 87 unclassified Rand books, reports, and memoranda on Latin America are listed in *A Bibliography of Selected Rand Publications: Latin America* (January, 1977), available free from the Washington office. (There are also specialized Rand bibliographies on energy, health, human resources, linguistics, population, foreign aid, foreign policy, and 44 other subject areas.) Individual titles can be purchased from Rand's Publications Department in Santa Monica.

M34 Research Institute on Immigration and Ethnic Studies (Smithsonian Institution)

1. *North Building, Room 2300*
955 L'Enfant Plaza, SW
Washington, D.C. 20560
381-4205

2.   Roy S. Bryce-Laporte, Director

4.   The Smithsonian's Research Institute on Immigration and Ethnic Studies conducts and supports interdisciplinary research on contemporary (post-1965) patterns of immigration into the United States and into territories under U.S. jurisdiction. The institute offers pre- and postdoctoral fellowships (consisting of office space and research assistance, but no stipend). Research supported recently has included the preparation of oral histories of West Indian laborers in the Canal Zone, and a study of ethnicity in the U.S. Virgin Islands.

The institute's research staff provides consultative services, and can refer researchers to immigrant organizations in the United States.

6.   Institute publications of potential interest to Latin Americanists include Roy S. Bryce-Laporte and Delores Mortimer (eds.), *Caribbean Immigration to the United States* (1976), Roy S. Bryce-Laporte and Stephen R. Couch (eds.), *Exploratory Fieldwork on Latino Migrants and Indochinese Refugees* (1976), Paul Meadows, *et al., Recent Immigration to the United States: The Literature of the Social Sciences* (1976), *Caribbean Immigration to the United States* (RIIES Occasional Paper No. 1, 1976), and the proceedings of a 1976 institute conference on "The New Immigration: Implications for the United States and the International Community" (forthcoming).

M35 Resources for the Future

1.   *1755 Massachusetts Avenue, NW*
      Washington, D.C. 20036
      462-4400

2.   Charles Hitch, President
      Lincoln Gordon, Senior Fellow

4.   Resources for the Future is a nonprofit research organization which studies—primarily from an economic perspective—domestic and international policy issues relating to natural resources, environmental quality, population, and energy. The staff numbers approximately 60 research personnel, plus a varying number of visiting scholars.

6.   The organization publishes a newsletter, *Resources* (three issues per year), and a series of books and research papers, including: Ronald Ridker (ed.), *Population and Development* (1976), Ronald Ridker (ed.), *Changing Resource Problems of the Fourth World* (1976), Pierre R. Crosson, Ronald G. Cummings, and Kenneth D. Frederick (eds.), *Selected Water Management Issues in Latin American Agriculture* (1978), Michael Nelson, *The Development of Tropical Lands: Policy Issues in Latin America* (1973), Raymond F. Mikesell, *Foreign Investment in Copper Mining: Case Studies of Mines in Peru and Papua New Guinea* (1975), Joseph Grunwald and Philip Musgrove, *Natural Resources in Latin American Development* (1970), Hans M. Gregersen and Arnoldo Contreras, *U.S. Investment in the Forest-Based Sector in Latin America: Problems and Potential* (1975), Ronald G. Cummings, *Water Resource Management in Northern Mexico* (1972), and Nathaniel Wollman, *The Water Resources of Chile: An Economic Method for Analyzing a Key Resource in a Nation's Development* (1968). The staff has also recently completed a study of the economic and

environmental consequences of population growth in Colombia. An annotated publications list is available on request.

M36 School of Advanced International Studies (SAIS) (Johns Hopkins University)—Center of Brazilian Studies

1. *1740 Massachusetts Avenue, NW*
Washington, D.C. 20036
785-6830

2. Riordan Roett, Director
Margaret Hayes, Associate Director

4. Inaugurated in 1978, the SAIS Center of Brazilian Studies serves as a research and discussion center for the analysis of Brazil's international political and economic relations. The center has working links with a counterpart organization in Rio de Janeiro: the Foundation for Foreign Trade Studies.

Two annual series of policy seminars are sponsored—one focusing on Brazilian international economic policies, the other on Brazil's role in the international political community. Other events include roundtable discussions, current-issues symposia, policy briefings by U.S. and Brazilian public officials, and special individual presentations. Events are usually attended by invitation only, but interested specialists may request to be placed on the center's mailing list.

Fellowship and exchange programs are anticipated.

5. The center intends to establish—within the SAIS Mason Library (see entry A48)—a Brazilian reference collection concentrating on periodicals and recent government serials on aspects of Brazilian economic development.

6. A publications program—consisting of a newsletter, occasional papers, and seminar-based monographs—is being developed. An international directory of Brazilianists is in preparation.

M37 School of Advanced International Studies (SAIS) (Johns Hopkins University)—Washington Center of Foreign Policy Research

1. *1740 Massachusetts Avenue, NW*
Washington, D.C. 20036
785-6276

2. Simon H. Serfaty, Director

4. The Washington Center of Foreign Policy Research, at Johns Hopkins University's School of Advanced International Studies, conducts research on major trends in international politics and problems in U.S. foreign policy. Nine SAIS faculty members, along with several associates and visiting fellows from public affairs, academic life, and journalism in the United States and foreign countries, participate in research projects, seminars, and weekly discussions.

6. The center publishes, through the Johns Hopkins University Press, a series entitled "Studies in International Affairs."

M38 Washington International Institute

1. *Suite 350*
    1900 M Street, NW
    Washington, D.C. 20036
    452-0818

2. James C. Keenan, President
    Alberto M. Piedra, Vice President and Director of Research

4. Created in 1976, the Washington International Institute is a nonprofit educational organization which seeks "to foster and promote in both the public and private sectors throughout the world, especially within the inter-American system, a better understanding and appreciation of private enterprise and the tradition of liberty under law." Programs of technical assistance and research were, as of this writing, still in the developmental stage. Links are being established with institutions in Mexico.

6. The organization plans to publish a monthly economic-outlook report on Mexico. Materials on Mexican art and culture may also be published.

M39 Washington Office on Latin America (WOLA)

1. *110 Maryland Avenue, NE*
    Washington, D.C. 20002
    544-8045

2. Joseph T. Eldridge, Director

4. The Washington Office on Latin America is a public-interest information center closely affiliated with various U.S. religious organizations. It monitors, and disseminates information on, United States policies toward Latin America, "seeking to promote conditions in Latin America favorable to the liberation of its people...by supporting those activities and policies of the United States government which permit and encourage respect for human rights, civilian-democratic rule, and a new international economic order." The organization disseminates its views through a variety of channels, including press releases to the news media, background briefings for the legislative assistants of key U.S. congressmen, research documentation for witnesses testifying in congressional committee hearings, and a bimonthly newsletter. Its interests have focused particularly on the nations of Central America and the southern cone. WOLA staff members can provide researchers with information on U.S. policy toward Latin America, pertinent legislation pending in Congress, and current conditions in Latin America. They can also supply information on the activities of Latin American activist groups and other private Latin American-oriented organizations in the Washington area.

    The organization sponsors an occasional conference (for example, on "human rights and U.S. policy toward the southern cone"), with governmental and non-governmental participants.

5. WOLA's reference file, consisting of some 4½ file cabinets of clippings, reports, and other miscellaneous materials on conditions in Latin America (organized by country), is available to researchers.

6.   A bimonthly newsletter, *Latin American Update,* contains analyses of important U.S. legislative matters affecting Latin America, together with summaries of, and commentaries on, Latin American news events. The newsletter will be sent, without charge, to anyone requesting to be placed on the mailing list.

M40   Woodrow Wilson International Center for Scholars

1.   *Smithsonian Institution Building*
1000 Jefferson Drive, SW
Washington, D.C. 20560
381-5613

2   James H. Billington, Director
Abraham F. Lowenthal, Secretary—Latin American Program

3.   Smithsonian Institution

4.   The Woodrow Wilson International Center for Scholars was established by Congress as an international institute for advanced study and as the nation's official "living memorial" to the 28th President, "symbolizing and strengthening the fruitful relation between the world of learning and the world of public affairs."

   Through its competitive Fellowship Program, the center brings from 80 to 100 men and women of intellectual distinction from the United States and other countries to Washington each year to work on major research projects. These fellows, from different disciplines and backgrounds, usually spend from four months to one year at the center. (There is also a Guest Scholar Program for short-term appointments.) Fellows work in two general divisions: Social and Political Studies, and Historical and Cultural Studies; and in four specific programs: the Environmental Studies Program; the Kennan Institute for Advanced Russian Studies; the Latin American Program; and International Security Studies.

   The Latin American Program, established in 1977, has two major aims: to support advanced research on Latin America, the Caribbean, and inter-American affairs by social scientists and humanists, and to help assure that fresh insights in these areas come to the attention of persons in governments, international organizations, the media, business, etc. The program awards about five fellowships each year in open international competition for research on topics which illuminate Latin American or inter-American realities—past, present, or future. Fellowship applications are reviewed by the program's nine-member Academic Council, composed of distinguished scholars from various disciplines and six countries. Central themes of particular interest are: a) the interplay between the international economic order and domestic political and economic choices in Latin America and the Caribbean; b) the nature and evolution of U.S.-Latin American relations, and Latin America's international role more generally; c) the causes and dynamics of authoritarianism in Latin America; d) the interplay between cultural traditions and political institutions in the region; e) the history of ideas in Latin America as they bear upon contemporary public policy choices; and f) the dynamics and viability of alternative development models in Latin America and the Caribbean.

   The center's activities include twice-weekly pre-luncheon "sherry hours"

5.

6.

(frequently featuring distinguished outside speakers), as well as periodic afternoon colloquia and evening dialogues—all aimed at creating a true "community of scholars." Within this framework, the Latin American Program sponsors its own colloquia, seminars, workshops, and conferences. These activities, some of which are by invitation, are announced in the center's monthly *Calendar of Events,* which Washington-area scholars may request to receive by mail.

5.   The Wilson Center has a 15,000-volume working library with basic reference works and essential monographs in the social sciences and humanities. The library subscribes to and maintains the backfiles of some three hundred scholarly periodicals. As part of a national Presidential Monument, it has special access to the collections of the Library of Congress and other government libraries. The librarian is Zdenek David (381-5850).

A Latin American Corner is maintained by the library for the Latin American Program. It contains important reference works, several Latin American newspapers, the *FBIS Daily Report: Latin America,* some two dozen scholarly journals for Latin American and Caribbean studies, published in the United States, Western Europe, and throughout Latin America, and scholarly monographs particularly in the fields of economics, history, and politics.

6.   In addition to its monthly *Calendar of Events,* the center publishes the *Wilson Quarterly,* an intellectual journal containing samples of research by center fellows plus abstracts or selections from important recent books and articles and news of major developments in the international intellectual community. The Latin American Program publishes its own semi-annual newsletter as well as a series of *Working Papers.* The center also sponsors a series of *Scholars' Guides to Washington, D.C.* which survey the collections, institutions, and organizations pertinent to the study of particular geographic areas, such as Russia/Soviet Union, Latin America and the Caribbean, East Asia, Africa, the Middle East, and other world regions.

M41   Woodstock Theological Center

1.   *1322 36th Street, NW*
Washington, D.C. 20057
338-8040

2.   Robert A. Mitchell, S.J., Director

4.   Woodstock Theological Center is a Jesuit "institute for research and reflection" on world problems of ethics, faith, and justice. The staff consists of eight full-time research fellows. Among the center's current research projects is a cross-cultural and interdisciplinary study of "human rights, needs and power in an interdependent world," which is being conducted in collaboration with several Jesuit research centers in Latin America. The project will attempt to develop "a new normative theory of human rights that takes into account the different cultural traditions of North and South America." Conferences and publications are expected to result from the project. The project director is Brian H. Smith, S.J.

5.   The Woodstock Theological Library is discussed in the "Libraries" section, entry A53.

M42 Worldwatch Institute

1. *Suite 701*
    1776 Massachusetts Avenue, NW
    Washington, D.C. 20036
    452-1999

2. Lester Brown, President
    Denis Hayes, Senior Researcher
    Erik Eckholm, Senior Researcher

4. The Worldwatch Institute is a nonprofit research organization which studies, from a global perspective, issues of population, energy, food, environment, and the changing roles of women. There are six researchers.

6. Research is published in *Worldwatch Papers* (approximately one per month) and in a book series. A subscription service is available.

Note: All of the research centers discussed in this section operate as nonprofit organizations. In addition, however, the Washington, D.C. area contains many private, commercial research, consulting, and technical assistance firms (of varying degrees of permanency) which specialize in international development, international marketing, etc., and which work under contract for U.S. government agencies and/or private business enterprises. There follows a partial list of such firms which have had Latin American interests:

C.A.C.I., Inc.
1815 North Fort Myer Drive
Arlington, Virginia 22209
841-7800

Checci and Company
1730 Rhode Island Avenue, NW
Washington, D.C. 20036
452-9700

Developing World Industry and Technology, Inc.
919 18th Street, NW
Washington, D.C. 20006
785-0620

Development Alternatives, Inc.
1823 Jefferson Place, NW
Washington, D.C. 20036
833-8140

Development Associates, Inc.
2924 Columbia Pike
Arlington, Virginia 22204
979-0100

Development Strategies Corporation
1825 Jefferson Place, NW
Washington, D.C. 20036
659-3457

Economic Associates, Inc.
1730 K Street, NW
Washington, D.C. 20006
223-2530

General Research Corporation
7655 Old Springhouse Road
McLean, Virginia 22101
893-5900

Hay Associates
1100 17th Street, NW
Washington, D.C. 20036
331-0430

Inter-American Services, Inc.
1750 Pennsylvania Avenue, NW
Washington, D.C. 20006
393-4350

International Business and Economic
Research Corporation
1819 H Street, NW
Washington, D.C. 20006
293-3344

International Development Corporation
600 New Hampshire Avenue, NW
Washington, D.C. 20037
337-2700

International Development Group, Inc.
2332 Tuckahoe Street
Arlington, Virginia 22205
532-6548

Latin American Affairs Consultants
National Press Building, Suite 1111
529 14th Street, NW
Washington, D.C. 20004
628-9439/9440

Robert R. Nathan Associates, Inc.
1200 18th Street, NW
Washington, D.C. 20036
833-2200

Planning and Development Collaborative
  International (PADCO)
1834 Jefferson Place, NW
Washington, D.C. 20036
296-0004

Practical Concepts, Incorporated (PCI)
1730 Rhode Island Avenue, NW
Washington, D.C. 20036
833-1040

TEMPO Center for Advanced Studies
  —Economic and Population
  Studies Group
General Electric Corporation
Suite 600
777 14th Street, NW
Washington, D.C. 20005
637-4511

Westinghouse Health Systems
P.O. Box 866
American City Building
Columbia, Maryland 21044
(301) 992-3100

N. Academic Departments and Programs

Academic Department and Program Entry Format

1. *Address; telephone numbers*
2. Chief official and title
3. Degrees and subjects offered; program activities
4. Library/research facilities

N1   American University—Latin American Studies Program

1. *School of International Service*
   American University
   Washington, D.C. 20016
   686-2475

2. John J. Finan, Director

3. American University awards an undergraduate degree in Latin American
   area and language studies. In addition, AU's School of International Service
   offers programs leading to BA, MA, and Ph.D. degrees in international
   studies, within which students may select a field of concentration in Latin
   American studies. The university offers undergraduate and some graduate-
   level courses in Latin American anthropology, economics, government and
   international relations, history, literature, and sociology.

   On approximately a monthly basis during the academic year, the School of
   International Service sponsors an evening lecture series on current Latin
   American issues, featuring outside speakers. The series may be attended by
   invitation only.

   LACASA, the university's Latin American student association, sponsors
   occasional social and cultural programs each semester. The organization can
   be contacted through the office of the director of Latin American Studies.

4. See entry A6.

N2   Catholic University—Ibero-American Studies Program

1. *c/o Department of History*
   The Catholic University of America
   Washington, D.C. 20064
   635-5484

2. James D. Riley, Director

3. Catholic University offers programs leading to the BA and MA in Ibero-American Studies, with courses in anthropology, economics, history, and literature. Doctoral programs with concentration on Latin America are offered by individual departments.

    The university's Latin American Student Association (which has an office in the International Students' Center at 701 Monroe Street, NE; telephone: 635-5444) sponsors social and cultural events on an ad hoc basis.

4. See entries A11 and A42.

N3 George Mason University—Latin American Studies Program

1. *c/o Department of Public Affairs*
    George Mason University
    4400 University Drive
    Fairfax, Virginia 22030
    323-2000

2. Robert P. Clark, Coordinator—Latin American Studies Committee

3. George Mason University offers an undergraduate program leading to the BA in Latin American Studies, with courses in anthropology, economics, geography, history, literature, and music.

N4 George Washington University—Latin American Studies Program

1. *Building I, Room 200*
    George Washington University
    Washington, D.C. 20052
    676-6185/6186

2. Marvin F. Gordon, Chairman

3. George Washington University offers BA and MA degree programs in Latin American Studies, with courses in anthropology, demography, economics, geography, history, literature, and political science. Doctoral programs with Latin American concentration are offered by individual departments.

    In addition, graduate students in GW's School of Public and International Affairs (SPIA) (676-6240) may concentrate on Latin America within programs leading to the MA and Ph.D. in international affairs.

4. See entry A21.

N5 Georgetown University—Latin American Studies Program

1. *132 Nevils Hall*
    Georgetown University
    Washington, D.C. 20057
    625-4675

2. G. Harvey Summ, Director

3.   Georgetown University offers undergraduate and graduate-level courses in Latin American economics, geography, history, literature, politics, and sociology/demography. The university's Latin American Studies Program awards an MA degree in Latin American Studies. In addition, the university's Walsh School of Foreign Service (625-4218) offers multidisciplinary programs leading to the BS and MS in international affairs, within which students may select a Latin American field of concentration. Doctoral programs with a Latin American concentration are administered by individual departments.

      The Latin American Studies Program sponsors a monthly forum for selected students, faculty, and outside specialists (by invitation only). The program's Latin American Studies Student Organization holds weekly meetings, occasionally featuring speakers. In addition, the university's Latin American Student Union sponsors a variety of social and cultural events each academic year. (The Latin American Student Union can be reached through the university's Student Activities office [625-4308]). Finally, the Walsh School of Foreign Service sponsors occasional lectures, seminars, and conferences on Latin American and/or international topics, most of which are open to interested scholars. Contact the office of the dean (625-4218) for information on upcoming events.

4.   See entry A22.

N6 Howard University—Caribbean/Latin American Studies Program

1.   *c/o Department of Economics*
Howard University
Washington, D.C. 20059
636-6718

2.   Ransford W. Palmer, Acting Director

3.   Although Howard University has no formal degree program in Latin American Studies, undergraduate and some graduate-level courses on Latin America are offered in anthropology and sociology, economics, geography, history, literature, political science, and interdisciplinary Afro-American Studies. Included are a number of courses focusing on Caribbean history, culture, and economic development.

      The newly created Caribbean/Latin American Studies Program plans to sponsor an informal seminar series on political, economic, and social issues, featuring guest speakers.

      The university's Caribbean Student Association can be contacted through the Office of Student Life (636-7000).

4.   See entries A23 and A24.

Inter-American Defense College See entry L5

N7 Maryland University

1.   *College Park, Maryland 20742*
454-0100

3. No formal Latin American Studies program has been established at the University of Maryland, although undergraduates may, on an individual basis, concentrate on Latin America within a program of independent study. The university offers Latin American-related courses (undergraduate and some graduate-level) in anthropology, art, economics, geography, government and politics, history, and literature.

    The university's Latin American Student Union (454-4392) sponsors ad hoc lectures, films, dinners, dances, and other social gatherings. The organization maintains an office in the university's Student Union building.

4. The University of Maryland library is discussed in the Libraries section, entry A34. In addition, the Department of Spanish and Portuguese (454-4305) maintains a separate library collection containing approximately 3,000 volumes of Iberian and Latin American literature.

National Defense University (National War College) See entry J8

N8 School of Advanced International Studies (SAIS) (Johns Hopkins University)—Latin American Studies Program

1. *1740 Massachusetts Avenue, NW*
    Washington, D.C. 20036
    785-6265

2. Riordan Roett, Director

3. The School of Advanced International Studies, a graduate division of Johns Hopkins University, offers programs leading to the MA and Ph.D. in international studies, within which students may select a field of concentration in Latin American Studies. Courses are offered in Latin American economics, history, politics, and international relations, with special attention to Brazil.

    SAIS sponsors a variety of conferences and lectures with occasional Latin American focus, including an annual "Christian A. Herter Lecture Series" on a selected topic in world affairs, an annual six-week "Seminar in Diplomacy" for young Latin American diplomats from embassies in Washington, and several annual forums in which corporation executives, government officials, and scholars discuss the overseas operations of U.S. business. The Latin American Studies Program also periodically sponsors specialized conferences and seminars, participation in which is usually by invitation only.

4. See entry A48.

State Department—Foreign Service Institute See entry J28

N9 Washington, D.C. Consortium of Universities—Washington Center for Latin American Studies

1. *School of International Service*
    American University
    Washington, D.C. 20016
    686-2482

2.   Dorothy Dillon, Director

3.   Students enrolled at any of the Washington, D.C. Consortium of Universities' member-universities—including American, Catholic, George Washington, Georgetown, and Howard—may take courses for credit at any other member institution. The Consortium's new Washington Center for Latin American Studies is an outgrowth of the Consortium Committee on Latin American Studies. Director Dorothy Dillon will attempt to rationalize, expand, and upgrade the Latin American Studies programs of the member-universities. Activities will include sponsorship of guest lecturers from Latin America, development of Consortium-wide courses and seminars, and other projects. The center should prove to be an excellent centralized source of information on academic programs in Latin American Studies in the Washington area.

APPENDIXES

Appendix I. Publications and Media

Publications and Media Entry Format

1. *address; telephone number*
2. publisher
3. chief official/key staff members
4. frequency of issue
5. content

Introductory Note

The following represents a selective list of those periodicals published in the Washington area which are devoted *primarily* to Latin American and/or Caribbean topics of potential scholarly interest. No attempt has been made to repeat bibliographic citations to all of those periodicals (international-relations journals, U.S. government agency publications, association newsletters, etc.) discussed elsewhere in this volume which include Latin America within a broader geographic coverage of world affairs. Nor has any attempt been made to include specific information on the large and ever-changing corps of Latin American press representatives stationed in Washington. For current names and addresses of the accredited Washington correspondents of Latin American and Caribbean newspapers, magazines, wire services, and television networks, see the semiannual *Resident Foreign Media Directory: Press-TV-Radio Correspondents in the United States,* which is compiled by the International Communication Agency's Foreign Press Center (724-1640), located in Room 202 of the National Press Building, 14th and F Streets, NW, Washington, D.C. 20045. Copies are available on request.

1. AACCLA Report

   1. *1615 H Street, NW*
      Washington, D.C. 20062
      659-4637
   2. Association of American Chambers of Commerce in Latin America
   3. Keith Miceli, Editor
   4. Semiannual
   5. Newsletter of the activities of the Association of American Chambers of Commerce in Latin America, including country reports from U.S. chambers of commerce in Latin America.

2. Action

1. *Cafritz Building, Suite 622*
   1625 Eye Street, NW
   Washington, D.C. 20006
   381-8651/8652
2. Pan American Development Foundation
4. Irregular
5. Newsletter covering technical-assistance program activities of the Pan American Development Foundation (see entry 128).

3. AIFLD Report

1. *1015 20th Street, NW*
   Washington, D.C. 20036
   659-6300
2. American Institute for Free Labor Development (AFL-CIO)
3. Edwin Palenque, Editor
4. Bimonthly
5. Newsletter

4. Américas

1. *General Secretariat*
   Department of Publications
   Organization of American States
   Washington, D.C. 20006
   381-8513/8175
2. OAS General Secretariat
3. Arbon Jack Lowe, Editor
4. Monthly (10 issues per year)
5. Illustrated magazine, published in English, Spanish, and Portuguese editions, with articles, book reviews, and notes about inter-American affairs and the art, music, literature, history, and social/economic development of Latin America.

5. The Americas: A Quarterly Review of Inter-American Cultural History

1. *Box 34440*
   Washington, D.C. 20034
   365-1763
2. Academy of American Franciscan History.
3. Antonine S. Tibesar, OFM, Editor
4. Quarterly
5. Scholarly journal containing articles, book reviews, and notes on Latin American history and the history of inter-American relations.

6. Argentina

1. *1600 New Hampshire Avenue, NW*
   Washington, D.C. 20009
   332-7100

2. Embassy of Argentina
4. Monthly
5. Current-events newsletter.

---

7. **Argentina**

    1. *1600 New Hampshire Avenue, NW*
       Washington, D.C. 20009
       332-7100
    2. Embassy of Argentina
    4. Irregular
    5. Magazine

---

8. **Barbados News Bulletin**

    1. *2144 Wyoming Avenue, NW*
       Washington, D.C. 20008
       387-7373
    2. Embassy of Barbados
    4. Irregular
    5. Current-events newsletter

---

9. **Boletín de la Oficina Sanitaria Panamericana**

    1. *525 23rd Street, NW*
       Washington, D.C. 20037
       331-5441
    2. Pan American Health Organization (PAHO)
    3. Clare Harley, Editor
    4. Monthly
    5. Technical journal (primarily in Spanish) containing articles, abstracts, news items, and book notices pertaining to public health and preventative medicine in the Western Hemisphere.

---

10. **Boletín de Precios Internacionales de Productos Básicos**

    1. *General Secretariat*
       Department of Publications
       Organization of American States
       Washington, D.C. 20006
       381-8813/8814
    2. OAS International Trade Program
    3. José Numar Zapata González, Editor
    4. Monthly
    5. Bulletin containing statistical information on commodity prices.

---

11. **Brazil Today**

    1. *3006 Massachusetts Avenue, NW*
       Washington, D.C. 20008
       797-0100

2. Embassy of Brazil
4. Irregular
5. Newsletter

12. Bulletin of the Pan American Health Organization

41. *525 23rd Street, NW*
    Washington, D.C. 20037
    331-5441
2. Pan American Health Organization (PAHO)
3. Clare Harley, Editor
4. Quarterly
5. Technical journal (English only) featuring articles, abstracts, news items, and book notices pertaining to public health and medicine in the Western Hemisphere.

13. *Carrollton Press, Incorporated*—Declassified Documents Reference System

1. *1911 Fort Myer Drive*
   Arlington, Virginia 22209
   525-5940
3. William Buchanan, President
   Annadel Wile, Executive Editor—*Declassified Documents Reference System*
5. The commercial Carrollton Press compiles declassified U.S. government documents and sells hard- and microfiche copies on a commercial subscription basis. Its "Declassified Documents Reference System" currently contains some 16,000 documents from the State Department, CIA, Defense Department, National Security Council, White House, Treasury Department, FBI, etc. Holdings range in date from the end of World War II to the 1970s, with the majority pertaining to the Eisenhower, Kennedy, and Johnson administrations (including many documents relating to Guatemala [1954], Brazil [1964], the Dominican Republic [1965], and Cuba). The collection is growing at a rate of approximately 2,000 documents per year.
   Finding aids include cumulative subject indexes and a quarterly catalog of abstracts. A newsletter, *Declassified Document News* (one or two issues per year), is disseminated to subscribers. Local Washington-area subscribers include the State Department Library (see entry A49), the Army Library (entry A7), the Defense Intelligence Agency Library (entry J8), and the Library of Congress (entry A33). Information brochures are available on request.

14. CECON Trade News

1. *General Secretariat*
   Department of Publications
   Organization of American States
   Washington, D.C. 20006
   381-8813/8814
2. OAS International Trade Program
3. Renato Tovar, Editor

4. Monthly

5. Bulletin containing current information on the OAS Special Committee for Consultation and Negotiation (CECON), hemispheric tariffs and customs duties, and trade legislation pending before the United States Congress.

15. Chile Economic News

1. *1736 Massachusetts Avenue, NW*
   Washington, D.C. 20036
   785-1746

2. Embassy of Chile

4. Monthly

5. Economic bulletin

16. Chile Today

1. *1736 Massachusetts Avenue, NW*
   Washington, D.C. 20036
   785-1746

2. Embassy of Chile

4. Quarterly

5. Newsletter

17. Ciencia Interamericana

1. *General Secretariat*
   Department of Publications
   Organization of American States
   Washington, D.C. 20006
   381-8733

2. OAS Department of Scientific Affairs

3. Rafael Mencia, Editor

4. Quarterly

5. Reviews of scientific and technological developments in the hemisphere.

18. Colombia Today

1. *2118 Leroy Place, NW*
   Washington, D.C. 20008
   387-5828

2. Embassy of Colombia

4. Monthly

5. General-information and economics newsletter.

19. La Educación

1. *General Secretariat*
   Department of Publications
   Organization of American States
   Washington, D.C. 20006
   381-8661

2. OAS Department of Educational Affairs
3. Jaime Ospina Ortíz, Editor
4. Quarterly
5. Journal containing general-interest articles on education in the hemisphere, progress reports on OAS educational programs, and reviews of books and periodicals.

20. Educación Médica y Salud

1. *525 23rd Street, NW*
   Washington, D.C. 20037
   331-5441
2. Pan American Health Organization (PAHO)
3. Clare Harley, Editor
4. Quarterly
5. Journal containing information on developments in public-health education in the Americas.

21. *Embassy of Brazil* Boletím

1. *3006 Massachusetts Avenue, NW*
   Washington, D.C. 20008
   797-0100
4. Irregular
5. Current-events news digest

22. *Embassy of Ecuador* Boletín de Noticias

1. *2535 15th Street, NW*
   Washington, D.C. 20009
   234-7200
4-5. Monthly newsletter

23. *Embassy of Guyana* Embassy News

1. *2490 Tracy Place, NW*
   Washington, D.C. 20008
   265-6900
4-5. Bimonthly newsletter.

24. *Embassy of Honduras* Carta Mensual

1. *Suite 408*
   4301 Connecticut Avenue, NW
   Washington, D.C. 20008
   966-7700
4-5. Monthly newsletter

25. *Embassy of Surinam* News in Brief

1. *Suite 711*
   2600 Virginia Avenue, NW
   Washington, D.C. 20037
   338-6980
4. Irregular
5. Current-events newsletter

26. Estadística

1. *General Secretariat*
   Department of Publications
   Organization of American States
   Washington, D.C. 20006
   381-8360
2. Official organ of the Inter-American Statistical Institute of the Organization of American States
3. Maria Alicia de Madariaga, Editor
4. Trimestral
5. Journal containing articles (in English, Spanish, Portuguese, or French) on inter-American statistical administration, official statistical practices, theory and method. Also includes news notes from government statistical offices and other statistical organizations, as well as bibliographic material.

27. *Foreign Broadcast Information Service (FBIS)*—Daily Reports

1. *P.O. Box 2604*
   Washington, D.C. 20013
   527-2368
   351-3577 (Information)
   351-2878 (Latin American Daily Report)
2. U.S. government
4-5. The U.S. government's Foreign Broadcast Information Service publishes a series of *Daily Reports,* containing translations of significant foreign-language material monitored from foreign media: radio and television broadcasts, press agency transmissions, newspapers, magazines, and journals. Included are translations of the speeches of foreign leaders; government statements; official communiques and interviews; major editorials, articles, and commentaries; news reports on important political, economic, cultural, and scientific developments; and a broad range of other reportage and writings. *Daily Report* Volume VI: *Latin America* is assembled by FBIS field monitoring stations in Panama, Paraguay, and Key West, Florida. A short version is available to the public, on a subscription basis, through the National Technical Information Service (NTIS) (see Appendix II: Bookstores). In addition, the FBIS Analysis Group publishes a classified weekly *Trends in Communist Media* which contains material on Cuba (as does the *Daily Report*). *Trends in Communist Media* is automatically declassified after six months and made available to the public through NTIS.

   There is no index to FBIS publications on Latin America. Individual FBIS reports are available at the Library of Congress.

28. Handbook of Latin American Studies

1. *Hispanic Division*
    Library of Congress
    10 1st Street, SE
    Washington, D.C. 20540
    426-5410

2. Published cooperatively by the Library of Congress and the University of Florida Press.

3. Dolores Martin, Editor

4. Annual

5. Bibliographic descriptions of recent books and articles dealing with Latin America. Annual volumes alternate their coverage between the social sciences and humanities.

---

29. Hispamérica: Revista de Literatura

1. *1402 Erskine Street*
    Takoma Park, Maryland 20012
    434-3806

3. Saul Sosnowski, Editor

4. Three issues per year

5. A Spanish-language journal devoted exclusively to Spanish-American literature, with articles on theory and criticism, interviews with authors, bibliographic notes, short stories, poems, and plays.

---

30. IDB News

1. *808 17th Street, NW*
    Washington, D.C. 20577
    634-8154

2. Inter-American Development Bank

3. Carlos Hirsch, Editor

4. Monthly

5. Newsletter

---

31. Inter-American Arbitration

1. *310 Federal Bar Building West*
    1819 H Street, NW
    Washington, D.C. 20006
    293-1455

2. Inter-American Commercial Arbitration Commission

4. Quarterly

5. Newsletter covering recent developments pertaining to arbitration of inter-American commercial disputes.

---

32. *Inter-American Bar Association* Letter to Members

1. *Suite 315*
    1730 K Street, NW
    Washington, D.C. 20006
    293-1340

4. Three or four issues per year.
5. Newsletter

33. *Inter-American Commission of Women* Informational Bulletin

1. *Paramount Building, Room 730*
   1735 Eye Street, NW
   Washington, D.C. 20006
   381-8847/8440
2. OAS Inter-American Commission of Women
4. Monthly

34. *Inter-American Council* Newsletter

1. *c/o Hispanic Division*
   Library of Congress
   10 1st Street, SE
   Washington, D.C. 20540
   426-5397
4. Monthly, except during summer months
5. Announcements of Inter-American Council activities (see entry H27).

35. Inter-American Economic Affairs

1. *P. O. Box 181*
   Washington, D.C. 20044
2. Inter-American Affairs Press
3. Simon G. Hanson, Editor
4. Quarterly
5. Scholarly journal containing articles and reviews on hemispheric economic relations and economic history.

36. Inter-American Review of Bibliography

1. *General Secretariat*
   Department of Publications
   Organization of American States
   Washington, D.C. 20006
   381-8668
2. Organization of American States' Department of Cultural Affairs
3. Elena Castedo-Ellerman, Editor
4. Quarterly
5. A "journal of humanistic studies" devoted to the study of hemispheric culture, featuring articles, book reviews, and selected bibliographies on Latin American topics from books acquired by the OAS' Columbus Memorial Library, the Library of Congress, the U.S. National Agricultural Library, and the libraries of Harvard and Columbia universities.

International Communication Agency—Foreign Press Center
See entry J17

37. Jamaica Newsletter

1. *1666 Connecticut Avenue, NW*
   Washington, D.C. 20009
   387-1010
2. Embassy of Jamaica
4. Monthly
5. Current-events newsletter

38. *Joint Publications Research Service (JPRS)*—Translations on Latin America

1. *1000 North Glebe Road*
   Arlington, Virginia 22201
   841-1050 (Information)
   841-1064 (Latin American Desk)
2. U.S. government
4-5. The U.S. Joint Publications Research Service provides translations and abstracts of foreign-language political and technical publications to U.S. government agencies, particularly within the U.S. intelligence community Many of its products are classified.

   In addition, however, JPRS publishes serial reports—*Translations on Latin America* (approximately three or four per week)—on major political, economic, and social developments in Latin America as reported primarily from Latin American newspapers and periodicals. These are available to the public, on a commercial subscription basis, through the National Technical Information Service (NTIS) (see Appendix II: Bookstores). JPRS also publishes intermittent serial translations of foreign-language press coverage relating to narcotics and dangerous drugs, law of the sea, environmental quality, and epidemiology (also available through NTIS).

   JPRS publications are available at the Library of Congress and in the JPRS reading room (open 8 A.M.-4:30 P.M., Monday-Friday). Lists of JPRS ad hoc publications can be found in the NTIS semimonthly publication *Government Reports Announcements and Index*. In addition, the Bell and Howell Micro Photo Division (Old Mansfield Road, Wooster, Ohio, 44691) publishes a monthly *TRANSDEX Index* to JPRS publications and sell individual documents on microfiche or hard-copy.

39. Journal of the Inter-American Foundation

1. *1515 Wilson Boulevard*
   Rosslyn, Virginia 22209
   841-3800
3. Michele St. Clair, Editor
4. Three issues per year.
5. Articles on development projects and problems.

40. Juventud

1. *General Secretariat*
   Department of Publications
   Organization of American States
   Washington, D.C. 20006
   381-8375
2. OAS Office of Youth Affairs
3. George Meek, Editor
4. Semiannual
5. Bilingual (English/Spanish) journal containing articles, book reviews, statistics, and news notes on inter-American youth and sports activities.

41. LADOC

1. *1312 Massachusetts Avenue, NW*
   Washington, D.C. 20005
   659-6812
2. United States Catholic Conference
3. Sister Pauline Frei, Editor
4. Bimonthly
5. "Latin American Documentation"—consisting of English translations of recent Latin American Catholic Church documents, pastoral letters, episcopal statements, etc.

42. Latin American Index

1. *1835 K Street, NW*
   Washington, D.C. 20006
   223-6500
2-3. Frank A. Schuler, Jr., Publisher and Managing Editor
4. Semimonthly
5. Current-events newsletter, containing political and economic news coverage. Semiannual index compiled.

43. Latin American Update

1. *110 Maryland Avenue, NE*
   Washington, D.C. 20002
   544-8045
2. Washington Office on Latin America (WOLA)
4. Bimonthly
5. Newsletter surveying current U.S. legislative activities affecting Latin America, as well as summaries of, and commentaries on, Latin American news events.

44. OAS Chronicle

1. *General Secretariat*
   Department of Publications
   Organization of American States
   Washington, D.C. 20006
   381-8513/8175
2. OAS General Secretariat's Office of *Américas* magazine.
3. Mario Barraco Marmol, Editor
4. Monthly (10 issues per year)
5. Newsletter containing current information on major inter-American events and the texts of important official OAS documents.

45. Pan American Health

1. *525 23rd Street, NW*
   Washington, D.C. 20037
   331-5441
2. Pan American Health Organization (PAHO)
3. Clare Harley, Editor
4. Quarterly
5. Magazine (in English and Spanish) devoted to developments in public health throughout the Americas.

46. Partners

1. *2001 S Street, NW*
   Washington, D.C. 20009
   332-7332
2. Partners of the Americas
4. Quarterly
5. Newsletter describing the program activities of the Partners of the Americas organization (see entry I 29).

47. Peruvian Embassy Bulletin

1. *1700 Massachusetts Avenue, NW*
   Washington, D.C. 20036
   833-9860
4-5. Monthly newsletter

48. Public Sector (formerly Development Financing)

1. *General Secretariat*
   Department of Publications
   Organization of American States
   Washington, D.C. 20006
   381-8547
2. OAS Public Sector Program
3. Raúl A. Gochez, Editor

4. Quarterly

5. Review of OAS technical assistance activities, with information on Latin American development programs, budgeting, revenue, capital markets, taxation, etc.

49. Times of the Americas

1. *830 Woodward Building*
   733 15th Street, NW
   Washington, D.C. 20005
   638-4119/466-5440

3. Clarence Moore, Editor

4. Biweekly

5. English-language newspaper containing coverage of Latin American current events. Microfilm copies of the *Times of the Americas* and predecessor newspapers (*Times of Havana, Times of Havana-in-Exile*), 1957-present, are available from the Bell and Howell Micro Photo Division (Old Mansfield Road, Wooster, Ohio 44691). Editor Clarence Moore will make his collections of back-issues and photographs available to researchers.

50. Venezuela Today (Venezuela Ahora)

1. *2445 Massachusetts Avenue, NW*
   Washington, D.C. 20008
   265-9600

2. Embassy of Venezuela

4-5. Monthly newsletter

51. Venezuela Up-to-Date

1. *2445 Massachusetts Avenue, NW*
   Washington, D.C. 20008
   265-9600

2. Embassy of Venezuela

4. Irregular

5. Magazine

Voice of America See entry J17

52. Washington Post

1. *1150 15th Street, NW*
   Washington, D.C. 20071
   223-6000 (Information)
   223-7400 (Foreign News)

3. Benjamin Bradlee, Executive Editor
   Howard Simons, Managing Editor

4. Daily

5. The *Washington Post* newspaper has two staff correspondents (currently Charles Krause and Karen D. Young) and two "stringers" (Larry Rohter in

Rio de Janeiro and Marlise Simons in Mexico City) in Latin America. Washington staff members Lewis Diuguid, Terri Shaw, and Joanne Omang also have Latin American experience and are accessible to researchers.

The *Washington Post* library—which contains over five million newspaper clippings and 600,000 photographs—is, regrettably, open only to accredited newspaper correspondents and *Post* staff members. The library operates 10:30 A.M.-7 P.M., Monday-Friday, and for a few hours on Saturday and Sunday. Mark Hannan is the librarian. Interlibrary loan services are available.

The Bell and Howell Micro Photo Division (Old Mansfield Road, Wooster, Ohio 44691) publishes a *Newspaper Index* to the *Washington Post, 1971-*present.

53. Washington Star

1. *225 Virginia Avenue, SE*
   Washington, D.C. 20003
   484-5000 (Information)
   484-4231 (Foreign News Desk)

3. Murray Gart, Editor
   Sidney Epstein, Executive Editor

4. Daily

5. The Washington *Star* newspaper relies on wire services and "stringers" for its Latin American coverage. Washington staff member Jeremiah O'Leary has Latin American experience.

   The Washington *Star* library (484-4375) is restricted to staff use. Exceptions *might* be made in individual cases. The facility is staffed 24 hours per day. Angelina O'Donnell is the librarian.

   The Microfilming Corporation of America (21 Harristown Road, Glen Rock, New Jersey 07452) has indexed the *Star* for the period 1852-1973.

54. Weekly Epidemiological Report

1. *525 23rd Street, NW*
   Washington, D.C. 20037
   331-5441

2. Pan American Health Organization (PAHO)

3. Clare Harley, Editor

5. Review (in English and Spanish) of information about communicable diseases in the Americas.

55. West Watch

1. *305 4th Street, NE*
   Washington, D.C. 20002
   543-2070

2. Council for Inter-American Security

3. Robert E. Moffit, Editor

4. Bimonthly

5. "Report on the condition of liberty and security in the Western Hemisphere," with coverage of hemispheric-defense issues and Marxist activities in Latin America and the Caribbean.

56. *Woodrow Wilson International Center for Scholars*—Latin American Program Newsletter

1. *Smithsonian Institution Building*
   1000 Jefferson Drive, SW
   Washington, D.C. 20560
   381-4321

4. Semiannual

5. Program activities of the Wilson Center's Latin American Program (see entry M40).

Appendix II. Bookstores

Bookstore Entry Format

1. address; telephone number

2. hours

3. stock

Introductory Note

The following is a selective list of local bookstores which feature materials of special interest to Latin Americanists.

AMERICAN UNIVERSITY BOOKSTORE

1. Anderson Hall
   Massachusetts and Nebraska Avenues, NW
   Washington, D.C. 20016
   686-2660

2. Hours vary.

3. Academic course materials in Latin American anthropology, economics, government, history, international relations, literature, and sociology.

CATHOLIC UNIVERSITY BOOKSTORE

1. McMahon Hall
   4th Street and Michigan Avenue, NE
   Washington, D.C. 20064
   635-5232

2. Academic year: 9 A.M.-5 P.M., Monday-Friday

3. Academic course materials in Latin American anthropology, economics, history, and literature.

GEORGE WASHINGTON UNIVERSITY BOOKSTORE

1. Marvin Center
   21st and H Streets, NW
   Washington, D.C. 20052
   676-6870

2. Academic year:
   8:45 A.M.-6:30 P.M. Monday-Thursday
   8:45 A.M.-5 P.M. Friday
   Summer:
   8:45 A.M.-5 P.M. Monday-Friday

3. Academic course materials in anthropology, demography, economics, geography, history, literature, and political science.

GEORGETOWN UNIVERSITY BOOKSTORE

1. Lauinger Library
   37th and Prospect Streets, NW
   Washington, D.C. 20057
   625-4068

2. 9 A.M.-5 P.M. Monday-Friday

3. Academic course materials in Latin American economics, geography, history, literature, politics, and sociology/demography.

GLOBE BOOK SHOPS—FOREIGN LANGUAGE CENTER

1. 1700 Pennsylvania Avenue, NW
   Washington, D.C. 20006
   393-1490

2. 9:30 A.M.-6:30 P.M. Monday-Friday
   10 A.M.-5 P.M. Saturday

3. Foreign-language learning aids and some Latin American literature. A branch store at 888 17th Street, NW, carries magazines and a few newspapers from Latin America.

HOWARD UNIVERSITY BOOKSTORE

1. 2801 Georgia Avenue, NW
   Washington, D.C. 20059
   636-6656

2. 9 A.M.-5 P.M. Monday-Friday

3. Academic course materials in Latin American, Caribbean, and Afro-American anthropology, economics, geography, history, literature, political science, and sociology.

INTERNATIONAL LEARNING CENTER

1. 1715 Connecticut Avenue, NW
   Washington, D.C. 20009
   232-4111

2. 10 A.M.-7 P.M. Monday-Saturday
   8 A.M.-5 P.M. Sunday

3. English-language titles in Latin American area studies—primarily economics, history, international relations, and politics. Also language materials, recordings of Latin American folk music, and some Spanish-American literature (in Spanish).

LATIN AMERICAN BOOKS OF WASHINGTON, D.C.

1. P. O. Box 39090
   Washington, D.C. 20016
   363-1666/362-2973

3. Used and out-of-print scholarly materials (approximately 50,000 titles) on Latin America, Spain, and Portugal. All fields, disciplines, and geographic areas are represented, as are U.S. and Latin American government publications, and publications of international organizations. Materials range from 18th-century imprints to recent works. Approximately half of the inventory is in Spanish or Portuguese.

The company operates by mail-order sales only. Customers are asked to submit lists of specific titles or subject-areas in which they are interested.

Contact owner David Clark for further information.

MARYLAND UNIVERSITY BOOKSTORE

1. Student Union Building
   Campus Drive
   College Park, Maryland 20742
   454-3222

2. Academic year:
   8:30 A.M.-7 P.M. Monday-Thursday
   8:30 A.M.-4:15 P.M. Friday
   10 A.M.-4 P.M. Saturday
   (Summer hours vary.)

3. Academic course materials in Latin American anthropology, art, economics, geography, government and politics, history, and literature.

MODERN LANGUAGE BOOK AND RECORD STORE

1. 3160 O Street, NW
   Washington, D.C. 20007
   338-8963

2. 10 A.M.-7 P.M. Monday
   10 A.M.-5:30 P.M. Tuesday-Friday
   10 A.M.-5 P.M. Saturday

3. A good selection of Latin American literature (in Spanish), and some Latin American social-science literature (also in Spanish).

NATIONAL TECHNICAL INFORMATION SERVICE (NTIS)

1. Operations Center
   5285 Port Royal Road
   Springfield, Virginia 22161
   557-4650 (Information)
   557-4642 (bibliographic search service)

   NTIS Information Center and Bookstore
   Suite 620
   425 13th Street, NW
   Washington, D.C. 20004
   724-3382 (Information)
   724-3383 (after-hours orders)

2. Springfield Operations Center:
   7:45 A.M.-4:15 P.M. Monday-Friday

   NTIS Information Center and Bookstore:
   9 A.M.-4:30 P.M Monday-Friday

3. The U.S. Department of Commerce's National Technical Information Service serves as the principal distribution center for the public sale of research

reports and analyses prepared, sponsored, or funded by U.S. government agencies. It currently has available for sale more than one million titles acquired by NTIS since 1964. The majority are scientific and technical materials, but also included are Commerce Department foreign-market airgrams and international market-share reports, Foreign Broadcast Information Service and Joint Publications Research Service reports relating to Latin America, EPA foreign environmental reports, research on international energy matters, and some Agency for International Development research studies. In addition, NTIS is attempting to collect Latin American-originated research materials on industrial technology and rural development (agriculture, nutrition, sanitation, etc.). The organization is also preparing to include in its collection selected State Department cables and airgrams on foreign political, economic, social, cultural, and military affairs (to be indexed by country and subject), as well as some unclassified Central Intelligence Agency research studies.

Items can be purchased in hard copy or microfilm. A computerized bibliographic search service is available for a fee.

Finding aids include a biweekly *Government Reports Announcements and Index* (with annual cumulation), containing summaries of recently acquired research titles; and *NTISearch Catalog,* a subject index to more than 1,000 published NTIS bibliographies produced by previous computer searches. A regularly updated descriptive brochure, *NTIS Information Services General Catalog,* is available without charge.

SIDNEY KRAMER BOOKS

1. 1722 H Street, NW
   Washington, D.C. 20006
   298-8010

2. 9 A.M.-6 P.M. Monday-Wednesday, Friday
   9 A.M.-7:30 P.M. Thursday
   10 A.M.-4 P.M. Saturday

3. A good selection of recent English-language social-science literature on Latin America. Particularly strong in economics, politics, international relations, and history. Some literature in translation.

U.S. GOVERNMENT PRINTING OFFICE (GPO) BOOKSTORES

1. Main Bookstore
   710 North Capitol Street, NW
   Washington, D.C. 20402
   783-3238 (General orders and inquiries)
   275-3030 (Congressional documents orders and inquiries)

   [Mail: Superintendent of Documents
   U.S. Government Printing Office
   Washington, D.C. 20402]

   GPO Commerce Department Bookstore
   14th and E Streets, NW
   377-3527

   GPO Health, Education, and Welfare Department Bookstore
   330 Independence Avenue, NW
   472-7899

   GPO International Communication Agency (formerly USIA) Bookstore
   1776 Pennsylvania Avenue, NW
   724-9928

GPO Pentagon Bookstore
Pentagon Building
557-1821

GPO State Department Bookstore
21st and C Streets, NW
632-1437

2. Main Bookstore:
   8 A.M.-4:30 P.M.
   (Branch bookstore hours vary.)

3. The U.S. Government Printing Office publishes and sells the reports and publications of U.S. government agencies and the U.S. Congress. Some 25,000 titles are currently available. See the *Monthly Catalog of United States Government Publications* (with semiannual indexes and annual cumulations) for individual listings. Free "Subject Bibliographies" are available for more than 250 topics, including agriculture, anthropology and archeology, foreign education, foreign investments, foreign languages, foreign trade and tariffs, U.S. foreign relations, maps, film and audiovisual information, national defense and security, the national and world economy, statistical publications, treaties and other U.S. international agreements, and U.S. intelligence activities. For further information, see the brochure *Consumers Guide to Federal Publications,* also free on request.

Note: Out-of-print books on, and from, Latin America can also be purchased— often at bargain prices—at several major book sales held in the Washington area each year. Perhaps the most significant of these events for Latin Americanists is the State Department Book Sale, sponsored by the Association of American Foreign Service Wives, and held during the autumn (usually October) at the State Department Building. Also note the Vassar College and Brandeis University book sales, which take place during the spring at varying sites. Each sale lasts for four or five days, and is announced in advance in local newspapers.

Appendix III. Library Collections: A Listing by Size of Latin American Holdings

Library Collections: A Listing by Size of Latin American Holdings

500,000 volumes or more:
  Library of Congress (A33)

100,000-500,000 volumes:
  Organization of American States—Columbus Memorial Library (A43)

50,000-100,000 volumes:
  Oliveira Lima Library (A42)

25,000-50,000 volumes:
  Inter-American Development Bank Library (A26)
  Pan American Health Organization Library (A47)
  State Department Library (A49)

10,000-25,000 volumes:
  Academy of American Franciscan History Library (A1)
  Georgetown University Library (A22)
  Joint Bank-Fund Library (A31)
  Maryland University Library (A34)
  National Agricultural Library (A35)
  Organization of American States—Department of Educational Affairs—
    Documentation and Information Service Library (A44)
  Woodstock Theological Center Library (A53)

Appendix IV. Standard Entry Forms

A. Library Entry Format

1.   General Information
   a. *address; telephone numbers*
   b. hours of service
   c. conditions of access (including availability of inter-library loan and reproduction facilities)
   d. name/title of director and heads of relevant divisions

2.   Size of collection
   a. general
   b. Latin American

3.   Description and Evaluation of Collection
   a. narrative assessment of Latin American holdings—subject and area strengths/weaknesses
   b. tabular evaluation of subject strength:

Subject Category	*Number of Titles (t.)*	*Rating (A-D)*
1. Philosophy and Religion		
2. History		
3. Geography and Anthropology		
4. Economics		
5. Sociology		
6. Politics and Government		
7. International Relations		
8. Law		
9. Education		
10. Art and Music		
11. Language and Literature		
12. Military Affairs		
13. Bibliography and Reference		
14. Argentina		
15. Bolivia		
16. Brazil		
17. Caribbean (excluding Cuba)		
18. Central America		
19. Chile		
20. Colombia		
21. Cuba		
22. Ecuador		

23. Guianas (Guyana, Surinam, French Guiana)
24. Mexico
25. Paraguay
26. Peru
27. Uruguay
28. Venezuela

 *A—comprehensive collection of primary and secondary sources (Library of Congress collection to serve as standard of evaluation)

 B—substantial collection of primary and secondary sources; sufficient for some original research (holdings of roughly one-tenth those of the Library of Congress)

 C—substantial collection of secondary sources, some primary; sufficient to support graduate instruction (holdings of roughtly one-half those of B collection)

 D—collection of secondary sources, mostly in English; sufficient to support undergraduat instruction (holdings of roughly one-half those of C collection)

4. Special Collections
 a. periodicals
 b. newspapers
 c. government documents
 d. miscellaneous vertical files
 e. archives and manuscripts
 f. maps
 g. films
 h. tapes

5. Bibliographic Aids (catalogs, guides, etc.) facilitating use of collection

B. Archive Entry Format

1. General Information
 a. *address; telephone numbers*
 b. hours of service
 c. conditions of access
 d. reproduction services
 e. name/title of director and heads of relevant divisions

2. Size of holdings pertaining to Latin America

3. Description of holdings pertaining to Latin America

4. Bibliographic aids (inventories, calendars, etc.) facilitating use of collection

C. Museum, Gallery, and Art-Collection Entry Format

1. General Information
 a. *address; telephone number*
 b. hours of service
 c. conditions of access

    d. reproduction services
    e. name/title of director and heads of relevant divisions

2.   Size of holdings pertaining to Latin America

3.   Description of holdings pertaining to Latin America

4.   Bibliographic aids facilitating use of collection

D. Music Collection Entry Format

1.   General Information
    a. *address; telephone numbers*
    b. hours of service
    c. conditions of access
    d. name/title of director and key staff members

2.   Size of holdings pertaining to Latin America

3.   Description of holdings pertaining to Latin America

4.   Facilities for study and use
    a. availability of audiovisual equipment
    b. reservation requirements
    c. fees charged
    d. reproduction services

5.   Bibliographic aids facilitating use of collection

E. Map Collection Entry Format

1.   General Information
    a. *address; telephone number*
    b. hours of service
    c. conditions of access
    d. reproduction services
    e. name/title of director and heads of relevant divisions

2.   Size of holdings pertaining to Latin America

3.   Description of holdings pertaining to Latin America

4.   Bibliographic aids facilitating use of collection

F. Film Collection Entry Format

1.   General Information
    a. *address; telephone number*
    b. hours of service
    c. conditions of access
    d. name/title of director and key staff members

2.   Size of holdings pertaining to Latin America

3.   Description of holdings pertaining to Latin America

4.   Facilities for study and use
   a. availability of audiovisual equipment
   b. reservation requirements
   c. fees charged
   d. reproduction services

5.   Bibliographic aids facilitating use of collection

G. Data Bank Entry Format

1.   General Information
   a. *address; telephone numbers*
   b. hours of service
   c. conditions of access (including fees charged for information retrieval)
   d. name/title of director and key staff members

2.   Description of data files (hard-data and bibliographic-reference) pertaining to Latin America

3.   Bibliographic aids facilitating use of storage media

H. Association Entry Format

1.   *Address; telephone numbers*

2.   Chief official and title

3.   Programs and activities pertaining to Latin America

4.   Library/reference collection

5.   Publications

I. Cultural-Exchange and Technical-Assistance Organization Entry Format

1.   *Address; telephone numbers*

2.   Chief official and title

3.   Programs and activities pertaining to Latin America

4.   Publications

J. United States Government Agency Entry Format*

1.   General Information
   a. *address; telephone numbers*
   b. conditions of access
   c. name/title of director and heads of relevant divisions

2.   Agency functions, programs, and research activities (including in-house research, contract research, research grants, and employment of outside consultants)

3.   Agency libraries and reference facilities

4.   Internal agency records (including unpublished research products)

5.   Publications
    a. published reports, periodicals, and series
    b. bibliographies

        *In the case of large, structurally-complex agencies, each relevant division/bureau will be described separately in accordance with the above entry format.

K. Latin American and Caribbean Embassies Entry Format

1.   General information
    a. *address; telephone*
    b. hours

2.   Reference facilities

3.   Publications

4.   Sponsored events and programs

L. International Organization Entry Format*

1.   General information
    a. *address; telephone*
    b. conditions of access
    c. name/title of director and heads of relevant division

2.   Organization functions, programs, and research activities (including in-house research, contract research, research grants, and employment of outside consultants)

3.   Libraries and reference facilities

4.   Internal records (including unpublished research products)

5.   Publications
    a. published reports, periodicals, and series
    b. bibliographies

        *In the case of large, structurally-complex organizations, each relevant division or sub-unit will be described separately in accordance with the above entry format.

M. Research Center and Information Office Entry Format

1.   *Address; telephone numbers*

2.   Chief official and title

3.   Parental organization

4.   Programs and research activities pertaining to Latin America

5. Library/research facilities
6. Publications

N. Academic Department and Program Entry Format

1. *Address; telephone number*
2. Chief official and title
3. Degrees and subjects offered; program activities
4. Library/research facilities

Bibliography

American Association of Museums. *Official Museum Directory*. Washington, D.C.: American Association of Museums, 1975.

American Council of Voluntary Agencies for Foreign Service, Inc. *U.S. Non-Profit Organizations in Development Assistance Abroad Including Voluntary Agencies, Missions, and Foundations*. New York: Technical Assistance Information Clearing House of the American Council of Voluntary Agencies for Foreign Service, Inc., 1971.

Ayer Press, '77 *Ayer Directory of Publications*. Philadelphia: Ayer Press, 1977.

Bartley, Russell H. and Wagner, Stuart L. *Latin America in Basic Historical Collections: A Working Guide*. Stanford, Calif.: Hoover Institution Press, 1972.

Benton, Mildred (ed.). *Library and Reference Facilities in the Area of the District of Columbia*. 9th ed. Washington: American Society for Information Science, 1975.

Brownson, Charles B. (comp.) *Congressional Staff Directory*. Mount Vernon, Virginia, 1976.

Chamberlin, Jim, and Hammond, Ann (eds.). *Directory of the Population-Related Community of the Washington, D.C. Area*. 3rd. ed. Washington, D.C.: World Population Society—D.C. Chapter, 1978.

Congressional Quarterly, Inc. *Washington Information Directory, 1977-1978*. Washington, D.C.: Congressional Quarterly, Inc., 1977.

Fisk, Margaret (ed.). *Encyclopedia of Associations*. 11th ed. Detroit: Gale Research Co., 1977.

Grayson, Cary T., Jr., and Lukowski, Susan. *Washington IV: A Comprehensive Directory of the Nation's Capital...its People and Institutions*. Washington, D.C.: Potomac Books, Inc., 1975.

Green, Shirley L. *Pictorial Resources in the Washington, D.C. Area*. Washington, D.C.: Library of Congress, 1976.

Hamer, Philip M. (ed.). *A Guide to Archives and Manuscripts in the United States*. New Haven: Yale University Press, 1961.

Haro, Robert P. *Latin Americana Research in the United States and Canada: A Guide and Directory.* Chicago: American Library Association, 1971.

Hilton, Ronald (ed.). *Handbook of Hispanic Source Materials and Research Organizations in the United States.* 2nd ed. Stanford: Stanford University Press, 1956.

Joyner, Nelson T., Jr. *Joyner's Guide to Official Washington.* 3rd ed. Rockville, Maryland: Rockville Consulting Group, 1976.

Mason, John Brown (ed.). *Research Resources: Annotated Guide to the Social Sciences.* Santa Barbara, Calif.: American Bibliographical Center, 1968-1971. 2 vols.

Palmer, Archie M. (ed.). *Research Centers Directory.* 5th ed. Detroit: Gale Research Co., 1975.

Sable, Martin H. *Master Directory for Latin America.* Los Angeles: UCLA Latin American Center, 1965.

Schmeckebier, Laurence Frederick, and Eastin, Roy B. *Government Publications and their Use.* 2nd rev. ed. Washington, D.C.: Brookings Institution, 1969.

Schneider, John H., Gechman, Marvin, and Furth, Stephen E. (eds.). *Survey of Commercially Available Computer-Readable Bibliographic Data Bases.* Washington, D.C.: American Society for Information Science, 1973.

Sessions, Vivian S. (ed.). *Directory of Data Bases in the Social and Behavioral Sciences.* New York: Science Associates/International, 1974.

Smith, David Horton (ed.). *Voluntary Transnational Cultural Exchange Organizations of the U.S.: A Selected List.* Washington, D.C.: Center for a Voluntary Society, 1974.

Tyler, William (ed.). *Data Banks and Archives for Social Science Research on Latin America.* Gainesville, Florida: Consortium of Latin American Studies Programs (CLASP), 1975.

U.S. Department of State, Office of External Research. *Foreign Affairs Research: A Directory of Governmental Resources.* Washington, D.C.: Department of State, 1969.

U.S. Department of State, Office of External Research. *Government-Supported Research on Foreign Affairs: Current Project Information, FY 1976.* Washington, D.C.: Government Printing Office, 1977.

U.S. Library of Congress, National Referral Center for Science and Technology. *A Directory of Information Resources in the United States: Federal Government.* Washington, D.C., 1974.

U.S. Library of Congress, National Referral Center for Science and Technology. *A Directory of Information Resources in the United States: Social Sciences.* rev. ed. Washington, D.C., 1973.

U.S. National Archives and Records Service, *United States Government Organization Manual, 1976/1977.* Washington, D.C., 1977.

Name Index

(Organizations and Institutions)

Entry symbols
correspond to the following sections of the text:

A—Libraries
B—Archives
C—Museums, Galleries, and Art Collections
D—Collections of Music and Other Sound Recordings
E—Map Collections
F—Film Collections
G—Data Banks
H—Associations
I—Cultural-Exchange and Technical-Assistance Organizations
J—United States Government Agencies
K—Latin American and Caribbean Embassies
L—International Organizations
M—Research Centers and Information Offices
N—Academic Programs and Departments

Academy for Educational Development I1
Academy of American Franciscan History A1, M1
Advanced International Studies Institute M2
Agency for International Development A3, F1, F13, G1, G2, J1
Agricultural Cooperative Development International I2
Agriculture Department B6, G3, J2
    See also National Agricultural Library
Air Force Central Still Photographic Depository F2
Air Force Department, B6, J8
    See also Air Force Central Still Photographic Depository; Office of Air Force History
American Anthropological Association H1
American Association for the Advancement of Science H2
American Association of Colleges for Teacher Education I3
American Association of Community and Junior Colleges H3

American Association of State Colleges and Universities I4
American Association of University Women H4
American Bar Association H5, I5
American Council of Young Political Leaders I6
American Council on Education H6
    See also Council for International Exchange of Scholars
American Council on International Sports I7
American Enterprise Institute for Public Policy Research M3
American Federation of Labor and Congress of Industrial Organizations (AFL-CIO) A4, I9
American Film Institute F3
American Foreign Service Association H7
American Historical Association H8
American Home Economics Association I8
American Institute for Free Labor Development I9
American Institute of Architects A5

Personal-Papers Index

Adams, John B4
Adams, John Quincy B4
Anderson, Chandler Parsons B4
Antrim, B. Jay B4
Arnao, Juan and Nicolás B4

Barrett, John B4
Barton, Clara B4
Bayard, Thomas B4
Beauregard, P.G.T. B4
Berlandier, Luis B4
Bingham, Hiram B7
Blaine, James G. B4
Blanco, Ramón B4
Brantz, Lewis B4
Buchanan, James B4
Buneau-Varilla, Philippe Jean B4
    See also Herrán, Tomás

Carr, Wilbur J. B4
Cervera, Pascual B4
Clay, Henry B4
Cleary, R. B4
Cleveland, Grover B4
Cline, Howard B4
Cockburn, George B4
Colby, Bainbridge B4
Connor, David B4
Connors, Philip A39
Corbin, Henry Clark B4
Crocker, William H. B8
Culbertson, William B4
Cunha Menezes, Manoel da B4

Daniels, Josephus B4
Deaderick, David B4
Dewey, George B4
Douglass, Frederick A24
DuVal, Miles A22, B9

Fillmore, Millard B4
Fish, Hamilton B4

Fletcher, Henry B4
Forrestal, James B9
Frelinghuysen, Frederick B4

Goethals, George Washington B4
Gomez, Máximo—See Arnao, Juan and
    Nicolás
Gorgas, William B4
Grant, Ulysses S. B4
Grimke, Archibald A24
Guggenheim, Harry F. B4
Gusmao, Alexandre de B4

Harding, Earl A22
Harding, Warren G. B4
Harrington, John P. B8
Harrison, Leland B4
Hatch, John B4
Haupt, Lewis B4
Hay, John B4
    See also Herrán, Tomás
Herrán, Tomás A22
Hilger, Inez B8
Howell, Glen F. B9
Hrdlicka, Ales B8
Hughes, Charles Evans B4
Hull, Cordell B4

Inman, Samuel Guy B4
Iturbide, Agustín de A11, A22, B4

Jones, William B4

Kennion, John B4
Kissinger, Henry B4
Knox, Frank B9
Knox, Philander C. B4
Krieger, Herbert B8

LaBarre, Weston B8
Lansing, Robert B4
Lardone, Francesco A11

Library Subject-Strength Index

This index groups the strongest library collections in the Washington, D.C. area by subject. Evaluation ("A" through "C") is based on the following criteria:

A—comprehensive collection of primary and secondary sources (Library of Congress collection to serve as standard of evaluation)

B—substantial collection of primary and secondary sources; sufficient for some original research (holdings of roughly one-tenth those of the Library of Congress)

C—substantial collection of secondary sources, some primary; sufficient to support graduate instruction (holdings of roughly one-half those of a "B" collection)

Categorization is based on standard Library of Congress subject-headings, or, in the case of geographic headings, on regional- and country-holdings in selected sub-categories of history, economics, political science, and literature. Some ratings are based on sub-categories of major subject-headings (for example: the Federal Reserve Board Research Library's holdings in finance are included within the "A" range in Economics). For further discussion of library-evaluation methodology, see the Introductory Note in the "Libraries" section. The reader's attention is also called to Appendix III—Library Collections: A Listing by Size of Latin American Holdings.

1. Philosophy and Religion
   A collections: A33, A43, A53
   B collections: A11, A22, A34, H38
   C collections: A6, A21

2. History
   A collections: A1, A24, A33, A43, A53
   B collections: A22, A34, A35, A39, A49
   C collections: A6, A11, A21, A47

3. Geography and Anthropology
   A collections: A33, A40, A43
   B collections: A34, E1

4. Economics
   A collections: A3, A12, A13, A17, A26, A29, A30, A31, A32, A33, A35, A43, A45
   B collections: A31, A49
   C collections: A6, A22, A34, A48

5. Sociology
   A collections: A12, A24, A33, A39, A43, A45, A47
   B collections: A22, A34, A49
   C collections: A6, A11, A21

6. Politics and Government
   A collections: A33, A43
   B collections: A49
   C collections: A6, A22, A34

7. International Relations
   A collections: A33, A43, A49

B collections: A6, A21, A22, A34, A48
C collections: A11

8. Law
A collections: A33
C collections: A26, A43

9. Education
A collections: A33, A43, A44
B collections: A38, I1
C collections: A49

10. Art and Music
A collections: A15, A33, A43
B collections: A34, A36, A40, C11

11. Language and Literature
A collections: A24, A33
B collections: A21, A43
C collections: A22, A34, N7

12. Military Affairs
A collections: A33, A43, L4
B collections: A49
C collections: A25

13. Bibliography and Reference
A collections: A1, A33, A43
B collections: A34, A49
C collections: A21, A22

14. Argentina
A collections: A33, A43
B collections: A22, A26, A35, A49
C collections: A31, A34

15. Bolivia
A collections: A33, A43, A49
B collections: A22, A26, A31, A35
C collections: A34

16. Brazil
A collections: A33, A42, A43
B collections: A10, A22, A35, A49, K5
C collections: A26, A31, A34

17. Caribbean (excluding Cuba)
A collections: A24, A33
B collections: A22, A31, A34, A35, A43, A49
C collections: A6, A21, A23, A26

18. Central America
A collections: A33, A43, A49
B collections: A22, A26, A31, A34, A35
C collections: A6, A21

19. Chile
A collections: A33, A43
B collections: A22, A26, A31, A35, A49, K6
C collections: A21, A34

20. Colombia
A collections: A33, A43
B collections: A26, A31, A35, A49
C collections: A21, A22, A34

21. Cuba
A collections: A33, A43
B collections: A34, A35, A49
C collections: A21, A22, A31

22. Ecuador
A collections: A33, A43
B collections: A26, A31, A35, A49
C collections: A22, A34

23. Guianas (Guyana, Surinam, French Guiana)
A collections: A31, A33, A35, A49
B collections: A34, A43
C collections: A21, A22

24. Mexico
A collections: A33, A43
B collections: A21, A22, A26, A34, A35, A39, A49
C collections: A6, A31

25. Paraguay
A collections: A33, A43
B collections: A22, A26, A31, A35, A49
C collections: A34

26. Peru
A collections: A33, A43
B collections: A26, A31, A34, A35, A49
C collections: A22

27. Uruguay
A collections: A33, A43
B collections: A26, A35, A49
C collections: A21, A22, A31, A34

28. Venezuela
A collections: A33, A43, K27
B collections: A26, A31, A35, A49
C collections: A6, A22, A34

Subject Index

The subject index which follows employs a topical rather than a geographic approach. It proved infeasible to include country-headings and other geographic index terms, because the vast majority of collections and organizations discussed in this volume focus on many or all of the nations of Latin America and the Caribbean rather than concentrating exclusively on any single country or group of countries. As a result, most entries included in the *Guide* can be expected to contain resources for country-specific research on all, or many, countries of the region. (For a geographically-structured assessment of major library collections in the Washington, D.C. area, see the preceding Library Subject-Strength Index.)

An effort has been made to break down major subject headings into narrower sub-categories of research fields. The historian, for example, can utilize the index from a broad chronological perspective (i.e., "History-Colonial," "History-19th Century," "History-20th Century") *and* from a more specific topical perspective (i.e., "Economic History—Colonial," "Political History—19th Century," "Social History—20th Century," "Church History," etc.). The economist will find pertinent data sources under "Economics" and under narrower sub-categories ("Finance," "Investment," "Multinational Corporations," "Trade," etc.).

Entry symbols correspond to the following sections of the text:

A— Libraries
B— Archives
C— Museums, Galleries, and Art Collections
D— Collections of Music and Other Sound Recordings
E— Map Collections
F— Film Collections
G— Data Banks
H—Associations
I— Cultural-Exchange and Technical-Assistance Organizations
J— United States Government Agencies
K— Latin American and Caribbean Embassies
L— International Organizations
M—Research Centers and Information Offices
N— Academic Programs and Departments

Africans A24, A33, D2
Agriculture A3, A19, A20, A26, A30, A31, A32, A33, A35, A43, B6, F7, F8, F20, G1, G2, G3, G6, H2, H31, H32, H37, I2, I11, I22, I23, I27, I30, J1, J2, J27, L6, L8, M24, M26, M30
Anthropology A15, A33, A40, A43, B8, C8, C11, F11, F12, F16, H1, H2, J14, J27
See also Archeology; Indian Languages

The author, Michael Grow, received B.S. (1966) and M.A. (1968) degrees from the University of Wisconsin, Madison, and a Ph.D. (1977) in Latin American history and U.S. diplomatic history from George Washington University in Washington, D.C. Since 1974 he has been an Assistant Professorial Lecturer in History at George Washington University. His publications include essays and reviews on aspects of Latin American history and inter-American relations.

Consultant William Glade is Professor of Economics and Director of the Institute of Latin American Studies at the University of Texas at Austin.

Consultant Martin C. Needler is Professor of Political Science and Director of the Division of Inter-American Affairs at the University of New Mexico.

Consultant Joseph S. Tulchin is Professor of History at the University of North Carolina at Chapel Hill, and Associate Editor of the *Latin American Research Review*.

Series Editor Zdenek David has been librarian of the Wilson Center since 1974. Previously, he served as the Slavic Bibliographer of the Princeton University Library, and as Lecturer in the Department of History at Princeton University.